Table of Contents

SECTION B: MODELS OF NATURALISTIC DECISION MAKING

Preface

Gary A. Klein
Judith Orasanu
Roberta Calderwood
Caroline E. Zsambok

This book was written to describe naturalistic decision making. This is our attempt to understand how human decision makers actually make decisions in complex real-world settings and to learn how to support those processes.

We believe there are four key features of naturalistic decision making: dynamic and continually changing conditions, real-time reactions to these changes, ill-defined goals and ill-structured tasks, and knowledgeable people. The focus of this book, as opposed to other works on decision making, is to present models and methods pertaining to these four features.

Early research on decision making had pursued purely mathematical models that analyzed decision making from the perspective of game theory and economics (von Neumann & Morgenstern, 1947), or that used statistical models to demonstrate decision biases (see Slovic, Fischhoff, & Lichtenstein, 1977). It is true that some researchers were looking at naturalistic settings and applications, but most of the research centered around laboratory-based experiments testing the mathematical and statistical models. The problem is that these experimental conditions were not very representative of field settings where the theories would have to be applied.

In 1985, the Army Research Institute (ARI) Office of Basic Research started a new research program on planning, problem solving, and decision making. The goal of this program was to make decision research more relevant to the needs of the applied community. In 1989, ARI sponsored a workshop to bring together researchers who had contributed substantially to understanding naturalistic decision making. The goal of this project was to document progress made in this line of research and to chart important research questions for the future. The workshop, organized by Klein Associates, was held in Dayton, Ohio, September 25–27, 1989, and over 30 professionals attended. They represented decision research being carried out by the military, NASA, private firms, and academic institutions. Their domains spanned tactical operations, medical decision making, weather forecasting, nuclear power-plant control, and executive planning, among others. One of the goals of the workshop was to define some common ground in this apparent diversity.

This book is a direct outcome of the workshop. In contrast to the usual procedure of having participants present research papers to each other, preliminary outlines for book chapters had been circulated prior to the workshop. The meeting time was reserved for discussing topics and clarifying the issues. We wanted to make naturalistic decision-making research available to a wider audience.

This book contains five sections.

Section A introduces the main themes of naturalistic decision making, describes classical decision theory in order to discuss some of its limitations, and presents examples of the types of decisions that need to be explained.

Section B presents examples of naturalistic research paradigms that have emerged within the last few years.

Section C examines a range of issues concerning our need to develop methodology to conduct research in naturalistic settings.

Section D examines applications and extensions of naturalistic decision making.

Section E attempts to evaluate the issues raised by this book.

Although each chapter finally had to be written by one or a few individuals, it was an explicit goal of the workshop for each chapter to reflect the expertise represented by the entire group of participants. This was accomplished by collecting comments and criticisms of panel members and workshop participants during and after the workshop about chapter outlines and drafts. The task of producing a cohesive book rather than a disjointed set of research papers was not easy, but we never assumed it would be. We are proud and appreciative of the efforts of this group of people in trying to accomplish this goal.

WORKSHOP PARTICIPANTS AND THEIR AFFILIATIONS

Lee Roy Beach, University of Arizona
Roberta Calderwood, Klein Associates Inc. (currently with SAIC, Albuquerque, NM)

Susan Chipman, Office of Naval Research

Jay J. J. Christensen-Szalanski, University of Iowa

Marvin S. Cohen, Decision Sciences Consortium, Inc. (currently at Cognitive Technologies, Inc.)

Terry Connolly, University of Arizona

Beth Crandall, Klein Associates Inc.

Michael Drillings, U.S. Army Research Institute

LorRaine Duffy, Air Force Human Resources Laboratory (currently with Naval Command Control and Ocean Surveillance Center)

Elliot Entin, Alphatech, Inc.

Jeff Grossman, Naval Command Control and Ocean Surveillance Center

Stan Halpin, U.S. Army Research Institute Field Unit, Ft. Leavenworth

Kenneth R. Hammond, University of Colorado–Boulder

T. Owen Jacobs, U.S. Army Research Institute

Gary A. Klein, Klein Associates Inc.

Raanan Lipshitz, University of Haifa, Israel

Ronald J. Lofaro, U.S. Army Research Institute, Aviation Research and Development Activity, Ft. Rucker (currently with Federal Aviation Administration)

Barbara Means, SRI International

David Noble, Engineering Research Associates

Judith Orasanu, U.S. Army Research Institute (currently with NASA/Ames Research Center)

Jens Rasmussen, RISO National Laboratories, Denmark

William B. Rouse, Search Technology, Inc.

Eduardo Salas, Naval Training Systems Center

Daniel Serfaty, Alphatech, Inc.

Robert J. Shively, NASA/Ames Research Center

Jerry Singer, Uniformed Services University of the Health Sciences

Marvin L. Thordsen, Klein Associates Inc.

Martin A. Tolcott, Decision Sciences Consortium, Inc. (retired)

Tom Triscari, Rome Air Development Center, Griffis AFB

John Valusek, Air Force Institute of Technology (currently with First Bank Systems, Minneapolis, MN)

David D. Woods, The Ohio State University

Caroline E. Zsambok, Klein Associates Inc.

In addition, chapters were prepared by several researchers who were not able to attend the workshop:

Michael E. Doherty, Bowling Green State University
Reid Hastie, University of Colorado–Boulder
Henry Montgomery, University of Göteborg, Sweden
Nancy Pennington, University of Colorado–Boulder

Acknowledgments

We first extend our appreciation to the Army Research Institute for the Behavioral and Social Sciences for providing the necessary funding for this project, and especially to Michael Kaplan, Michael Drillings, and Edgar Johnson for their continued encouragement and support. Thanks also to Battelle Memorial Institute at Research Triangle Park, NC, for their efficient and helpful administration of our funding from the Army Research Office Scientific Support Program.

In addition to the diligence and calibre of the book's authors, the book's strengths result in large part from the many helpful comments, criticisms, and suggestions provided by a host of reviewers. The chapter authors themselves read and commented on drafts of each others' manuscripts. Michael Doherty and Reid Hastie did an especially thorough review. Workshop participants other than chapter authors who deserve special mention for their reviews of individual chapters include: Susan Chipman, Elliot Entin, Jeff Grossman, Daniel Serfaty, Jerry Singer, Marvin Thordsen, and Martin Tolcott. We would also like to thank Len Adelman, Stephen Andriole, Rex Brown, Arthur Elstein, Andrea Granitz, Robert Helmreich, Chuck Layton, Ben Morgan, Andrew Sage, and John Stewart, who were not at the workshop, for their many constructive comments.

A special thanks is due the staff at Klein Associates for their months of untiring and highly professional efforts. Mary Alexander and Vicky Shaw assisted in manuscript preparation. Paula John provided administrative support from the time the workshop was first planned to final manuscript preparation. Buzz Reed gave us editorial suggestions and strategies for manuscript preparation. Karen Getchell-Reiter prepared the subject index. Barbara Gasho was invaluable as our production editor, keeping track of every draft of every chapter across several continents.

We would also like to thank Barbara Bernstein, Carol Davidson, and Sharon Jehlen at Ablex Publishing Corporation for their expertise and guidance in the publication process.

Section A

Introduction

Chapter 1

The Reinvention of Decision Making

Judith Orasanu
NASA-Ames Research Center

Terry Connolly
University of Arizona

Consider the following three scenarios:

Scenario 1: A firefighting crew arrives at the scene of a reported fire in a four-story apartment building. The commander of the crew surveys the front of the building, sees no smoke or flames, and goes around the side. There he sees through a basement window that the laundry chute is on fire, and that fire has spread to the basement ceiling. He orders his crew into the first and second floors of the building to extinguish the fire from above with hoses. As they enter, the crew report back that the fire has spread above the second floor. Back at the front of the building, the commander sees that smoke now pouring from the eaves: The fire must have spread via the laundry chute to the fourth floor, and down the corridor from the back to the front of the building. The commander realizes that he will need help, and calls in another unit. He also orders his team to drop their efforts at suppressing the fire, and to concentrate instead on a room-by-room search for people trapped in the burning building. They succeed in evacuating all the occupants, but the building is gutted, despite the arrival within 10 minutes of a second unit.

Scenario 2: A 45-year-old banker wakes one night with a blinding pain, the worst he has ever felt, running across the left lower side of his face and jaw. His face is agonizing to the touch, and he can hardly bear to open his mouth. His wife rushes him to the emergency room of the university hospital two miles away, where he is examined by the admitting physician who prescribes a pain killer and a sedative. The physician is unable to make a firm diagnosis, but suspects the attack to be psychosomatic, associated with the intense work stress the patient has recently been suffering. Two hours later, the pain starts to subside, and the banker finally goes home. After two similar but longer episodes in the following month, the banker consults with his internist who refers him to a dentist. The dentist discovers two deteriorating molar fillings on the lower right side, and replaces them. When the attacks persist, he refers his patient to an endodontist who carries out a root canal on a third tooth. None of this helps the banker whose attacks continue to get worse. Finally, the banker, now virtually an invalid and in constant pain, is referred by his internist to a consulting neurologist who, within 5 minutes, diagnoses a classic case of trigeminal neuralgia. With the drug he prescribes, the banker is pain-free within 2 weeks, and makes a complete recovery.

Scenario 3: Alphadrive Industries, Inc. is a developer and manufacturer of computer memories and related equipment. They are finally getting ready to start production of their first major new product in 3 years, an automatic back-up device for desk-top computers. The technology development has been difficult, but they think they have a winning product, with patent protection for the crucial elements, and they anticipate getting to market 6 to 9 months ahead of their major competitor, Betamem. However, 2 months before Alphadrive is ready to start production, Betamem drops a bombshell: They announce that they will be showing a similar product at the upcoming Atlantic Computer Fair, ready for immediate shipment. Their specifications and price will clearly beat Alphadrive's product. Alphadrive's Marketing Department proposes a flat-out effort to beat Betamem to market and establish market share. They propose moving up the production start, and putting the device into production before final tests, meanwhile launching a high-priced advertising campaign offering the units as available now. The Development Group, on the other hand, argues that Betamem may be overly optimistic or simply bluffing, and that Alphadrive's reputation for reliability could be ruined if they introduce an untested product. They argue for sticking to the original schedule. After a fierce battle lasting over an entire weekend, involving virtually the entire management group, Alphadrive's CEO comes down on the side of the Development Group. The device is launched 4 months later, after significant last-minute engineering changes correct some problems discovered on final testing. Betamem later announces that its introduction will be delayed by unforeseen technical problems. They ultimately abandon their effort to enter this market.

There is nothing especially unusual about these three sketches (the first adapted from Klein, 1989a, the second from Klawans, 1988, the third a fictionalized composite of several stories). They present, in brief outline, people trying to figure out what to do in the face of difficult circumstances. When we speak of *decision making,* it is activities like these that we have in mind. The activities are complex, the stakes often high, and the effects on lives likely to be significant. It is not surprising that substantial research effort has been devoted to understanding and assisting people to make decisions.

A respectable research library may hold hundreds of books and thousands of articles on various aspects of decision making. Some will be highly mathematical, some deeply psychological, some full of wise advice about how to improve. What is surprising is how difficult it is to apply much of this learning to the sorts of decision tasks described in the three scenarios. The research intends to address activities labeled "decision-making." And it does. Yet the correspondence between what is found in these research reports and the three scenarios we have presented is surprisingly low. Why is the relevance of one to the other so remote?

The central argument of this chapter, and of this book, is that the basic cause of the mismatch is that traditional decision research has invested most of its energy in only one part of decision making, which we shall refer to the *decision event.* In this view, the crucial part of decision making occurs when the decision maker (generally a single individual) surveys a known and fixed set of alternatives, weighs the likely consequences of choosing each, and makes a choice. The decision maker evaluates the options in terms of a set of goals, purposes, or values that are stable over time, and that he or she knows quite clearly. Research on decision events tends to focus on the ways in which decision makers pull together all available information into their choice of a best alternative.

The decision-making activities suggested by the three scenarios offer few clean examples of decision events. It is possible to shoehorn the activities into this mold, but something gets lost. For example, consider the firefighting scenario rewritten from a decision event perspective. The fireground commander's goal would be to choose the best course of action, given his values and objectives. Possible actions might include: sending firefighters to the basement or to the roof to extinguish the blaze, searching for and evacuating residents, calling in additional fire companies, wetting down the roof, or protecting adjacent structures. Each possible action would be evaluated according to all evaluative dimensions, such as saving lives of occupants, preserving structures, minimizing risk to firefighters, conserving resources, or keeping the fire from spreading. Importance weights would be assigned to each evaluative dimension, and then the ratings and weights would be combined to yield the best course of action.

Klein's research (1989a, this volume, Chap. 6) shows that the decision event model does not characterize what fireground commanders report they actually do. Their efforts focus on defining the situation—what kind of fire do they face? Based on experience with similar fires, the commander selects the most plausible action for reaching his goal, given the constraints of the situation. The candidate course of action is evaluated by projecting forward its likely consequences, and looking for undesirable effects. If none is found, the action is implemented.

The approach Klein has observed differs from a decision event model in at least three ways: much effort is devoted to situation assessment, or figuring out the nature of the problem; single options are evaluated sequentially through mental simulation of outcomes; and options are accepted if they are satisfactory (rather than optimal). In contrast, the decision event approach emphasizes concurrent evaluation of multiple options; relies on analytical methods for integrating values and probabilities associated with each option; and seeks an optimal solution.

The Alphadrive CEO in Scenario 3 shows some of the decision event activities, in that she finally made the go/no go decision. But we find ourselves as interested in how the Marketing and Development people tried to control the CEO's information, and in the cunning effort by Betamem to trick them into a premature product launch. Traditional decision approaches can be stretched to connect with these everyday scenarios, but critical aspects are ignored. The reason is that the real-world processes have a number of features not explicitly considered by the basic decision event model.

The most fundamental difference is that in everyday situations, decisions are embedded in larger tasks that the decision maker is trying to accomplish. Decision event research in the laboratory tends to require decisions apart from any meaningful context. In natural settings, making a decision is not an end in itself. Usually it is a means to achieving a broader goal. Decisions are embedded in task cycles that consist of defining what the problem is, understanding what a reasonable solution would look like, taking action to reach that goal, and evaluating the effects of that action. As Brehmer (1990) states in describing his research on dynamic decision making,

> The study of decision making in a dynamic, real time context, relocates the study of decision making and makes it part of the study of action, rather than the study of choice. The problem of decision making, as seen in this framework, is a matter of directing and maintaining the continuous flow of behavior towards some set of goals rather than as a set of discrete episodes involving choice dilemmas. (p. 26)

A fundamental contention of this volume is that decision performance in everyday situations is a joint function of two factors: (1) *features of the task,* and (b) the subject's *knowledge and experience* relevant to that task. Past decision research has neglected these two elements in varying degrees. In this chapter we describe some important naturalistic task features and the role of experience in decision making. Next, we examine how research methods affect conclusions about the nature of decision-making processes. Then, we discuss the value of traditional decision paradigms, and conclude with some findings from naturalistic decision-making (NDM)research.

CHARACTERISTICS OF NATURALISTIC DECISION SETTINGS

Eight important factors characterize decision making in naturalistic settings, but frequently are ignored in decision-making research.[1] It is not likely that all 8 factors will be at their most difficult levels in any one setting, but often several of these factors will complicate the decision task.

1. Ill-structured problems
2. Uncertain dynamic environments
3. Shifting, ill-defined, or competing goals
4. Action/feedback loops
5. Time stress
6. High stakes
7. Multiple players
8. Organizational goals and norms

1. *Ill-structured problems:* Real decision problems rarely present themselves in the neat, complete form the event model suggests. The decision maker will generally have to do significant work to generate hypotheses about what is happening, to develop options that might be appropriate responses, or even to recognize that the situation is one in which choice is required or allowed. Observable features of the setting may be related to one another by complex causal links, interactions between causes, feedback loops, and so on. The fireground commander in Scenario 1, for example, knew almost nothing of the problem he

---

[1] These features overlap with those specified by Sternberg (1985, 1986) for teaching critical thinking skills outside the classroom.

faced when he arrived at the scene, and was guided heavily by his developing understanding of the location, type, and severity of the fire. The internist in Scenario 2 was clear about the surface symptoms of his patient's problem, but spent a great deal of time testing hypotheses about underlying causes in order to guide the patient to the right professional. When he did so, the problem was quickly solved. In Scenario 3, the crucial step was when Alphadrive's CEO decided that they were probably facing a bluff, not a rival's engineering breakthrough—a crucial reading of a complex, ambiguous set of tangled cues. When a task is ill-structured, there are typically several equally good ways of solving the same problem. There is no one accepted procedure to use, and it is necessary to select or invent a way to proceed. Moreover, there is no single correct or best answer. Ill-structured problems frequently are made more ambiguous by uncertain dynamic information (feature 2 below) and by multiple interacting goals (feature 3 below).

2. *Uncertain dynamic environments:* Naturalistic decision making typically takes place in a world of incomplete and imperfect information. The decision maker has information about some part of the problem (the firefighting units available, the costs of a product), but not about others (the current extent of the fire, the probable market for the product). Information may be ambiguous or simply of poor quality: Observers are unsure of what they saw; diagnostic tests leave open a range of possible diseases.

Two additional factors make the problem still harder. First, the task is likely to be dynamic—the environment may change quickly, within the time frame of the required decision. For example, a small fire five minutes ago may be a large fire now. Second, the validity of the information may be suspect if it is generated by an intelligent adversary, as in Betamem's attempt in Scenario 3 to make Alphadrive think they were facing a critically short deadline for introducing their new product.

3. *Shifting, ill-defined, or competing goals:* Outside the laboratory, it is rare for a decision to be dominated by a single, well-understood goal or value. We expect the decision maker to be driven by multiple purposes, not all of them clear, some of which will be opposed to others. The fire chief would like to save the building, but not expose his crew to unnecessary danger. Time may be important, but it is unclear how it should be traded off against danger and property damage. The design engineers want to test their new product comprehensively, but not to delay its introduction. These conflicts and tradeoffs may arise in laboratory-based decision making, of course, but are especially tricky in NDM because they are often novel and must be resolved swiftly, and because the situation may change quickly, bringing new values to the

fore. As the fire develops, the commander's goals may shift from protecting property to saving lives. Often, larger goals will provide direction, since decisions typically are embedded in broader tasks.

4. *Action/feedback loops:* The traditional decision models are concerned with an *event,* a point in time at which the single decisive action is chosen. In NDM, in contrast, it is much more common to find an entire *series of events,* a string of actions over time that are intended to deal with the problem, or to find out more about it, or both. This is not just a matter of gathering information until one is ready for the decisive action. Physicians, for example, will often consider a line of treatment as both an attempt to cure the patient and a part of diagnosis: "If the patient responds to Drug A, the infection was clearly Disease X. If not, we'll move to Drug B, which should help if the problem is Disease Y, the next most likely candidate, and so on." The fact that there are multiple opportunities for the decision maker to do something may be helpful in that early mistakes generate information that allows corrective action later (including dealing with side effects of the early actions). Action/feedback loops may also generate problems. Actions taken and results observed may be only loosely coupled to one another, making it hard to attribute effect to cause. These action/feedback loops are quite characteristic of NDM problems. They may make the problems easier (when outcomes are tightly coupled to actions) or harder (when outcomes are loosely coupled to action), but they certainly require a new view of how decisions are made.

5. *Time stress:* An obvious feature of many NDM settings is that decisions are made under significant time pressure. This may be at the level of needing action in minutes or seconds (as in Scenario 1), or of compressing review of crucial corporate strategy into a single weekend (as in Scenario 3). This time pressure has several obvious but important implications. First, decision makers in these settings will often experience high levels of personal stress, with the potential for exhaustion and loss of vigilance. Second, their thinking will shift, characteristically in the direction of using less complicated reasoning strategies (Payne, Bettman, & Johnson, 1988). Decision strategies that demand deliberation—for example, the extensive evaluation of multiple options recommended by many decision theorists—are simply not feasible. Studies of decision making such as that of fireground commanders in Scenario 1 show that very few options (perhaps only one) are analyzed, and those only in nonexhaustive ways. It seems unlikely that reflective thought is the key to successful action in firefighting conditions. Other modes of picking actions seem more appropriate.

6. *High stakes:* The examples sketched in the three opening scenarios each involve outcomes of real significance to the participants:

preserving substantial property or life in Scenario 1, the loss of one's career or perhaps one's life in Scenario 2, the future of an entire company in Scenario 3. Obviously, there are plenty of everyday decisions where the stakes are much smaller than these. Our interest is in cases where the stakes matter to the participants who are likely to feel stressed but who will take an active role in arriving at a good outcome. Our concern is that much decision research involves subjects who are not invested in the task to the same level that they would be outside the laboratory.

7. *Multiple players:* Many of the problems of interest to NDM researchers involve not a single decision maker, but several, perhaps many, individuals who are actively involved in one role or another. Parties may be simply a decision maker and an immediate subordinate acting together to divide the work between them. The group may expand to an entire management committee or team trying to act together as one decision maker. Alphadrive's Marketing and Development groups in Scenario 3 took on such team decision-making roles. A decision may be distributed over a set of partly cooperative, partly competitive individuals who try to coordinate their activities, as in geographically separate regional managers for a single national organization. It can be hard to make sure all team members share the same understanding of goals and situational status so that relevant information is brought forward when needed in the decision process.

8. *Organizational goals and norms:* As the discussion so far has indicated, naturalistic decision making frequently takes place in organizational settings. The organizational setting is relevant to the decision-making process in two ways. First, the values and goals that are being applied will not be simply the personal preferences of the individuals involved. Second, the organization may respond to the decision maker's various difficulties by establishing more general goals, rules, standard operating procedures, "service doctrine," or similar guidelines. These factors are difficult to incorporate into artificial environments (see Hackman, 1986).

These eight characteristics fall short of providing a strict definition of NDM. We list them here to suggest the types of decision situations of interest in this volume, which we believe have been neglected in past decision-making research, yielding perhaps a truncated view of human decision making. Extreme values on these eight features present a "worst case scenario" for the decision maker. However, as the opening scenarios show, it is easy to find real-world examples that embody extreme values on several characteristics.

THE IMPORTANCE OF EXPERTISE

In addition to looking at naturalistic task conditions, it is also important to understand how people use their knowledge and experience in coping with complex decision tasks. This volume is concerned with decisions made by individuals who know a lot about the problem domain. That does not mean they are expert decision makers (such as decision analysts), but they are familiar with the tools and information sources relevant to making a decision.

Relatively little research has been done on the role of expertise in decision making (but see the Hammond, Hamm, Grassia, & Pearson, 1987, study of highway engineers; the Lusk, Mross, & Hammond, 1989, study of weather forecasters; and Shanteau's, 1987, summary of expert decision making). In contrast, researchers studying problem solving have been much more interested in expertise (for a review see Chi, Glaser, & Farr, 1988). The latter group presents findings that contradict those of many decision researchers. Problem-solving studies show fundamental differences between novices and experts in how problems are interpreted, what strategies are devised, what information is used, memory for critical information, and speed and accuracy of problem solving. Experts can see underlying causes and have more complex models of the problem than novices (Larkin, McDermott, Simon, & Simon, 1980). These findings are drawn from fields as diverse as electronics, chess, physics, medicine, foreign policy, and baseball. In contrast, decision researchers have found that expertise confers little advantage in the judgments of clinical psychologists, college admissions officers, or economic forecasters. What can account for such radically different conclusions?

We must look to the kinds of tasks used in the two types of research. Studies that conclude no advantage to experts usually require integration of large amounts of data to discern correlations or to judge outcome probabilities in highly uncertain environments. Especially difficult are situations that provide no feedback on the decision. Many studies have shown that this type of task requires significant computational resources, and that experts, no matter how knowledgeable, are simply not equipped to perform well. Mathematical solutions achieved by computers typically do a much better job (Dawes, 1971, 1979). However, when the task requires problem structuring, interpretation of ambiguous cues within the expert's domain, and reliance on underlying causal models, experts surpass novices who lack the knowledge base to guide their performance (Johnson, 1988). In summing up the differences, Dawes (1971) has observed that, "people are better at selecting and coding information than they are at integrating it." For example, Crandall and Calderwood (1989) found that experienced neonatal intensive-care unit nurses could recognize the onset of life-threatening infection in premature infants 24–48 hours before the diagnosis could be confirmed through laboratory tests.

Johnson (1988) has made a convincing case that findings about expertise from the problem-solving literature generalize to judgment and decision making, particularly when the tasks have elements in common. Johnson also points out that most research on expert problem solving has focused on the *process* by which solutions are reached and how knowledge is used. In contrast, decision research has typically focused on the quality of the *outcome*—how close it comes to an ideal solution (see also Brehmer, Jungermann, Lourens, & Sevon, 1986). However, outcome-oriented research offers few clues about the psychological processes that produce those outcomes.

Research on expert problem solving has shown that a significant aspect of what specialists do when functioning in their everyday complex environments is to use their knowledge and experience to size up the situation, determine if a problem exists, and, if so, whether and how to act upon it. Experience enables a person to seek information that will be helpful in coping with the situation, and to generate a limited set of plausible diagnoses, options, or hypotheses, rather than wasting precious time and energy on low-payoff leads (Chi, Farr, & Glaser, 1988). In fact, Klein (1989a, this volume, Chap. 6) has found that whereas experts use a "recognition-primed" or perception-based decision process to retrieve a single likely option, novices are more likely to use an analytical approach, systematically comparing multiple options (cf. Larkin et al., 1980).

What is needed, and what this book is about, is research and theory that will contribute to a fuller understanding of how people use their knowledge and experience to make decisions in complex dynamic situations. Previous research has chronicled the many ways in which reasoners can go wrong; now we need to balance that work with an account of how they can go right.

THE ISSUE OF RESEARCH METHODS
(OR, DIFFERENT METHODS =
DIFFERENT CONCLUSIONS)

As MacDougall observed in 1922,

> Science has no royal road. . . . If lab experimentation involves any essential disturbance of the phenomenon, the psychologist must lay aside his

plans of formal simplification and study the event under its natural conditions accepting whatever complications the change introduces into his problem. (1922, pp. 351–352; cited in Gillis & Schneider, 1966)

Why do we think it's so important to examine decisions made in environments containing the features listed earlier and by decision makers with knowledge and experience relevant to the task? The primary reason is that phenomena observed in complex natural environments may differ substantially from those observed in the laboratory based on decontextualized tasks performed by novices with little stake in the outcomes. Ideally, laboratory tasks involve micro environments that abstract essential variables from the broader environment to which the experimenter wants to generalize (see Hammond, 1980, and this volume for a discussion of Brunswik's representative design). In fact, critical variables may be missing or changed in the lab, with major consequences for the behavior of interest.

A case in point comes from a study of birdsong in territorial behavior of the *Nuttall* subspecies of the white-crowned sparrow (Petrinovich, 1980). Using ethological methods, Petrinovich examined factors that influence birdsong and its effects on invaders. He found that significant behavioral variations depended on the stages of the breeding cycle (courting, nest building, mating, incubation, and tending the young). Previous laboratory-based work, however, had shown conflicting and theoretically uninterpretable results. Petrinovich's major findings had not been observed before, because *Nuttall* does not reproduce in the laboratory. This example shows how carefully controlled laboratory experimentation can obscure the most interesting and significant phenomena.

Less striking, but more relevant to decision research, is Ebbesen and Konecni's (1980) finding that judges and parole officers recommended different criminal sentences in a laboratory simulation and in the courtroom. Their lab studies left out variables that were critical in the natural decision environment. In this case, different conclusions would be drawn about the operation of variables from the two research environments.

Our concern for research environments and methods is that very different conclusions may be drawn about the fundamental nature of human decision making depending on the tasks, methods, and participants in the studies. As in the laboratory study of birdsong, contradictions abound. Some researchers have concluded that people are hopelessly irrational and need help in making logical decisions. Yet human experts can solve certain classes of difficult problems that powerful computers can't approach. How can both conclusions be true?

Recent experiments have shown how "rational" behavior can be manipulated by features of the task and people's knowledge relevant to it. If tasks tap into everyday forms of reasoning about particular topics, people appear to reason in a rational manner. When tasks are relatively uninterpretable to the subjects, their performance appears irrational. For example, considerable research on heuristics and biases has shown the limitations of human reasoning (see Kahneman, Slovic, & Tversky, 1982). Much of the work involves statistical reasoning, which requires an appreciation of the role of chance, as in lotteries. This body of work suggests that human reasoning is essentially flawed.

However, other research shows that people may reason fully in accord with rational principles when they understand that the events they are judging are in fact randomly generated. Gigerenzer, Hell, and Blank (1988) showed subjects random samples being drawn, which led to fully rational judgments. Nisbett, Krantz, Jepson, and Kunda (1983) point out that experts can reason statistically within their own domain because they have a better understanding of which events are truly random and which are causal. Thus, experts know when to apply statistical reasoning and when to apply knowledge-based reasoning strategies. Likewise, on tasks of formal logic, people perform poorly if the problems are presented in abstract symbolic form (if p, then q). However, if structurally identical problems are clothed in meaningful content, people reason quite logically (Wason & Johnson-Laird, 1972). The critical factor seems to be problem representation. As Huber (1986) put it, "Decision behavior seems to depend on the decision maker's representation of the system, and the goal(s), plans, actions, etc. which are based upon the representation and goal(s)" (p. 121). Manipulations that influence how people represent the problem have major consequences for how they reason (see also Einhorn & Hogarth, 1986).

In an effort to explain the contradictions between rational and irrational performance, Anderson (1990) has offered the notion of "adaptiveness of cognition," a notion relevant to this volume. He contends that the human cognitive apparatus, including perception, classification, memory, and problem solving, has evolved adaptively to cope with certain kinds of tasks found in everyday environments. Thus, to understand cognition we must understand the demands and critical features of the environment as they relate to cognitive processes.

From an adaptionist perspective, [some researchers] have chosen a strange set of tasks to focus on. There are the puzzles and games, such as chess, Tower of Hanoi, Rubik's cube and the eight puzzle—and there are the academic activities, like math and science problem solving. . . . Such problem solving has little adaptive value, and one can question whether our problem solving machinery has evolved to be adapted to such tasks.

Indeed, one might argue, in the case of puzzles and games, that they are played because they are challenging, and they are challenging precisely because we are not adapted to succeed in such domains. (p. 192)

A similar argument could be made for many of the statistical reasoning tasks used in decision event research that lead to "irrational" thinking.

Understanding naturalistic decision making requires that research methods must expand beyond the study of naive subjects in context-limited environments. Existing research greatly overrepresents the problem solving and choice processes of college students working unfamiliar tasks for modest stakes. While such studies can provide useful understanding of the early stages of skill acquisition, they cast little light on the performance of the expert operating in his or her regular environment with normal decision aids, time sequences, cue sets, and so on.

A broader range of research methods will be needed to capture phenomena at varying levels of complexity. These may include various observational methods such as ethnography, realistic simulations, and computer modeling to test theories. Some researchers maintain that the best way to understand complex phenomena is to break them down into simple components, understand how these function, and then to reassemble them. But the complex world is not just an aggregation of the simple. Certain reasoning processes emerge only in complex environments, and are not available for study in simple tasks. For instance, certain classes of errors, such as fixation or tunnel vision, emerge only in a dynamically changing situation (Woods, 1988).

An urgent need exists for research on complex decision making both within and outside the laboratory. We look forward to multidisciplinary "full-cycle" research approaches (Warneryd, 1986) as the norm in the future, with investigations moving back and forth between the field and the laboratory. The generality of findings discovered in the lab would be evaluated in realistic environments, and, where possible without distorting the phenomena, hypotheses derived from observations in real-world situations would be tested in the laboratory. Experimental laboratory research would still play an important role, but the tasks and subjects would be selected to reflect critical aspects of operational situations.

THE VALUE OF CLASSICAL
DECISION-MAKING PARADIGMS

Traditional approaches to decision research have evolved to serve specific functions, and their contributions should not be ignored. Analytical approaches, derived from economic theory, have been used to study tasks for which the researchers could determine the optimal choice (see Einhorn & Hogarth, 1981; Keeney & Raiffa, 1976; and Slovic, Fischhoff, & Lichenstein, 1977, for reviews). Economic theory assumes that the decision maker seeks to optimize the outcome of choice and that the options, criteria, and values are known. Normative theories do not tell us how people actually make decisions, but provide formal methods for reaching optimal solutions. Many prescriptive decision aids have been developed on the basis of normative decision theories (Brown, 1989a).

For example, if you are interested in buying a car, you might use a normative strategy called a multiattribute utility analysis (MAUA, see Edwards & Newman, 1982). In brief, you would identify the factors that distinguish among the models you are considering, such as cost, size, gas mileage, style, safety, and fun. Then you'd rate each model on each dimension and assign an importance weight to each dimension. A mathematical formula would combine the values and ratings to identify your ideal car, based on your stated values.

A MAUA is considered a compensatory decision strategy because high values on a less important evaluation dimension can be balanced by low values on a more important dimension; all information is factored into the equation. However, compensatory analyses are typically very time-consuming. They are useful when context is limited, time pressure is low, and expertise is low. In fact, when time is limited, people often adopt noncompensatory strategies (Payne, Bettman, & Johnson, 1988). That is, they do not evaluate all options on all dimensions, but adopt short-cuts for arriving at a satisfactory choice. Dominance structuring (Montgomery, this volume) and elimination by aspects (Tversky, 1972) are two such strategies. Nevertheless, normative-prescriptive methods have proven valuable in helping policymakers identify the factors that must go into a complex decision, and in helping diverse stakeholders develop a common framework to select a course of action that benefits them all. Decision analysis based on normative models is useful when an optimal decision is desired, particularly when the consequences are critical, such as siting a nuclear power plant (Keeney, 1982).

Normative decision theory also serves as a benchmark for evaluating the rationality of people's unaided decisions. The criterion for rationality is logical consistency. The tasks used to assess rationality typically require people to integrate large amounts of information and to reason statistically, that is, to revise their probability estimates of outcomes as additional information is provided, according to Bayes theorem (Edwards, 1954). In general, people's intuitive statistical judgments do not conform to the rational consistency of formal models, though recent research shows that experts can reason statistically within their own domains under certain task conditions (Nisbett et al., 1983).

Other research grounded in normative theories examines the psychological short-cuts people take in order to get around their own information-processing limitations when dealing with probability judgments in highly uncertain situations. These heuristics often lead to systematic biases or errors compared to normative standards (Kahneman, Slovic, & Tversky, 1982). Chapters in the next section will address this issue specifically from an NDM perspective.

In this book we will not be covering decisions based on normative models, because the topic has been well studied in other work and because the assumptions of the normative-prescriptive approach do not fit our focus. What characterizes research within the normative model is that the problem is defined by the experimenter, including the task framework, the options, and often the evaluation dimensions. Moreover, the focus is on the decision outcome rather than on how people come to decide that a choice or action is needed, what influences their goals, how the options are generated, or how the choice fits within the broader framework of reasoning about the situation.

A traditional approach that is included in this volume is the social judgment theory (Brehmer, 1984; Hammond et al., 1975, 1980). This theory addresses the process by which people select, weigh, and combine ambiguous cues to make judgments about uncertain events. Its focus is on the psychological processes of knowing, usually when people cannot manipulate the environment to get more information. Because of the significance of perceptual and interpretive processes in situation assessment in many theories described later in this book, this approach is clearly relevant to NDM. Social judgment theory is represented by Hammond's chapter in this volume.

THE NEW GENERATION OF DECISION RESEARCH

This volume and the workshop on which it is based reflect initial ventures in the scientific study of decision making in complex natural environments. Several findings have emerged from these efforts that either contradict the accepted wisdom from earlier decision-event-centered research, or provide new insights brought about by the shift to studying more complex decision situations using different methodologies. Here are some examples that are documented in detail in later chapters:

1. In contrast to procedures prescribed by normative models, experts in field decision situations tend not to generate and evaluate several courses of action concurrently to determine the best choice. Rather, based on their classification of the problem, they generate a single highly likely option and evaluate its appropriateness to the current conditions (Klein, 1989a, this volume, Chap. 6; Lipshitz, this volume, Chap. 9). If it is appropriate, they act on it; if not, it is modified or a second option is generated and the cycle is repeated.

2. The major factor that distinguishes experienced from less experienced decision makers is their situation assessment ability, not their reasoning processes per se (Chi et al., 1988; Klein, 1989; Orasanu, 1990). Experts in a field can look at a situation and quickly interpret it using their highly organized base of relevant knowledge. The identification of situation type carries with it retrieval of one or more action alternatives that constitute appropriate responses.

3. Because of situational and organizational constraints, decision makers usually use a "satisficing" (Simon, 1955) rather than an optimizing strategy (Hickson, Butler, Cray, Mallory, & Wilson 1986). That is, they select a good enough, though not necessarily the best, choice. While at first blush this might seem lazy or hazardous, the fact is that in most ill-defined complex situations, there is no single correct answer. Many paths will lead to the same goal or to parallel and satisfactory goals, which generally involve tradeoffs in time, risk, or resources.

4. Reasoning is "schema-driven" rather than driven by a computational algorithm. Even for problems with many novel elements (typical of NDM situations), decision makers use their knowledge to organize the problem, to interpret the situation, and to define what information is valuable for solution (Larkin et al., 1980; Noble, 1989, this volume). Some information may be selected or distorted to fit the existing schema, a potential source of error (Tolcott et al., 1989a). But it also enables speedy assessment, search, selection, and interpretation of relevant information, a definite advantage when faced with information overload and time pressure. A critical feature of the schema-driven approach is that people create causal models of the situation. They try to understand the significance of events and information by inferring causal relations (Hastie & Pennington, 1987, this volume; Thagard, 1988; Thüring & Jungermann, 1986). This enables them, for example, to interpret intentions of other participants, either friend or foe, and to evaluate proposed actions by anticipating their future consequences (Lipshitz, this volume).

5. Finally, reasoning and acting are interleaved, rather than segregated (Connolly & Wagner, 1988; Weick, 1983). Instead of analyzing all facets of a situation, making a decision, and then acting, it appears that in complex realistic situations people think a little, act a little, and then evaluate the outcomes and think and act some more (cf. Connolly & Wagner, 1988). This *decision cycle* approach reflects the incomplete knowledge, dynamically changing conditions, and competing goal structures that characterize NDM situations. Decision event models assume all options, outcomes, and preferences are known in advance and thus are amenable to evaluation. The decision cycle approach treats the development of this knowledge as an integral part of decision making.

We have referred to our general approach as a reinvention of decision making to signal the contrast between the traditional and the naturalistic paradigms. Differences lie in the importance assigned to experience, task complexity, and demands of naturalistic settings. The NDM orientation is a sharp departure from the way decision research has been and generally still is conducted with naive subjects, performing artificial tasks that lack meaningful consequences. The purpose of this volume is to describe the naturalistic decision-making approach, to examine its potential as well as its limitations, and to point the way to future research and applications.

KEY POINTS

- Classical decision-making research focuses on the *decision event:* choice from among a fixed set of known alternatives based on stable goals, purposes, and values.
- NDM research focuses on decisions that are embedded in larger dynamic tasks, made by knowledgeable and experienced decision makers.
- It is not feasible to apply classical decision research analyses to many real-life situations, as illustrated by three case studies.
- Naturalistic decision-making research examines settings that include many of the following characteristics:
  — problems are ill-structured
  — information is incomplete, ambiguous, or changing
  — goals are shifting, ill-defined, or competing
  — decisions occur in multiple event-feedback loops
  — time constraints exist
  — stakes are high
  — many participants contribute to the decisions

— the decision maker must balance personal choice with organizational norms and goals

- Naturalistic decision-making research has yielded new findings:
  — In naturalistic dynamic settings, experts frequently generate and evaluate a single option rather than analyze multiple options concurrently.
  — Experts are distinguished from novices mainly by their situation assessment abilities, not their general reasoning skills.
  — Because most naturalistic decision problems are ill-structured, decision makers choose an option that is good enough, though not necessarily the best.
  — Reasoning is "schema-driven," that is, guided by the decision maker's knowledge, to search and assess information, and to build causal models of events.
  — Deciding and acting are interleaved.

Chapter 2

Why Classical Decision Theory is an Inappropriate Standard for Evaluating and Aiding Most Human Decision Making

Lee Roy Beach
University of Arizona

Raanan Lipshitz
University of Haifa

It is customary to attribute two roles to the formal, axiomatic, rational actor theory of decision evaluation and choice, a normative role and a prescriptive role. For brevity, we will call the formal theory *classical decision theory,* by which we mean the collection of axiomatic models of uncertainty and risk (probability theory, including Bayesian theory), and utility (utility theory, including multiattribute utility theory), that prescribe the optimal choice of an option from an array of options, where optimality is defined by the underlying models and the choice is dictated by an explicit rule, usually some variant of maximization of (subjective) expected utility.

In its normative role, classical decision theory is an abstract system of propositions that is designed to describe the choices of an ideal hypothetical decision maker—omniscient, computationally omnipotent Economic Man—given the theory's very specific assumptions about the nature of the decision task. In this role the theory actually has little relevance to real-world decisions. It merely is an internally consistent, logical system that, perhaps unfortunately, reflects its origins as an attempt to rationalize observed decisions (Bentham, 1789/1970) by being couched in terms that also are commonly used to describe the behavior of human decision makers.

Since the publication of the theory of games by von Neumann and Morgenstern (1947), followed by Edwards' (1954) introduction of classical decision theory to psychology, it has become common to attribute a prescriptive role to classical decision theory. By *prescriptive* it is meant that the way that Economic Man would make decisions is assumed to be the uniquely appropriate way, the only "rational" way. Indeed, the optimality of humans' decisions usually is judged by whether the decisions conform to the prescriptions of the theory. The assumption that classical theory is prescriptively appropriate has motivated nearly 40 years of empirical behavioral research—every study that has evaluated the quality of human decision making using the prescriptions of classical theory as the standard of comparison has been a reaffirmation of this assumption.

Implicit in the prescriptivity assumption is the further assumption that, if decision makers behaved as they "should," classical decision theory would not only be normative and prescriptive, it also would be descriptive of human decision behavior, thus coming full circle from Bentham (1789/1970) and the Utilitarians. However, starting with the work of Allais (1953) and Ellsberg (1961) on through the recent work of Kahneman and Tversky (1979) and subsequently, it has been repeatedly demonstrated that decision makers only infrequently behave as they "should." That is, decision behavior does not appear to conform consistently, or even often, to the logic of classical theory or to the operations implied by that logic. Of course, classical theory is mathematically precise and it is unreasonable to expect the same precision in the behavior that is compared to it. Quite beyond this understandable lack of conformity, however, it doubtless is the case that human decision making cannot be described adequately using classical theory as a descriptive theory.

This lack of conformity, this inability to use classical theory as a descriptive theory, has prompted four responses from decision researchers. One response is merely to damn the behavior: "If your procedures or decisions or feelings are intransitive or otherwise discordant with subjective expected utility, they are incoherent, 'irrational,' or whatever you want to call it, and trying to justify them as coherent or find other rationalities is a waste of time" Pratt (1986, p. 498). This view saves the theory and rejects the behavior. Some scholars who hold this view do so because they prize the theory and simply are uninterested in the behavior—a position to which they certainly are entitled. Others who hold this view, but who prize the theory *and* are interested in the behavior, strive to reduce the gap between theory and behavior by changing the behavior. This is the second response to the nonconformity of behavior to theory, and it has given rise to decision analysis as an art and profession, as well as to a sizable array of decision aids that are designed to help people make their decision processes conform to classical theory.

The third response has been to retain the general logic and structure of classical theory but to make modifications of some of the theory's components and operations in light of the research findings. Scholars who have provided this response prize the theory but are more interested in the behavior—hence, their willingness to compromise the theory in order to better understand decision behavior. This is the position taken by behavioral economics (Bell, 1982; Loomis & Sugden, 1982; Machina, 1982), of which prospect theory (Kahneman & Tversky, 1979) is perhaps the most famous example. As pointed out by Beach and Mitchell (1990, Beach, 1990), while this response follows a time-honored tradition in science (i.e., modifying theory in light of evidence), it also runs the risk of hanging on to a point of view (in this case the logic and structure of classical theory) that may not be as valuable as it once appeared. To be sure, history provides examples of theories being improved by modification in light of evidence. It also provides examples of theories being repaired and shored up until all but the True Believers lose interest in the increasingly pedantic arguments that signal the theory's impending death. One example is the overlong extension of the Ptolemaic theory of the solar system; stimulus–response theories of learning are another example. (Indeed, one sign of theoretical moribundity may be that True Believers begin to talk almost exclusively to each other.)

The fourth response is represented by attempts to more accurately describe the process involved in real-world decision making by individuals acting alone or in groups. The underlying notion is that, by knowing what decision makers actually are attempting to do, they perhaps can be helped to do it better. Scholars who have provided this response are almost wholly interested in understanding behavior. Because classical decision theory has been found of limited help in achieving such understanding, it has been either completely replaced or relegated to the back of the stage. Of course, many of these scholars retain a great deal of respect for classical theory; they acknowledge that it is appropriate for some decision tasks and that human decisions sometimes conform to its prescriptions. However, they are unconvinced (or, more often, have lost the conviction) that classical theory always is the standard against which decision behavior should be judged. Rather, they have come to believe that it is misdirected to force every or even most decision tasks into the rather limited mold that classical theory provides.

Herbert Simon (1955) led the way in the formulation of this fourth response, and organizational theorists of various stripes were the first to carry it forward (e.g., Cohen, March, & Olsen, 1972; Cyert & March, 1963; Gore, 1964; Janis & Mann, 1977; Lindblom, 1959; March & Simon, 1958; Steinbruner, 1974; Weick, 1979). Most of these earlier efforts focused heavily upon group processes, and it is only recently that theories formulated as part of this fourth response have widened their focus to include individuals. The theories described in Chapter 5 of this volume are the most recent examples of this fourth response.

WHEN BEHAVIOR AND CLASSICAL THEORY DIFFER

Even the most casual reader of the decision literature is aware of the research on decision heuristics and biases. This work, started in large part by Ward Edwards, Daniel Kahneman, and Amos Tversky, and subsequently carried on both by them and by many other researchers, focuses primarily upon judgment rather than decision making. However, insofar as it has examined decision making per se, it suggests or documents discrepancies between decision behavior and classical theory. Add to this the more pertinent literature on "choices among bets," in which decision makers' choices between gambles often are found to be governed by factors that are irrelevant to the theory's prescriptions, and the picture looks pretty dismal. Of course, that picture is framed, if you will, by classical theory.

Because the heuristics and biases research will be examined in detail in Chapters 3 and 4, there is no need to discuss it here. Instead, let us consider the results of another literature that often is overlooked by the decision research establishment and that the causal reader might not know exists—a literature that has important implications for the results of choices between gambles as a source of insight into decision behavior. This second literature does more than merely document the lack of conformity of decision behavior to theoretical prescriptions. It suggests that human decision making consists of many tasks that are quite different from the gambling task for which classical theory peculiarly was designed. In short, this literature demands that the unthinkable be thought; classical theory frequently may be an inappropriate standard for evaluating and aiding human decision making.

Most of this second literature does not come from laboratory experiments. Rather it comes from observation of decision makers engaging in routine, on-the-job decisions. As a result, each study is perhaps less compelling than an experiment would be, but the consistency of the results across studies argues for their overall credibility. For example, Mintzberg (1975), observing business managers, found that most of the decisions involved only one option rather than multiple options, and the decision was whether to go with that option rather than a choice from an array of competing options. Moreover, few decisions required or received the careful balancing of losses and gains, let alone explicit use of probability, that are central to classical theory.

Peters's (1979) observations of managers yielded the same conclusions, and, in addition, he found that most decisions are elements of a larger endeavor that is directed toward achieving some desired state of affairs, with each decision providing a small step in the appropriate direction. That is, decisions are not determined solely by the relative attractiveness of their potential outcomes, they are determined by how those potential outcomes fit into a larger scheme of things. It is compliance with this larger scheme that is the chief criterion for decisions. Findings by Donaldson and Lorsch (1983) in an extensive study of the executives of 12 major corporations corroborate these conclusions. In addition, numerous observers have noted that the decision process consists more of generating and clarifying actions and goals than of choosing among prespecified alternative actions (options). And the research consistently suggests that the decision-making manager acts primarily as a promoter and protector of the organization's values rather than as a relentless seeker of maximal payoffs (Donaldson & Lorsch, 1983; Peters, 1979; Selznick, 1957).

It is illuminating that, even when they have been trained to use classical decision theory (and even when they have decision aids available to help them apply it), managers rarely use it. And even when they do use it, they seldom follow prescriptions that disagree with their own subjective intuitions (Isenberg, 1984, 1985). These are competent, intelligent, successful executives, not college students who have been dragooned into laboratory studies. Their unwillingness to use classical theory suggests that something is wrong. The usual view is that *they* are what is wrong—they ought to be using the theory. On the other hand, they know how, they have aids available, and yet they resist. To use the theory's own terms, the executives appear to regard the costs of using the theory to be greater than the benefits. One must wonder why.

Certainly, one reason decision makers resist using the theory is that its prescribed operations are cumbersome and time consuming, and the decision maker's time and resources (and patience) simply are insufficient. Phillips (1985, 1986, 1989) suggests an additional reason. Like Isenberg (1984, 1985), Phillips observed that corporate decision makers usually rely upon the "subjective mode" to make decisions, even when extensive, computerized technology is available. His discussions with executives suggest that, because the databases for deriving probabilities and projecting trends consist of records of past events, the probabilities and trends are "backward looking" and therefore are of questionable pertinence to decisions that often concern time frames of up to 20 years or more into the future. In a rapidly changing world the relative frequencies of past events may provide little guidance for decisions about such an extended future, and decision makers rely upon their own vision of what the future holds. By the same token, reliance upon data about the past assumes that the world is static—the data are useful only for predicting what will happen if the future looks a great deal like the past, or if identified trends continue. Strategic decisions are made in order to *act* upon the world, to make sure that the future does *not* look like the past. Decision makers go to great lengths to insure that they have the ability to control key future events, and controllability is factored into their decisions. As it turns out, the issue of control is an important key to why classical theory frequently is neither an appropriate standard by which to evaluate decision behavior nor a relevant model for decision aiding.

CONTROL IN DECISION BEHAVIOR

To understand why control is important, let us turn to an incisive critique of classical theory by Shafer (1986). Shafer directs his analysis at Savage's (1954) conclusion that it is optimal to make choices that maximize subjective expected utility (i.e., the version of classical theory that uses subjective probabilities and utilities), and that to do otherwise is to behave irrationally.

The vehicle used by Savage (1954), and many others, is the gamble. That is, decisions under uncertainty are regarded as gambles, and the analysis of the decisions is the same as that that would be appropriate for gambles. For example, a familiar decision dilemma (Behn & Vaupel, 1982) pits the status quo (the certain alternative) against an alternative that could, with some uncertainty, eventuate in either an outcome that is better than the status quo or an outcome that is worse than the status quo. Classical theory views the latter as a gamble that should be preferred to the status quo if its subjective expected utility is greater than the utility of the status quo.

Shafer argues that analysis of a decision in terms of subjective expected utility is an argument by analogy, an analogy between what the decision maker must do to decide and what a gambler must do to bet on an analogous game of chance. He points out that, sometimes, such an analogy is cogent, but at other times it is not.

Note that, in most games of chance, the gambler does not influence events—he or she must assay the circumstances, make his or her bet, and wait for some external process to determine whether he or she won or lost. In short, the gambler exerts little or no control over the events of interest. This is in marked contrast to the control that is so much a part of most human decisions, and insofar as such control exists, the analogy between those decisions and gambling is not cogent.

The analogy is vulnerable on at least two additional points. First, in real-life decisions, subjective probabilities and utilities seldom are independent (Slovic, 1966). This is intuitively reasonable because "the process of formulating and adopting goals creates a dependence of value on belief, simply because goals are more attractive when they are feasible" (Shafer, 1986, p. 479). The second point is that basing decisions upon the alternatives' expected values may not be appropriate for unique decisions (Lopes, 1981).

The expectation for a gamble is a weighted mean of the gains and losses that may result from choosing it, where the weights are the probabilities of the gains and the losses occurring. As such, the expectation is wholly imaginary for any single gamble—the gambler will receive *either* the gain *or* the loss, but *not* their weighted mean. In contrast, for a series of similar gambles, the expectation is the amount that the gambler is likely to end up with in the long run—and it therefore has meaning for each gamble as part of the series.

The argument is that, if a decision is not one of a series of highly similar gambles, it is not in the least clear that it is "rational" to decide by maximizing expectation, and decision makers appear to realize this. Research shows that, even when decisions are explicitly about gambles, bets on unique gambles tend not to be based upon their expected values. Keren and Wagenaar (1987) had participants choose between pairs of gambles (e.g., $100 with 99% certainty, or $250 with 50% certainty). In one condition the chosen gamble would be played only once (unique), and in the other condition the chosen gamble would be played 10 times (repeated). The gambles were designed so that the one with the highest expected value had the lower probability of winning. If the participants' decisions conform to the prescriptions of classical theory, they would choose the higher expected value gamble whether or not it was unique or repeated (e.g., $250 with 50% certainty, which has an expectation of $125 but also has the lower probability of winning, rather than $100 with 99% certainty, which has an expectation of $99). However, the data showed that, across study conditions, 71% of the participants chose the higher expected value gamble when it was to be repeated, but only about 57% chose it when it was unique. In further studies it was found that neither students nor casino gambles rely very heavily upon expected value in making wagers (Keren & Wagenaar, 1985; Wagenaar & Keren, 1988; Wagenaar, Keren, & Pleit-Kuiper, 1984; Wagenaar, Keren, & Lichtenstein, 1988). As Wagenaar

(1988; Beach, Vlek, & Wagenaar, 1988) has emphasized, if even real gamblers fail to conceive of real gambles in the way classical decision theory prescribes, it is a bit far-fetched to assume that other decision makers conceive of other decisions according to those prescriptions. All told, it is difficult to sustain much belief in the gamble analogy as a universal characterization of risky decision making—at least from the point of view of human decision makers. Whether or not their views count is, of course, a question.

DO DECISION MAKERS' VIEWS COUNT?

The conclusions reached above rely heavily upon the differences between how decision makers and classical theory view the demands and structure of various decision tasks. It can be argued that the very reason for using classical theory as a prescriptive model is that human decision makers' views of their decision tasks are flawed and therefore their views do not count for much. But, what is the evidence for this "flawed view" argument? The major evidence is its subjective appeal. Most of us feel uneasy about our decisions, primarily because we have made decisions that did not turn out well and we live with the clear understanding that we will someday regret decisions that we have not even made yet. However, classical decision theory does not address the question of making correct decisions, it merely addresses the question of making decisions correctly—that is not the same thing. That is, classical theory is about making the best bet given conditions at the moment; it is specifically about process and only indirectly about outcome. As in casino gambling, "you bet your money and take your chances," and some failures are the price of playing. Certainly, it is an article of faith that, in the long run, "proper" process (i.e., classical theory) will result in a greater number of satisfactory decisions than will any other process, but this merely is faith until it has been empirically demonstrated. And it has not been empirically demonstrated. On the contrary, research (Paquette & Kida, 1988; Payne, Bettman, & Johnson, 1988; Thorngate, 1980) shows, both in computer simulations and in solid laboratory experiments, that a variety of alternative decision methods yield results comparable to or, under short deadlines, even superior to classical theory.

The second reason that decision makers' views often are not considered to count derives from the literature on flawed judgment and decision making. However, *flawed* is defined as a deviation from classical theory, and the possibility that the theory is inappropriate is seldom entertained. With the possible exception of sociobiology, it is difficult to think of any discipline that has made its central theoretical viewpoint so unassailable.

Make no mistake, in its normative role, prescribing decisions for hypothetical Economic Man, classical theory is not subject to these criticisms. It is when behavioral scientists assume that these prescriptions apply to any and all human decisions that the mischief is done. Because its prescriptive role is assumed to have the same status as in its normative role, the legitimacy of the theory is not questioned when behavior does not conform to its prescriptions. Instead, it is concluded that the behavior, and thus the decision maker, is wrong or irrational and must be made to conform to the theory. If the rules that hold in other branches of science were to be applied here, the possibility that the theory is not universally appropriate as a standard for evaluating and aiding decision behavior would have to at least be considered.

Our point, and the point made by the literature that has been briefly presented above, is that it may not be sufficient to conclude that real decision makers lack the superhuman cognitive powers of omniscient, computationally omnipotent Economic Man, and that they therefore fall short of the classical decision theory's perfection. While human frailties must be duly noted, the difficulty may not be wholly attributable to human shortcomings. The strong suspicion is that classical theory does not provide the conceptual depth that is needed to deal with real-world complexity; in some ways people seem far more capable than the theory.

The naturalistic decision theories described by Lipshitz in Chapter 5 are attempts to break the stranglehold of classical theory on both the scientific analysis, and the real-world practice, of decision making. This is in contrast to behavioral economics, which appears satisfied with tinkering with classical theory to make it fit laboratory data. However unsystematically, the development of naturalistic decision theory has been marked by attempts to make theory more sensitive to the constraints imposed by the environments in which decisions arise. In the process it has become increasingly clear that how the decision maker perceives or *frames* (Minsky, 1968) those environmental constraints is central to understanding decision making, and that different decision strategies follow from those perceptions. Because it is cumbersome, perhaps impossible, to adequately include those constraints and perceptions within the confines of classical theory, the theory often fails to be useful when the time comes to apply it in naturalistic decision settings. Therefore, its prescriptions often are inappropriate either as guides for action or as standards for the evaluation or aiding of human decision behavior.

A CASE STUDY: THE DOWNING OF A LIBYAN
AIRLINER BY ISRAELI DEFENCE FORCES

Having critiqued classical theory, we turn now to a case study of a naturalistic decision. The decision resulted in Israeli fighter jets forcing a Libyan airliner to crash-land in the Sinai peninsula, killing all but one person aboard. The tragic incident, which caused considerable furor both within Israel and internationally, permits us to contrast the classical decision theoretic description of the decision with that of the person who made the decision, Air Force General "Motti" Hod. The exercise for the reader is to judge whether classical theory adequately captures General Hod's recounting of how the decision was made.

The Public Record

At midday on February 21, 1973, a Libyan airliner began its trip from Bengazi to Cairo. At about 2:00 p.m. the plane flew over Port Touafic (at the southern end of the Suez Canal), deviating considerably from its prescribed course. The plane had been spotted by Israeli radar before it crossed into the Israeli-occupied Sinai peninsula, and two F-4 Phantom fighters were sent to intercept it. The presence of the airliner was particularly alarming, because Israeli Intelligence had been warned of a terrorist plan to hijack an airplane and explode it over a populated area, such as Tel Aviv, or over an important military installation. Moreover, even though the airliner had violated Egyptian airspace, Egypt's air defense system had made no response. What is more, when the F-4s made contact with the plane, no passengers could be seen, because all of the window shades were down.

After making contact with the airliner, the F-4s signaled the pilot to land at Refidim air base. At first the pilot seemed to obey—he descended and lowered the plane's landing gear. Suddenly he turned back in the direction from which he had come, as if trying to escape. Despite warning shots across its path, the plane continued to fly west. General Hod did not want what was by then assumed to be a terrorist plane to escape. After telephoning his superior for concurrence, he ordered the F-4s to force the plane to land by shooting at its wing-tips. The airliner continued westward even after its right wing was hit. The F-4s then shot at its wing base which forced an attempted crash landing. The plane touched down successfully, but slid into a sand dune. There was only one survivor out of 113 passengers and crew.

Later, when the plane's "black box" was recovered, it became apparent that the airline pilot was confused about where he was and what was happening. He thought the Refidim air base was Cairo's international airport. He thought the American-built Israeli F-4s were Russian-built Egyptian MIGs. He misunderstood the signals from the Israeli pilots about what he was to do. Of course, all of this was unknown to General Hod, who was primed for a terrorist air attack.

The Classical Description

The dilemma facing the Israeli decision maker can be viewed as turning upon his uncertainty about whether the airliner was innocent and merely off course, or a terrorist bomb aimed at Tel Aviv or a military target. The decision itself depends upon the probabilities the decision maker assigned to the two 'states of nature' and the utilities he assigned to the potential outcomes. Classical theory prescribes choice of the action that has the larger subjective expected utility.

General Hod's Description

(From a slightly condensed translation of a talk given by the General.) The plane was detected in an area from which there previously had been sorties of Egyptian fighter planes. The radar warning was "hostile intrusion" with no qualifications about what kind of plane it was. The system worked automatically; F-4s were dispatched. I was at headquarters, where the intruder was tracked flying at jet speed. (Civilian airplanes fly at approximately the same speed as military planes on long-range penetrations.) We checked and found that there was no traffic on the military communication channels. Suspecting a civilian airplane, we checked the civilian airwaves and again found nothing. We could see that the plane was passing over very sensitive Egyptian locations with no reaction on the part of the Egyptian air force. All of these are indicators of a hostile intrusion.

The plane did not pass over our ground-to-air missile bases, which would have shot it down automatically. The F-4s intercepted the airliner midway between the Gulf and Refidim, and reported that it was a Libyan Boeing 727. They asked the plane to identify itself, but it could not be reached by radio. The fact that the plane was Libyan raised a warning flag for us; we had information on a terrorist plan to hijack an airliner to attack civilian targets or to pressure Israel to release imprisoned terrorists.

At this stage the F-4s were ordered to communicate with the pilot by hand signals. One fighter flew 2–3 meters away from the right side of the airliner and signaled the co-pilot to land. The fighter pilot reported that the Libyan looked straight at him and that the plane's undercarriage was lowered, indicating that the Libyan understood the signal.

At this point we did not know who was in the airliner's cockpit. In fact the crew consisted of a French captain and flight engineer, and a Libyan co-pilot who did not speak French. Visual contact was with the co-pilot, who sat on the right.

Now there began a deaf person's dialogue between me and the captain . . ., You have to realize the psychology of a captain who is responsible for 130 passengers. There is a maxim in civilian aviation that even the slightest risk to passengers' safety should be avoided. That is why airplanes are hijacked so often merely with toy guns and empty plastic boxes—the pilot simply does what the hijacker wants so as not to endanger the passengers. Given such commitment, there is no question but what the plane should land. But something else is going on here. The Captain sees—we figure that he must see—the Star of David painted on the F-4s, and he can see the airfield. He understands that we want him to land, since he releases the undercarriage and approaches the tarmac. But then he lifts the undercarriage and flys off!

The airliner did not fly away directly but first turned to circle the air base. We figured that he wanted to make a better approach. But then he turned and started to fly west. We ordered the F-4s to approach the plane again, establish eye contact, and then when the pilot is looking to shoot in the air to signal unequivocally that the plane should land. The F-4 shot, and reported that the airliner was continuing westward—even though the pilot must have seen the tracer bullets.

I passed all of this information to General Elazar [Chief of Staff of the Israeli Defence Forces], and we discussed what we should do with this rascal. He knew that we wanted him to land, saw Refidim, communicated his understanding to us, and then tried to escape. Uncertainty gradually transformed to a certainty: that plane wished to avoid landing at Refidim at all costs. But given that this was its interest, ours became to land it there at all costs. It was implausible that a captain with 130 passengers would refuse to land. The F-4s approached, and the F-4 pilot reported that he could not see anything [passengers]. All the airliner's window shades were down. There cannot be a civilian airplane with all the window shades down. Some, even the majority, may be down, they never are all down unless someone orders that they be. When the pilot reported that all the shades were down, he was ordered to shoot at the wing tips to convince the guy that we sincerely wanted him to land. Our uncertainty diminished every minute. Assuming that he understood us, it made no sense; there was absolutely no explanation why a captain would not land. Therefore, we were not going to let him escape. All of this took only a few minutes, but time seemed to pass very slowly.

At this stage we tried to establish communication with Cairo on all the emergency channels. We failed, both there and in other places. The F-4 shot at the wing tip, but the Libyan remained indifferent and proceeded westward. This convinced us absolutely that he had such an excellent reason not to land at Refidim that this was the key to the whole affair. We felt compelled to force it to land to find out why he was so obstinate.

A few months earlier an Ethiopian airliner strayed into the Egyptian ground-to-air missile system and the poor thing was shot down. An American private airplane also was shot down by missiles above the Delta. Several other planes were fired at when they penetrated areas where the maps warn that you will be shot at without warning. Pilots are familiar with these free-fire zones, and airline captains stay far away from them because of their obligation to passengers' safety. And here was this plane despite all the warnings. That's how all uncertainty dissipated—he certainly had something to hide from us.

Let us now move to the cockpit, in view of what we learned from the plane's "black box." There sat the French captain and flight engineer and the Libyan co-pilot. The first two converse in French, which the co-pilot does not understand, and ignore him altogether. They drink wine and find themselves approximately 70 miles off course without a clue to their whereabouts. When they see the F-4s they identify them as MIGs, and when the co-pilot tells them to land they reassure him that there is no problem, since these are MIGs and they are flying to Cairo. Everything is in French, and the co-pilot doesn't understand a word.

Our communication is with the Libyan co-pilot, and the Frenchmen ignore him, and everything else, because they know that Egypt and Libya are on such good terms that under no circumstances will Egyptian fighters shoot down a Libyan airliner. When the F-4s start to shoot the Captain and engineer panic, thinking that the MIGs have gone berserk. When they finally decide to land, they crash into the sand dune and almost all aboard are killed.

Should there have been a different decision, in retrospect? I confess that if an unidentified airplane penetrated the same area today, flying in the identical direction, and under a similar intelligence warning, I would react in precisely the same way. Who can claim today that it was unwise to shoot the plane down then and there? It was well known that the general area was highly sensitive, and that airplanes—not civilian but military airplanes—had been shot down there before. Lastly, was the decision made under time pressure? Not really, because time is relative. When you flirt with a girl, 2½ minutes pass in a flicker, but when you are in a dog-fight they sometimes are an eternity.

In terms of the features of the naturalistic decision models: Most of General Hod's description underscores efforts to assess the situation, to figure out what was going on. In part this involved past experience: the Six-Day War, previous intrusions, knowledge about airline pilots' protectiveness of their passengers. In part it involved information procurement, monitoring military and civilian radio channels, attempts to communicate with the airliner itself and with Cairo, and the F-4s' surveillance of the intruder. And in part it involved inferences based upon available information—inferences about the airline captain's motivation and intent in an attempt to make his actions make sense, inferences about the meaning of the closed window shades, inferences about meaning of the aborted landing and the attempt to fly back toward Egypt.

As events unfolded, the general's initial uncertainty decreased until, at the time that he ordered the F-4s to force the airliner down, he was no longer uncertain about the plane and its hostile intent. In retrospect he was incorrect, but he was certain nonetheless. In short, he was not making a bet—he was acting upon what seemed to him to be a sure thing. He was not considering two alternative actions—he was doing the single action that followed directly from his appraisal of the situation. To a large degree there was no decision in the classical sense.

A recent account of this incident (Lanir, 1991) helps us to tie up some loose ends and complete the story, even though it does not affect the analysis of the decision making of the Israeli generals. It appears that the Libyan airline crew believed their plane was over Egypt, and the pilot interpreted the Israeli jets as Egyptian MiGs. Cairo has a military airport to the east, and the civilian airport is to the west. As the airliner was preparing to land, the pilot noticed that it was a military base, and believed he was making a blunder, which explained the presence of the military aircraft around him. Suddenly, everything fit together. That is why he pulled up and headed west. He was looking for the civilian airport on the other side of Cairo. Given his situation assessment, it was the obvious action to take.

SUMMARY

For almost half a century the study of human decision behavior has been dominated by a single standard, the prescriptions of classical decision theory. The purpose of this chapter was to argue that this domination no longer is viable and that it is time to move on to new ways of thinking about decision making. To this end, we have presented a critique of the appropriateness of classical decision theory as a standard against which to measure the adequacy of human decision making. The critique was drawn from the decision literature and focused upon the theory's adequacy for describing decision behavior in both laboratory studies, usually involving students as subjects, and in observational studies, usually involving practicing managers as subjects. The conclusions are listed below. In light of these, it seems clear that classical theory cannot continue to be used as the standard for evaluating all decision behavior. The theory has its place, of that there can be no doubt. But where its use as the single standard may have once been justified because so little was known about decision making and about human cognition, circumstances have changed. It is time to stop patching and propping an inappropriate theory. It is time to create a more useful theory.

KEY POINTS

- Real-life, naturalistic decision tasks frequently differ markedly from the task for which classical decision theory was designed.
- Even when they know how, professional decision makers seldom rely upon classical theory to make decisions.
- The fundamental role of control in naturalistic decisions belies classical decision theory's reliance upon gambles as an all-purpose analogy for decisions.
- The assumption that use of classical decision theory necessarily will improve decision success is empirically unproven and questionable.
- The features of naturalistic decision settings described in Chapter 1 are not adequately addressed by classical decision theory.

Chapter 3

Three Paradigms for Viewing Decision Biases

Marvin S. Cohen
Cognitive Technologies, Inc.
Arlington, VA

I. EVALUATING DECISIONS

Decisions can, and do, go wrong: A doctor misdiagnoses a patient's illness; a new product fails in the marketplace; a military commander mistakenly engages a civilian aircraft. Undesirable outcomes, however, do not necessarily imply faulty decision making; consider General Hod's decision to shoot down a Libyan airliner (described at the end of the last chapter). Even though the aircraft turned out *not* to be on a hostile mission, his conclusion that it was hostile might have been justified by the information he had at the time, by his efforts to gather further relevant data, and by the costs of a terrorist incident. It can also happen, of course, that a bad decision works out well. It is natural, then, for psychologists to look for a way of evaluating the decision itself, or the process that led to the decision, as distinct from its outcomes: to point, for example, at false prior beliefs, inappropriate priorities, shaky inferences from data, or even logical inconsistencies, rather than simply a bad outcome.

A widely accepted research paradigm in psychology (e.g., Kahneman, Slovic, & Tversky, 1982) has taken Bayesian decision theory as the standard by which reasoning is to be judged, and has identified pervasive *patterns* of error, called *biases,* in laboratory performance. According to these researchers, unaided decision processes employ rules of thumb (or *heuristics*) that under many (but not all) conditions lead to "severe and systematic errors" (Tversky & Kahneman, 1974). The bottom line of this research has been a rather pessimistic view of human reasoning. To illustrate, let us extrapolate some of the laboratory results on biases and their interpretation to a hypothetical physician:

- In assessing the probability that she will encounter cases of diseases A, B, and C among her patients, the physician may rely on the ease with which she can recall or imagine instances of each disease. This is the so-called *availability heuristic,* postulated by Tversky and Kahneman (1972). Availability may be influenced by factors like the recency or salience of the physician's own experiences, which do not reflect the true relative frequencies of the diseases in the relevant population.
- In estimating a quantity, such as the required length of treatment for disease B, the doctor may first generate her best guess, then adjust it upwards and downwards to allow for uncertainty, e.g., 10 days plus or minus 2. This is the *anchoring and adjustment* heuristic. According to Tversky and Kahneman (1974), adjustments are typically insufficient. The result is an *overconfidence* bias (Lichtenstein, Fischhoff, & Phillips, 1982), for example, 95% confidence intervals that contain fewer than 95% of the actual cases.
- If the description of a patient's symptoms resembles the stereotypical picture of disease C, the physician may assign C a high probability, even if it is in fact extremely rare in comparison to diseases A and B. This is called *base rate neglect,* and may result from the *representativeness heuristic,* a tendency to judge probabilities by the similarity of a sample or instance to a prototype of its parent population (Kahneman & Tversky, 1972).
- Once she has arrived at an opinion about the illness that is causing the patient's symptoms, the doctor may fail to revise her opinion in the light of new symptoms or test results that conflict with it; she may even find ways to explain away the apparently conflicting data. This is the so-called *belief bias,* or *confirmation bias,* extensively reviewed in Nisbett and Ross (1980). Tversky and Kahneman (1980) attribute it to the compelling nature of causal beliefs.
- In evaluating different treatment alternatives, the doctor may take her most important objective first (e.g., reducing the size of a tumor by x%) and eliminate options that fail to achieve it; she may then compare the surviving options to her next most important goal (e.g., avoiding certain side-effects), and so on until only one option is left. This is the *elimination-by-aspects* strategy (Tversky, 1972). It may lead the doctor to overlook important compensatory relationships; for example, she may reject an option that just misses one goal but that is outstanding in other respects.
- The doctor may regard a treatment more favorably if she happens

to think of the outcomes in terms of potential gains, such as chance of survival, and less favorably if she happens to think of those same outcomes in terms of potential losses, such as chance of death. This is the *reference effect*, discussed by Tversky and Kahneman (1981). They attribute it to predecisional processes that select a neutral reference point for the representation of outcomes, and to judgmental processes that weight losses with respect to the reference point more heavily than comparable gains.

On what grounds do psychologists claim that the doctor's assessments, inferences, and choices in these examples are mistaken? In some cases (e.g., availability, anchoring and adjustment) the doctor's probability assessments may be compared to actual frequencies of the relevant events (i.e., disease types and treatment durations, respectively). In other cases (such as the examples of base-rate neglect and confirmation bias) the relevant events are more complex and one-of-a-kind, and empirical frequencies will often be unavailable. Nevertheless, whether frequencies are available or not, the doctor's judgments or inferences can be evaluated in terms of their internal coherence. Bayesian probability theory provides a normative standard that is accepted by many researchers, and which specifies how a person's beliefs *should* be related to one another. Similarly, Bayesian decision theory (which includes probability theory as a part) provides a standard for evaluating the rationality of the doctor's *choices* among treatment options, even when a large sample of actual choice outcomes is not available, in terms of the internal coherence among her beliefs, preferences, and actions.

According to this research, a decision bias is not a lack of knowledge, a false belief about the facts, or an inappropriate goal; nor does it necessarily involve lapses of attention, motivation, or memory. Rather, a decision bias is a systematic flaw in the internal relationships among a person's judgments, desires, and/or choices. Human reasoning depends, under most conditions, on heuristic procedures and representations that predictably lead to such inconsistencies. It follows that human reasoning processes are error prone *by their very nature*.

Few recent areas of psychological research have had as much impact on psychology as the work on heuristics and biases, or have been as widely cited in the literature of other fields and in the popular press (as noted by Berkeley & Humphreys, 1982; and by Lopes, 1988). Perhaps more importantly, this research has motivated efforts to help people make better decisions, by automating or supporting the "normatively correct" methods for processing information (e.g., Edwards, 1968). Nevertheless, there is a growing chorus of dissent (e.g., Anderson, 1986; Berkeley & Humphreys, 1982; Einhorn & Hogarth, 1981; Jungermann, 1983; Lopes, 1988, Shanteau, 1989; and many others). Some of the original investigators have begun to emphasize methodological and conceptual problems in the research on biases, and have concluded that, at the very least, human shortcomings have been exaggerated at the expense of human capabilities (e.g., Kahneman & Tversky, 1982a; von Winterfeldt & Edwards, 1986).

A focus on naturalistic decision making adds a new perspective to this debate, opening to question some of the basic assumptions of the decision bias research. For example, what is the actual impact (or lack of impact) of each bias in real-world domains? Can we predict when errors will be serious and when not? Does the dynamic and open-ended quality of real tasks, as opposed to laboratory tasks, help reduce the effects of biases? Are biases sometimes mitigated by task-specific knowledge? Do they sometimes occur as side effects of using knowledge effectively? Do biases sometimes reflect a decision maker's capacity limitations or adaptations to the cost of information processing? How are such costs measured, and how is such adaptation achieved? Finally, are we really sure what a decision-making "error" is? What conclusions follow if we look more closely at how people actually reason before fitting a normative model that says how they "ought" to reason?

These questions are by no means settled. Nor is there any assurance that the answers, when they come, will support a more optimistic view of decision making; for example, errors may be worse rather than better in dynamic, open-ended environments. Nevertheless, these questions establish the need for research that is both carefully controlled and representative of real-world decisions. It is surely worthwhile to consider seriously an alternative to the standard view, which, although not proven, is consistent with all the evidence we now have. According to this alternative picture, *people tend to use decision-making strategies that make effective use of their substantive knowledge and processing capacity; such strategies are generally subject to incremental revision and improvement in dynamic environments;* and *the net result is performance that is usually adequate, though subject to improvement in specific respects.* Such a picture, by exposing and challenging assumptions underlying the standard view, may be a fruitful stimulus to research that is both more valid and ultimately, more useful. Moreover, if this picture is true, even in part, *decision aiding and training should be targeted at strengthening the decision maker's preferred approach to a problem rather than replacing it altogether.*

Our discussion of these topics is organized as follows. Section II of this chapter will describe three alternative paradigms for viewing decision biases—comparing the paradigms with respect to the types of normative and explanatory models they utilize, and the style of empirical research they encourage. The next chapter will explore the "naturalistic paradigm" in more depth, discussing six challenges to the prevailing "rationalist" view of decision biases. These challenges emphasize the information-rich and dynamic character of the decision environment, the capacity limitations and knowledge of the decision maker, and the importance of cognitive and behavioral criteria in the selection of an appropriate normative benchmark. Taken together, these challenges lead to a more convincing and more useful, naturalistic concept of decision bias. In Chapter 15, I turn finally to the implications of the naturalistic paradigm for decision aiding and training.

II. A TALE OF THREE PARADIGMS

Recent demonstrations of decision errors have been dramatic, but not because anyone had really thought that humans were perfectly rational. Discrepancies between behavior and apparent normative constraints had been well known to an earlier generation of researchers. By the same token, recent researchers on biases have not painted an unremittingly gloomy picture. What happened may be best illuminated by the metaphor of a *paradigm shift* (cf. Lopes, 1988): Research on decision biases has changed the way conflict between behavior and normative models is *interpreted;* it has also changed the character of psychological models, and the style of empirical research. New work may now be causing all of these to change once again.

There are three basic paradigms, or filters, through which this subject may be viewed: the *formal-empiricist* paradigm, which preceded the research on biases as the standard approach to decision making; the *rationalist* paradigm, which has spawned most of the present controversy; and the *naturalistic* paradigm, which is now emerging and, we argue, offers the most fruitful perspective.

The Formal-Empiricist Paradigm

Up to the late 1960s, researchers on decision making wanted their theories to do double duty: both to fit empirically observed behavior and to have normative plausibility. If behavior failed to fit a model, they did not condemn the behavior as "irrational"; instead, they regarded the *model* as inadequate—both to describe behavior and to evaluate it (Barclay, Beach, & Braithwaite, 1971; Beach, Christensen-Szalanski, & Barnes, 1987; Lee, 1971). The experimenter's task was to devise a new formal description of the anomalous behavior that brought out its good features—that provided a *rationale*.

Paradoxes, in which carefully considered judgments or decisions clashed with a model, were occasions to question, and possibly to improve, the model. According to a proposed normative rule for choice under uncertainty, for example, one should select the option that has the highest *expected value*. The expected value of an option is an average obtained by adding the payoffs associated with each possible outcome, while weighing each outcome by its probability of occurrence. (If a lottery ticket pays $1000 to the winner, and there is a 1 in 10,000 chance of winning, the expected value of the ticket is: (.0001) ($1000) + (.9999) ($0) = $0.10; a rational decision maker, according to the expected-value rule, should be willing to pay no more than 10 cents for such a ticket.)

Many features of ordinary behavior—such as purchasing insurance and gambling—are inconsistent with maximization of expected value. Instead of heralding these as *decision biases*, Bernoulli tried to make sense of them (focusing in particular on a famous problem called the St. Petersburg paradox). In 1738 he proposed replacing the *objective* measure of preference (e.g., money) with a *subjective* one (utility), and assumed that the utility of each additional dollar is smaller as the number of accumulated dollars increases. The same rule, with more elaborate assumptions about the way utility is related to dollars or other objective payoffs, is still used today to reconcile the normative model with ordinary intuitions and behavior. Upon such technical threads hangs the rationality of an enormous set of everyday decisions.

Although utility is subjective, *probability* might be defined objectively, in terms of the relative frequency of an event (e.g., heads) in some sample space (e.g., a series of coin tosses). Yet people also find it meaningful to talk about, and make decisions that depend on, probabilities of unique events; for example, "Bush will probably be re-elected President." (Even the "objective" notion of probability seems to depend on judgment in selecting an appropriate sample space.) The next major step in the evolution of formal-empiricist models replaced frequency-based probabilities with *subjective probabilities*, or personal degrees of belief. As a price for accommodating unique events and individual differences in decision making, normative models could no longer dictate the *content* of a person's beliefs or preferences.

What *did* normative models do? De Finetti (1937/1964) and Savage (1954) developed formal systems for merging subjective preferences and subjective probabilities in a new normative rule, maximization of *subjectively expected utility* (SEU). This rule looks the same as maximization of expected value, except that subjective probabilities and utilities are substituted for objective probabilities and payoffs, respectively. The surface similarity disguises an important difference, however. Unlike maximization of expected value, the SEU "rule" does not imply a *procedure* for decision making: Probabilities and utilities are defined by reference to a decision maker's choices among gambles; they do not guide such choices. There is no longer a rationale for starting with probabilities and preferences as inputs and deriving choices, or measures of the desirability of options, as outputs; the decision maker could just as well start with the desirability of an option and assess probabilities and utilities afterwards. What the SEU rule and the associated laws of probability do is specify *consistency relationships* that probabilities and utilities (and the choices that define them) should satisfy.

Savage and De Finetti successfully showed that behavior satisfying these consistency relationships had certain very general attractive features, which they described in postulates or axioms: For example, judgments about the *probability* of an event are the same regardless of changes in *preference* for that event (Savage's independence postulate). Conversely, de Finetti and Savage showed (by derivation of the SEU rule from such postulates) that, if you want your decisions to have the attractive features, then your judgments and decisions *must* satisfy the SEU rule and the laws of probability.

Psychologists tested formal-empiricist models by asking subjects to make choices in sets of interrelated gambles that varied in their uncertain events and payoffs (e.g., Davidson, Suppes, & Siegel, 1957). If a subject's choices were consistent with the SEU axioms, then utilities of the payoffs, and subjective probabilities of the events, could be said to exist and could be numerically defined for that subject. (For example, if a subject was indifferent between $.40 for sure and a gamble with a 50–50 chance of winning $1.00, the utility of $.40 would be one-half the utility of $1.00 for that subject.) Experimental tests, however, typically showed deviations from the formal-empiricist predictions (e.g., Marks, 1951; Mosteller & Nogee, 1951; Swets, 1961; Tversky, 1967). One conclusion, according to a review by Peterson and Beach (1967), was that humans were pretty good, but not perfect, "intuitive statisticians." Another response was to continue to loosen the constraints imposed by models of decision making: for example, to introduce a notion of probabilistic choice (obeying a weaker set of axioms) in place of deterministic choice (Luce, 1959, 1977), or to include the variance among outcomes as an attribute affecting the desirability of a gamble (Allais, 1953).

Table 3.1.   Three Paradigms for Decision-Making Research

	Formal-Empiricist Paradigm	Rationalist Paradigm	Naturalistic Paradigm
Criteria of Normative Evaluation	Behavioral and Formal	Formal Only	Behavioral, Cognitive, and Formal
Style of Psychological Modeling	Formal	Cognitive-Eclectic	Cognitive-Integrated?
Style of Empirical Observation	(a) Systematic Variation of Model Parameters (b) Artificial Tasks	(a) Demonstrations of Formal Errors (b) Simplified "Real World" Tasks	(a) Study of Decision Processes and Outcomes (b) Complex Real-World Tasks

The formal-empiricist paradigm focussed on behavioral testing of formal models, not on the cognitive processes actually underlying decisions. Little effort, for example, was made to collect concurrent think-aloud protocols from subjects as they made decisions, to interview them afterwards about the reasons for their choices, or even to vary parameters that might affect performance but which were not in the formal model. The models themselves, as already noted, impose mathematical consistency constraints on a subject's judgments and preferences, but make no reference to actual psychological steps or representations. Not surprisingly, then, some psychologists have questioned the cognitive plausibility of SEU even in cases where it fits behavior. Lopes (1983; Schneider & Lopes, 1985), for example, has argued that real decision makers are less concerned with an option's average outcome than with the outcomes that are most *likely* to occur.

In sum (as shown in the first column of Table 3.1), the formal-empiricist paradigm: (a) allowed human intuition and performance to drive normative theorizing, along with more formal, axiomatic considerations; (b) used the resulting normative theories as *descriptive* accounts of decision-making performance; and (c) tested and refined the descriptive/normative models by means of systematic variation of model parameters in artificial tasks.

The Rationalist Paradigm

Since Plato and earlier, "rationalist" philosophers have found ordinary reasoning riddled with flaws, and held out the promise of a more rigorous method for establishing the truth. At least since Descartes, the preferred method has involved replacing intuitive leaps of thought by short, logically self-evident steps. Both of these elements—the disparagement of ordinary reasoning and the promotion of a more valid methods—have flourished, somewhat independently, in the last 20 years.

Decision analysis has "come of age" as a body of techniques for applying decision theory in management consulting (Ulvila & Brown, 1982). In contrast to the purely formal constraints of decision theory, decision analysis specifies procedures: for example, Bayesian inference (for drawing conclusions or making forecasts based on incomplete or unreliable evidence), decision tree analysis (for choices with uncertain outcomes), and multiattribute utility analysis (for choices with multiple competing criteria of evaluation) (see Brown, Kahr, & Peterson, 1974; Keeney & Raiffa, 1976; Raiffa, 1968). The prescribed problem-solving strategy is to decompose a problem into elements, to have appropriate experts or decision makers subjectively assess probabilities and/or utilities for the components, and then to recombine them by the appropriate mathematical rule.

The prevailing concept of decision biases emphasizes the other side of rationalism: errors in unaided decision making. Errors have now taken on a more dramatic and important role than in previous research. Underlying this change was a paradigm shift in the relationship between normative and descriptive theorizing. The rationalist paradigm takes decision theory as a norm that is fully justified by its formal properties (i.e., the postulates that entail it), not by its fit to the way people in fact make decisions; rationalism attributes discrepancies between behavior and a model to the irrationality of decision makers, not to flaws in the model.

What motivated the change in attitude toward normative theories? According to Kahneman and Tversky (1982a), the goal of their work was to make the psychology of decision making more cognitive. The formal-empiricist paradigm had combined normative and descriptive functions in the same formal models; the rationalist paradigm separates the functions of (cognitively) describing or explaining behavior and (formally) evaluating it. To make their case for a cognitive approach to explanation, however, Kahneman, Tversky, and other researchers had to do more than show divergence between the normative model and actual decisions: after all, in the formal-empiricist paradigm a model could always be revised. Decision bias researchers foreclosed this possibility by promoting a picture of normative theory as a fixed benchmark, immune to descriptive influence. The emphasis on human irrationality was a by-product.

Part of the appeal of rationalist research has been its use of easily understood demonstrations of errors. Everyday problems replaced artificial choices about lotteries; systematic variation of model parameters gave way to the less tedious presentation of a few simple variants of the same problem, sufficient to demonstrate inconsistency, though not to fit a model (Lopes, 1988). Readers can thus confirm conclusions about "biases" by checking their own intuitions. Nevertheless, the realism of these experiments is limited. Stimuli, although ostensibly drawn from real life, typically involve unfamiliar situations briefly described to college or high school students; moreover, they are usually prestructured and prequantified, and involve a single response to a static rather than an unfolding situation: that is, the problems specify numerical frequencies, probabilities, and/or payoffs, and subjects are asked to make one-time decisions about explicitly identified hypotheses or options.

Consider the following problem, used to demonstrate base rate neglect by Tversky and Kahneman (1980, p. 162):

A cab was involved in a hit-and-run accident at night. Two cab companies, the Green and the Blue, operate in the city. You are given the following data:
(i) 85% of the cabs in the city are Green and 15% are Blue;
(ii) A witness identified the cab as a Blue cab. The court tested his ability to identify cabs under the appropriate visibility conditions. When presented with a sample of cabs (half of which were Blue and half of which were Green) the witness made correct identification in 80% of the cases and erred in 20% of the cases.
Question: What is the probability that the cab involved in the accident was Blue rather than Green?

According to Tversky and Kahneman, the probability that the guilty cab is Blue is computed from Bayes' Rule as follows:

$$(.15)(.80) \: / \: ((.15)(.80) + (.85)(.20)) = .41$$

where .15 is the base rate of Blue cabs, and .85 is the base rate of Green cabs. The base rates in this case strongly favor Green and should outweigh the witness's testimony that the cab was Blue. Most subjects, however, inferred the probability of Blue to be at or near .80, apparently ignoring base rates. In a different variant of the problem, however, when the witness (item ii) was omitted from the problem, subjects did use base rates. Subjects also paid more attention to base rates when (i) was replaced by a more "causally relevant" base rate, the frequency of accidents attributed to Blue and Green cabs.

It is perhaps no surprise that in such experiments unaided human decision making has been found wanting. Biases have been observed in virtually every context that a statistician could imagine, including:

Assessment of probabilities—
- overconfidence in estimating probabilities of simple events,
- overconfidence in estimating probability distributions for quantities,
- reliance on ease of recall or generation (i.e., availability) in estimating frequencies of events in a class,
- overestimating, after an event has actually occurred, the probability that would have been assessed for the event before it occurred (hindsight bias),
- relying on theoretical preconceptions rather than data in estimating correlations between events (illusory correlation);

Inference—
- disregarding prior statistical information in responding to a single piece of evidence (base rate neglect),
- disregarding or discounting evidence that conflicts with a prior hypothesis (belief bias),
- confirmation bias in selecting observations to test a hypothesis;
- failing to update belief sufficiently in the light of new evidence (the conservatism bias),
- disregarding sources of uncertainty: acting "as if" earlier conclusions were known with certainty when reasoning proceeds in stages; adopting the most likely hypothesis as a "best guess,"
- ignoring sample size in assessing the accuracy of estimates or the probability of a sample,
- overestimating the probabilities of compound events (the conjunction fallacy),
- mistaken conceptions of randomness in estimating the probabilities of chance sequences of events: overestimating the probability of sequences with many alternations and representative proportions,
- overextreme predictions (neglecting regression to the mean) when predicting one quantity based on its correlation with another quantity,

Choice—
- effect on decisions of changes in the reference point for describing simple outcomes: for example, risk aversion if outcomes are described as gains, risk seeking if the same outcomes are described as losses,
- effect on decisions of how multiple events are grouped together and associated with options as their outcomes ("psychological accounts"),
- effect on decisions of ignorance regarding true probabilities; resort to "worst-case" or "best-case" strategies in defining outcomes (Ellsberg's paradox),
- a greater effect on preference of reducing the probability of an outcome by a given ratio when the outcome was certain, than when it was not certain (the certainty effect, or common ratio effect),
- effect on decisions of how outcomes are sequenced in time; evaluating outcomes as if earlier, uncertain contingencies were known to occur (the pseudo-certainty effect),
- effect on decisions of changes in the payoff for an outcome that is the same regardless of which option is chosen (Allais' paradox, or the common consequence effect).

We will touch on some of these errors in the discussions that follow; reviews can be found in Einhorn and Hogarth (1981); Hogarth and Makridakis (1981); Slovic, Fischhoff, and Lichtenstein (1977); Smithson (1988); Tversky and Kahneman (1974).

At the deepest level, biases are violations of consistency constraints imposed by probability theory or decision theory. (Even in the case of assessment biases, such as overconfidence and availability, agreement with empirical frequencies is relevant only if it is expected according to the formal theory.) For example, in one condition of the cab study (when the witness's testimony was included), subjects regarded base rates as irrelevant, while in another condition (when the witness was omitted), they regarded the same base rate data as relevant. In this example, as in many others, the formal equivalence between conditions is implicit, resting on the experimenter's assumptions about the subjects' other beliefs and/or preferences (e.g., that frequency data do not become less relevant due to the presence or absence of a witness).

From an explanatory point of view, however, biases have been attributed to any of a rather large number of cognitive processes. Base rate neglect, for example, is explained in the cab problem by preference for information that can be interpreted causally (Tversky & Kahneman, 1982). In other cases the same formal error (base rate neglect) is explained by the tendency to assess probabilities in terms of "representativeness," or the similarity of a sample to its population (Tversky & Kahneman, 1982). Other explanatory hypotheses (which we have already alluded to) include availability (assessing the probability of a class by the ease of recalling or generating instances), anchoring and adjustment (beginning the estimation process with a salient anchor point and insufficiently adjusting it to allow for other factors), and representation processes that distort the decision maker's use of probabilities and payoffs in choice problems (Kahneman & Tversky's "Prospect Theory," 1979).

Rationalist experiments, unlike formal-empiricist ones, often study factors not contained in the normative model: one example is the comparison of a "causally relevant" base rate with a "statistical" one in the base rate neglect study. Such manipulations expose additional reasoning errors (when the manipulated variable has an effect even though it should not) and also help test hypotheses about the cognitive processes underlying performance (e.g., the reliance on causal problem representations). Nevertheless, such manipulations fall far short of a systematic investigation of cognitive mechanisms. The primary goal of the experiments is simply to compare rival hypotheses of normatively "correct" versus "incorrect" behavior. As in formal-empiricist experimentation, there has been virtually no effort to explore cognitive processes more directly—by means of verbal protocols, interviews, or other process-tracing techniques (e.g., eye-movements or information requests).

The result, ironically, has been a failure by the rationalist paradigm to successfully integrate decision making research with the rest of cognitive psychology. Attention has focussed on classification of an ever-growing array of biases, defined negatively as deviations from "the" normative theory (Anderson, 1986); there has been insufficient effort to test alternative psychological explanations (Shanteau, 1989), to systematically study how and when the postulated heuristics and representation processes occur (Fischhoff, 1983), or to develop underlying theoretical principles and links with other areas of psychology such as problem solving and learning (Wallsten, 1983).

The rationalist paradigm promoted a desirable transition to cognitively oriented theories of performance by adopting a less desirable tactic: creating a rigid normative concept as a straw man, and designing experiments that often do little more than discredit the straw man. In sum (as shown in the second column of Table 3.1), the rationalist paradigm (a) adopts a static and purely formal view of normative standards, (b) gives an explanatory account of reasoning in terms of a diverse set of unrelated cognitive mechanisms, and (c) experimentally demonstrates errors with prestructured and prequantified "real-life" stimuli.

The Naturalistic Paradigm

The argument of this book is that a third paradigm is now emerging, distinguished from both the formal-empiricist and the rationalist paradigms by a more pronounced concern for decision making in realistic, dynamic, and complex environments (see Chapter 1), and the adoption of research methodologies that focus more directly on decision processes, as well as their real-world outcomes (see Woods, this volume). In this section and in the next chapter, I will explore the implications of that new paradigm for the notion of decision-making "error."

The naturalistic point of view involves more than simply looking for the same biases and heuristics in realistic settings. From the naturalistic perspective, an unquestioning acceptance of the relevance of classical normative standards is untenable, because real-world decision makers appear to use qualitatively different types of cognitive processes and representations. If these decisions are to be evaluated, other standards may often be appropriate. The new paradigm thus breaks the spell of classical probability/decision theory. Research is not tethered to it either as an explanatory model (the formal-empiricist paradigm) or as a straw man (the rationalist paradigm).

The naturalistic paradigm agrees with the rationalist approach (and differs from the formal-empiricist approach) in its explanatory emphasis on cognitive representations and processes. But it gets there without reliance on the tactic of looking for human irrationality under every behavioral stone. Formal models fail, not because people irrationally violate them (as the rationalists argue), but because the models themselves do not capture the adaptive characteristics of real-world behavior. By focusing on the way people actually handle complex environments, the naturalistic paradigm illuminates the *functions* that cognitive processes serve. As a result, it stands a better chance of developing a successful and coherent set of explanatory models. One by-product is a decreased emphasis on relatively ad hoc cognitive procedures, like heuristics, and more focus on an integrated picture of how knowledge structures are created and adjusted in dynamic environments.

The naturalistic point of view does not wholly banish the idea that errors occur when people make decisions—or even the idea that those errors are systematic: Everything "natural" is not good. In many respects, decision making in naturalistic settings is surely more difficult than in laboratory tasks (e.g., options, hypotheses, goals, and uncertainties may all be unspecified), and there is still a need to both evaluate and improve performance. The notion of a *decision bias* may yet prove useful in both respects. From the naturalistic perspective, however, evaluation of reasoning is more subtle and demanding: no longer a cookie-cutter comparison between performance and an unquestioned normative template. In the naturalistic framework, the reciprocity between normative and descriptive concerns that characterized the formal-empiricist approach can be retained—and even expanded—*if cognitive as well as behavioral criteria are incorporated into normative modeling*. Normative theories are intellectual tools whose justification depends in part on how well they fit a particular decision maker's goals, knowledge, and capabilities in the task at hand (cf. Shafer & Tversky, 1988); they are products of a negotiation between competing sets of intuitions about specific problems, general principles, and cognitively plausible methods.

We suspect that decision biases have not been satisfactorily identified, described, or explained within the prevailing rationalist approach. If errors are perceived where they do not exist and if other, perhaps more important types of error are overlooked, then decision aiding and training cannot hope to be effective or accepted. The naturalistic paradigm may cause us to see decision-making errors in a new light.

KEY POINTS

- Traditional research in decision making was derived from two paradigms: formalist-empiricist and rationalist.
- While neither paradigm has successfully described decision making in real settings, each paradigm offers a perspective worth retaining.
- While the formal empiricist paradigm tailored formal models to fit decision behavior, the rationalist paradigm uses formal models to critique decision behavior.
- The naturalistic paradigm rejects a purely formal approach, whether for describing or for evaluating decisions.
- The nature of errors that people make in real settings is different from the biases described by rationalist research. People are not hopelessly irrational.
- Naturalistic decision making research stands a better chance of producing a coherent set of explanatory models of decision making in ill-understood, novel, and changing task environments.

Chapter 4

The Naturalistic Basis of Decision Biases

Marvin S. Cohen
Cognitive Technologies, Inc.
Arlington, VA

Research within the rationalist paradigm has thrown a spotlight on decision-making errors. But if the rationalist understanding of decision errors is inadequate, as I claimed in Chapter 3, what can we put in its place? A convenient strategy is to break down the rationalist argument and examine the assumptions that seem most questionable from the naturalistic point of view. Out of this discussion, a new, naturalistic notion of decision bias will emerge.

The rationalist paradigm starts with the claim that unaided decisions are often formally inconsistent, and draws two conclusions. The rationalist argues, first, that the decision processes that predictably lead to such decisions are flawed. From the same premise, the rationalist also concludes (at least implicitly) that the outcomes to which such decisions lead will be undesirable. Both of these conclusions, as well as the original premise of formal inconsistency, can and have been challenged. Each of them, I will argue, disregards important characteristics of real-world environments, real-world decision makers, and real-world tasks.

> Rationalist claim: Inconsistent decisions lead to undesirable outcomes.
> - Challenge (1): A desirable overall outcome can be achieved in *real-world problem domains,* even though some individual decisions have undesirable outcomes.
> - Challenge (2): *Real-world environments* facilitate desirable outcomes from *individual* decisions.
> Rationalist claim: Decision processes are flawed because they lead to inconsistent decisions.
> - Challenge (3): The inconsistency of decisions is mitigated

by the benefits of using the decision maker's *real-world knowledge*.

- Challenge (4): Constraints on the decision maker's *information-processing capacity* justify use of non-Bayesian procedures.

Rationalist claim: Decisions are often formally inconsistent.

- Challenge (5): There are *alternative Bayesian models* that better capture the subject's understanding of specific tasks.
- Challenge (6): There are *alternative, non-Bayesian normative concepts* that justify the decision maker's way of approaching specific tasks.

Such challenges are not mutually exclusive. They vary, however, in where they draw the line against rationalist pessimism: that is, at outcomes [Challenges (1) and (2)]; more aggressively, at the decision processes that lead to the outcomes [Challenges (3) and (4)]; or, more aggressively still, at the very notion of an inconsistent decision [Challenges (5) and (6)].

Challenges (1) and (2) focus on the failure of the rationalist research to take account of the effects of decisions in real-world environments. By themselves, (1) and (2) do not challenge the rationalist paradigm very profoundly: They agree that decisions are often inconsistent, and that decision processes are therefore biased, but ask only how much it really matters in real task domains or in specific tasks. Challenges (3) and (4) go further; they focus on the failure of rationalist research to take full account of the "internal environment" with which the decision maker must deal. Decision processes may be justified, even though they sometimes produce inconsistent decisions because they reflect effective use of the decision maker's knowledge or efficient rationing of her cognitive effort. Challenges (5) and (6) criticize the rationalist approach for disregarding or misunderstanding important elements of the decision task, from the point of view of the decision maker. Appropriate modeling of the decision maker's beliefs and preferences concerning a task, whether within a Bayesian or non-Bayesian framework, shows that decisions are not flawed even in the narrowest sense. Challenge (6) questions the underlying relationship between descriptive and normative concerns that has been central to the rationalist paradigm.

The naturalistic paradigm criticizes the rationalist concept of decision error, but it also proposes a replacement. Each challenge (except 5) is associated with a new concept of how decision making can go wrong, which is more plausible and ultimately more relevant to decision aiding and training than the rationalistic emphasis on formal inconsistency. Successful decision making does not require a logically complete formal model of every problem; what it does require is the ability to adapt: to focus attention where one's knowledge will have the most impact, and to adjust to new information, environmental changes, and shortcomings that may appear in one's problem-solving approach. I will try to pull together the threads of these concepts into the outline of an alternative, naturalistic synthesis: at the descriptive/explanatory level, a set of recognition processes and metacognitive strategies that manage the deployment of knowledge and capacity in evolving situations [Challenges (1), (2), (3), and (4)]; at the normative level [Challenges (5) and (6)], a process of assumption-based reasoning which accommodates the effort by decision makers to extend their knowledge into ill-understood, novel, and changing task environments.

I. DO INCONSISTENT DECISIONS LEAD TO BAD OUTCOMES?

Challenge (1): A desirable overall outcome can be achieved in real-world problem domains even though some individual decisions have undesirable outcomes.

Challenge (1) looks at the overall level of achievement of goals in a task domain, and concludes that the rationalist paradigm has overstated the frequency and the importance of biases: They are rare and, on average, inconsequential (Christensen-Szalanski, 1986). There are both (a) methodological and (b) formal arguments for this conclusion.

Variant (a): Methodological. In most research on biases, stimuli are not selected randomly, but are designed to maximize the chance of detecting suboptimal processes (Lopes, 1988). The answer given by an experimental subject to a problem nearly always points unambiguously to either the normatively correct decision process or to a heuristic. Such studies are efficient but biased: that is, they will be systematically nonrepresentative of domains in which heuristics and normative methods generally give the *same* answers. Subjects are also selected nonrandomly (i.e., they are typically students) and do not represent the range of experience ordinarily found in a domain. In addition, the use of between-subjects designs makes it unclear whether any individual subject actually shows the bias under study (Fischhoff, Slovic, & Lichtenstein, 1979; Scholz, 1987).

Another consequence of the rationalist effort to demonstrate errors has been stress on the statistical significance of effects rather than on their size, *measured on some meaningful scale.* Christensen-Szalanski (1986) has argued that researchers should provide domain-specific measures of the importance of a bias, and estimates of its prevalence in a domain. He cites the example of an impressive cluster of biases discovered in medical diagnosis, whose opportunities for occurrence turned out to be "embarrassingly small" and whose effects on treatment choices when they did occur were found to be negligible. Yates (1982; Centor, Dalton, and Yates, 1984) concluded empirically that overconfidence errors in estimating the probabilities of events were of little practical consequence. Even if biases occasionally cause large errors, they may reflect a reasonable tradeoff among goals in a task domain. For example, Klein (1989b) speculates that the "belief bias" may be a by-product of efficient expectancy-based processing that increases speed of response at the cost of errors in a minority of tasks.

Biases may also seem more frequent than they are because of the way in which findings are cited. Christensen-Szalanski and Beach (1984) found that studies reporting poor performance were cited preferentially in the social sciences literature over studies reporting good performance. Moreover, researchers in other fields (e.g., behavioral auditing; Shanteau, 1989) have tended to accept the "heuristics and biases" framework even when it provides only a poor fit to their own data.

Variant (b): Formal. In fact, there are theoretical reasons to expect that suboptimal strategies and normative models often agree in their *outcomes.* Von Winterfeldt and Edwards (1973) showed that it is unnecessary to be very precise or accurate in the estimation of parameters (e.g., importance weights) for many normative models; large errors will have a negligible effect on the decision maker's expected payoffs. Similarly, Dawes and Corrigan (1974) showed that simply counting the attributes or variables in a linear model is virtually as good, on average, as using the normatively correct weights. Moreover, simple linear models are robust enough to accurately describe many nonlinear processes (Dawes, 1979; Goldberg, 1968). When there is random error in the assessment of parameters, simple but incorrect linear models can actually outperform complex models that correctly describe interdependencies among variables (Makridakis & Hibon, 1979; unpublished research by Paul Lehner, personal communication, 1990). Thorngate (1980) showed with a Monte Carlo simulation that "biased" choice strategies can often select the same alternative as the Bayesian model, even when the biased strategies omit significant amounts of information. Large errors may occur, on the other hand, when important variables are omitted (Dawes & Corrigan, 1974) or if information is not utilized to eliminate grossly inadequate alternatives (von Winterfeldt & Edwards, 1975). These results suggest that using "optimal" procedures and accurately assessing parameters for them may be less important in successful performance than gross knowledge of what factors are relevant.

Even more critically, it is possible to anticipate the conditions under which suboptimal strategies will lead to bad results. For example, Payne, Bettman, and Johnson (1989) found that simply counting favorable aspects or outcomes of an option is not a bad strategy when aspects or outcomes do not differ much in importance or probability: for example, house A is better located and has more rooms, house B is less expensive and prettier and available sooner; since house B has more advantages, choose house B. But elimination-by-aspects (which screens options by the more important aspects or more probable outcomes first) is a better approximation to normative methods when aspects or outcomes do differ significantly. Elimination-by-aspects rejects options that do not achieve cutoffs or aspiration levels on various dimensions (e.g., not enough rooms, not pretty enough, too expensive, etc.); it does not consider how much the decision maker would be prepared to give up on one dimension (e.g., cost) in order to gain a certain amount on another dimension (e.g., more rooms). Elimination-by-aspects in turn works well unless tradeoffs are crucial; that is, it is significantly suboptimal only when there are options that just miss achieving a goal on one dimension but that are outstanding in other respects.

This ability to pinpoint the undesirable outcomes to be expected and their conditions of occurrence for different strategies has an important implication for decision aiding and training: it opens the possibility of helping decision makers avoid the specific pitfalls that are associated with their preferred problem-solving method, rather than forcing them to radically alter the method itself. The very fact of using a nonnormative decision strategy can no longer be regarded as an "error"; the failure to compensate for its known shortcomings can be.

Challenge (2): Real-world task environments facilitate desirable outcomes from suboptimal decisions.

Still more optimistically, Challenge (2) argues that apparently suboptimal decision processes lead to desirable outcomes even in a single task, if we adopt a bigger picture of the task environment. Real-life tasks are not the "snapshot" decisions studied in the laboratory (Hogarth, 1981). Rather, "decisions" are typically (a) made in information-rich environments, for example, they are stretched out in time, with redundant cues, incremental stages of commitment, feedback from earlier actions, and shared responsibility; (b) the underlying circumstances of the task may themselves be changing; and (c) important consequences of the decision maker's actions may only be apparent over long time periods. The overall process may be unbiased, even though small time-windows are not.

Variant (a): Information richness. Many biases appear to reduce the amount of information utilized by the decision maker, or to reduce the impact of the information that the decision maker does use. Such biases would be exacerbated in a spare laboratory environment (where each cue is essential) and attenuated in an information-rich, highly redundant real-world environment (Einhorn, Kleinmuntz, & Kleinmuntz, 1979; Hoch & Tschirgi, 1983; Wright & Murphy, 1984). These considerations apply to biases in inference, multiattribute choice, and planning.

In the case of inference, two biases, conservatism (Edwards, 1968) and the belief bias (e.g., Tolcott, Marvin, & Lehner, 1987), both involve a failure to update beliefs based on the full normative impact of new evidence. But in dynamic environments they may reflect an approach to belief revision that relies on feedback from initial guesses, additional redundant clues, and opportunities for subsequent correction. Tversky and Kahneman (1974) regard the *anchoring and adjustment* heuristic as a source of bias due to insufficient adjustment. But in a continuous environment, iterated adjustments may move assessments progressively closer to the normative target (Lindblom, 1959). Similarly, the availability heuristic may involve taking initial direction from the cues that first come to mind (i.e., instances of a class that are easily recalled) and adjusting later when other cues are encountered (Hogarth, 1981). In organizations, the effects of multiple players and multiple constituencies may offset the effects of individual errors in a similar manner (Lindblom, 1959).

In choice, elimination-by-aspects can be thought of as a failure to evaluate options based on the full normative implications of one's preferences. The decision analytic technique called *multiattribute utility theory* (Keeney & Raiffa, 1976) requires the up-front development of a full numerical model, incorporating precise tradeoffs among different criteria, and its application in one fell swoop to all options. Elimination-by-aspects, however, evaluates options by their performance on individual goals, without reference to tradeoffs. Similarly, Simon (1955) described another heuristic strategy called *satisficing,* in which decision makers set goals on a few relevant dimensions and accept the first option they find that is satisfactory on them all. The apparent disadvantages of elimination-by-aspects and satisficing are: (a) no option may survive on all criteria, or (b) too many options may survive. In a dynamic environment, however, decision makers can adjust their goals as they encounter options, raising aspirations if they find it easy to discover satisfactory alternatives and lowering aspirations if they find it difficult (Simon, 1955). Such dynamic adjustments constitute a form of *learning* about preferences that is analogous to the learning about evidence discussed in the previous paragraph. From a rationalist point of view, it may violate Savage's postulate on the independence of beliefs and utilities, but it may nonetheless produce highly adaptive results.

Finally, decision makers seldom stop to plan out all their options *planning* and all the contingencies that might befall them; in short, they fail to make full "normative" use of all the available information about options and future outcomes. Fortunately, as Connolly and Wagner (1988) point out, only a few decisions (e.g., having a child, waging nuclear war, committing suicide) require once-and-for-all, nonreversible commitment; more typically, tentative actions are possible, errors can be corrected, choices do not entirely close off other options, and what has been accomplished along one path might even be useful if one changes direction. In these latter cases (e.g., choosing a career, courting a potential mate, hiring a new employee, adopting a foreign policy), a full-scale analysis of all options, including the probability and desirability of each possible outcome, may be less successful than a more exploratory approach.

There is no guarantee, however, that an incremental approach will always be successful—in inference, choice, or planning. Incremental commitment has its own dangers, for example, that irreversibility will creep in without being noticed (Brown, 1989b), that "good money will be thrown after bad," or that feedback will be ineffective (Einhorn, 1980). Nevertheless, the availability of successful incremental strategies in dynamic environments once again forces a revision in the notion of a decision-making error. The failure to fully model a problem beforehand is not per se an error; what is an *error,* though, is failing to incrementally improve one's understanding of relevant beliefs, preferences, and options as the problem evolves.

Variant (b): Change in the world. Variant (a) emphasizes the opportunity, in continuous problem environments, to learn about a world that is assumed to be fixed while we learn about it. Another important aspect of continuous environments is the possibility of change in the underlying processes that we are trying to learn about. The possibility of change increases the adaptiveness of strategies that do not immediately make full normative use of evidence, current goals, or available options and contingencies. Biases that appear to involve insufficient reaction to new evidence may serve the decision maker well in the face of possible real-world changes that affect the reliability of evidence and its significance. In choice, shiftable reference points and aspiration levels may help decision makers cope with changes in the real-world conditions that determine what can be achieved by an action (Hogarth, 1981). Contingency plans that try to anticipate every possible change tend to be either unmanageably complex or unrealistically oversimplified (Brown, 1989b); overplanning can suppress the variability that is necessary for learning, and the ability to innovate if the unexpected occurs. In all three cases, a strategy of tentative, incremental commitment, improvising in the face of the unexpected, may work better.

Variant (c): Long-term consequences. Static laboratory studies preclude the observation of long-term consequences that may arise from real-world decisions. Anderson (1986) and others, for example, have noted the social advantages of overconfidence in one's ability to control events. Tribe (1971) has argued that explicit quantification of the probability of a defendant's guilt or innocence during a trial may eventually undermine society's confidence in the judicial process. In still other contexts, formal inconsistencies in judgments and decisions may involve processes of trial and error that help decision makers determine what cues are important and what strategies will work (Hogarth, 1981). Inconsistency may have other adaptive consequences, too: for example, to promote unpredictability of one's own behavior in competitive situations.

II. ARE DECISION PROCESSES FLAWED BECAUSE THEY PRODUCE INCONSISTENT DECISIONS?

Challenge (3): The inconsistency of decisions is mitigated by the benefits of using the decision maker's real-world knowledge.

This challenge is more optimistic still: real-world task environments need no longer come to the rescue of flawed decision processes. Decision processes lead to adaptive decisions, because they draw on decision-maker knowledge. There are (at least) four variants of this challenge: (a) People are more likely to be normatively consistent in tasks with which they are familiar or expert; (b) people are more likely to be normatively consistent when they have been explicitly trained in the use of appropriate general-purpose intellectual tools, such as decision analysis; (c) applying knowledge or expertise to a task is frequently associated with nonnormative behavior, but the contribution of domain-specific knowledge to the quality of decisions offsets the effects of normative inconsistency; and (d) people do not use normative procedures because such procedures demand types of knowledge that people often do not have. According to (a) and (b), special-purpose or general-purpose knowledge, respectively, causes people to adopt normatively correct procedures; according to (c) and (d), the appropriate handling of knowledge and/or ignorance is what makes people adopt nonnormative (but justified) procedures. All four variants, however, reject the idea of universal, pure decision processes, which operate in the same way in the real world and the laboratory, independent of what people know.

Variant (a): Domain-specific knowledge reduces biases. A number of researchers have supported the idea that decision-making knowledge is embodied in special-purpose packages, such as schemas, frames, or scripts (e.g., Minsky, 1975; Schank & Abelson, 1977). On this view, there is no general cognitive machinery that ensures consistency with respect to probability theory (or logic or any other normative standard). Rather, there are a large number of specialized structures that, most of the time, happen to produce normatively consistent performance. An experimental task that uses artificial materials, even if it seems formally identical to a corresponding real-life task, may fail to elicit an appropriate knowledge package (Simon & Hayes, 1976); hence, performance may be qualitatively different and, perhaps, defective. Even more strikingly, Ebbesen and Konecni (1980) showed how performance by experienced decision makers could be dramatically different in a simulated laboratory version of a task and in the real world.

Some support for the idea that normative consistency depends on domain-specific knowledge has come in the area of logical reasoning. Wason (1968) showed subjects four cards, which (they were told) had a letter on one side and a numeral on the other. Subjects were asked to test rules of the form, "If a card has a vowel on one side, then it has an even number on the other." For example, if the four cards showed an A, B, 4, and 7, logic, according to Wason, dictates that subjects select the cards with A and 7—since rules of the form *If-p-then-q* are false only if p is true and q is false. Nevertheless, most subjects turned over the cards with A and 4. Wason interpreted this as a confirmation bias: choosing to collect information that can only confirm rather than disconfirm a hypothesis. The card showing 4 cannot disconfirm the rule regardless of what is on the other side; the card showing 7 (which the subjects neglected) could disconfirm the rule if its other side had an A. This bias, however, seemed to disappear when concrete materials were substituted for the meaningless letters and numbers; in a study by Johnson-Laird, Legrenzi, and Legrenzi (1972) subjects correctly tested rules such as "If an envelope is addressed on one side, it must be stamped on the other." Cheng and Holyoak (1985) argued that valid performance does not depend on the familiarity of the stimuli as such, but on the ability of the subjects to apply learned relationships, called *pragmatic reasoning schemas,* such as those associated with obligation, permission, or causality.

The notion that people are less "biased" in familiar tasks has been tested elsewhere, with mixed results. For example, an effect of using between-subjects designs is that individual subjects are never able to *become* familiar with a task. When studies on base rate neglect and on the effects of sample size were replicated using a within-subjects design instead of a between-subjects design, the bias was reduced, presumably because the salience of relevant variables was heightened for individual subjects who experienced all conditions (Fischhoff et al., 1979; Birnbaum & Mellers, 1983; Leon & Anderson, 1974). Base rate neglect is also reduced when subjects experience actual events instead of being given statistical summaries (Nisbett, Borgida, Crandall, & Reed, 1976). May (1986) provides an empirical and theoretical analysis that attributes overconfidence in probability estimates to substantive ignorance regarding specific items, rather than to an abstract shortcoming in probabilistic reasoning. Shanteau (1989) summarizes studies with auditors that show nonexistent or reduced effects of biases associated with representativeness, availability, and anchoring and adjustment.

There is other evidence, however, supporting the importance of knowledge about uncertainty handling itself, in addition to knowledge of the problem domain. For example, weather forecasters have been found to be well calibrated in their probability estimates; but bankers, clinical psychologists, executives, and civil engineers did show overconfidence, despite their experience in their respective domains, presumably because of lack of training in probability judgment per se (cited in Fischhoff, 1982). Finally, as Evans (1989) points out, schema theory simply does not account for some people's ability, at least some of the time, to reason correctly about abstract or unfamiliar material.

Variant (b): General-purpose knowledge reduces biases. As we have seen, domain-specific knowledge does not guarantee normatively correct performance. In any case, the real world contains unfamiliar as well as familiar tasks; Fischhoff (1982) argues that artificial laboratory studies in which biases occur are not necessarily unrepresentative of real-world novelty. Real-world decision makers, however, have another sort of knowledge available to them that laboratory subjects typically do not: the use of general-purpose "intellectual tools" (von Winterfeldt & Edwards, 1986). This view rescues human rationality by emphasizing human malleability: The heuristics and biases literature overlooks the ability to bring one's thinking into line with an appropriate tool.

Von Winterfeldt and Edwards regard the attempt to study pure "statistical intuitions," unassisted by the customary use of technical knowledge, books, calculators, notes, or other "external" aids, as misguided. They argue that a cognitive process is not a fixed method, but a "learned intellectual or judgmental skill executed with whatever tools seem necessary" (p. 554). The boundary of the skin is arbitrary: Education moves information and processing from outside to inside; technology (paper and pencil, calculators, computers) moves them outside again. L. J. Cohen (1981) makes a related point: People cannot be condemned as "irrational" or "biased" when they fail to utilize principles that they have not been taught and whose discovery required mathematical sophistication and even genius. Shafer (1988; Shafer & Tversky, 1988) has argued that unaided human intuitions are not precise or definite enough to be regarded as either coherent or incoherent with respect to normative theories; rather, people learn how to construct precise and definite judgments by using normative theories. The metaphor of *intellectual tools* thus shifts the emphasis from human shortcomings to the natural ability to improve—culturally by inventing new tools, individually by learning how to use them, and on a particular occasion by using the tools to build a model of one's preferences and beliefs.

The tool metaphor is important, because it rescues the idea of decision aiding from paradoxes that are implicit in both the formal-empiricist point of view and in the rationalist point of view. If people's beliefs, preferences, and choices are already (pretty nearly) consistent with respect to normative standards, as the formal-empiricists supposed, then there is no need for decision aiding. On the other hand, if beliefs, preferences, and choices are inconsistent with respect to the normative theory, as the rationalists suppose, there is still no good rationale for decision aiding! Decision aids themselves depend on subjective inputs regarding probabilities and utilities; but if these inputs are subject to bias, then how can the conclusions of an aid be trusted? As far as normative decision theory is concerned, modifying the inputs is just as good a way of achieving consistency as adopting the conclusion.

The tool metaphor breaks out of this dilemma by rejecting the premise (accepted by both formal-empiricists and rationalists) that decision makers have preexisting definite and precise beliefs and preferences about every relevant issue. Decision aiding is useful, then, simply because it helps decision makers generate beliefs and preferences that they aren't sure about from beliefs and preferences that they are sure about. A successful normative model matches up with the pattern of a decision maker's knowledge and ignorance: it demands as inputs things the decision does know, and produces as outputs things the decision maker wants to know.

The tool metaphor, interestingly enough, undermines the *formal* justifications of decision *theory* offered by Savage (1954/1972), De Finetti (1937/1964), Lindley (1982), and others—since these all depend on the assumption of definite and precise beliefs and preferences about everything. But the tool metaphor substitutes something that might be better: a *cognitive* justification for *decision analysis.*

Unfortunately, the case for the cognitive plausibility of decision analytic procedures is less than overwhelming. Rationalist research on biases suggests that people do have strong intuitions about the solutions to problems that conflict with their own inputs to standard decision analytic models; moreover, people often fail to agree with the normative rule itself when it is explicitly presented to them (Kahneman & Tversky, 1982a) and are unpersuaded by arguments in support of the normative rule (Slovic & Tversky, 1974). Finally, as we will see, decision makers do not utilize, and do not have precise knowledge about, many of the *inputs* required in decision analytic models. In the face of these difficulties, one can persist in hoping that intuition can be "educated" to become decision analytic (von Winterfeldt & Edwards, 1986), or one can look for *other* tools in addition to decision analysis that may, at least for some users in some tasks, provide a better fit to their own particular patterns of knowledge and ignorance.

Some researchers have argued, ironically, that it is difficulty in using decision analysis, by contrast to more natural methods for handling uncertainty, that causes biases. Artificiality in the presentation of information about uncertainty, by means of numerical probabilities, may degrade performance. Zimmer (1983) argues that people ordinarily describe uncertainty verbally, in terms of such expressions as *highly probable, likely, quite possible,* and so on, rather than with precise numerical probabilities. Zimmer applied a measurement technique for matching these expressions to ranges of numerical probabilities. His subjects turned out to be reasonably well calibrated (not overconfident or underconfident) when allowed to use the verbal labels instead of numbers. Zimmer also claims that the "conservatism" bias, that is, a failure to adequately update beliefs in the light of new evidence (Edwards, 1968), was reduced when subjects used verbal labels instead of numerical probabilities. In a study of the *regression fallacy,* that is, overextreme predictions of one quantity based on another, Zimmer asked subjects not only for a precise prediction (as in Kahneman & Tversky, 1973), but also for a verbal assessment of degree of confidence and the likely direction of error. Subjects showed considerable awareness of the pitfalls in the precise estimate: Confidence was generally low, and almost all subjects were aware that the true values would probably be less extreme. Subjects' descriptions of their own reasoning (in a different experiment) suggested that verbal and numerical response modes prompted quite different problem-solving processes. Subjects using verbal labels took into account a wider range of qualitative variables than subjects using numbers (cf. Hammond, 1988).

In sum, general-purpose knowledge about decision making may sometimes reduce biases—whether because a decision maker has subjected his or her thinking to a technical discipline, or because the problem lends itself to problem-solving techniques that are already embedded in the language and the culture.

Variant (c): Effective handling of domain-specific knowledge causes biases. On another view, biases, instead of being eliminated by knowledge, are the by-products of domain-specific knowledge; they are caused by the knowledge structures (such as schemas) or cognitive processes (such as pattern matching) that people use to solve problems. An important implication of this view is that people might be unable to apply their knowledge effectively if they were to change their ways of thinking; performance might *suffer* on the whole if people were to adopt standard normative procedures in place of natural methods.

One process that is key to human problem solving (but neglected in standard normative theories) is pattern matching or recognition. There is evidence that expertise in a variety of fields depends on the ability to recognize important features of the problem and to directly retrieve appropriate actions or solution techniques; in contrast, the more analytical approach of sophisticated novices requires explicitly generating and evaluating alternative methods for reaching a goal (e.g., Larkin, McDermott, Simon & Simon, 1980). Chess masters, for example, may be distinguished from novices at least in part by their ability to recognize a very large number of familiar patterns, reducing the need to search through a tree of possible moves and countermoves (de Groot, 1965, 1978; Chase & Simon, 1973). Polya (1945), Newell (1981), Klein (1980), and Noble, Truelove, Grosz, and Boehm-Davis (1989) have emphasized how new problems may be solved by recognizing their similarity to older, better understood problems and by appropriately transforming the old solution to take account of differences. Experts, unlike novices, perceive similarities in terms of the fundamental laws or principles in a domain rather than in terms of superficial features (Chi, Feltovich, & Glaser, 1981). According to Lopes and Oden (in press) the virtues of pattern-based reasoning include robustness under conditions of noise or error, general applicability without stringent preconditions, and practicability with brainlike hardware

[handwritten margin note: This is why we use adjective - to add weight to a direction of thought re the topic]

(e.g., massive parallel processing versus step-by-step serial processing).

Pattern-based reasoning may provide an explanation of a broad range of biases. In the *conjunction fallacy* (Tversky & Kahneman, 1983), for example, people estimate the probability of two statements both being true (e.g., "she is a feminist lawyer") as higher than one of the individual statements ("she is a lawyer"). Lopes and Oden (in press) speculate that the tendency to overestimate the probability of conjunctive classifications may be due to the improved match between conjunctive labels and experimentally provided descriptions of people (e.g., *feminist lawyer* is a better match than simply *lawyer* to the description of a woman who is "single, outspoken, and very bright," and who is "deeply concerned with issues of discrimination and social justice"). Leddo, Abelson, and Gross (1984) accounted for overestimation of the probability of conjunctive explanations in terms of improved matches with schemas that specify the components expected in a good explanation (e.g., a statement of both the crime and the motive is judged more probable than a statement of the crime alone).

Pennington and Hastie (1988) have argued that jurors evaluate evidence by fitting it into a story that is constructed in accordance with explanatory schemas. The *belief bias*, in which new evidence is interpreted to fit the currently held hypothesis, may reflect such a process. More generally, research in cognition suggests that prior expectations play a normal and important role in interpreting data. Expectations fill gaps and help organize experiences in perception (Bruner, 1957), recall (Bransford & Franks, 1971), everyday reasoning (Minsky, 1975), and science (Kuhn, 1962). Schemas, frames, scripts, and other knowledge structures permit successful action under conditions of incomplete and noisy data and limited time. The cost of these benefits is an occasional error when the schema is inappropriate.

Expectancy-based processes may also account for "distorted" concepts of randomness. When asked to produce random sequences, for example, of heads and tails, subjects provide too many alternations and too few runs of all heads or all tails, in comparison to "truly random" (binomial) processes like tossing a coin (Wagenaar, 1972). When asked to estimate the probability of a particular sequence of "random" events, such as the birth order of girls and boys in a family, subjects overestimate the probabilities of sequences that contain equal numbers of each kind, and the probabilities of sequences that contain many alternations (Kahneman & Tversky, 1972). Lopes (1982a) attributes such errors to powerful top-down processes that account for our ability to detect patterns against a background of noise.

An alleged bias in choice involves the assignment of outcomes to "psychological accounts" (Tversky & Kahneman, 1981). In one problem, some of the subjects were asked to imagine that they purchased a $10 ticket to a play, and on entering the theater discovered they have lost it; other subjects were asked to imagine that they decided to see the play, and on entering the theater to purchase a ticket found that they have lost a $10 bill. Subjects who lost the $10 bill were much more likely to purchase a ticket than subjects who lost their original ticket (worth $10). Nevertheless, the "total asset positions" that would result from buying the ticket is the same for the two sets of subjects, and that is what should, according to normative theory, determine the decision. According to Tversky and Kahneman, however, people do not lump all the consequences of their actions into a single pool. When they lost a ticket, subjects included the cost of the original ticket in the "account" containing the new ticket price, raising the psychologically perceived price of the show to $20; on the other hand, when $10 was lost, they regarded it as irrelevant to the cost of the ticket. Psychological accounts appear to group outcomes that belong together according to causal schemas or goal-oriented *scripts*. Such groupings may facilitate learning significant correlations between one's actions and the events that they cause, and also help people keep track of different attitudes toward risk in different psychological accounts, for example, avoiding risks in accounts that pertain to major investments, while seeking risks within accounts allocated for risky investments, vacations, luxury items, and so on (von Winterfeldt & Edwards, 1986).

The reference effect involves an effect on choice due merely to changes in the way actions or outcomes are described; for example, description in terms of "chance of survival" may lead to risk aversion, whereas description in terms of "chance of death" may lead to risk seeking. Such effects might occur because different action or outcome descriptions match different internal knowledge structures, activating different arguments for or against an action (Shafer, 1988).

More generally, and perhaps more importantly, the heuristics cited by Kahneman and Tversky to account for decision biases may be better understood as integral parts of schema-based processing, rather than as isolated and somewhat ad hoc explanatory mechanisms. The availability heuristic corresponds to the retrievability of a schema; representativeness corresponds to the degree of similarity between the current situation and a schema; and anchoring and adjustment involve transformations of the solution associated with a schema to accommodate a mismatch with the current situation.

Variant (d): Effective handling of domain-specific ignorance causes biases. According to variant (c), normative models might interfere with the effective use of knowledge. The other side of the coin is that normative models may interfere with effective handling of *ignorance;* in effect, they force the decision maker to pretend that he or she knows things that he or she does not know. Presupposing the existence of precise probabilities and preferences, as required in standard normative theories, may prematurely close off the possibility of *learning* about one's beliefs and preferences in dynamic environments, through subsequent experience or reflection (March, 1988; Levi, 1986). But even when decisions must be made on the spot, decision makers may be more successful when they do not adopt a false precision.

Decision makers may have little or no knowledge from which to assess the scores, weights, and probabilities required by decision analytic models for the integration of different evaluative dimensions and uncertain outcomes. Frequently they adopt strategies that require much less precise information (Svenson, 1979; Tyszka, 1981): for example, satisficing requires only yes-or-no judgments about alternatives on each dimension (e.g., does the alternative achieve a goal or not?) and no comparisons at all among different dimensions; elimination-by-aspects merely adds a requirement for rank ordering dimensions by importance; the *lexicographic decision rule* (i.e., pick the best candidate on the most important dimension; if there is a tie, go to the next most important dimension, etc.) adds a requirement for rank ordering alternatives on a given dimension but remains far less demanding than decision analytic modeling. Similarly, in the *regression fallacy,* when decision makers provide overly extreme predictions of one quantity based on another, they may simply not know enough to estimate the degree of correlation between the known variable and the variable to be predicted (especially if there is a possibility of change in the underlying process). In the *belief bias,* decision makers may feel unsure of the reliability of a source of apparently disconfirming evidence, and thus discount it. In *base rate neglect,* decision makers may be unsure of the reliability of frequency data, and thus disregard it.

The inputs required by a decision analysis often do not correspond to what a decision maker knows with confidence. But is the output of a decision analysis worth the effort? Sometimes, at least, it seems not. The end result of a decision analysis is usually an "average" hypothesis, outcome, or preference, which has little meaning in terms of what decision makers need to do or know (Cohen, Leddo, & Tolcott, 1988). They can avoid, plan for, and/or react to specific situations or outcomes, not an unrealizable average. In planning a defense, for example, it is useful for a general to know that the main enemy force might be planning to attack at point A or else at point B; they may try to predict how well various defensive options will fare in each of those cases. But they will have little use for a prediction of enemy intent in terms of the probability-weighted average future enemy force at each location, or for an evaluative score reflecting a defensive plan's success averaged across the two situations. It is plausible to speculate that there is a "basic level" of description, neither too detailed nor too general, that is most usefully linked to the rest of a decision maker's knowledge in a particular task (cf. Rosch, Mervis, Grey, Johnson, & Boyes-Braem, 1979). Simon (1972) observed that normative models of chess, which attempt to summarize all the implications of a move with a single abstract evaluative measure, are less successful than nonnormative models, which ignore some possible outcomes and explore a small number of well-chosen paths to an appropriate depth.

In sum, variant (d) implies that decision analysis is, on at least some occasions, not a good intellectual tool: It fails to match the pattern of what a decision maker knows and needs to know. Variant (c)—that nonnormative behavior flows from schema-based processing—underscores this conclusion, implying that decision analysis conflicts with the way people ordinarily use what they know in order to solve problems and make decisions. All four variants of this challenge imply a redefinition of the notion of a decision-making *error:* not in terms of logical inconsistency, but in terms of the failure to effectively exploit one's knowledge in the service of one's needs.

We may, nevertheless, be somewhat uncomfortable with a picture of "natural" reasoning that is exclusively focused on knowledge. Such a view may fall short in accounting for the flexibility that decision makers sometimes display in novel situations. For example, while experts may "recognize" familiar problems, recognition itself is not simple: It may incorporate a series of transformations and retransformations of the problem until the expert finally "knows" how to solve it. Physics experts, according to Larkin (1977), first sketch the superficial objects and relations in a problem; if the depicted system is still not familiar, they may transform it into an idealized, free-body diagram; if recognition still does not occur, they may switch to a more novice-like strategy of means–ends analysis. Once they have solved a problem, physics experts draw on a variety of strategies to verify its correctness, for example, by checking whether all forces are balanced, whether all entities in the diagram are related to givens in the problem, and so on. There is abundant evidence that recognitional processes are not inflexibly automatic but involve a fairly continuous stream of optional processes that evaluate and guide the application of prestored knowledge.

Challenge (4): Constraints on the decision maker's information-processing capacity justify use of non-Bayesian procedures.

Challenge (4) brings flexibility front and center. It adopts an optimistic stance toward human rationality without appeal to factors (such as intellectual tools, knowledge, or incremental commitment and feedback) that operate primarily in real-world settings. It implies that a wider understanding even of the laboratory context helps make normative sense of "biased" performance: Herbert Simon (1955, 1972) argued that strategies such as satisficing that might seem irrational in the absence of information-processing constraints are perfectly sensible, given the presence of such constraints. According to the effort/accuracy tradeoff hypothesis, adoption of suboptimal strategies may itself be justified at a second-order level, given the cognitive demands of calculating an optimal solution and the "almost as good" quality of simplifying strategies.

Payne (1976) carried Simon's idea one step further: Individuals appear to utilize not one, but a variety of simplifying strategies in response to varying task characteristics. Beach and Mitchell (1978) proposed that decision strategies are selected on the basis of a cost–benefit calculation that balances the demand for accuracy in a particular task against the cost of being accurate in that task. Payne et al. (1989) have shown (through an analytical model of effort and Monte Carlo simulation of accuracy) how different choice strategies might in fact trade off in terms of accuracy and effort under different task conditions. No single heuristic does well across all decision environments; but a decision maker can maintain a reasonably high level of accuracy at a low level of effort by selecting from a repertoire of strategies contingent upon situational demands (Payne et al., 1989).

Experimental data suggest that people do in fact adaptively adjust their processing strategies in response to changes in such variables as the number of options (Payne, 1976), or the variance among probabilities and importance weights (Payne et al., 1989). A number of studies have shown that time stress causes selective focussing on negative attributes/outcomes (Leddo, Chinnis, Cohen, & Marvin, 1987; Wright, 1974) and adoption of alternatives that hedge against the worst case (Leddo et al., 1987; Ben Zur & Breznitz, 1981). Display features can also make some strategies harder and others easier (Hammond, 1988; Tyszka, 1980). For example, when information about alternatives is presented numerically, subjects are more likely to compare alternatives directly to one another (as in the lexicographic rule); but when less precise verbal descriptions of alternatives are given, alternatives are compared to a goal, as in elimination-by-aspects (Huber, 1980).

Even in applications where comparable research on effort/accuracy tradeoffs has not been done, it is clear that adaptation to constraints on capacity is necessary. For example, as noted above, some choice biases involve assigning outcomes to different "psychological accounts," based on causal or goal relationships, rather than considering the decision maker's total asset position (Tversky & Kahneman, 1981). If limited capacity is taken into account, we might ask: How could it be otherwise? Changes in one's total assert position may be occurring continuously—for example, paychecks, retirement accumulations, appreciation of one's home and investments, depreciation of one's car, changes in inheritance prospects, and so forth; it would hardly be worth the effort to try to model the impact of all these events on every decision (von Winterfeldt & Edwards, 1986).

Biases in inference and probability assessment may also be adaptive responses to capacity limitations. For example, the belief bias could result in principle from the impossibility of questioning every belief in the light of each new experience: some beliefs (e.g., the currently active schema) must be left unquestioned in order to evaluate others (Quine, 1960). With even a small number of beliefs, examination of all combinations of their truth and falsity rapidly becomes impossible in principle (Cherniak, 1986). The same problem would explain some cases of base rate neglect. For example, in fitting causal models to correlational data, the number of possible causal arrangements grows very rapidly with the number of variables (Glymour, Scheines, Spirtes, & Kelly, 1987) (e.g., the factors that might cause cancer, such as smoking, diet, geographical location, health care, etc., might also have causal effects on one another). It is impossible to assess base rates for all the possible causal arrangements; and the assessment of a catch-all hypothesis (e.g., *everything else*) is hardly satisfactory if we do not know what hypotheses it contains. As a result, decision makers (including scientists) must *satisfice*, that is, look for satisfactory rather than optimal models. In a continuous environment inference may become more like *design:* instead of choosing among a pregiven set of hypotheses, an original hypothesis or small set of hypotheses will be revised and/or elaborated incrementally as shortcomings are discovered.

The effort/accuracy theory introduces still another notion of decision error: the failure to appropriately balance accuracy and effort in the choice of decision strategies. Formal inconsistency per se is not an error in this sense; adopting a highly inaccurate strategy, when only a small amount of effort would be required to adopt a more accurate strategy, may sometimes be an error. But then again, in other contexts, with other payoffs, it might be an error to expend more effort in order to improve accuracy.

There is a curious disconnection between the effort/accuracy tradeoff hypothesis [Challenge (4)] and schema-based views of problem solving that emphasize the role of substantive knowledge [Challenge (3)]. As noted above, there is evidence that expertise consists, at least in part, in the ability to recognize a large store of situations and to retrieve appropriate solutions (e.g., Larkin, 1981; Chase & Simon, 1973). By contrast, the effort/accuracy tradeoff model emphasizes rationality at the level of metacognitive or higher order decisions about how to decide. Schema-based approaches seem to emphasize automatic activation of relevant knowledge structures, leaving little room for conscious monitoring and control (e.g., Anderson, 1982), while the effort/ accuracy model defines both of its central concepts (effort and accuracy) without reference to knowledge.

We think that each approach needs to be supplemented by concepts from the other. Experts are skilled not only in recognition, but in metacognitive processes that enhance the *likelihood* of recognition and that verify, critique, modify, and/or abandon the results. The primary function of metacognitive processes is to control the application of knowledge, not to choose among knowledge-independent analytical strategies.

A Synthesis: The Interaction of Recognition and Metacognition

From the naturalistic point of view, several aspects of the effort/accuracy approach to biases bear questioning: its commitment to a measure of effort that ignores how much the person *knows* about a problem; its use of decision analytic strategies as the standard for evaluating accuracy; and its emphasis on conscious higher order selection of strategies as opposed to local choices about what to do/think next. A Recognition/Metacognition model revises each of these features.

(a) *A notion of effort that incorporates knowledge.* Payne et al. (1989) have measured effort abstractly, in terms of the number of generic EIPs (*elementary information processes,* such as *read, compare, add*) required by a strategy; they have validated the model in laboratory studies in which tasks do not involve expertise or experience, and in which all relevant information is predigested (e.g., as probabilities and payoffs) rather than inferred or generated from the decision maker's own memory. This model incorporates individual differences in *general-purpose* ability to perform EIPs and in ability to combine them into strategies (cf. Beach & Mitchell, 1978). In a more naturalistic setting, however, the decision maker's estimate of the difficulty of a strategy will reflect what he or she believes about his or her own knowledge of a specific task and of the relevant domain. The decision maker chooses to deploy attention selectively to certain aspects of the problem, to mentally recode or physically transform certain problem materials, and to selectively "rehearse" some of the materials rather than others—because he or she believes that those aspects or materials are more likely to activate knowledge that will activate other knowledge, and so on, until he or she arrives at a solution. EIPs for retrieving and transforming knowledge must be incorporated into the theory of mental effort.

The overconfidence bias in estimating the probability of a conclusion might result from metacognitive choices that reflect the effort required to retrieve or generate ways that the conclusion could be false (Pitz, 1974). The overconfidence bias is reduced when subjects are explicitly asked to generate reasons why the conclusion they favor might be wrong (Koriat, Lichtenstein, & Fischhoff, 1980; Hoch, 1985); as new reasons are demanded, subjects exert more effort, selectively activating new knowledge structures, and questioning increasingly fundamental premises of the original conclusion (Cohen, 1990). Similarly, metacognitive choices may underlie the top-down processing that is characteristic of the belief bias, in which apparently conflicting data are perceived as supporting a favored hypothesis. More effort would be required to activate and test alternative explanatory schemas. The optional (or metacognitive) character of the belief bias is suggested by Tolcott and Marvin's (1988) finding that simply briefing subjects on the existence of the bias reduced its effect. More recently, Tolcott and his colleagues have found that subjects who were required to actively select evidence bearing on a hypothesis were less likely to interpret conflicting evidence as confirming, than subjects who had evidence passively presented to them; the former subjects may have been induced to attach a higher value to truly testing the hypothesis.

Other biases may involve a similar metacognitive balance between effort and accuracy. Reference effects in choice may reflect the difficulty of accessing alternative ways of describing outcomes when one way of describing them is strongly activated by the wording of the problem. The availability bias, by its very definition, refers to ease of recall of instances as a determinant of probability estimates for a class (Tversky & Kahneman, 1973; Beyth-Marom & Fischhoff, 1977). The hindsight bias might result from the effort that would be required in tracking and undoing the effects of a past event on all the relevant components of a person's knowledge (Fischhoff, 1982).

Different choice strategies may also reflect different metacognitive choices about the most efficient access to relevant knowledge. In one strategy, called *dominance structuring* (Montgomery, 1983), decision makers start by provisionally selecting an option; they then work backward, adding and dropping attributes, revising scores, and so on in an effort to show that the selected candidate is as good as or better than other candidates in all respects; if they fail, they select another option, and so on. Such a strategy may be quite easy when decision makers have precompiled, intuitive "knowledge of what to do," but have less direct access to knowledge about the attributes that justify such a choice. By the same token, elimination-by-aspects would be easier in domains where knowledge is organized by goals and the means of achieving them, and satisficing would be easier in domains where knowledge is organized by options and what they are good for. Even compensatory strategies, which require comparisons across different dimensions, may be easier when decision makers have readily accessible knowledge upon which they can base judgments of the relative importance of criteria; for example, a military commander might evaluate the cost of losing one of his or her own units compared to the value of destroying an enemy unit in terms of the relative numbers of the two forces known to be present in a battle area (Cohen, Bromage, Chinnis, Payne, & Ulvila, 1982).

(b) Replacement of decision theory by dynamic adjustment as a benchmark for performance. According to the effort/accuracy model, decision analytic procedures are the ideal from which decision makers deviate under high workload. But decision makers do not necessarily adopt decision analytically correct methods even when workload demands are low (e.g., Cohen et al., 1988); and decision makers often reject normative rules and arguments for those rules when they are explicitly presented (Kahneman & Tversky, 1982a; Slovic & Tversky, 1974). Kahneman and Tversky have cited such results as support for the claim that biases are deeply rooted in our cognitive systems, on the analogy of perceptual illusions. An alternative, naturalistic view is possible, however: Under conditions of low workload, decision makers might adopt more effective variants of nonoptimal strategies. Increased effectiveness may result from iterative improvements in a dynamic environment.

Decision makers might deal with tradeoffs among evaluative dimensions, for example, by adopting a more dynamic and self-critical variant of satisficing or elimination-by-aspects. In these variants, a decision maker starts out with relatively high aspirations on all dimensions; if all goals cannot be achieved, aspirations on particular attributes might be revised downward, in small steps, to accommodate options that just miss a goal but are outstanding in other respects. Such a metacognitive process would accommodate the compensatory relations that are relevant for the problem at hand, without requiring the explicit assessment of a large number of precise weights that are not relevant (Cohen, Bromage, Chinnis, Payne, & Ulvila, 1982; Cohen, Laskey, & Tolcott, 1987).

In the same way, more sophisticated variants of nonoptimal inference strategies might be adopted in low-stress conditions. In the belief bias, people seem to use an existing hypothesis to interpret new evidence in a top-down manner, producing a more definitive picture of the situation, in contrast to continuously shifting Bayesian probabilities. The natural improvement of this strategy might be to make it dynamic and self-critical: to keep track of the evidence that has been provisionally "explained away," or to maintain a cumulative assessment of the degree of doubt in the current conclusion, and to initiate search for an alternative hypothesis when the amount of explained-away evidence, or the degree of cumulative doubt, reaches a high-enough level (Cohen, 1989, 1990). This strategy allows more effective use of decision-maker knowledge in building a coherent explanation/prediction of events; at the same time, it guards against being locked into seriously mistaken conclusions.

Ironically, a Recognition/Metacognition framework has less trouble than the effort/accuracy hypothesis in accounting for cases where people *do* use decision-theoretically optimal procedures. Normatively correct behavior might be *easy* (rather than effortful) when readily activated knowledge structures in a particular domain happen to fit normative rules (Cheng & Holyoake, 1985), or when the decision maker is well versed in general-purpose normative techniques (von Winterfeldt & Edwards, 1986).

(c) Local choices rather than deliberative higher order selection of strategies. The effort/accuracy hypothesis has typically assumed that strategies are selected by a top-down, conscious process, in which normative constraints are satisfied. By contrast, Simon (1972) rejected the notion of a second-order level of decision making that normatively derives heuristics, on the grounds that it would require difficult assessments beyond those needed simply to carry out the heuristic itself; the effort involved would be better devoted to improving the knowledge that is directly exploited in the heuristic. There is also controversy among researchers in the related area of "metacognition" regarding the degree to which higher order regulative processes involve conscious awareness: whether they are completely automatic (Sternberg, 1984), involve awareness of the first-order cognitive events being regulated (Gavelek & Raphael, 1985), or involve awareness of both first-level and higher-level processes (Kuhn, Ansel, & O'Loughlin, 1988). Think-aloud protocols suggest that top-down selection of decision strategies, based on features of the task, does sometimes occur (Payne et al., 1989). There is also evidence in the problem-solving literature that experts are better than novices at assessing the difficulty of a task (Chi, Glaser, & Rees, 1982). Nevertheless, Payne et al. (1989) have themselves recently suggested that, in some cases, decision strategies may be "constructed" step by step in the course of the decision maker's interaction with a problem, rather than explicitly selected (cf. Connolly & Wagner, 1988). In such an incremental, iterative process, decision makers would utilize feedback from previous cognitive actions to make local decisions about what to do next.

Metacognition does not mean that people are conscious of all the knowledge that makes them effective or expert. It does suggest that people have higher level schemas (which may themselves sometimes be domain specific and largely automatic) that gauge the familiarity and difficulty of problems or subproblems, and that incorporate responses (a) to enhance the chance of recognition, and (b) to control the process of validating a potential problem solution. The metacognitive processes embodied in these schemas are governed by an implicit balancing of effort against expected results, in a way that takes account of such factors as the available time for a decision, the likelihood of errors, the stakes of the decision, the opportunity for feedback and midcourse corrections, and the structure of relevant knowledge representations.

In a naturalistic version of the effort/accuracy hypothesis, heuristics may sometimes be both *less* effortful and *more* accurate than normative models. If knowledge influences both effort and accuracy, then reasonably efficient decision-making strategies might sometimes emerge simply by "doing what comes to mind." Tradeoffs between effort and accuracy arise in more novel situations, where effective decision makers must be skilled in selecting the parts of their knowledge to be explored, monitoring progress toward a solution, recalling relatively inaccessible parts of their knowledge, and making revisions in beliefs and strategies where necessary (Larkin, 1981; Glaser, 1989; Brown & DeLoache, 1978).

Adaptation: Imperfect, but Important

Challenges (1), (2), (3), and (4) all depend at bottom on the notion of adaptation—to internal capacity constraints, to the requirements of applying knowledge, to dynamic and rich task environments, and to the performance of a decision strategy across the overall spectrum of tasks in a domain. Deviations from formal consistency may turn out to be adaptive or at least neutral in these contexts, if the benefits associated with them outweigh the harm they do.

The challenges differ in how the adaptation is supposed to take place. Consider a simple analogy: Both squirrels and humans put away valuable objects for safekeeping. On some level the function, or adaptive consequence, of burying nuts and putting jewelry in a safe (or money in the bank, etc.) is the same. Yet the squirrel's behavior is controlled by a genetically inherited program. He will try to bury nuts even in situations where the behavior does not have any adaptive consequences, for example, in an enclosure with a concrete floor, or where no competitors for nuts exist. Humans will vary their "squirreling away" behavior (up to a point) to fit their individual circumstances.

Similarly, biases may reflect relatively coarse-grained adaptations: that is, fixed cognitive traits that do reasonably well across all tasks that humans encounter, and which do not change from task to task. Challenges (1) and (2) require no more than this. For example, if overconfidence is an inherited or culturally conditioned trait with social advantages (Anderson, 1986), we would not expect an individual's overconfidence to be reduced in occasional situations where it is no longer socially advantageous (e.g., in a psychology laboratory). (However, if the environment of the species or the culture were consistently changed, then overconfidence might eventually disappear, over a much longer time period.) Challenges (3) and (4) demand a more fine-grained, flexible adaptation: biases reflect strategies that change in response to features of a task and decision maker, that is, the familiarity of the task and the effort it demands. Finally, as we shall see in the next section, Challenges (5) and (6) address an even more fine-grained and flexible adaptiveness, in which performance changes in response to detailed beliefs and preferences regarding the specific task.

It is obvious that having adaptive consequences, at whatever level, does not mean that a characteristic of decision making is "optimal": there may always be a more fine-grained level and a more refined adaptation. Even *at their own level,* adaptations may not be the optimal solutions. Natural selection, like cultural evolution and like human decision makers, is a satisficer, not an optimizer, and there is always likely to be room for improvement.

The naturalistic challenges, while rejecting rationalist pessimism, have left considerable leeway for error. Indeed, they make more sense of the notion of decision error than either the formal-empiricist framework (in which it is not clear when performance is in error and when the model is wrong) or the rationalist framework (according to which error is simply formal inconsistency). Challenge (1) introduced the notion of error as a failure to guard against specifically identified pitfalls in a suboptimal strategy. Challenge (2) emphasized the potential failure to respond to feedback or to make midcourse corrections in order to incrementally improve performance in dynamic environments. Challenge (3) stressed the failure to effectively exploit one's own knowledge. And Challenge (4) highlighted the failure to appropriately weigh effort against accuracy in the selection of strategies. The Recognition/Metacognition framework incorporates all four kinds of error: biases represent a failure of metacognitive processes that facilitate problem recognition and retrieval of appropriate solutions, that monitor for potential problems in a decision process, and that verify and revise proposed solutions. The point, then, is not to paint unaided decision makers in a rosy glow. The argument is simply this: Decision-making errors are better understood against a pattern of generally successful adaptation to real-world contexts, rather than as deviations from a largely irrelevant abstract standard.

It has been argued, however (e.g., Einhorn & Hogarth, 1981), that claims about adaptation are scientifically unacceptable. These critics argue (a) that such claims are "unfalsifiable," since the post-hoc invention of adaptive consequences is all to easy; and (b) that failure to adapt is consistent with natural selection through such phenomena as "genetic drift," persistence after ceasing to be adaptive, and "hitch-hiking" of some traits upon the adaptiveness of others (e.g., Gould & Lewontin, 1979). I think these complaints are misguided.

Adaptive claims would be unscientific if they implied that the function or adaptive purpose of a characteristic is, by definition, whatever consequence it happens to have. (In that case decision strategies would be trivially adaptive, since they have consequences.) The hypothesis of adaptation requires, at a minimum, that a characteristic, such as using a particular decision strategy in certain sorts of tasks, exists because of the adaptive consequences it had in the past. This usually has the following testable implication: If conditions are changed so that the consequence no longer occurs, then the characteristic will change (over the appropriate time period, which may involve the species, the culture, or the individual). Empirical or theoretical research can support specific claims of this sort regarding the adaptiveness of specific characteristics. Some work has been done, for example, changes in decision-making strategies due to task features that measurably affect effort (Payne, 1976), or due to different degrees of familiarity with a task (Larkin, 1977); more work is obviously needed.

The truly insupportable claims (as noted by Dawkins, 1983) are the negative propositions that a decision-making characteristic has no important adaptive function, or that there is no decision strategy more effective than (the current variant of) decision analysis.

What is most misleading is the suggestion (e.g., in Einhorn & Hogarth, 1981) that the burden of proof is on the adaptationist. On the contrary: The assumption of adaptation has had enormous heuristic value in the life sciences. The relevance of natural selection is not diminished just because evolution *can* produce nonadaptive traits; on the whole, evolution is adaptive, though there is lots of "noise" over short time periods (Dennett, 1983). To my knowledge, no case has *ever* been made in biology for the heuristic value of assuming dysfunctionality.

Tversky and Kahneman (1974), however, argue that the study of errors (in the sense of formal inconsistency) can shed light on information-processing mechanisms, by analogy to the study of perceptual illusions. But the analogy has been criticized on at least two grounds: Standards of normative correctness are far less well understood in decision making than in perception, so it is not so clear what counts as an error in this sense (Smithson, 1989); and in any case, the "correct" process does not play a causal role in decision making the way the physical stimulus does in perception, where mechanisms can be thought of as transforming (or distorting) the stimulus (Shanteau, 1989; Anderson, 1986). Demonstrations of error in the rationalist paradigm show that a particular mathematical model does not fit performance, and (from an explanatory point of view) that is about all. No light is shed on cognitive mechanisms.

Perhaps an alternative is to disregard the question of functionality altogether, and to focus directly on mechanisms. But that would be comparable to studying the eye without any idea of what it was used for. Where would one even begin? What aspects would be worthy of attention? When would an explanation be complete? What would it mean to improve its performance? We think that the study of decision processes without reference to problem domains, task environments, knowledge, or capacity, is a dead end.

From the practical point of view, two kinds of errors are possible: thinking that adaptiveness is there when it isn't, and missing it when it is there. Eliminating an adaptive behavior (though training or "aiding") may be every bit as bad as letting a defective behavior go uncorrected. Moreover, when decision-making behavior does go wrong, corrective steps are more likely to be successful if they take its normal function into account. We turn in the next section to "normative" theories and what they may have to say about critiquing or improving the decision-making process.

III. ARE DECISIONS FORMALLY INCONSISTENT?

Challenge (5): There are alternative Bayesian models that better capture the subject's understanding of the problem.

Rationalist experimenters use decision analytic or logical models to evaluate their subjects' decisions; and thus far, for the sake of argument, we have accepted the validity of these normative standards. The use of a suboptimal decision strategy might be justified if it leads to satisfactory outcomes, even if the strategy itself is not inherently correct [Challenges (1) and (2)]; or a suboptimal strategy might be justified because it effectively exploits knowledge under conditions of limited capacity [Challenges (3) and (4)]. From this point of view, alternative, naturalistic concepts of decision error *coexist* with the rationalist concept of error as formal inconsistency. The previous challenges claimed that error in the rationalist sense is often outweighed, in the evaluation of performance, by the *absence* of error in the naturalistic sense (i.e., decision makers successfully compensate for specific weaknesses in decision strategies; they incrementally improve their knowledge of the problem; they efficiently use knowledge and capacity). Challenges (5) and (6), however, go farther: they attack the idea that decision processes are biased even in the narrow, rationalistic sense.

Challenge (5) accepts Bayesian decision analysis as a normative standard, but argues that in many cases of alleged biases, it has not in fact been violated. Variants of this challenge are something of a grab bag: They include (a) subjects' misconstruing the instructions of the experimenter and the experimenter's misunderstanding the knowledge and goals of the subjects, as well as (b) more serious errors by the experimenter in modeling the problem. These challenges have the flavor of the formal-empiricist paradigm: deviations of strong intuitions from a decision analytic model are taken as causes for concern about the decision analytic model rather than signs of irrationality by decision makers (e.g., Bell, 1981). To the extent that these arguments are convincing, decision analysis and ordinary decision-making performance may be reconciled. We think, in fact, that the challenges are not always fully convincing: The formal constraints of decision theory are too restrictive; as a result, formally adequate decision analytic models turn out not to be cognitively plausible. It is perhaps more important, however, that these challenges illustrate the dynamic character of "normative" modeling, and point the way to a more interactive process of decision aiding that does not so much dictate to decision makers as negotiate with them.

(a) Subject/experimenter misunderstanding. The normative force of decision theory is not to tell a decision maker what to believe, value, or do. Rather, it indicates when beliefs, preferences, and choices are inconsistent with one another. Consistency itself is relative to a selected model or structure; for example, if a subject (acting as decision maker) perceives a dependence between judgments that the experimenter regards as independent, or if he or she values attributes of an option that the experimenter has ignored, then apparently inconsistent behavior may in fact be quite rational. It is strange, then, that

decision-making research in the rationalist tradition has only rarely sought direct evidence of the way subjects/decision makers represent a problem. Process-tracing methodologies, for example, in which subjects think out loud as they work a problem, have been used only rarely (e.g., Svenson, 1979; Payne, 1976; Scholz, 1987); subjects are seldom asked at the conclusion of a study why they answered as they did; finally, there is little or no systematic study of the answers in their own right in order to get a better picture of the underlying processes. The only assurance that subjects and experimenters share an understanding of the problem is the instructions, and this is a frail reed. As Berkeley and Humphreys (1982) argue, there is no way that a written description of a problem can remove all ambiguity. The contrast with applied decision analysis is instructive: Numerous iterations and extensive interaction between analyst and client are required, before they can mutually agree on an appropriate model (e.g., Phillips, 1982).

Instructions may in fact cause biases, as Kahneman and Tversky (1982a) acknowledge. In the real world, things are said for a reason; in an experimental context, therefore, subjects may naturally draw inferences from the verbal description of a problem that they would not draw if the "same problem" were actually experienced. One convention that governs ordinary conversation (Grice, 1975), for example, allows the listener to assume that the speaker is trying to be relevant. As noted by Kahneman and Tversky (1982a), this makes it difficult to study how subjects handle information that is supposed to be "irrelevant." For example, the finding that subjects interpret supposedly neutral cues in accordance with their favored hypothesis (an effect of the belief bias) may, in part at least, be due to the assumption that the cue would not have been presented if it did not have some bearing on the question at hand. A similar complaint could be raised about studies in which "irrelevant" individuating evidence causes subjects to ignore base rates (Kahneman & Tversky, 1973). Some instances of overconfidence, in which subjects are given an anchor, may also reflect reasoning of this kind. One group of subjects were asked the probability that the population of Turkey was greater than 5 million; another group was asked the probability that it was less than 65 million; when both groups were subsequently asked for their best guess as to the population of Turkey, the median estimates were 17 million and 35 million for the low- and high-anchor groups, respectively. This may reflect a legitimate assumption that the phrasing of the question is itself evidence, rather than a bias caused by "insufficient adjustment" of an anchor. If subjects are uncertain of their answers in the first place, they would be foolish not to utilize such information (Macdonald, 1986).

Kahneman and Tversky (1982a) appear to defend the allegation of bias even in these examples; they cite an experiment in which an anchor that was randomly chosen (by the spin of a roulette wheel) in the presence of the subjects also influenced estimates, despite the fact that no subject "could reasonably believe that (the anchor) conveys information." But it is far from clear that subjects accept assurances from experimenters regarding "randomness." In some cases, it may be quite reasonable for subjects to assume that the experimenter is lying. Gigerenzer and Murray (1987) cite base rate neglect experiments by Kahneman and Tversky (1973) in which subjects are told that personality sketches are selected from a population of engineers and lawyers at random. In fact, of course, the descriptions were deliberately constructed to match stereotypes of doctors and lawyers. If subjects suspect this (and, of course, they should), they will, as good Bayesians, ignore base rates.

The credibility of many experiments may be undermined by the unrealistic precision with which information is provided. For example, a well-known reference effect experiment (Tversky & Kahneman, 1981) asks subjects to choose between two medical options for fighting a disease that is expected to kill 600 people. In one condition the choice is between program A, in which 200 people will be saved for sure, and program B, which has a $1/3$ chance of saving 600 people and a $2/3$ chance of saving none. In the other condition, the choice is between program C, in which 400 people will certainly die, and program D, which has a $1/3$ probability of no one dying and a $2/3$ probability that 600 people will die. The choices in the two conditions are identical, but outcomes are described in programs A and B in terms of gains (saving people), and outcomes are described by C and D in terms of losses (people dying). Despite this identity, people tend to choose program A in the first condition and program D in the second. As Smithson (1989) points out, however, it is highly implausible to predict exact numbers of deaths in this kind of forecast; subjects may thus read unintended ambiguity into the outcome predictions. Berkeley and Humphreys (1982) argue that the description of program A suggests that at least 200 people will be saved, and that actions may be discovered that could result in saving more; the description of program C suggests that at least 400 people will die, but possibly more. Under this interpretation, A and C are not identical *to the subjects*. A similar interpretation of ambiguous outcomes may affect experiments on "psychological accounts." Subjects who lose a $10 ticket may be less likely to buy a new ticket than subjects who lose a $10 bill because a variety of subsequent options are relevant (and ethically appropriate) in the case of the lost ticket: for example, they might instead try to convince a box office clerk to replace the ticket or an usher to seat them (Berkeley & Humphreys, 1982).

In all these examples, the subjects' rationality is rescued by more complex decision analytic structures: taking the wording of instructions as evidence for the correct answer, taking frequency data as imperfect evidence for the true base rate (conditional on random selection), and elaborating a decision tree with subsequent acts. To varying degrees, these are somewhat ad hoc adjustments; the problems that they address have the flavor of "experimental artifacts," which might be corrected simply by more carefully controlled experimental procedures (e.g., Fischhoff, 1982). The more important underlying lessons, however, concern the importance of understanding the way subjects represent the problem and of studying decision making in contexts that are sufficiently similar to the real world that subjects know how to represent them.

(b) Experimenter mismodeling. Bias findings may also be inconclusive due to deeper and more general errors in decision analytic modeling. A number of criticisms of the bias literature take on a quite formal and technical character. But they have in common with the issues examined above an emphasis on factors that may be important to subjects but overlooked by experimenters, and which can be incorporated into ever more complex decision analytic models.

Discrepancies between experimenters and subjects in the perceived structure of a problem may occur because of differences in goals. Bell (1981, 1988) has developed a revision of expected utility theory that incorporates the feelings that a decision maker might expect to have after making a choice under uncertainty and discovering the actual outcome. Decision makers feel "regret" if they discover that a different alternative would have done better than the alternative they chose. They feel "disappointed" if the outcome they achieve does not match the outcome they expected. Avoiding regret or disappointment are goals that may trade off in a multiattribute utility framework with more standard goals such as financial gain. Bell uses these concepts to account for a variety of apparent decision "biases," including Ellsberg's (1961) paradox (in which decision makers prefer choices in which the probabilities of outcomes are known, to choices in which the probabilities of outcomes are unknown).

Discrepancies between subjects and experimenters may also occur in fundamental beliefs or assumptions, for example, about the possibility of change in model parameters. When people predict one quantity (e.g., next year's economic growth rate) based on another quantity (e.g., this year's growth rate), their predictions typically do not "regress to the mean" as they should, given that the two quantities are imperfectly correlated; a very bad year is typically expected to be followed by another very bad year, instead of by a more nearly average year (Tversky & Kahneman, 1974). In a dynamic context, however, the regression fallacy may reflect sensitivity to fundamental changes; for example, the next year could be worse than the present year if the economy is in fact declining. In many cases, the costs of missing such a change would be significantly greater than the costs of a false alarm.

Birnbaum (1983) has criticized the simple Bayesian updating rule that serves as a normative standard in base rate neglect studies (e.g., Kahneman & Tversky, 1973). The simple Bayesian model assumes, in the cab problem, for example, that the witness commits the very fallacy that the experimental subjects are accused of: that the witness did not consider base rates in making his own report! Birnbaum develops a more complex Bayesian inference model that uses signal detection theory to model the witness, and in which the witness balances the costs of different kinds of errors in light of the base rates; such a model leads to the "biased" answer preferred by subjects in this experiment.

There is a more fundamental problem with the base rate neglect studies. The experimenters assume that the frequency data provided in the instructions are decisive evidence for the "true" base rate (Niiniluoto, 1981; Birnbaum, 1983). Bayes's rule requires that the decision maker estimate the probability (before considering the witness's report) that a Blue cab would be responsible for an accident just like the one that happened, namely, hit-and-run, at night, at this location, and so on. But what they are given is quite different: the frequency of Blue cabs in the city. Subjects must decide for themselves whether this frequency is an accurate estimate of the required probability. They are free to discount it or disregard it, and should do so, for example, if they believe the larger company is likely to have more competent drivers than the smaller company, is less likely to have drivers who would leave the scene of an accident, and so forth (Gigerenzer & Murray, 1987).

The above explanation accounts for the finding that subjects do not neglect so-called *causal* base rates (the frequency of *accidents* by each cab company). This result is not necessarily a bias in favor of causal reasoning (Tversky & Kahneman, 1980); rather, subjects may have judged quite reasonably that information about the number of accidents is stronger evidence for the required base rate than information about the number of cabs (cf. Bar-Hillel, 1980). Unfortunately, however, this more elaborate decision analytic model still falls short. It does not explain why, if noncausal base rates are deemed irrelevant, subjects do use noncausal base rates when the witness is dropped from the story. To accommodate this, the decision analytic model would have to be elaborated further, so that the impact of the frequency data was dependent on the presence or absence of other evidence. While formal consistency might thus be restored, very little insight into the subjects' actual reasoning is provided.

Overconfidence is perhaps one of the more intuitively understandable decision biases. Yet Kadane and Lichtenstein (1982) argue that calibration sometimes violates Bayesian normative constraints. In particular, when there is no feedback regarding whether or not predicted events occur, and when the predicted events are nonindependent, a consistent decision maker should not be calibrated. Events can be nonindependent because their occurrence is influenced by some third event. For example, a pilot might believe that 90% of the airports in a given area will be closed if a storm intensifies, but that only 60% will be closed if it does not intensity. If the pilot thinks that the chance of intensification is 50 percent (and if he is a good Bayesian) he should predict the chance of closing for each airport to be (.5)(.9) + (.5)(.6) = .75. But the true frequency of closings will turn out to be either 60% (in which case the pilot was *overconfident*) or 90 percent (in which case he was *underconfident*). In calibration studies, the same kind of nonindependence could occur if a common cognitive model or reasoning method were utilized to assess the probabilities of different events. A Bayesian model that captured this would have to conditionalize probability assessments on the validity of specific aspects of the subject's own reasoning.

Lopes (1982) has argued that an overly rigid normative standard is used in studying intuitions about randomness (e.g., Wagenaar, 1972; Kahneman & Tversky, 1972). The principle function of a concept of randomness is to serve as a baseline against which significant patterns (i.e., nonrandomness) can be detected. Judgments of randomness, then, will depend on the types of nonrandomness that are likely in a particular problem domain. If random and nonrandom sets of patterns overlap (i.e., certain patterns could be either random or nonrandom), then the judgment will also depend on the relative costs of missing a significant pattern versus mistakenly identifying a random pattern as significant. So-called misconceptions of chance, then, may be the result of subjects and experimenters using different criteria of randomness. For example, all sequences of heads and tails of the same length are equally likely in a coin toss, yet Kahneman and Tversky (1972) found that subjects regard sequences with representative proportions of heads and tails (e.g., HTHTTH) as more probable than sequences with less representative proportions of heads and tails (e.g., HHHHTH). In most real-world domains, detecting nonrandom sequences is less important than detecting atypical proportions (e.g., of defective products off an assembly line). The subject might, therefore, have failed to understand that they were to deal with the sequence as such, instead classifying the coin tosses by the number of heads and tails. In that case, they were correct in regarding the event of five heads and one tail as less probable, hence more likely to be nonrandom, than the event of three heads and three tails. A more comprehensive Bayesian model of randomness judgments might require prior probabilities for different patterns of nonrandomness in the appropriate problem domain and a signal detection analysis of the costs of different kinds of errors. It is far from clear that such assessments could be meaningfully provided.

Discussions of the belief bias often sound as though classical logic or probability theory dictated the answer: Contradictory evidence should prompt rejection of a contradicted hypothesis (cf. Popper, 1959); disconfirming evidence should lower confidence in the hypothesis. Neither logic nor probability theory, however, is so definitive. The basic reason, in both cases, is that prediction from a hypothesis is always implicitly or explicitly dependent on auxiliary beliefs; the failure of the prediction to come true may therefore lead to the rejection to these other beliefs rather than rejection of the target hypothesis. The impossibility of definitive falsification is known in the philosophy of science as the *Quine-Duhem thesis* (Quine, 1961; Duhem, 1914/1962). An Army intelligence officer who has evidence that an attack will occur at a certain location, but who fails to discover in the photographic evidence the expected forward movement of the enemy's artillery, need not change his belief in the location of attack. Instead, he can question the reliability of the negative indicator: Perhaps the enemy plans to omit the initial artillery barrage for purposes of surprise, or artillery in some other location has a sufficient range to cover the attack area, or artillery equipment is unavailable or not in working order, and so on; perhaps artillery movement occurred but could not be detected photographically, because weather, foliage, and/or intentional camouflage masked its presence. We quite properly calibrate our trust in one source of information (e.g., a witness, a scientific experiment, an instrument, our own senses) by reference to its agreement or disagreement with other sources of information, and also by reference to its agreement or disagreement with our own beliefs (if a stranger tells me there is an elephant in the next room, I am unlikely to place much credence in anything he or she says). How could it be otherwise, since there is no directly revealed "ground truth"?

This kind of reasoning can in fact be accommodated within Bayesian models, although at great cost in complexity. The impact of each piece of evidence on the hypothesis may depend on all the other evidence that has been observed—that is, all potential observations may be combined into a single variable; the set of hypotheses may be expanded to include all combinations of truth and falsity of the original hypothesis and the auxiliary beliefs. In effect, such a model abandons the "divide and conquer" strategy of decision analysis (although Pearl, 1988, has made some efforts to simplify the modeling of some of these effects). Bayesian models may also permit the impact of evidence to depend on prior beliefs, by conditionalizing evidence assessments on the decision maker's own probability judgments (e.g., French, 1978)— but at the price of even greater loss of economy. A final source of complexity is the requirement to explicitly model all the possible temporal orders of the evidence, since two conflicting pieces of evidence may be interpreted differently depending on which is experienced first (Woodcock, Cobb, Familant, & Markey, 1988). It is extremely implausible to suppose that decision makers have explicit and exact models of this sort in their heads that anticipate their potential reactions to every possible state of affairs. Such models provide no real insight into the reasoning of decision makers: they do not tell us what it is that does or does not make sense about belief bias behavior.

A *confirmation bias* has also been found in the process of collecting information to test a rule. As noted above, Wason (1968) used rules of the sort: If there is a vowel on one side of a card, there is an even number on the other. Of four cards, showing an A, B, 4 and 7, respectively, subjects chose to turn over the cards with A and 4. According to Wason's simple logical model, the card showing a 4 cannot falsify the rule, whereas the card showing a 7 could (if there were a vowel on the other side). There is strong reason, however, to doubt the general applicability of such a simple model. A scientist testing the hypothesis that "All ravens are black" will hardly set out collecting nonblack things to determine whether they are ravens (this has been called the *paradox of confirmation;* Hempel, 1965). Even if the hypothesis under investigation is really false (hence, there is a nonblack raven somewhere), the scientist will find the nonblack raven faster by looking at ravens than by looking at nonblack things. The reason lies in knowledge about the domain: If the rule is false, the proportion of nonblack things that turn out to be ravens will still be much smaller than the proportion of ravens that turn out to be nonblack. A fairly complex Bayesian model is required to represent such beliefs (Horwich, 1982, pp. 53–62), but they appear to be quite general across problem domains: Useful rules link reasonably specific classes to one another (e.g., ravens and blackness), while the complements (nonravens, nonblack things) will be larger and more diverse. If subjects (mistakenly) carry over these strategies to the card task, turning over the 7 would be rejected as an inefficient method for rule falsification. Klayman and Ha (1987) provide a similar analysis of a rule discovery experiment by Wason (1960).

In all these examples, experimenters appear to have applied an overly simple decision analytic model to their own problems—perhaps as a sort of satisficing in the face of complexity. Potentially important factors are not captured by these models. In particular, subjects do not accept information provided to them at face value; they evaluate instructions, randomness, base rates, conflicting evidence, and potential tests of hypotheses in the light of real-world knowledge (sometimes inappropriately extrapolating from familiar to unfamiliar settings). Subjects' performance can, in principle, be accounted for by more complex decision analytic models—indeed, virtually any decision-making performance could be captured by some decision analytic model, given the freedom in choosing structure and inputs (Glymour, 1980). For this very reason, of course, the exercise of inventing a decision analytic model to predict subjects' responses does not prove that their decision processes are "rational."

In the absence of more systematic investigation, however, the very existence of alternative models compels us to suspend judgment about which model is appropriate. It is at least equally arbitrary to assume that subjects' beliefs and goals are best fit by the models adopted by experimenters. Abstractly fitting performance to a convenient normative template is of little help in evaluating a reasoning process. The flexibility of decision analytic modeling is a virtue if one is looking for an intellectual tool, but is a drawback if one is looking for a Platonic test of rationality.

It seems implausible, to say the least, that subjects would be able or willing to provide the many precise assessments demanded by the models that fit their behavior. In other words, the models that make the subjects' behavior appear rational are not very successful as potential intellectual tools. But it shouldn't be necessary to prove that subjects were actually using (or could use) the hypothesized models. It would be enough to show that they are sensitive in an roughly appropriate way to the variables contained in the model. Developing such models highlights variables to which subjects might in fact be sensitive, such as the credibility of base rates and evidence, or the different types of "nonrandomness" that characterize different domains. The question to which we now turn is whether there are simpler and more illuminating (but also normatively plausible) processing strategies in which such variables might be incorporated.

Challenge (6): There are alternative, non-Bayesian normative concepts that justify the decision maker's way of approaching the problem.

Challenge (6) represents the most fundamental criticism of the decision bias paradigm. It rejects the definition of formal consistency that has been used to characterize and define decision biases. It argues, in essence, that *rationality* cannot be equated with decision theory; decision theory is one of a set of competing claims regarding what it means to make rational decisions. An extreme variant is (a) that biases are not possible *in principle,* because the chief criterion for adopting a normative theory is its fit to actual decision making behavior (L. J. Cohen, 1981); if (nonstressed) behavior disagrees with the model, the model must be automatically dropped. A more moderate position is (b) that a variety of alternative normative frameworks and prescriptive concepts now exist for decision making (e.g., Zadeh, 1965; Shafer, 1976; L. J. Cohen, 1977), and some of these may shed more light than decision analysis on the thought processes that decision makers actually utilize, and perhaps provide a more adequate tool for helping them make better decisions.

(a) The possibility of biases. In the previous chapter, we discussed different paradigms for the relationship between normative and descriptive. When decision-making behavior disagrees with a normative model, the rationalist paradigm condemns the behavior; the formal-empiricist paradigm will consider changing the model—as long as the new model has some degree of formal plausibility. L. J. Cohen's position seems to drop the latter qualification: the model *must* be changed if it disagrees with behavior. Before addressing Cohen's challenge, let us back up and ask what we mean by "normatively correct" decisions. What basis is there for choosing among competing normative frameworks? It is helpful to distinguish three kinds of arguments, which may be loosely described as formal, cognitive, and behavioral:

- Formal: justifies models like Bayes' rule of maximization of subjectively expected utility by deriving them from "self-evident" axioms. This is the *only* kind of normative justification according to orthodox Bayesians. Not coincidentally, Bayesian theory has a preeminent claim to validity on this basis. De Finetti (1937/1964), for example, showed that, unless your beliefs and choices conform to the rules of decision theory, a clever opponent could turn you into a "money pump," that is, devise a set of gambles in which you would inevitably lose. Savage (1972), Lindley (1982), and others have provided derivations of decision theoretic constraints from other axioms. Axiomatic justifications of other normative approaches have also been developed, however (e.g., fuzzy set theory: Bellman & Giertz, 1973; Nau, 1986).
- Cognitive: justifies a model (e.g., Bayes's rule or multiattribute utility analysis) in terms of its own face validity and practicality. Two kinds of cognitive considerations have been advanced in recent discussions: (a) Does the model require inputs about which the decision

maker has confident and precise intuitions (von Winterfeldt & Edwards, 1986)? (b) Are the operations applied by the model to the inputs plausible—that is, is there a strong analogy between the problem at hand and "canonical examples" of the application of the model (Shafer, 1981, 1982; Shafer & Tversky, 1988)? For some theorists, normative justification is exclusively at this cognitive level—although there is disagreement among them on whether decision analytic models will always come out on top (von Winterfeldt & Edwards) or whether alternatives might sometimes be justified (Shafer). For orthodox Bayesians, cognitive concerns are important, too, but merely from an engineering, not a normative, standpoint: Bell, Raiffa, and Tversky (1988) and Brown (1989a) propose a "prescriptive" science to bridge the gap between "normative" constraints (thought of as purely formal) and "descriptive" shortcomings of real decision makers.

• Behavioral: justifies a model in terms of the match between its *outputs* and the actual performance of decision makers (under non-stressed conditions); a normative theory must be revised if it does not describe "human intuitions in concrete, individual cases" (L. J. Cohen, 1981). Systematic flaws in decision-making competence (i.e., biases) are ruled out by definition; errors can only be the by-products of ignorance about the correct methods or of *performance* limitations such as fatigue, lapses of memory, inattention, and lack of motivation. L. J. Cohen has championed this position in its most extreme form, but arguments are quite common in the mainstream normative literature for the superiority of one or another framework based on the plausibility of its conclusions in specific examples (e.g., Zadeh, 1984; Bell, 1982; Ellsberg, 1961).

For each of these levels—axioms, models, and outputs—there are theorists who regard it as the exclusive touchstone of rationality. But no one of these levels, I argue, is adequate by itself:

• Limitations of the formal level: Axiomatic derivations say that if you accept the axioms, you must accept the model (e.g., Bayesian inference, maximization of SEU); but if you don't accept the axioms, you need not accept the model. Yet every derivation in the literature requires one or more axioms that have no inherent plausibility. For example, Savage (1972) assumes that decision makers always know their preferences among gambles; they either prefer gamble A to gamble B, prefer gamble B to gamble A, or are indifferent—but they are never *ignorant* (Shafer, 1988). Lindley (1982) makes an equivalent assumption: that uncertainty is to be measured by a single number (although at least two numbers would be needed to measure the decision maker's *confidence* in her own probability assessments).

What do we gain by giving up the noncompelling axioms? Non-Bayesian systems may have attractive features, especially at the cognitive level, that Bayesian decision theory lacks: alternative, richer frameworks may more adequately represent types of uncertainty that characterize real-world problems, such as incompleteness of evidence, vagueness, and imprecision. Even Bayesians must implicitly give up formal justification (which requires the assumption that all probabilities and preferences are precisely known) in order to make sense of applied decision analysis as a tool for generating unknown probabilities and preferences from known ones.

How much do we lose by rejecting the noncompelling axioms? Systems that permit ignorance about beliefs and preferences (i.e., which measure uncertainty by more than one number), such as fuzzy logic or Shafer-Dempster belief functions, may still possess the attractive properties contained in the other axioms, for example, independence of beliefs and preferences. Is a framework which is consistent with *all the other* axioms really *less justified* than decision theory? The only thing such frameworks lack, by comparison with Bayesian theory, is the demonstration of their uniqueness via axiomatic derivation. Being a doctrinaire Bayesian, from this point of view, is like preferring to live in a *uniquely tiny* house instead of in a comfortable house that is the same size as your neighbors'.

- Limitations of the cognitive level: Cognitive criteria emphasize the fit between the inputs required by a model and the decision maker's knowledge, and between the processing required by the model and the decision maker's judgments of plausibility: that is, normative models are good "tools" for generating needed probabilities and preferences from known probabilities and preferences. But the tool metaphor, taken by itself, has trouble with a crucial features of real decision aiding: The iterative process by means of which initial models are replaced by better ones until both analyst and decision maker are satisfied. What partially drives this process is the fact that decision makers often come to a problem with intuitions not only about the *inputs* to a model, but about the *answer* as well. When a model gives answers that are widely discrepant from intuitions, decision makers quite properly want to reexamine the model and improve it. A direct judgment or choice regarding the answer to the problem might sometimes capture the decision maker's knowledge more effectively than a more detailed analysis. It may sometimes make sense to resolve inconsistency by changing the model.

- Limitations of the behavioral level: According to the behavioral criterion, we should *always* abandon a model when we don't like the answers. But if this were true, decision making (under nonstressed conditions) could never be improved by analysis; the status quo would always be best. In fact, however, models can and do cause decision makers to change their minds. Models can be persuasive because they have certain very general attractive properties (e.g., independence of preferences and beliefs), or—perhaps more importantly—because they seem to organize all the relevant factors in a particular problem in a reasonable way. It is arbitrary to take intuitions about specific cases seriously, as L. J. Cohen (1981) urges, but to dismiss more general intuitions about the fit between the problem and a model (the cognitive level) and the more abstract intuitions about formally desirable properties. (L. J. Cohen, 1983, himself seems to have come around to such a view.)

Formal, cognitive, and behavioral criteria are all, in the end, "intuitions" (Einhorn & Hogarth, 1981)—it is hard to justify the absolute epistemological priority to one set over the other. According to one view of justification (Goodman, 1965; Rawls, 1971; Daniels, 1979), normative judgments involve an equilibrium between general principles and performance: We amend the general principles if they imply a practice we are unwilling to accept, and we amend practice if it violates a principle we are unwilling to amend. "The process of justification is the delicate one of making mutual adjustments between (principles and practices); and in the agreement achieved lies the only justification needed for either" (Goodman, 1965, p. 64).

Some writers have been alarmed at the "relativistic" implications of this view; any practice is justified if it fits the principles a decision maker happens to accept (e.g., Stich & Nisbett, 1980). This criticism confuses the *process* of justification with *successful* justification. We need not regard a behavior as successfully justified simply because an equilibrium of this sort has been achieved. One equilibrium can be more convincing than another—if it draws on a wider range of more plausible theories (the formal level), if it organizes more of the decision maker's knowledge (the cognitive level), and if it fits a wider range of behavior. The success of the behavior in achieving real-world goals (cf. Thagard, 1988) is also a legitimate indicator of the validity of a normative framework; in fact, our intuitions may themselves be the product of an evolutionary past comprising a long series of actual successes and failures.

What are the implications of this view for decision biases? How people *actually* make decisions is a relevant consideration in evaluating a normative model of how they *ought* to decide. Is the normative evaluation of decision making, therefore, completely circular? Must systematic decision-making errors be dismissed as impossible? No. The reason is that other criteria besides the behavioral also contribute legitimately to the evaluation of normative models: that is, at the formal level—desirable general properties; and at the cognitive level—a match of the model's required inputs and modes of processing to the knowledge representations and plausibility judgments of decision makers. Because of these other criteria, normative models may survive behavioral disagreement; if cognitive or formal criteria strongly support the model, behavioral disagreement may cause us to amend the behavior.

Nevertheless, L. J. Cohen (1981) was not all wrong. When behavior clashes with a normative model, there is always a force of at least some magnitude pulling away from the "error" verdict: *The more systematic the "errors," and the more prevalent they are among successful practitioners or experts, the greater the feeling that we should modify theory rather than condemn the practice.* Like other tradeoffs (see the discussion of challenge 3 above), precise and confident judgments of the relative importance of these criteria may simply not be realistic. In the real world (e.g., applications of decision aiding or training), we may have to decide on a case-by-case basis. The most constructive strategy is to use conflicts between behavior and model as a prompt for expanded understanding of both. For example, in our discussion of challenge 5, violations of behavioral consistency led to revised decision analytic models. Some of these new models proved to be unpersuasive on the cognitive level, however, because of their complexity and the difficulty of the inputs they required. The next step is to look at revisions at the formal level, that is, non-Bayesian normative frameworks that may shed more light on decision making processes than complex Bayesian models.

(b) Alternative normative concepts. In the past two decades there has been a lively debate in the normative research community regarding alternative concepts and methods for reasoning with uncertainty (e.g., Smithson, 1989; Cohen, Schum, Freeling, & Chinnis, 1985; Kanal & Lemmer, 1986). This ongoing competition among normative concepts has been largely, though not entirely, disregarded by psychologists concerned with studying human decision biases (but see Shafer & Tversky, 1988). Yet one of the key issues of that debate has been decision making under varying conditions of knowledge and ignorance; some of the suggested solutions may, therefore, illuminate un-

aided decision making in the real world. We will focus here on one such approach: a framework for assumption-based reasoning that formalizes effective metacognitive control over the application of knowledge.

Classical Bayesian theory has no easy way to represent the amount of knowledge or ignorance underlying an uncertainty judgment. A .5 probability that Jones will beat Smith in a tennis match may represent thorough knowledge of the capabilities of the two players, leading to the conclusion that they are evenly matched, or it might reflect complete ignorance (Gardenfors & Sahlin, 1982). Similarly, a .9 probability might be based on a lot of evidence or very little. From a Bayesian point of view, choices should be unaffected by decision makers' confidence or lack of confidence in their own beliefs: the decision maker whose .5 probability represents a large amount of knowledge should act in precisely the same way as the decision maker whose .5 probability represents virtually no knowledge at all. Nevertheless, real choices are affected, not just by probability, but by degree of knowledge (Ellsberg, 1961). People may prefer to bet on *either* player in a tennis match in which the opponents are known rather than bet on *either* player in a match whose players are unknown, even though the "probabilities" should be 50–50 in each case. These choices violate the probability axioms: the less well-understood "probabilities" appear to sum to less than 1.0. Yet such choices can seem quite reasonable on reflection.

According to a number of normative theorists (e.g., Ellsberg, 1961; Gardenfors & Sahlin, 1982; Levi, 1986), under conditions of ignorance decision makers are entitled to fall back on non-decision-analytic criteria of choice. One such criterion, for example, involves comparison of options in terms of their worst-case outcomes. A worst-case strategy would reduce the desirability of betting on either of the unknown players in a tennis match: Since both Smith and Jones are unknown, it is possible that Jones is much worse than Smith, *and* it is possible that Smith is much worse than Jones. An alternative, equally permissible, decision strategy is to evaluate unknown probabilities in terms of the best case. More generally, to the extent that a decision maker's knowledge does not specify exact probabilities, preferences, or actions, she is free to adopt *assumptions* within the range permitted by her knowledge.

Assumption-based reasoning has received considerable attention from the artificial intelligence community as a method for handling incomplete information (e.g., Doyle, 1979; deKleer, 1986). Unfortunately, in these assumption-based systems, the process of metacognitive control, for example, revising assumptions when they lead to contradictory results, is largely arbitrary. Cohen (1986, 1989) has proposed a system that provides for higher order reasoning (i.e., meta-cognition) about the assumptions in quantitative models; in turn, quantitative measures of the reliability of beliefs, the magnitude of the conflict, and the responsibility of particular assumptions for the conflict guide the processes by which assumptions are adopted, evaluated, and revised.

Techniques of this sort may capture aspects of naturalistic reasoning more successfully than the decision analytic paradigm. In particular, the notion of assumption-based reasoning fits several recently proposed models of naturalistic decision making quite well (see Lipshitz, this volume). According to Lipshitz (in his theory of decision making as *Argument-Driven Action*) and Klein (in his theory of *Recognition-Primed Decision Making*), decisions do not involve explicit comparison and choice among alternatives. Instead, a single action is generated by matching the current situation to known cases; this is followed, optionally, by a process of verifying or critiquing the generated action, rebutting the critique, and (if necessary) modifying or rejecting the option. Similarly, I have proposed (Cohen, 1989) that in inference problems, a "first-blush" or normal reaction to a piece of evidence is followed, optionally, by consideration of possible exception conditions or rebuttals, and possibly by a revised interpretation of the evidence. More generally, an action or inference, once it has been generated, is assumed appropriate, until reasons are found to believe otherwise.

In the last section, we observed patterns of behavior that violated simple decision analytic models, but which could be accommodated within far more complex (but less plausible) decision analytic models. For example, a first step toward handling "base rate neglect" was a Bayesian model that explicitly evaluates the reliability of the experimentally provided frequency data as evidence for the true base rate. This model fails, however, to accommodate the apparent inconsistency in evaluation from one condition to another: when individuating evidence (the witness) was available, frequency data were apparently regarded as unreliable; but when no individuating evidence was present, frequency data were apparently regarded as reliable. A far more complex model is required at this point, which anticipates every possible combination of evidence and frequency data. *An account in terms of ignorance and assumption-based reasoning, by contrast, stays simple: It divides the work of the complex model between simple first-level beliefs and simple metalevel rules.*

In the base-rate studies, it is reasonable to suppose that subjects are unsure about the reliability of the frequency data: They are not told the source of the information or how recent it is; they are told nothing about other relevant factors that could distinguish the two cab companies (e.g., competence of drivers, training not to leave the scene of an accident); finally, they have virtually no experience with information of this kind in comparable settings (either experimental or real world). Nevertheless, in the absence of any other information, they may well be prepared to *assume* that the frequency data are reliable and relevant. Such an assumption, however, is not equivalent to a belief based on knowledge: it is subject to change. In particular, conflict between the frequency data (e.g., the proportion of Blue cabs in the city = .15) and individuating evidence (e.g, the witness says the guilty cab was Blue) triggers a process of problem solving in which the assumptions that contributed to the conflict are reexamined and possibly revised. In the presence of individuating data, therefore, subjects may retract their assumption that the frequency data are reliable. There is no inconsistency in beliefs, only a quite reasonable change in assumptions.

The so-called *belief bias,* in which new evidence is reinterpreted to fit a prior hypothesis, is subject to a very similar analysis. This phenomenon can also be handled in a decision analytic model; within such a model, evidence items will not be independent of one another conditional on the hypothesis, as they are in standard Bayesian models; in fact, evidence and prior probabilities would not be independent either. Such a model, however, is often intractably complex and requires precise assessments of how the decision maker will respond to every combination of internal prior judgments and external events; the model must be complicated even further if the temporal order of the evidence is taken into account.

The most plausible way to handle belief bias behavior is not to impose complex Bayesian models of belief change, but to introduce a notion of assumption-based reasoning. Decision makers are not completely confident ahead of time about the meaning of every piece of evidence they are likely to encounter. In the normal course of events, assumptions are adopted in order to facilitate the smooth incorporation of new data into a preexisting framework, or schema (as in Piaget's *assimilation* or Thomas Kuhn's *normal science*). Sometimes the requirement to assimilate data conflicts with the assumptions usually adopted (e.g., that a source of information is reliable until proven otherwise, or that the worst case outcome will occur); the usual interpretation may then be overridden (either by an automatic, expectancy-driven process or by conscious reflection) and the data "explained away." The same piece of evidence may thus have a different interpretation as a function of the context of other evidence and beliefs in which it occurs. Assimilation, however, can be carried too far. In a dynamic environment, if a long series of apparently conflicting pieces of evidence has been explained away, the decision maker may grow uneasy. At some point, he or she may realize that a simpler overall set of beliefs and assumptions can be achieved by rejecting the favored hypothesis. Examples of this sort of "Gestalt shift" are the "scientific revolutions" referred to by Kuhn (1962).

According to Fischhoff and Beyth-Marom (1983), people choose to perform tests that, no matter what information they actually obtain, will be interpreted as confirming their favored hypothesis. Baron, Beattie, and Hershey (1988) found that subjects consistently overestimated the value of questions that were regarded as useless by a Bayesian value-of-information model. Another possibility, however, is that the Bayesian value-of-information model missed the point. In that model, the potential impact of an observation is based on the interpretation that the decision maker assigns to it *at the present time*. But the present interpretation of the evidence may depend on assumptions, which are subject to change. Suppose, for example, that subsequent evidence continues to be interpreted as confirming the hypothesis, but that more and more work to "explain away" is required to do this. At some point, the decision maker does change her mind: the cumulative effect of all this "confirming" evidence is a disconfirmation! The tests that produced that evidence clearly did have value, even if no single one of the tests could have caused any perceptible change in belief *at the time it was performed*.

A similar approach might illuminate the dynamic aspects of choice behavior. According to multiattribute utility analysis, precise preferences among criteria exist in the decision maker's head waiting to be elicited; when the appropriate algorithms are applied to such preferences, one and only one option (barring exact ties) always turns out to be best. Choice in the real world, however, is often a dynamic process, in which changing assumptions about goals and options reflect increasing understanding of preferences. This process may involve rather sophisticated and active problem-solving steps. For example, when goals are in conflict (i.e., no single alternative satisfies all the criteria), decision makers may reexamine assumptions: they may drop some goals or change their priority, they may relax or qualify the scoring of alternatives on various criteria, or they may try to discover alternative means to the same ends. By contrast, when evaluative criteria are incomplete (i.e., an insufficient number of options have been eliminated), decision makers may look for additional plausible assumptions: they may explore reasons to strengthen one or more of the original goals; they may look for additional goals; they may scrutinize the performance of candidates on various criteria more closely;

they may even find a way to make more precise tradeoff judgments. A multiattribute utility analysis, by giving a definitive answer prematurely, may forestall rather than facilitate improved understanding.

The same principles may apply to a variety of other biases in inference and choice. Assumptions regarding predictability and change in underlying processes may affect the so-called *regression fallacy,* in which *overextreme* predictions of one quantity are made based on another quantity. Assumptions about various possible exceptions to a conclusion may influence *overconfidence* (such assumptions are necessary, under certain conditions, for the achievement of calibration). Assumptions about the types of nonrandomness to be expected in particular domains may influence judgments of randomness. Assumptions about the representativeness of recalled instances may underlie availability effects. In many experiments, subjects may make assumptions about the relevance or credibility of experimentally provided information.

On what grounds do I claim that a system of assumption-based reasoning can be "normative"? Clearly, anyone for whom Bayesian decision theory and/or logic are normative *by definition* will be unmoved by such a claim. From a naturalistic point of view, however, we consider the cognitive and behavioral plausibility of a proposed normative framework in addition to its more formal virtues. From this point of view, assumption-based reasoning is entirely defensible:

- Formally, it retains the more compelling axioms underlying decision analysis, since many important inconsistencies are attributed to changes in assumptions rather than to firm beliefs and preferences (Levi, 1986; Kyburg, 1968/1988). Changes in preferences, for example, as the decision maker learns which options are feasible can be accommodated without sacrificing the independence of (firm) preferences and (firm) beliefs.
- Cognitively, assumption-based models require more natural inputs and provide more plausible processing of those inputs than decision analytic models. First, they do not demand assessments (e.g., of the reliability of information) that are more precise than the decision maker's knowledge or capacity permits. Assumption-based reasoning is tailored to limited-capacity processing, in which it is not possible to marshall all the information that may conceivably be relevant for every decision. Assumptions help a person make more effective use of the knowledge that is available, by permitting selective focus on hypotheses, outcomes, and dimensions about which she has the most information (by assuming, provisionally, that unexamined possibilities contain no surprises). Problems with the first-

pass solution prompt activation of additional parts of the decision maker's knowledge, or additional external information collection.

The assumption-based approach also seems inherently more plausible than the standard decision analytic model. Bayesian updating handles conflicting evidence, in effect, by taking an average; there is never a definitive picture of the situation, in which conflict is explained or resolved. Assumption-based reasoning, by contrast, takes conflict as a symptom that something might be wrong in the reasoning that led to the conflict, and uses it as a stimulus to find and correct mistakes (Cohen, 1986, 1989). It exploits the opportunity for self-correction in dynamic environments.

- Finally, the assumption-based model matches actual decision-making performance far more closely. If one doctor says a child has the mumps and the other says she has measles, parents might differ in their responses: some might assume one doctor was correct, and disregard the other; other parents would look for a third doctor, investigate the credentials of the two conflicting doctors, or explore the reasons for their diagnoses in more depth. But very few parents would take an average (i.e., settle for an inconclusive assignment of probabilities to the two possibilities). If both doctors happened to assign a very small probability to a third disease, a Bayesian model would assign full support to the "compromise"—even though neither doctor regarded it as an important possibility (Zadeh, 1984).

Assumption-based strategies also pervade highly successful "expert" reasoning. For example, scientists seek a coherent picture of nature rather than an assignment of probabilities to alternatives: They try to explain unexpected new observations by means of minimal adjustments in existing theory (Quine, 1960); and they adjust (or "calibrate") experimental procedures until the procedures produce theory-predicted results (Greenwald, Pratkanis, Leippe & Baumgardner, 1986). The alternative to these practices is a "disbelief bias," that is, abandoning a theory at the first sign of trouble, probably crippling science's ability to find (or impose) regularities in nature. The relatively sudden shifts that characterize "scientific revolutions" suggest a process of initially explaining away conflicting data, then reexamining and revising assumptions—as opposed to the continual changes in probability characteristic of Bayesian models.

By fitting a variety of actual behaviors into the framework of assumption-based reasoning, however, we by no means imply that all decision-making performance is normatively correct. The preponderance of evidence suggests that actual behavior will not perfectly fit any normative model that is also plausible on cognitive and/or formal grounds. *The goal is to devise normative models that are illuminating and insightful: that is, they must provide a close enough fit to actual decisions and decision processes so that the discrepancies really do seem like errors that are worthy of attention.*

What kinds of decision errors, then, does an assumption-based theory of decision making identify? Biases, from this point of view, are defects in the metacognitive processes that control the verification and revision of conclusions. In the assumption-based model, as in Bayesian decision theory, errors involve formal inconsistency; but the system within which consistency is now defined has been tailored to fit the processes and constraints that affect real-world problem solving. For example,

- Belief bias: It is not automatically an error when decision makers "explains away" an apparently conflicting piece of evidence; however, they may explain away "too much" conflicting evidence, and (especially in a time-stressed environment) fail to maintain a sense of "cumulative doubt" that triggers the reassessment of a favored hypothesis. Moreover, the opposite error is also possible: they may take evidence literally when they should have questioned it—that is, explained it away.
- Overconfidence: In assessing uncertainty, decision makers, may overlook important exceptions to a conclusion (overconfidence); alternatively, however, they may take far-fetched possibilities too seriously, paralyzing effective inference and action.
- Satisficing, elimination-by-aspects: It is not automatically an error for decision makers to adopt goals on evaluative dimensions and to neglect tradeoffs; however, it is an error if they fail to raise or lower their goals realistically in the light of their achievability. Once again, adjusting their goals too much or too soon may also be an error.
- Ellsberg's paradox: By focusing on the worst case, decision makers may miss important opportunities; or by focusing on opportunities (the best case), they may overlook risks. However, they may also go wrong by trying to summarize multiple outcomes or dimensions by an abstract average (incorporating both worst and best cases) that is poorly correlated with successful action.

The assumption-based approach formalizes and refines our understanding of the kinds of errors we have already identified, in our discussion of the other challenges: failure to compensate for shortcomings of decision strategies, failure to make midcourse corrections in an inference or choice, failure to effectively exploit knowledge and to efficiently deploy capacity. Systematic errors of this type may well exist, but such "decision biases" are clearly not the ones to which we have grown accustomed. The "cure" may also be different from what is usually supposed: It need not require the imposition of decision analytic models. Decision making should be both understood and improved in its own terms.

KEY POINTS

- Even if decisions are inconsistent or biased, real-world environmental factors may often prevent undesirable outcomes.
- Formally inconsistent decision processes can lead to a useful outcome because they embody the decision maker's real-world knowledge.
- The benefit of reduced cognitive effort in decision making can often justify the use of a formally deficient procedure.
- Appropriate normative modeling of tasks may show that decisions should not be regarded as flawed in even the narrowest sense.
- Improvements in decision making need not require imposing analytic methods.

Section B

Models of Naturalistic Decision Making

Chapter 5

Converging Themes in the Study of Decision Making in Realistic Settings

Raanan Lipshitz
University of Haifa

How do people actually decide in realistic settings? In Chapter 1, Orasanu and Connolly described why such decisions are sometimes so tough: time pressures, ill-structured problems, uncertain and incomplete information, shifting goals, action–feedback loops, high stakes, multiple players, and organizational context. The list is formidable, yet people carry on—and sometimes excel—under these circumstances. How do they do it?

So far there is no unified "decision theory" that can answer this puzzle and I do not intend to propose one in this chapter. What I do is review some partial answers that have been proposed by different researchers in the form of models of decision making in various settings. I describe the models and discuss their differences and similarities, so that, by the end of the chapter you should have a clearer idea of how decisions are actually made and how proficient decision makers can be counted on to do a good job. The chapter reviews nine models: Noble's model of situation assessment (Noble, 1989; Noble & Mullen, 1987; Noble, Grosz, & Boehm-Davis, 1987); Klein's model of Recognition-Primed Decisions (Calderwood, Crandall, & Klein, 1987; Klein, 1989; Klein, Calderwood, & Clinton-Cirocco, 1986); Pennington and Hastie's model of explanation-based decisions (Pennington & Hastie, 1986, 1988); Montgomery's dominance search model (Dahlstrand & Montgomery, 1984; Montgomery, 1983, 1989a; Montgomery & Svenson, 1989a); Beach and Mitchell's image theory (Beach, 1990; Beach & Mitchell, 1987; Beach, Smith, Lundell, & Mitchell, 1988); Rasmussen's model of cognitive control (Rasmussen, 1983, 1985, 1989); Hammond's cognitive continuum theory (Hammond, 1986a, 1988; Hammond, Hamm, Grassia, & Pearson, 1987; Lusk, Stewart, & Hammond, 1988); Connolly's model of decision cycles (Connolly, 1982, 1988; Connolly & Wagner, 1988); and my own model of argument-driven action (Lipshitz, 1989). Why have I chosen these models rather than others? First, and foremost, they all deal with real-world decision making, that is, with decisions that are meaningful to the decision makers who have some relevant knowledge or expertise in regard to them. Second, I am not interested in models that grew out of classical decision theory (Hogarth, 1987; Kahneman, Slovic, & Tversky, 1982), because I think that the growing doubts on their applicability to real-world decisions indicate that it is time to try a different approach (Beach & Lipshitz, this volume; Cohen, this volume; Einhorn & Hogarth, 1981; Fischhoff, Goitein, & Shapira, 1982; Funder, 1987; Klein, 1987; March, 1978; Wallstein, 1983). Third, I wish to keep the scope limited to decision making by individuals and so omitted models that were geared to the group or organizational level (Chapters 19 and 20 in this volume cover team decision making). Undoubtedly there are other models that can be added, but my goal is not to write an exhaustive literature review. I simply wish to explore the extent of agreement between some recently developed models of how decisions are actually made.

Reading descriptions of nine different models can be quite confusing. To reduce the confusion, I group the models in two basic categories. The first category consists of *process models,* which describe the sequence of phases in which decisions are made. The second category consists of *typological models,* which classify decision processes (e.g., as intuitive or analytic) and discuss the contingencies under which each type is—or ought to be—used. Although some models fit both categories, I retain the dichotomy for ease of presentation and to highlight the principal features of the various models.

After reviewing the nine models, I identify their common features and evaluate the extent to which they address the features of real-world settings discussed by Orasanu and Connolly in Chapter 1. Lastly, the review focuses on the *conceptual* aspects of the nine models. To learn more about their associated research and applications, you should read the chapters by the individual authors in this volume and the literature referenced at the beginning of this chapter.

PROCESS MODELS

Five models are grouped in this category. The models are similar in that all depict decision making as a sequence of activities. They differ in terms of the type of decisions and the nature of the sequences which they describe.

1. Noble: Situation Assessment

Suppose that a formation of airplanes is detected flying westward across the Iraqi–Jordanian border by Israeli radar. How would—or should—Israel respond to this information? The answer, suggests David Noble, depends on how the situation is assessed or "sized up." Thus, Noble's model of situation assessment focuses on a crucial aspect of decision making. The process of situation assessment unfolds as follows (Figure 5.1): First, concrete information on the situation (e.g., information that is read from a radar screen) is combined with additional background or "context" information (concerning e.g., current Arab–Israeli tensions) and general knowledge retrieved from the decision maker's memory (e.g., on Iraqi offensive doctrine and bombers' characteristics) to form a tentative interpretation ("representation") of the situation. Assume, for a moment, that the initial representation created this way is that these are Iraqi bombers en route to attack Israel. This representation implies certain expectations concerning, for example, the future direction, altitude, and speed of the suspected bombers. These expectations are tested by additional information from the radar and other sources. To the extent that the expectations do not match this information, the representation is refined or rejected in favor of a new representation that is tested, retained, refined, or rejected in turn. Thus people can sometime decide what to do by observing that the current situation is similar to other previously observed situations, and that actions that worked in those situations may also work in the new one.

Noble conducted a set of psychological experiments to test the validity of his model, but his interests, and the interesting aspects of his work, lie elsewhere. Noble's objective is to develop computer software capable of accurate assessment of complex situations. The interesting aspect of his work is that he chose not to use sophisticated statistical methods that are applicable to this problem. Instead he chose to emulate the seemingly suboptimal process of human situation assessment, because he sought to develop a system that could "combine information of different types and from different sources, even when this information is vague, unreliable, incomplete, partially inconsistent, and deliberately misleading" (1989, p. 1). Preliminary tests of his computerized system in operational environments indicate that it does, in fact, have these hoped-for characteristics.

Figure 5.1. Situation Assessment: A Schematic Representation

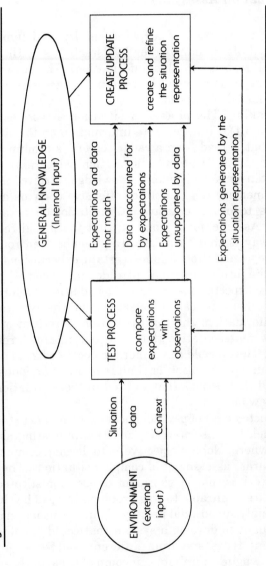

From *Application of a Theory of Cognition to Situation Assessment*, by D. Noble, 1989. Copyright © 1989 by Engineering Research Associates. Reprinted by permission.

Since computers and human brains function very differently, Noble's system does not actually simulate how people go through the stages specified in Figure 5.1, but just follows them in its own, very different way. Gary Klein and his associates, whose work I review next, developed a model that describes how people actually base their decisions on situation assessment.

2. Klein: Recognition-Primed Decisions (RPD)

Klein is interested in how proficient decision makers manage to be effective under high stress and time pressure. To this end he and his associates carefully interviewed and observed experienced fireground commanders, tank platoon leaders, and design engineers. In addition they compared the decision-making processes of experts and novices.

Klein's principal conclusion is that, contrary to the traditional definition of *decision making* as choosing among alternatives, proficient decision makers rarely compare among alternatives. Instead they assess the nature of the situation and, based on this assessment, select an action appropriate to it. This process, which Klein calls *recognition-primed decision making,* consists of three phases: situation recognition, serial option evaluation, and mental simulation (Figure 5.2).

Situation recognition. At this stage the decision maker recognizes (i.e., classifies) the situation as typical or novel. The process is recognition primed because recognition is, to a certain extent, its most crucial element: Typical situations lead to typical (or well-rehearsed) actions, whereas novel situations pose a new challenge that cannot be countered effectively by employing old routines. To recognize the situation and guide the selection of proper action, the decision maker identifies critical cues that mark the type of the situation and causal factors that explain what is happening and what is going to happen. Based on these, he or she sets plausible goals (which can be achieved in his or her particular situation) and proceeds to select an appropriate action given his or her goals and expectations.

Serial option evaluation. In this phase the decision maker evaluates action alternatives one at a time until a satisfactory one is found. Actions are selected from an *action queue* where they are arranged according to this *typicality.* Thus, the first action evaluated is that rated as the most typical response in the particular situation. The process by which actions are evaluated is mental simulation.

Mental simulation. To evaluate if an action is satisfactory, the decision maker acts it out in his or her imagination. He or she mentally simulates the successive steps to be taken, the potential outcomes of these steps, the problems that are likely to be encountered, and if and

Figure 5.2. Recognition-Primed Decision (RPD) Model

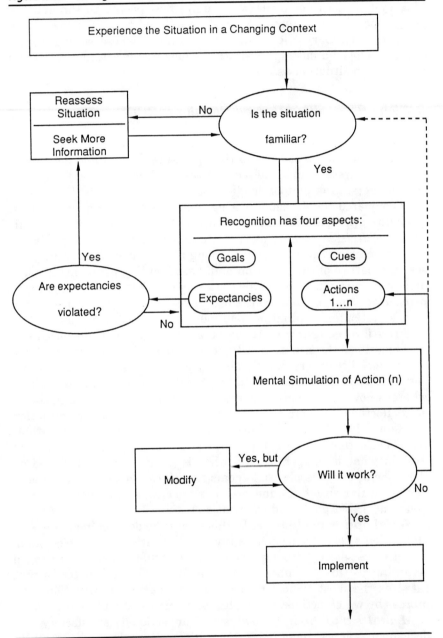

From "Recognition-Primed Decisions," by G. Klein, 1989. *Advances in Man-Machine Systems Research*, Vol 5, p. 50. Reprinted by permission.

how these problems can be handled. As a result of the simulation the decision maker either implements the action as is, modifies it, or rejects it altogether and turns to examine the next action in his or her action queue. Another outcome of mental simulation is a reassessment of the situation, as previously unnoticed aspects of the situation surface in the process of imagining future developments.

The RPD model is a descriptive model; that is, it does not prescribe how decisions ought to be made but how they are actually made by experienced practitioners in certain domains. Nevertheless, the model explains how these people make effective decisions in stressful conditions, where many things change rapidly or happen at the same time. First, focusing on critical cues and identifying causal factors reduces the information overload and sense of confusion that paralyze novice decision makers in such situations. In addition, the identification of causal factors helps to establish accurate expectations, which, together with plausible goals, are essential for selecting an appropriate action. The main advantage of the second step in the model, serial selection on the basis of typicality, is that a reasonably matching action can be implemented in short order. The last step in the model, mental simulation, guards against the mistakes that result from uncritical thinking.

The RPD model underscores the crucial role of domain-specific knowledge or experience in proficient decision making: No step in the model can be executed effectively without such knowledge. Thus, the model has interesting implications regarding the nature of expertise. The critical features of expert decision making in realistic settings in general, and in stressful situations in particular, are not superior analytical or computational skills. Rather, these features include making finer distinctions and setting plausible goals within situations, drawing better analogies among situations, imagining richer potential developments, producing appropriate action, and recognizing inappropriate action more quickly.

Klein emphasizes that RPD is not a universal model of decision making. It is a model that is more suitable and likely to be encountered under time pressure and with high levels of expertise. It is less likely to be encountered if these conditions are not met, if the decisions are naturally presented as choices, and if the decision maker feels a need to optimize or justify the decision. The next model to be reviewed was developed by studying decision making in a very different context.

3. Pennington and Hastie: Explanation-Based Decisions

Pennington and Hastie began by developing a model of how individual jurors make their decisions which they then expanded to a general model of decision making. The model was developed by asking people on jury duty to think aloud as they watch a condensed video taped version of a real murder trial. Analysis of the think-aloud protocols (as this type of data is technically labeled) revealed a three-phase process corresponding to the three stages of the trial: processing the evidence, defining the verdict alternatives, and determining the verdict.

Processing the evidence. During the trial, jurors are presented piecemeal with a large and sometimes contradictory body of evidence. Pennington and Hastie found that jurors make sense of the evidence by organizing it in the form of a coherent story of what apparently has happened. About one-half of the events in the stories were testified to directly in the evidence. The remaining events were inferred actions, mental states, and consequences that were added to make the story coherent by filling gaps in the evidence. Although different jurors may construct different stories, they all reveal the same underlying "episode schema" (Figure 5.3). The elements of an episode schema are connected by temporal or causal relations and consist of the *initiating events* and *physical state* of the main characters (e.g., the defendant argues with the victim in the neighborhood bar); the *psychological states* and *goals* of these characters (as both become increasingly agitated and hostile, the defendant decides to kill his adversary); their actions and the consequences of these actions (the defendant goes home, takes his gun, and shoots the victim, who dies on the way to the hospital).

Defining verdict alternatives. Following the presentation of evidence, the judge instructs the jury on the possible verdicts that apply to the case and the jury, then defines the attributes that must be satisfied for handing down each verdict. Different verdicts within the same category of trial (e.g., murder trials) are defined in terms of the same set of attributes. For murder trials the attributes consist of the *identity* of the murderer, his or her *actions* and *mental* state, and the *circumstances* of the murder. The corresponding attributes of a first degree murder for example, are (a) the defendant is the murderer, (b) he or she killed the victim, (c) he or she had an intention to kill, and (d) he or she did so without sufficient provocation on the part of the victim.

Determining the verdict. The verdict is selected by finding which verdict has the best match with the story constructed from the evidence. Matching can be done directly, owing to the correspondence between verdict attributes (identity, actions, mental states, and circumstances) and the elements of the episode schema (characters, actions, mental states, initiating events, and physical states). Thus, a juror will vote for a verdict of first degree murder if and only if,

Figure 5.3.   Abstract Episode Schema

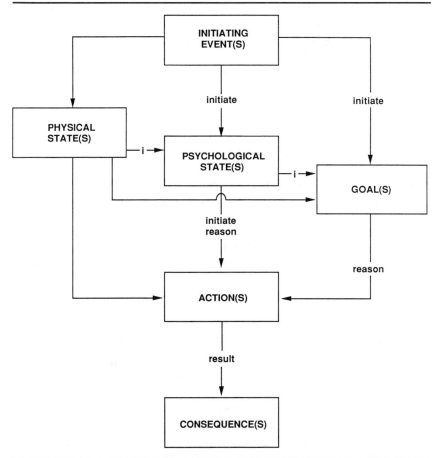

From "Evidence Evaluation in Complex Decision Making," by N. Pennington & R. Hastie, 1986. *Journal of Personality and Social Psychology, 51,* 242–258. Reprinted by permission.

according to the juror's reconstruction of the case, the defendant had an intention to kill.

Pennington and Hastie validated their model by showing that jurors organize the evidence in story form, and that jurors who chose different verdicts constructed stories with different initiating events and different conceptions of the defendant's goals and psychological states. As predicted by the model, differences between stories corresponded to differences between the attributes of the verdicts chosen by the jurors.

Pennington and Hastie suggest that the story-based decision-making process is a special case of how decisions are generally made in situations where people have to process large amounts of information that is incomplete, piecemeal, and presented sequentially in a jumbled temporal sequence. To cope with this situation, people construct a causal explanation based partly on the evidence and partly on inferences and general knowledge. The particular form of the causal model depends on the specific task or domain. The use of stories by jurors, for example, can plausibly be attributed to their task of deciding on the basis of "what had actually happened" and to the fact that information on this type of questions is most easily remembered in the form of a story.

In conclusion, despite some apparent dissimilarities that can be attributed to different contexts of study, Noble's, Klein's, and Pennington and Hastie's models share an emphasis on the role of situation assessment, and recognition or explanation, in the decision-making process. The next model focuses on what traditionally has been conceived as the essence of decision making—making a choice among alternatives.

4. Montgomery: Search for Dominance Structure

Montgomery is interested in how decisions are actually made when several alternatives are available as, for example, when purchasing a car or an apartment. His answer, in a nutshell, is that, in this situation, people search for a *dominant* alternative. An alternative is said to be dominant if it is at least as attractive as its competitors on all relevant attributes, and exceeds each of them on at least one attribute. The search for a dominant alternative goes through four phases: preediting, finding a promising alternative, dominance testing, and dominance structuring (Figure 5.4). At each stage the decision maker employs different decision rules (i.e., rules for adopting, rejecting, or preferring one alternative to another).

Preediting. In the preediting phase the decision maker selects the attributes (i.e., criteria) that are important for his or her decision and uses them first to screen alternatives that are obviously unacceptable. For example, if he or she wants to rent an apartment, he or she may use size and price to screen available apartments that are either too large, too small, or too expensive. (This type of rule for excluding alternatives is known as a *conjunctive decision rule*.)

Finding a promising alternative. At this stage the decision maker picks an alternative that seems to be most promising, because it is most attractive on a particularly important attribute, for example, an especially inexpensive apartment. (This type of rule for admitting alternatives is known as a *disjunctive decision rule*.)

Figure 5.4.   A Dominance Search Model of Decision Making

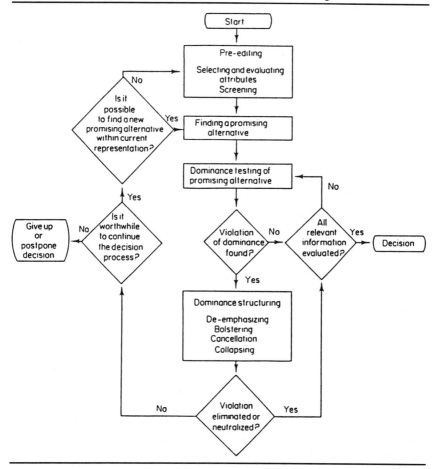

From *Process and Structure in Human Decision Making*, by H. Montgomery & O. Svenson, 1989. Reprinted with permission of John Wiley & Sons, Ltd.

Dominance testing. At this stage the decision maker tests if the promising alternative is in fact the best available option according to the criterion of dominance. If the criterion holds, the alternative is selected. If the promising alternative falls short of this criterion, the decision maker proceeds to the stage of dominance structuring.

Dominance structuring. If a promising alternative is not found to be dominant, the decision maker tries to make it to one by reinterpreting its standing compared with its competitors. There are several methods for restructuring the relative standing of competing alternatives on the attributes by which they are compared. These include *deemphasizing* the likelihood that the inferiority of the promising alternative on a certain attribute will materialize ("apartment B does have a better location, but its owner seems reluctant to sell"); *enhancing* the significance of the attributes on which it is superior by the use of vivid images ("I think that the price factor is particularly important—my uncle recently got into real trouble because he took a risk and bought above his means"); *cancelling* (i.e., calculating tradeoffs between advantages on one attribute and disadvantages on another); and *integrating* several attributes into a single comprehensive attribute ("it may be more difficult to obtain a good mortgage for this apartment, but when you consider the monetary factor as a whole, it is still cheaper than the other apartments"). Montgomery suggests that deemphasizing and bolstering are more likely to involve rationalization (and a distortion of reality by wishful thinking) than collapsing and cancellation.

Basically, then, Montgomery thinks of decision making as the process of finding a good argument for acting in a certain way, first by a quick selection of a promising alternative and then by testing or ensuring the dominance of this alternative. Why do people make decisions this way? According to Montgomery, the search for dominance structure has two advantages. First, it is compatible with the limited capacity of human information processing: focusing on a limited number of alternatives and attributes and accentuating the differences between them makes it easy to identify the preferred alternative with no further calculations. Second, and more importantly, the availability of a dominant alternative helps decision makers to persist in its implementation. Thus, the search for dominance structure is particularly suitable in realistic settings where changing circumstances, conflicting or ambiguous goals, and the presence of competing interests in and out of one's organization continuously challenge the accomplishment of difficult goals.

The obvious similarity between the RPD and dominance search models is that both portray decision making as a quick selection and further evaluation of a single alternative. The obvious differences between them are that the RPD model suggests selection and evaluation based on suitability to current or projected conditions, whereas in the dominance search model these are based on the relative standing of different alternatives on a set of common attributes. Another interesting difference between the models is that in the RPD model detection of an unsatisfactory alternative leads to its modification or replacement by others, whereas in the dominance search model it leads to reinterpretation of the available information, even at the risk of distortion of reality.

Are the RPD and dominance search models incompatible? Not necessarily. The RPD model was developed by interviewing and observing experienced practitioners who exercise relevant knowledge and skills under stress and time pressure. The dominance search model was tested by asking subjects in laboratory studies to think aloud or specify information that they require as they choose between different alternatives (e.g., apartments) on the basis of a set of common attributes. Future research will tell if the RPD and dominance search models are valid for different contexts and domains of decision making. Meanwhile they complement one another by pointing to different dangers to effective decisions. The RPD model suggests that decision makers may fail owing to faulty situation assessment and mental simulation. The dominance search model emphasizes that weighing the pros and cons of different alternatives may be determined (or seriously attenuated) by quick selection of a promising candidate. A considerable body of evidence indicates that this danger is indeed ubiquitous outside the laboratory (Alexander, 1979; Janis & Mann, 1977; Soelberg, 1967; Webster, 1964).

5. Beach and Mitchell: Image Theory

Image theory summarizes more than 15 years of research in which Beach, Mitchell, and their associates studied real-life decisions in widely different domains including whether or not to have another child, whether to commute to work by bus or car, which job offer to accept, which organizational policies should be adopted, and how financial-auditing decisions are made. It is therefore more comprehensive than the three models so far reviewed but is strikingly compatible with them. I shall discuss these similarities after presenting the basic concepts of the model: *images, adoption decisions, progress decisions,* and *frames* (Figure 5.5).

Images. Images are cognitive structures (technically labeled *schemata*) that organize decision makers' values and knowledge and guide their decisions. Image theory distinguishes three types of images. The *value image* consists of the decision maker's *principles,* namely, his or her notions about what is right and wrong and the ideals to which he or she aspires. The *trajectory image* consists of concrete goals that the decision maker attempts to achieve. The *strategic image* consists of *plans* and *tactics* (sequences of activities and specific behaviors required to achieve a goal) as well as *forecasts* (the anticipated outcomes of implementing a plan). The principles, goals, and plans that drive a certain decision correspond to the answers to "why?" "what?" and "how?" respectively.

Figure 5.5.   A Schematic Representation of Image Theory

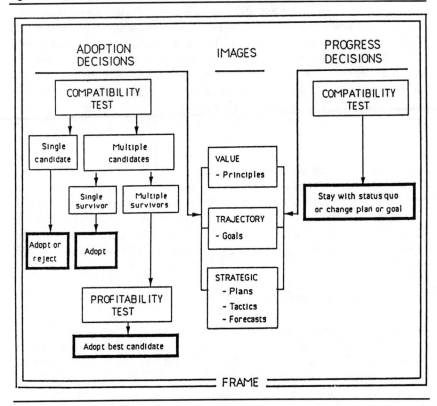

Adoption decisions. These decisions concern the addition of goals and plans to the decision maker's current agenda. Adoption decisions are primarily based on a *compatibility test:* A candidate goal or plan is adopted if it does not violate the decision maker's three images beyond a threshold (which varies from one decision maker and one situation to another). The compatibility test is designed to screen out unacceptable goals and plans. If more than one candidate survives this test, the decision maker selects the best of them by using a test of *profitability,* a collective label for various methods of choosing among alternatives. Profitability tests range from intuitive methods (which require little time and effort) to analytic methods, and are either compensatory (allowing for the advantages of an alternative to compensate for its disadvantages) or noncompensatory. Image theory suggests that real decisions are primarily made on the basis of compatibility. What it has to say on profitability is basically summarized by the following four propositions: (a) Decision makers use profitability tests only if they cannot decide on the basis of compatibility. (b) Compatibility tests and profitability tests are made essentially independently; that is, decision makers tend to ignore information which they used in testing for compatibility when they move on to choose on the basis of profitability. (c) The greater the complexity of a decision, the greater the decision makers' tendency to use intuitive noncompensatory tests of profitability. (d) Decision makers use different tests of profitability in order to make reasonably good quality decisions at a minimal level of effort.

Progress decisions. There are two types of progress decisions, and both pertain to plans. First, progress decisions are used to support adoption decisions by projecting forward in a similar fashion to Klein's mental simulation: What problems is the plan likely to meet? Will it, for example, conflict with existing constituents of the trajectory and strategic images? If the answer is no, the plan is added to the strategic image. If it is yes, it is either adopted after revision or replaced by another candidate. The second type of progress decisions are used to decide if an implemented plan actually achieves its objectives. If the answer is yes, the decision maker will make no changes. If the answer is no, he or she will adapt either the plan or his or her goals accordingly. Both types of progress decisions are made by test of compatibility.

Frames. A *frame* is a subset of the decision maker's principles, goals, and plans that he or she brings to bear on a particular decision. At any point in time the current frame defines the status quo. Image theory suggests that decision makers have a proclivity towards the status quo: Other things being equal, people prefer existing goals and plans to potential alternatives.

There are obvious similarities as well as important differences between image theory and the preceding models. For example, based on Pennington and Hastie, Beach and Mitchell suggest that people frame the knowledge and values that affect particular decisions in the form of stories; like Noble and Klein, they suggest that decision makers tend to focus on one alternative at a time; and like Montgomery, they agree that, when decision makers do choose among alternatives they rely primarily on dominance as the criterion of profitability. The most significant difference between image theory and the preceding models is the role that it accords to the decision maker's principles, that is, his or her personal values and ideals (in early versions the theory referred to the value image as *self-image*). Thus, image theory recognizes that many decisions are best understood as expressive behavior, that is, actions taken not as means towards desired ends but to express or actualize cherished values and ideals. It is plausible that image theory developed this way because many of the decisions studied by Beach and Mitchell (e.g., child bearing and job selection) speak more to one's values than to one's expertise.

In his recent book on image theory, Beach (1990) cautions that Figure 5.5, which summarizes the theory, is a fictitious expositional convenience: Real decisions never follow such an orderly linear process. As it is reasonable to assume that Noble, Klein, Pennington and Hastie, and Montgomery would subscribe to the same caution in regard to their models, an interesting question presents itself: Are these models truly *descriptive* if the processes they present are *fictions* (or, to be more precise, *idealizations*) combining features of how decisions are actually made in forms that actually are rarely encountered?

Let us consider this question more concretely. Some of the cases studied by Klein consisted of both phases of the RPD model, namely, situation recognition followed by mental simulation. Other cases, however, consisted of series of actions based only on situation recognition. Do the latter cases invalidate the model? Not necessarily, since Klein explicitly states that pure recognition, or "intuitive" decisions, are likely to be encountered under certain conditions (e.g., routine decisions and time pressure). The following four models suggest typologies of different types of decision processes (e.g., intuitive vs. analytic) and discuss the conditions under which each type is likely to be encountered or can be properly used.

TYPOLOGICAL MODELS

6. Rasmussen: The Cognitive Control of Decision Processes

Rasmussen is interested in the decision-making processes of human operators of complex automated systems. As errors in supervising such systems as nuclear power plants may cost dearly both materially and in human lives, understanding these particular decision processes is very important.

Extensive analysis of actual accidents and think-aloud protocols obtained by means of simulators led Rasmussen to distinguish between three types of behavior that are controlled by qualitatively different cognitive mechanisms: Skill-based behavior, rule-based behavior, and knowledge-based behavior (Figure 5.6). Using this distinction it is possible to gain better understanding of human errors in running complex systems and reduce the likelihood of such errors with suitable decision support systems.

Skill-based behavior. This type of behavior includes expert sensorimotor performance (e.g., speaking, bicycle riding), which runs

Figure 5.6. Schematic Model of Three Different Levels of Human Information Processing

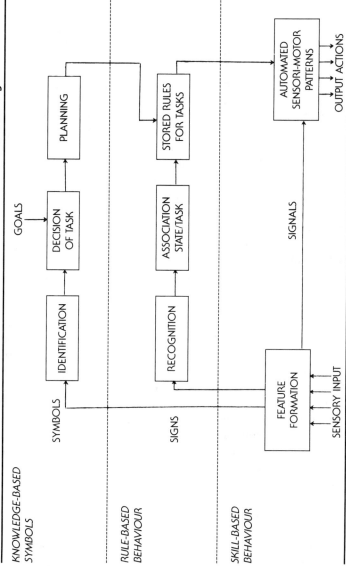

Skills, Rules, Knowledge: Signals, Signs, and Symbols, and Other Distinctions in Human Performance Modelling, by J. Rasmussen, 1983. *IEEE Transactions on Systems, Man and Cybernetics, SMC-13*(3), 257–267. Reprinted by permission of IEEE.

smoothly and efficiently without conscious attention. Skill-based behavior is controlled by a dynamic *mental model* that depicts the decision maker's movements and environment in real time, thereby enabling him or her to adjust rapidly to feedback from his or her actions. Information (sensory input) at this level is processed as *signals:* It triggers action directly without explicit consideration of what the information means or what the decision maker's goals are.

Rule-based behavior. This type of behavior is controlled by rules and know-how that can be stated explicitly by the decision maker. Both skill-based and rule-based behaviors are characteristic of expert performance. The fuzzy boundary between them depends on the extent to which behavior is executed automatically or attentively. Information at the level of rule-based behavior is processed as signs indicating that the situation is of a certain kind (recognition), thereby invoking a rule that dictates the enactment of a certain behavior (cue-task association) based on past experience or formal training. Whether a decision maker operates at the skill-based or rule-based level is largely a function of his or her expertise and familiarity with the situation.

Knowledge-based behavior. Whereas skill-based and rule-based behaviors are appropriate for familiar situations, effective action in novel situations requires deeper understanding of the nature of the situation and explicit consideration of objectives and options. Information at the level of knowledge-based behavior is processed as *symbols,* which are used to construct mental models representing causal and functional relationships in the environment (e.g., the technological system operated by the decision maker). Analysis of verbal protocols shows that such models are constructed at different levels of *abstraction* and *decomposition.* The abstraction (or means–ends) dimension denotes the fact that operators of technological systems sometimes focus on concrete physical aspects of the system (e.g., its appearance and material composition), and at other times they consider abstract properties such as information flow within the system and its general purpose. The decomposition dimension denotes the fact that operators sometimes focus on specific components and at other times focus on larger units or the entire system. Figure 5.7 traces the reasoning process of a technician trouble-shooting a malfunctioning computer within five levels of abstraction and five levels of decomposition.

The distinction between skill-based, rule-based, and knowledge-based behaviors allows very detailed analysis of possible human malfunction in particular events or situations. As Figure 5.8 shows, each level of behavior is characterized by different types of errors, and a particularly important type of error is failure to recognize the need to move from one level to another. Clearly, failure to recognize which

Figure 5.7.   Levels of Modeling Human Performance

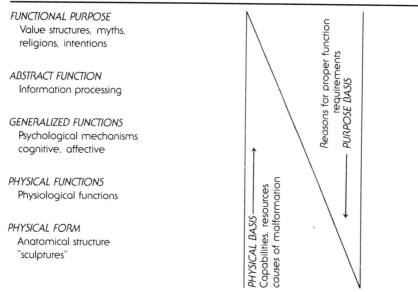

FUNCTIONAL PURPOSE
Value structures, myths,
religions, intentions

ABSTRACT FUNCTION
Information processing

GENERALIZED FUNCTIONS
Psychological mechanisms
cognitive, affective

PHYSICAL FUNCTIONS
Physiological functions

PHYSICAL FORM
Anatomical structure
"sculptures"

Skills, Rules, Knowledge; Signals, Signs, and Symbols, and Other Distinctions in Human Performance Modelling, by J. Rasmussen, 1983. *IEEE Transactions on Systems, Man and Cybernetics, SMC-13* (3), 257–267. Reprinted by permission of IEEE.

error had actually caused an accident may lead to recommending inappropriate corrective measures. Rasmussen also points out that different kinds of decision support systems are appropriate for different levels of abstraction and decomposition. For example, structural diagrams are useful for locating a malfunctioning component but not very useful for inferring the component's intended use. Thus he developed a family of decision aids to assist decision makers at the various levels at which they operate.

Rasmussen suggests that social systems are most properly represented at the higher levels of abstraction, since human behavior is heavily influenced by values and goals (i.e., ends). Consistent with this suggestion, the five process models that we reviewed above are mostly models of knowledge-based behavior. Two exceptions are Noble and Klein, who depict the early (recognition) phases of situation assessment as rule-based behavior.

One of the important contributions of Rasmussen's model is, therefore, the attention that it draws to the extent to which decision makers operate habitually or even automatically, particularly when they exercise well-rehearsed skills. The model to which we now turn is largely

Figure 5.8. Guide for Event Analysis to Identify the Internal Mechanisms of Human Malfunction

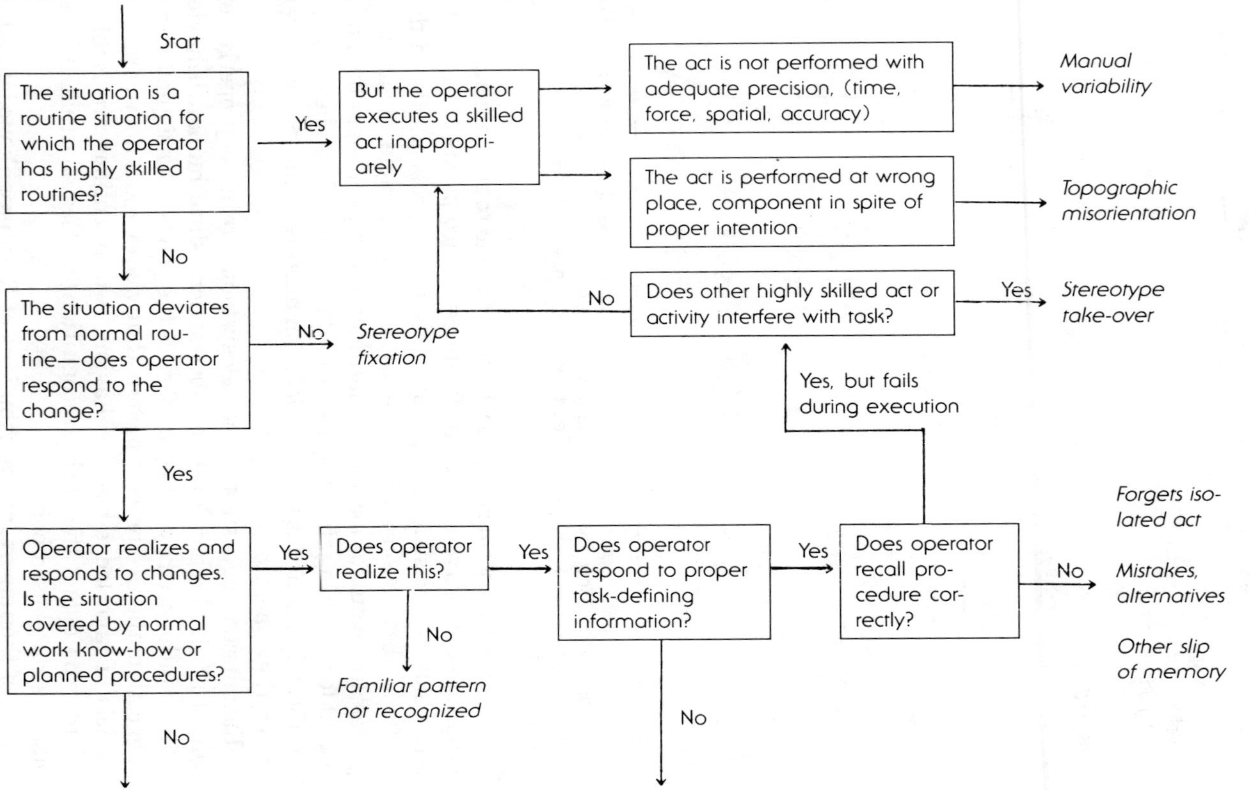

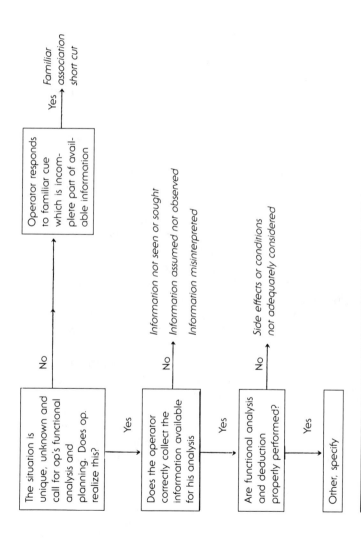

The situation is unique, unknown and call for op's functional analysis and planning. Does op. realize this?

No → Operator responds to familiar cue which is incomplete part of available information → **Yes** *Familiar association short cut*

Yes ↓

Does the operator correctly collect the information available for his analysis

No →
Information not seen or sought
Information assumed not observed
Information misinterpreted

Yes ↓

Are functional analysis and deduction properly performed?

No →
Side effects or conditions
not adequately considered

Yes ↓

Other, specify

From "Human Errors: A Taxononary for Describing Human Malfunctions in Industrial Installations," by J. Rasmussen, 1982. *Journal of the Occupational Association*, pp. 311–333. Reprinted by permission.

concerned with the question, under which conditions is acting in such an "intuitive" fashion effective?

7. Hammond: Task Characteristics and Human Cognition

Hammond is interested in how decision processes change as a function of changes in the decision task or environment. His work is an extension of social judgment theory, which describes the relationships between the objective environment (or task system), the information that is available on this environment, the subjective perception and integration of this information, and the judgments and decisions to which they lead. Figure 5.9 describes this sequences in regard to the prediction of microbursts (brief, localized windstorms) by metereologists. Two questions that particularly interest Hammond are the extent to which decisions are made *intuitively* or *analytically* and whether the decision maker seeks *patterns* or *functional relations* in assessing the situation.

Intuitive vs. analytical decisions. Hammond suggests that the cognitive processes that guide decision making can be located on a *cognitive continuum* which ranges between intuition and analysis. Hammond suggests several criteria to determine the extent to which a cognitive process is intuitive. A process is *more* intuitive (or less analytical) to the extent that it is executed under low control and conscious awareness, rapid rate of data processing, high confidence in answer and low confidence in the method that produced it, and two additional criteria that pertain to the nature of errors in judgment and organization of information. Hammond suggests further that whether decisions are made more or less intuitively is a function of two factors. The first factor is failure: Decision makers tend to become more analytical when snap judgments fail, and more intuitive (i.e., begin to guess) when careful analysis fails. The second factor is the nature of the decision maker's task. According to Hammond's *inducement principle,* certain task characteristics induce the use of more intuitive (or less analytical) processes. For example, tasks that require processing large amounts of information in short time periods induce intuition, and tasks that present quantitative information in sequential fashion induce analysis. Thus, cognitive processes can be arranged on a cognitive continuum as more or less intuitive (or analytical), and tasks can be arranged on a task continuum which represents the extent to which they induce more or less intuition or analysis. Hammond has devised two indices, the *cognitive continuum index* (CCI) and the *task continuum index* (TCI), which can be used to locate specific tasks and decision processes on their respective continuums.

Figure 5.9. Sequence of Phases in Microburst Forecasting

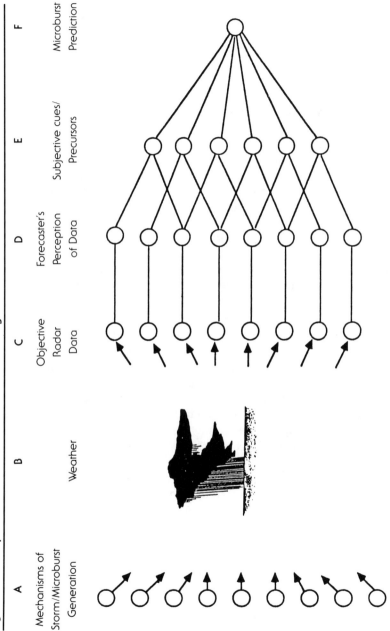

A	B	C	D	E	F
Mechanisms of Storm/Microburst Generation	Weather	Objective Radar Data	Forecaster's Perception of Data	Subjective cues/ Precursors	Microburst Prediction

From *Toward the Study of Judgment and Decision Making in Dynamic Tasks: The Case of Forecasting the Microburst*, by C. M. Lusk, T. R. Stewart, & K. R. Hammond. 1988. Reprinted by permission.

The inducement principle explains why decision makers oscillate between intuitive and analytical decision making as task characteristics change. It also raises an interesting question: Is it always better to be analytical? Typically, methods to improve decision quality require analysis, implying that the answer is yes. In contrast, Hammond's *correspondence-accuracy principle* suggests that the answer is no. The principle argues that judgments are most accurate (and hence decision making is most effective) when the location of the cognitive process on the cognitive continuum matches the location of the decision task on the task continuum. Thus, changes in the characteristics of tasks lead to predictable changes in the nature of cognitive processes, and changes in the extent to which the two are compatible lead to predictable changes in the latter's accuracy. Hammond does not bring extensive theoretical justification for the correspondence-accuracy principle. He does report evidence supporting it from a carefully conducted study.

Pattern vs. functional relations seeking. Hammond suggests that, in addition to inducing *more or less* intuitive cognition, task characteristics induce seeking *either* patterns *or* functional relations in the situation. Pattern seeking is induced if the situation provides information that is highly organized (e.g., a picture or a story) and if the person is required to produce coherent explanations of events or situations. Functional relations seeking is induced if the information is not organized in a coherent fashion and if the person is required to provide descriptions or predictions (e.g., of velocities of objects).

In sum, Hammond suggests that real-world decisions are made in a quasirational mode, namely a mixture of intuition and analysis. Thus, the models which were reviewed before describe quasirational processes. Quasirational processes cannot be defended in the same way as analytic models, which can be formally shown to produce optimal decisions—if the underlying assumptions are satisfied. Nevertheless, as Hammond's own research and the other models show, quasirational processes are defensible if they match the decision maker's skill, the nature of the decision task and the context of the decision.

Hammond's descriptive model has two important contributions. It points to the importance of analyzing the nature of the decision task and it explicates the nature and role of intuition in dynamic decision processes. The next model to be reviewed takes this analysis further.

8. Connolly: Decision Cycles

Connolly argues that, since processes of making real decisions are dynamic, it is improper to analyze them as isolated instances of choos-

Figure 5.10.   The Two-Cycles Model

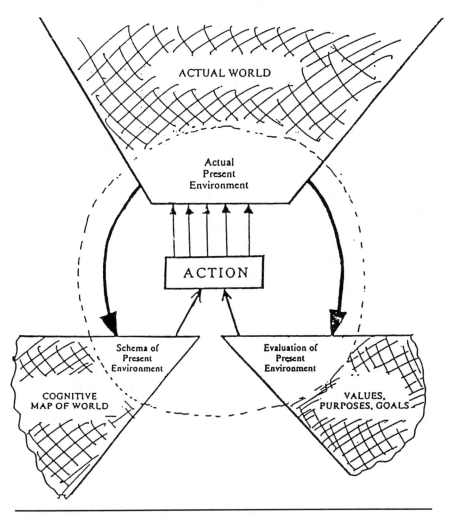

From "Decision Cycles," by T. Connolly & W. G. Wagner, 1988, in *Advances in Information Processing in Organizations*, edited by R. I. Caddy, S. M. Puffer, & M. M. Newman, 1988. Reprinted by permission of JAI Press.

ing among alternatives. Properly conceived decision making consists of cyclical interplay between situation assessment, evaluation of alternatives, and action. This is the essence of Connolly's decision cycles model, which is presented graphically in Figure 5.10. The decision cycles model consists of three domains and two cycles (or levels). The domains are the actual world, the decision maker's cognitive map (or subjective image) of this world, and his or her values. The two cycles are the *perceptual cycle* and the *decisional cycle*. In the perceptual cycle feedback on the consequences of action adjusts the cognitive map on which action was based. In the decisional cycle the same feedback adjusts the goals for which it was taken. Thus, Connolly is similar to Noble, Klein, Pennington and Hastie, and Rasmussen in assuming that the decision maker's cognitions (i.e., his or her cognitive map, situation assessment, explanations, or mental models) guide his or her actions. He is also similar to Montgomery and Beach and Mitchell in assuming that action is determined by the decision maker's values. The particular contribution of the Decision Cycles model is its emphasis on the role of exploratory action and the consequences of action on shaping both cognitions and values.

Since acting and thinking are intertwined in the decision cycles model, Connolly suggests distinguishing between two qualitatively different decision processes, action-last or *tree-felling,* and action-first or *hedge-clipping.* Tree-felling exemplifies decisions that are made, at one fell swoop following a period of planning or deliberation, because the decision is consequential, its goals are well defined, and there is a clear way of achieving them. In contrast, hedge trimming exemplifies decisions that are made *incrementally* in a series of steps. Hedge-clipping has several advantages. When it is hard to define precise goals (e.g., the exact final shape of the hedge) and outcomes of isolated actions are relatively inconsequential, it makes more sense to find your ways as you go along than to invest time and effort in thinking thoroughly ahead. Plans are of limited value (and sticking to them is downright dangerous) when the future is uncertain and goals are ambiguous, and reacting to feedback requires less cognitive effort than exhaustive planning.

Connolly suggests using the concept of *decision paths* to describe how real-world decisions unfold as decision makers move, thinking or acting first between the three domains and two levels of the decision cycles model. Consider, for example a person who wishes to buy a VCR and who has a clear idea on the relative values of its different features and how much he or she wants to spend. The decision path of this person would probably focus on perceptual exploration, as he or she has much to gain from finding which brands are available that may satisfy his or her preferences. In contrast, the decision path of a person who has only a vague notion that he or she wants a VCR is likely to include more evaluative exploration, as he or she will try to discover what actually the benefits of owning a VCR or the value of this or that feature are.

So far Connolly has not tested his ideas empirically. However, he cites numerous research showing that managers prefer hedge-clipping to tree-felling in making their decisions. Since they often have to reconcile conflicting goals and operate under high uncertainty concerning both present situations and future consequences, managers prefer to proceed incrementally, adjusting their actions and adapting their goals as they get to understand the environment better through exploratory action.

9. Lipshitz: Decision Making as Argument-Driven Action

Lipshitz developed the conceptualization of decision making as argument-driven action from analysis of written self-reports of decision making under uncertainty obtained from officers in the Israel Defense Forces. Although the cases could be interpreted as making *consequential choice* (choosing among alternatives in terms of expected outcome), they could be also interpreted at least as plausibly as *matching* (selecting an action on the basis of its appropriateness to the situation) and *reassessment* (reevaluating the appropriateness of an action because of objections to its implementation). Lipshitz suggests that consequential choice, matching, and reassessment are three generic modes of making decisions that differ in terms of six basic attributes of decision processes: *framing* (how the decision problem is defined), *form* (how action is selected), *uncertainty* (the nature of the doubt which has to be resolved in order to act), *logic* (the underlying rationale for acting in this way), *handicaps* (the barriers to making quality decisions), and *therapies* (the methods of improvement that are compatible with the preceding five characteristics). Table 5.1 shows how each of the three generic modes is characterized in terms of the six basic attributes.

Consequential choice. Consequential choice problems are framed as forward-looking choices: Which of several available alternatives has the best consequences? The decision process thus takes the form of comparing among alternatives and uncertainty pertains to the likelihood and attractiveness of future outcomes. The logic underlying this type of reasoning is teleological. It is captured by the expression "Think ahead," which reflects a belief that people act wisely when they visualize the future and plan accordingly. A principal handicap to deciding well this way is the limited human information-processing ability. A variety of therapies for this limitation have been designed, based on formal models of optimal choice and psychological research on judgment under uncertainty (Chapters 2, 3, and 4 in this volume discuss various consequential choice models).

Matching. Matching problems are framed as situation assessment:

Table 5.1.   Attributes of Consequential Choice, Matching and Reassessment

Parameter/Mode	Cons. Choice	Matching	Reassessment
Form	Comparison among alts. Consideration of future consequences	Situation assessment Serial rule based evaluation of action	Evaluating and satisfying objections to a certain action
Problem framing	Choosing from an available set of alternatives	Responding appropriately to a problem or situation	Countering objections to an (at least tentatively) selected action
Uncertainty	Likelihood and desirability of future outcomes	Nature of the situation and corresponding proper action	Same as in consequential choice and matching
Logic	Teleological	Deontological	Nonjustificational
Handicaps	Limited info. processing capacity; sub-optimal biases and heuristics	Ambiguous situations; Improper matching rules	Binding precommitment; Unrecognized assumptions
Therapies	Decision Analysis MAUT analysis	Training; Expert systems	Critical inquiry (e.g., devil's advocate; reflection in action)

What should be done in this situation? The question invokes a rule which dictates proper conduct based on personal experience, professional standards or social norms. Matching is blocked by uncertainty concerning the nature of the situation or which action it calls for. The underlying logic is *deontological,* which is captured by the expression "Those who do not learn from the past are condemned to repeat it." This logic reflects a belief that people act wisely when they use their experience or the experience of others, and the principal compatible therapies are training and expert systems (which frequently employ matching rules technically known as *production systems*).

   Reassessment. Reassessment problems are framed as objections to a certain course of action owing to uncertain present or future circumstances. This mode is distinct in that the decision maker is already committed to a certain course of action, which means that the principal handicap to high-quality decisions is uncritical implementation owing to past decisions or wishful thinking. The therapies called for include various methods for enhancing critical thinking whose underlying logic is known as *nonjustificational*. This logic is captured by the expression "How can I know what I want until I hear what I say," reflecting a belief that prescience is impossible, acting often precedes thinking, and the best that we can do is reflect critically on our values and assumptions.

Table 5.1 shows that defining decisions and analyzing them only as choosing among alternatives is an overgeneralization, as they are often made in at least two fundamentally different modes. Thus a more inclusive conceptualization is required to do justice to the variety of ways in which decisions are actually made. To this end, Lipshitz suggests defining decisions as purposeful action driven by action arguments of the general form "Do 'A' because 'R,'" where "A" and "R" denote an action and reasons for acting this way respectively. This definition is inclusive because different decision modes correspond to different action arguments. Thus, consequential choice corresponds to the argument "Do 'A' because it has better expected consequences than its alternatives;" matching corresponds to the argument "Do 'A' because it is appropriate to the situation," and reassessment corresponds to the twin arguments "Do 'A' either because there are no objections to its implementation or because such objections can be rebutted."

So far the argument-driven model proved useful for the clinical analysis of cases from several perspectives. Its usefulness for research and training is still to be demonstrated.

SYNTHESIS: EMERGING COMMON TRENDS

The nine models reviewed in this chapter were developed by different researchers using different methodologies to study somewhat different questions in a variety of realistic settings. Nevertheless, it is possible to point to six themes that are common to some of the models and compatible with all of them. The six themes, which represent the kernel of a naturalistic decision theory, are *(a) diversity of form, (b) situation assessment, (c) use of mental imagery, (d) context dependence, (e) dynamic processes,* and *(f) description-based prescriptions.*

1. Diversity of form. The nine models suggest, singly and collectively, that real world decisions are made in a variety of ways. Klein's model includes both recognition based decisions and decisions that are based on further mental simulations of possible scenarios. Pennington and Hastie suggest that the process of decision making based on story construction is a special case of a large class of explanation-based decision making. Montgomery describes several methods of obtaining dominance structure. Rasmussen distinguishes between skill-based, rule-based, and knowledge-based decisions, and Hammond distinguishes between intuitive, analytical, and quasirational decisions which combine both of these. Beach and Mitchell distinguish between adoption and progress decisions and between tests of compatibility and tests of profitability. Connolly distinguishes between 'tree felling' and 'hedge cutting' decisions, and Lipshitz distinguishes between three generic modes of decision making.

The diversity of form among these models indicates that they agree on the futility of trying to understand and improve real-world decisions in terms of a single pliable concept such as maximizing (or seeking to maximize) expected utility.

The diversity of form (despite some admitted overlap) between models indicates that students of real-world decisions cannot quite agree on how they are actually made. What are the reasons for this disagreement? A possible source of variance, to which I had occasion to allude in the course of reviewing the models, is that one's model is partly determined by the type of decisions studied. For example, Klein and Rasmussen observed rule-based and recognition-primed decisions because they studied proficient practitioners who can bring to bear their expertise effectively in this manner. Beach and Mitchell noticed the influence of ideals and moral values because these are more important than expertise in the personal decisions which they studied. Pennington and Hastie discovered story-based decisions because this form is induced by the task of a jury that is to determine guilt or innocence on the basis of "what really happened." Despite the diversity that can be found both within and between the models, the four following themes are repeated in almost all of them.

2. Situation assessment. Situation assessment is the "sizing up" and construction of a mental picture of the situation. All nine models include an element of situation assessment, reflecting thereby a shift of focus from the laboratory, where problems are defined and presented by the experimenter to the real world, where they have to be identified and defined by the decision maker. Some tie it directly to the selection of action; others suggest that it is a preliminary phase that initiates a process of evaluation of alternatives. The former models include Noble, who suggests that the perceived nature of the situation directly determines which action is selected; Rasmussen's skill-based and rule-based behaviors; Hammond's intuitive decisions; and Lipshitz's matching mode decisions. Those who see situation assessment as a preliminary phase include Klein, who suggests that situation assessment sets the stage for serial selection and mental simulation; Pennington and Hastie, who suggest that the evaluation of alternative verdicts is preceded by assessing past situations through their reconstruction in story form; and Montgomery, and Beach and Mitchell, who refer to situation assessment as the process of preediting or framing the criteria for action selection respectively. Lastly, Connolly refers to situation assessment (i.e., cognitive mapping) as one of the levels of his decision cycles model. In sum, all nine models suggest that making decisions in realistic settings is a process of constructing and revising situation representations as much as (if not more than) a process of evaluating the merits of potential courses of action.

3. Use of mental imagery. The traditional conception of decision making as choosing among alternatives emphasizes the role of calculative cognitive processes (i.e., weighing the costs and benefits of alternative courses of action). The models that were reviewed in this chapter emphasize different cognitive processes that are related to creating images of the situation, most notably categorization (e.g., of situations, Noble, Klein, Rasmussen), the use of knowledge structures (e.g., schema, Beach & Mitchell, Connolly) and the construction of scenarios (for example in the form of storytelling and mental modeling (Klein, Pennington, & Hastie, Beach & Mitchell, Lipshitz).

4. Context dependence. Orasanu and Connolly point to the importance of context in trying to understand real-world decisions, and I used essentially the same argument to explain the diversity observed by students of these decisions. Some of the models also emphasize context effects. Rasmussen suggests that context familiarity determines whether decisions are made at a skill, rule, or knowledge level. He also suggests that the nature of the context (i.e., mechanical vs. social systems) influences the abstraction level of knowledge-based mental models. Hammond and Klein delineate situational and task characteristics that induce intuitive or analytic decision processes. Connolly suggests that interaction between the nature of the situation, the decision maker's knowledge, and his or her values determine both the use and the appropriateness of using tree-felling or hedge-cutting decision processes.

5. Dynamic processes. All nine models reject the notion that decisions are made as discrete isolated events. The dynamic quality of decisions is conceptualized in two basic fashions. Hammond, Rasmussen, and Connolly suggest that decision makers switch between intuitive and analytic decision making as a function of changing task requirements. Noble, Klein, Montgomery, Beach, and Mitchell, and Lipshitz suggest a two-phase sequence in which a (typically quick) preliminary selection based on matching or compatibility rules is followed by more deliberate evaluation that they term *updat-*

ing, mental simulation, dominance search, profitability testing, and *re-assessment,* respectively.

6. Description-based prescription. How decisions ought to be made, and how they can be improved, has been traditionally approached on the basis of analytical models that prescribe systematic problem definition, diagnosis, generation of alternatives, and choice. The fact that decisions are actually not made this way was considered immaterial to the validity of the prescriptions or as evidence for their necessity. The models described in this chapter were often motivated by disappointment with this approach (see Beach & Lipshitz, this volume). These models represent a belief that one cannot divorce prescription from description because (a) some of the methods which are actually used make good sense despite their imperfections (Noble, Klein, Montgomery, Hammond, Lipshitz, Connolly), and (b) people will find it difficult to apply methods which are too different from the methods which they customarily use (Rasmussen, Beach, & Mitchell).

If high-quality decisions are not necessarily compatible with the prescriptions of analytic models, where can we obtain criteria for such decisions and guidelines for their achievement? The development of description-based prescriptions begins by studying how experts make decisions in their areas of expertise and then developing methods for improving decision quality either by emulating these experts, or by designing decision support systems which are compatible with human information-processing and knowledge-representation methods (Klein, Rasmussen).

CONCLUSION

In Chapter 1, Orasanu and Connolly noted that classical decision theory fails to account for eight characteristics of real-world decision settings: Ill-structured problems; uncertain dynamic environments, shifting, ill-defined, or competing goals; action/feedback loops; time stress, high stakes; multiple players; and organizational goals and norms. In conclusion, let us examine how the alternative models reviewed in this chapter account for the first six characteristics. Since this chapter is concerned with models of individual decision making, multiple players and organizational roles and norms will not be examined. Note briefly however, that (a) the presence of multiple players is one of the causes of environmental uncertainty and goal conflicts, (b) Beach and Mitchell include organizational norms and goals as elements of the value and trajectory images of individuals who espouse them, and (c) Lipshitz suggests that matching rules are frequently socially determined norms, traditions, and standard operating procedures.

1. Ill-structured problems. Orasanu and Connolly argue that considerable work is done before a decision is cast as a choice among alternatives. The process models reviewed above refer to this work as recognizing or understanding the situation (Noble, Klein, Pennington, and Hastie, Connolly) and as setting or framing the relevant subset of values, actions, or action modes (Montgomery, Beach, and Mitchell, Klein, Hammond, Rasmussen). Other models suggest that decision problems are not necessarily structured as choices among alternatives (Klein, Pennington, and Hastie, Beach and Mitchell, Lipshitz), and that some decisions are made so quickly (or "intuitively") that they probably remain ill-structured throughout the decision process (Rasmussen, Hammond, Connolly). Lastly, Montgomery and Lipshitz suggest that considerable work is done after, as well as before, classical theory's "decision events." In conclusion, it is not clear whether resolving ill-structured decision problems is contingent on structuring them deliberately as is done, for example, in decision analysis. Indeed, some problems may well be structured neatly after the fact, to justify or enhance decisions which were already made.

2. Uncertain dynamic environments. Some of the models address specifically three of the four sources of uncertainty identified by Orasanu and Connolly: incomplete information, unreliable or ambiguous information, and rapidly changing situations. The fourth source, purposefully misleading information, is not addressed explicitly by any model. Since people have to make sense of the situation in order to make decisions (Noble, Klein, Pennington, and Hastie, Rasmussen, Connolly), these impediments should impair their effectiveness. Nevertheless, Noble decided to simulate human situation assessment precisely because people manage to make decisions under these conditions. How do they do it? The answer, put simply, is that decisions are only partly based on outside information. Incomplete, unreliable, or ambiguous information is compensated or corrected by coherent mental models (Rasmussen, Connolly), background information (Noble, Klein) and cognitive schemata (Noble, Pennington, and Hastie, Beach and Mitchell). Whereas researchers inspired by the classical theory are quick to point to the dangers of acting on this basis, the models reviewed in this chapter point to its advantages when information is either unavailable or fallible.

Another particularly suitable mechanism for handling uncertainty due to rapidly changing situations is action based on feedback and exploration. Noble, Klein, and Connolly pay particular attention to the role of feedback. I will return to this subject below in conjunction with action/feedback loops.

3. Shifting, ill-defined, or competing goals. These characteristics pose different obstacles to decision makers. Conflicting goals interfere with action selection at a certain point in time and implementation at later points in time. Shifting goals reduce the likelihood that actions which satisfied one's goals at an earlier point in time will be judged satisfactory later on. Two different methods for handling conflicting goals are setting priorities (to satisfy more important goals first, Klein) and dominance structuring (to reduce the conflict generated by competing demands, Montgomery). Noble, Klein, and Connolly stipulate explicitly that goals change as a function of feedback on the nature of the situation and the consequences of one's actions. Beach and Mitchell describe the mechanisms through which goals are added and deleted from one's value image.

4. Action/feedback loops. Orasanu and Connolly argue that real world decisions are not made as isolated decision events or moments of choice. All the models reviewed in the chapter concur with this argument. The models, however, describe decision making as a primarily cognitive process. Only two models refer explicitly to the role of action or action implementation in the process. Beach and Mitchell discuss the monitoring of implementation through progress decisions and note people typically prefer the status quo. Connolly suggests that action may precede thinking and emphasizes the role of exploratory action and its effect on revising both one's beliefs and values.

5. Time pressure. Several models specifically address this issue. Klein suggests that decision makers mange to act proficiently under time pressure by relying on domain-specific expertise, which enables them to identify the situation quickly and accurately and to act promptly by accessing an action queue that is arranged with the appropriate action on top. Klein, Beach, and Mitchell, Rasmussen, Hammond, and Connolly suggest that, as time pressure mounts, decision makers use more intuitive decision processes, which require less time and effort to act. Thus, the various nonanalytic decision-making processes described by these researchers are suitable for acting under time pressure.

6. High stakes. The concern here is primarily methodological. Because high-stakes decisions entail severe losses in case of failure, they cannot be studied in the laboratory. High stakes probably affect decision making in two ways. They increase vacillation prior to making a decision, and decrease the likelihood of abandoning it once made, particularly if the decision maker can be held responsible in case of failure.

What can we learn from laboratory studies that use contrived experimental tasks on making high-stakes decisions? Considering the context effect noted above, the answer must be "unfortunately, not much." This answer can be actually extended to making real decisions in general. One of the lessons that the nine models teach us is that the familiarity of the situation (or the expertise of the decision maker) is one of the most important factors in how decisions are actually made. Thus, as difficult as it is, real-world decisions should be probably studied only in situ, or at least under laboratory conditions which replicate such conditions with high fidelity. Consistent with this conclusion, Klein and Lipshitz developed their models from descriptions of real decision cases; Pennington and Hastie, and Rasmussen, worked with high-fidelity simulators; and Beach and Mitchell, and Connolly, relied to a great extent on research conducted in realistic settings.

In conclusion, there is considerable affinity between the nine models of decision making in realistic settings reviewed in this chapter. Two challenges that lie ahead are the construction of a theory of decision making in the real world and learning to apply these models effectively to help decision makers make better decisions. To meet both challenges, it is necessary to progress from the high-level terminology that the models currently use (e.g., framing, pattern seeking, recognizing typicality, and matching) to more specific descriptions of how these processes are carried out.

KEY POINTS

- No unified theory has yet been proposed describing how individuals make decisions in naturalistic settings.
- This chapter reviews nine current models and assesses areas of agreement across them.
- These models have six common themes about naturalistic decision making:
  — Real-world decisions are made in a variety of ways.
  — Situation assessment is a critical elements in decision making.
  — Decision makers often use mental imagery.
  — Understanding the context surrounding the decision process is essential.
  — Decision making is dynamic—it does not consist of discrete isolated events or processes.
  — Normative models of decision making must derive from an analysis of how decision makers actually function, not how they "ought" to function.

Chapter 6

A Recognition-Primed Decision (RPD) Model of Rapid Decision Making*

Gary A. Klein
Klein Associates Inc.
Fairborn, OH

INTRODUCTION

Traditional models of decision making do not take into account many critical aspects of operational settings, as described in Chapter 1. Decision makers in operational settings are usually very experienced, in contrast to the naive subjects used in laboratory studies. In this chapter I present a recognitional model of decision making that shows how people can use experience to avoid some of the limitations of analytical strategies. This model explains how people can make decisions without having to compare options. It fuses two processes—situation assessment and mental simulation—and asserts that people use situation assessment to generate a plausible course of action and use mental simulation to evaluate that course of action. I believe this recognitional model describes how decision making is usually carried out in real-world settings. This conclusion is based on a series of studies in which it was found that recognitional decision making is much more common than analytical decision making. Finally, I contrast the strengths and weaknesses of recognitional and analytical decision strategies.

* Funding for the research cited in this chapter was received from the U.S. Army Research Institute for the Behavioral and Social Sciences, Contracts MDA903-86-C-0170 and MDA903-85-C-0327. However, the views, opinions, and/or findings contained in this chapter are those of the author and should not be construed as an official Department of the Army position, policy, or decision. I wish to thank Caroline Zsambok, Michael Doherty, and Reid Hastie for their helpful suggestions for improving this chapter.

RECOGNITIONAL DECISION MAKING

For the past several years, my colleagues and I have been studying command-and-control performance and have generated a *Recognition-Primed Decision* (RPD) model of naturalistic decision making. We began (Klein, Calderwood, & Clinton-Cirocco, 1986) by observing and obtaining protocols from urban fireground commanders (FGCs) about emergency events that they had recently handled. Some examples of the types of decisions these commanders had to make include whether to initiate search and rescue, whether to initiate an offensive attack or concentrate on defensive precautions, and where to allocate resources.

The fireground commanders' accounts of their decision making do not fit into a decision-tree framework. The fireground commanders argued that they were not "making choices," "considering alternatives," or "assessing probabilities." They saw themselves as acting and reacting on the basis of prior experience; they were generating, monitoring, and modifying plans to meet the needs of the situations. We found no evidence for extensive option generation. Rarely did the fireground commanders contrast even two options. We could see no way in which the concept of optimal choice might be applied. Moreover, it appeared that a search for an optimal choice could stall the fireground commanders long enough to lose control of the operation altogether. The fireground commanders were more interested in finding actions that were workable, timely, and cost effective.

It is possible that the fireground commanders were contrasting alternatives, but at an unconscious level, or possibly the fireground commanders were unreliable in their reports. We have no way of demonstrating that the fireground commanders weren't contrasting alternative options, but the burden of proof is not on us. There is no way to prove that something isn't happening. The burden of proof is on those who wish to claim that somehow, at some level, option comparison was going on anyway. The reasons we believe that the fireground commanders were rarely contrasting options are: it seems unlikely that people can apply analytical strategies in less than a minute (see, for example, Zakay & Wooler, 1984); each FGC argued forcefully that he or she wasn't contrasting options; and they described an alternative strategy that seemed to make more sense.

Clearly, the fireground commanders were encountering choice points during each incident. During the interviews the fireground commanders could describe alternative courses of action that were possible, but insisted that, during the incident, they didn't think about alternatives or deliberate about the advantages and disadvantages of the different options. Instead, the fireground commanders relied on their abilities to recognize and appropriately classify a situation, similar to the findings of Chase and Simon (1973) for chess players. Once the fireground commanders knew it was "that" type of case, they usually also knew the typical way of reacting to it. They would use available time to evaluate an option's feasibility before implementing it. They would imagine how the option was going to be implemented, to discover if anything important might go wrong. If problems were foreseen, then the option might be modified or rejected altogether, and another highly typical reaction explored.

We have described this strategy as a Recognition-Primed Decision (RPD) model (e.g., Klein, 1989a; Klein et al., 1986) of how experienced people can make rapid decisions. For this task environment, a recognitional strategy appears to be highly efficient. The proficient fireground commanders we studied used their experience to generate a workable option as the first to consider. If they had tried to generate a large set of options, and to systematically evaluate these, it is likely that the fires would have gotten out of control before they could make any decisions.

The RPD model is presented in Figure 6.1. The simplest case is one in which the situation is recognized and the obvious reaction is implemented. A somewhat more complex case is one in which the decision maker performs some conscious evaluation of the reaction, typically using imagery to uncover problems prior to carrying it out. The most complex case is one in which the evaluation reveals flaws requiring modification, or the option is judged inadequate and rejected in favor of the next most typical reaction. Because of the importance of such evaluations, we assert that the decision is primed by the way the situation is recognized and not completely determined by that recognition.

Orasanu and Connolly, in Chapter 1, presented one of the firefighting incidents we studied—a reported fire in the basement of a four-story apartment building. Upon arrival, the FGC assessed the problem as a vertical shaft fire in a laundry chute. Since there had been no sign of smoke from the outside, he judged that the fire was just getting underway. This situation assessment included plausible goals (he believed there was time to put it out before it got out of control), critical cues (he needed to find out how far the fire had spread up the shaft), expectancies (he believed that the firefighters could get above the fire in time to put it out), and an obvious course of action (send teams with hoses up to the first and second floors).

Unfortunately, the fire had just spread beyond the second floor, and the crews reported back that they were too late. The FGC then walked back to the front of the building, where he saw smoke beginning to

Figure 6.1. Recognition-Primed Decision Model

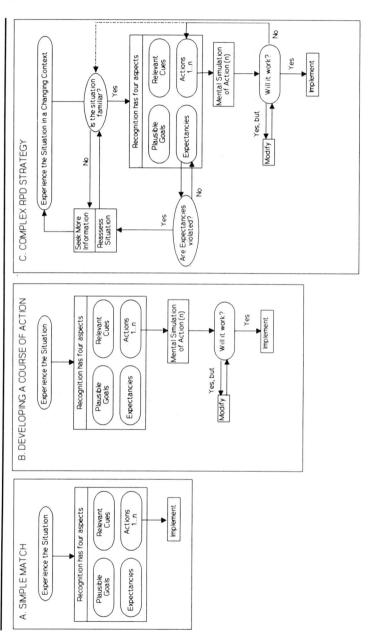

escape from under the eaves, just under the roof. He imagined how the fire had just reached the fourth floor, pushing smoke down the hall. His situation assessment shifted—this was no longer a simple vertical shaft fire. The whole building was being engulfed. The goals were now obvious—search and rescue. The critical cues included the front stairway as a prime evacuation route. The side stairway, previously the focus of activity, was now irrelevant. The expectancies now centered around the FGC's belief that spread of the fire might be too fast to ensure complete evacuation of the building. The course of action was straightforward—cease attempts to extinguish the fire, begin search and rescue operations, and call in a second alarm.

There seem to be four important aspects of situation assessment (a) understanding the types of goals that can be reasonably accomplished in the situation, (b) increasing the salience of cues that are important within the context of the situation, (c) forming expectations which can serve as a check on the accuracy of the situation assessment (i.e., if the expectancies are violated, it suggests that the situation has been misunderstood), and (d) identifying the typical actions to take.[1]

In the case of the laundry chute fire, the goals were partially determined by doctrine (e.g., when to conduct search and rescue) and partially by the nuances of the situation—the goal of trying to extinguish the fire did not prevent the FGC from later ordering his crews to begin search and rescue. But the FGC did have to make sure that the attack on the fire didn't take too long or become too exhausting. In addition, during the initial attempt to extinguish the fire, the crew members were all clustered around the rear stairway where the fire was spreading, so they were well positioned to shift into a search and rescue mode when necessary. The FGC had to be sensitive to a variety of goals at the same time. A simplistic decision analysis that separated different goals might have been misleading, whereas a more sophisticated decision analysis would be difficult to carry out under these time pressures.

Continuing with the discussion of Figure 6.1, if there is enough time the decision maker will evaluate the dominant response option by

---

[1] It should be noted that we had anticipated that the fireground commanders would rely on retrieval of analogue cases. But despite our probes, the fireground commanders rarely were able to identify analogues they had used. Each incident had so many unique aspects that there was no incident where an analogue matched the entire episode. Analogues were cited as occasionally helpful for aspects of an incident. For the most part, the vast experience of the fireground commanders had enabled them to merge the individual cases and to be able to use a judgment of familiarity or prototypicality that would not be present with the retrieval of an individual analogue case.

imagining it, conducting a mental simulation to see if it will work. If it does, it will be implemented. If it runs into problems, it will be modified. If it can't be fixed, then it will be rejected, and another likely option will be considered. If there is not adequate time, the decision maker is prepared to implement the course of action that experience has generated as the most likely to be successful. Note that this evaluation is context-specific. The evaluation is directed at how a course of action will fare in an actual situation, not at rating the advantages/disadvantages for various dimensions.

A recognitional decision process can also be seen in the example of the Libyan airliner incident, presented in Chapter 2. The Israeli general did not try to generate a set of options or evaluate the options in terms of utilities, probabilities, standard evaluation dimensions, or base rates. Instead, the focus was on forming a situation assessment. The general appeared to be willing to treat the airplane as being off course during a commercial flight, but the deviant behavior of pretending to land and then fleeing to the west challenged this interpretation. The general used mental simulation to try to imagine how a legitimate pilot would have taken such actions in good faith and could not come up with a plausible scenario. Using the failure to find a plausible story as evidence, the general concluded that the pilot was not on a legitimate flight. From this situation assessment, the goal was obvious— prevent the airplane from escaping. The course of action was also obvious—force the plane down. Even in retrospect, knowing the consequences, it is hard to specify a superior decision strategy.

Mental simulation is also used in evaluating a course of action. One incident from our study of forest fires involved a decision to use a key road to transfer crews to and from the fire line. A staff member noted that a slight shift in wind direction could quickly bring the fire right across the road. The other staff members saw this was a real danger, so they decided to close that road and transfer operations to another, less convenient road. This decision did not involve any comparison of the strengths and weaknesses of using each of the roads. Instead, there was a sequential evaluation in which the prime option was identified, mental simulation was carried out, the prime option was rejected, and was replaced by a second option.

There are a number of features that distinguish the RPD model from classical decision models.

- The RPD model focuses on situation assessment rather than judging one option to be superior to others.
- The RPD model describes how people bring their experience to bear on a decision.

- The RPD model asserts that experienced decision makers can identify a reasonably good option as the first one they consider, rather than treating option generation as a semi-random process, requiring the decision maker to generate many options.
- The RPD model relies on satisficing (Simon, 1955) rather than optimizing—finding the first option that works, not necessarily the best option.
- The RPD model focuses on serial evaluation of options and thereby avoids the requirement for concurrent deliberation between options that marks the focus on the "moment of choice."
- The RPD model asserts that experienced decision makers evaluate an option by conducting mental simulations of a course of action to see if it will work, rather than having to contrast strengths and weaknesses of different options.
- Finally, a recognitional strategy enables the decision maker to be continually prepared to initiate action by committing to the option being evaluated. Formal strategies require the decision maker to wait until the analyses are completed before finding out which option was rated the highest.

We have studied the use of recognitional decision making in a variety of tasks and domains, including fireground command, wildland fire incident command teams, U.S. Army Armored Division personnel (see Klein, 1989a, for a description of these), battle planning (Thordsen, Galushka, Klein, Young, & Brezovic, 1990), critical care nursing (Crandall & Calderwood, 1989), and chess tournament play (Calderwood, Klein, & Crandall, 1988).

These studies reflect a broad range of task constraints. The studies cover decisions made over several days as well as those made in less than 1 minute; decisions involving primarily a single individual and also teams of 5–9 people; decision makers with more than 20 years of command experience and newly promoted officers. Both qualitative and quantitative methods of investigation were employed in these studies, including semistructured interviews, on-site observations, and protocol analysis. The tasks performed ranged in the level of realism from the observations and interviews during an actual wildland fire requiring coordination of 4,000 crew members, to military exercises and computer simulations, to classroom planning exercises.

The results have provided support for the validity and utility of the model as it applies to individual decision makers. Table 6.1 reports the results of five studies that attempted to tabulate the incidence of RPD strategies vs. concurrent deliberation of options, for nonroutine decisions. We can see that the recognitional strategies were more frequent,

Table 6.1.   Frequency of RPD Strategies Across Domains*

Study	# Decision Points	Proportion of Decision Points Handled Using RPD Strategies
1. Urban Fireground Commanders (FGC-1)	156	80%
2. Expert Fireground Commanders (FGC-2)	48	58%
Novice Fireground Commanders (FGC-2)	33	46%
3. Wildfire	110	51%
4. Tank Platoon Leaders	55	42%
5. Design Engineers	51	60%

*These data were adapted from *Advances in Man-Machine Systems Research, 5,* 1989. Copyright © 1989 by JAI Press. Reprinted by permission.

even for these very difficult cases. This is true under circumstances where the coding system involved a liberal criterion for categorizing a decision as "analytical" (i.e., relying on concurrent generation and evaluation of options). If there was any indication that two or more options were contrasted, even if the decision maker abandoned the effort or used it for only a limited part of the incident, it was classified as analytic. Our coding methods were shown to be highly reliable; Taynor, Crandall, and Wiggins (1987) found intercoder agreement to be between 87%–94%.

For the first study in Table 6.1, Urban FGC-1, we looked at all the decision points in nonroutine incidents, including trivial decisions. These decision makers averaged 23 years of experience and showed 80% recognitional decisions. The second study (FGC-2) only examined the nonroutine command decision points of nonroutine incidents. The proportion of recognitional decisions was 58% for the experts and 46% for the novices. In Study 3, the functional decisions about fighting the forest fires showed 56% recognitional decisions, whereas the organizational decisions (whether to relieve someone of command) required more comparisons of different options. There the rate of recognitional decision making was only 39%, yielding an average of 51%. The incident commanders in this study averaged 24 years of experience. In Study 4, the tank platoon leaders were cadets in their first 10 days of training, and the proportion of recognitional decisions was below 50%. For Study 5, we found that experienced design engineers who were *not* under time pressure still relied heavily on recognitional decision making for difficult cases (60%). These data suggest that recognitional strategies are the most frequent, even for nonroutine decisions. Analytical strategies are more frequently used by decision makers with less experience.

STRENGTHS AND WEAKNESSES OF
RECOGNITIONAL DECISION MODELS

I am *not* proposing that there is a best decision strategy. Both recognitional and analytical approaches have their functions. Sometimes, both are applied within the same decision task. My claim is that recognitional strategies can be adaptive, can allow experienced decision makers to respond effectively, and should be acknowledged as a potential source of strength.

I have noted some limitations of analytical decision strategies. If they are used in the wrong conditions, they can leave the decision maker unable to react quickly and effectively. Conversely, the danger of misapplying recognitional decision strategies is that personnel will lack the experience needed to identify effective courses of action as the first ones considered, or will lack the ability to mentally simulate the option to find the pitfalls, or will fail to optimize when necessary. For example, the task of generating an operational order of battle requires speed and satisficing, and can be compromised by excessive use of analytical decision strategies. However, the task of anticipating the enemy's course of action requires optimizing to identify the worst thing that the enemy might do, and here recognitional processes can lead to tunnel vision and self-deception.

Studies by other researchers suggest that there are a number of factors affecting the use of analytical vs. recognitional decision "strategies" (e.g., Hammond, Hamm, Grassia, & Pearson, 1987). Our research has shown that recognitional decision making is more likely when the decision maker is experienced, when time pressure is greater, and when conditions are less stable. In contrast, analytical decision making seems to prevail when the available data are abstract and alphanumeric rather than perceptual, when the problems are very combinatorial, when there is a dispute between different constituencies, and when there is a strong requirement to justify the course of action chosen.

We do not believe that an RPD process approach should be taught, since the RPD model is already a description of what people do. Instead, we would argue that training is needed in recognizing situations, in communicating situation assessment, and in acquiring the experience to conduct mental simulations of options.

This chapter has tried to show that when people use recognitional rather than analytical strategies, it is not a sign of incompetence or irrationality. Recognitional strategies have strengths and value in naturalistic settings.

KEY POINTS

- Prescriptive decision strategies are not designed for ill-defined tasks or for time-pressured situations.
- A Recognition-Primed Decision (RPD) model describes how decision makers use their experience to avoid painstaking deliberations.
- Experience enables a person to understand a situation in terms of plausible goals, relevant cues, expectancies, and typical actions.
- Experienced decision makers usually try to find a satisfactory course of action, not the best one.
- Experienced decision makers can usually identify an acceptable course of action as the first one they consider, and rarely have to generate another course of action.
- Decision makers can evaluate a single course of action through mental simulation. They don't have to compare several options.
- Recognitional decision strategies are more appropriate under time pressure and ambiguity; analytical strategies are more appropriate with abstract data and pressure to justify decisions.
- In a variety of operational settings, recognitional decision strategies are used more frequently than analytical strategies, even for difficult cases.

Chapter 7

Image Theory: Personal and Organizational Decisions

Lee Roy Beach
University of Arizona

Image theory (Beach, 1990; Beach & Mitchell, 1987, 1990) is a descriptive theory of decision making, in contrast to classical theory, which is a normative, prescriptive theory (Beach & Lipschitz, this volume). The decision maker is viewed as having to make up his or her mind about what goals to pursue, how to pursue them, and, once pursuit has begun, whether adequate progress is being made. In some cases the decision maker operates privately, making decisions that pertain primarily to his or her personal interests, although even personal decisions often have implications for, and are influenced by, the interests of other persons. In other cases the decision maker acts for a group or organization, be it a family, a club, or a business. In these latter cases, the decision maker has to make up his or her own mind and then merge the decision with the individual decisions of other members of the organization who have a stake in the final decision. Image theory focuses upon the individual decision maker's decisions, rather than upon the merging of multiple individuals' decisions into a group decision.

The decision maker possesses three decision-related images, which are knowledge structures that constrain the decisions that he or she can make (see Beach, 1990, for a discussion of images as knowledge structures). The first is an image of how things *should* be and how people *ought* to behave. This image is composed of the decision maker's values, morals, ethics, and personal crotchets, which, for convenience, are collectively called *principles*. They are his or her bedrock beliefs about what is right and wrong, good and bad, proper and improper, appropriate and inappropriate—the absolutes that guide the decision maker's choices and actions. In organizational contexts these principles include beliefs and values that are held in common with other members of the organization, particularly in regard to the activities of the organization. It is only by sharing, or at least knowing about, the group's principles that the decision maker can participate successfully in the organization's decision making (Beach, Smith, Lundell, & Mitchell, 1988).

Principles run the gamut from the general ("Honesty is the best policy") to the specific ("We always meet the payroll on time"), from the admonitory ("Try to treat the customer as you would want to be treated") to the imperative ("Never discuss internal financial affairs with outsiders!). Principles are not all necessarily admirable ("Do unto others before they do unto you"), nor are they all necessarily rational— as Sigmund Freud tried to tell us. However, the principles that are deemed by the decision maker to be relevant to the decision at hand are the ultimate criteria for that decision. Potential goals and actions that are incompatible with relevant principles will be rejected.

The decision maker's second image is of the things that he, she, or the organization wants to accomplish, and the third image is of what is being done to accomplish them. The former consists of an agendum of *goals* to accomplish and timelines for accomplishing them. The latter consists of a roster of *plans* for reaching the goals. A major part of decision behavior consists of monitoring the implementation of these plans in an effort to assay their progress toward goal attainment— lack of progress triggers reexamination of the plan's adequacy or the goal's fundamental attainability, with an eye to replacement of either or both.

Decision making consists of accepting or rejecting potential goals and plans for addition to the second and third images, and of monitoring the progress of plans as implementation proceeds. Potential goals for addition to the second image arise from the need to satisfy principles ("We should try to accomplish X because it promotes fairness and equity"), or from an outside suggestion (from one's spouse, friend, boss), or from their being naturally correlated with other goals ("As long as my doctor insists that I lose weight, I might as well try to get back into shape too"). Potential plans for the third image, plans for accomplishing adopted goals, come from past experience (doing what worked before, with adjustments to fit the new circumstances), from instruction by someone who has relevant experience (training), or by flashes of creative inspiration. Ready-made plans for achieving commonly sought goals, either from past experience or instruction, are called *policies*.

Adoption of a potential goal or plan is based, first of all (and sometimes solely), upon whether it is even reasonable. That is, how compatible it is, how well does it fit, with what the decision maker values and with what he or she is already seeking and doing? Compatibility means that it is not contrary to relevant principles and that it does not cause foreseeable trouble for existing goals or plans. If it is not wholly compatible, how incompatible is it? If it is not too incompatible, it might work out all right. However, there is some degree of incompatibility, some degree of lack of fit, that exceeds the decision maker's tolerance and calls for rejection of the potential goal or plan (Beach, 1990; Beach & Mitchell, 1987, 1990; Beach et al., 1988; Beach & Strom, 1989; van Zee, Paluchowski, & Beach, in press).

Decision making begins with potential goals and plans being subjected to a test of their compatibility with the decision maker's three images in order to screen out those that do not warrant further consideration. If this initial screening involves only one potential goal and if that goal is judged to be sufficiently compatible, it is adopted, and the decision maker proceeds to seek a plan for its accomplishment—either an existing policy or a new plan. If the process involves more than one potential goal and only one is judged to be reasonably compatible, the situation is similar to having started with only one potential goal that was judged to be compatible—it is adopted and a plan is sought. If more than one potential goal is involved and more than one passes the initial screening on the basis of compatibility, it becomes necessary to choose among them. Any of a number of strategies may be used to choose the best of the survivors of screening; many involve comparison of the foreseeable payoffs of adopting each of the survivors and selection of the survivor that offers the greatest potential profit (Beach & Mitchell, 1978). Note that the theory posits two decision mechanisms: one that serves to screen out unacceptable goals, and one that serves to choose the best when there are multiple survivors of the screening decision.

These same two decision mechanisms are used in the adoption of plans.

Decisions about the progress of plan implementation involve forecasting where the plan will lead. If the forecasted result does not include the goal it is supposed to achieve, the plan must be revised to include it, or rejected and an alternative sought. If revision is impossible or unsuccessful and if no satisfactory alternative to the plan can be found, the goal itself must be revised or rejected. Decisions about the adequacy of progress rely upon compatibility between the forecasted result of plan implementation and the goal that the plan is supposed to achieve—the same decision mechanism that is used for screening of goals and plans.

Many decisions about goals, plans, and progress are straightforward and almost seem to make themselves. This occurs when the screening mechanism reveals that the potential goal or plan (or progress) is either so compatible or so incompatible with clearly relevant principles, existing goals, and ongoing plans that there is little question about what to do (Mitchell & Beach, 1990). Sometimes, however, decisions require more deliberation in order to clarify the relevant criteria and to identify the relevant characteristics of the potential goal or plan (Beach, Mitchell, Paluchowski, & van Zee, in press). Image theory is an attempt to identify the mechanisms common to both kinds of decisions.

IMAGE THEORY

Having outlined the theory rather informally, we turn now to a more formal presentation.

Images

To begin, image theory assumes that decision makers use three different schematic knowledge structures to organize their thinking about decisions. These structures are called *images,* in deference to Miller, Galanter, and Pribram (1960), whose work inspired image theory. The first of the three is the *value image,* the constituents of which are the decision maker's *principles.* These are the imperatives for his or her behavior, or the behavior of the organization of which he or she is a member, and serve as rigid criteria for the rightness or wrongness of any particular decision about a goal or plan. Principles serve to internally generate *candidate* goals and plans for possible adoption, and they guide decisions about externally generated candidate goals and plans.

The second image is the *trajectory image,* the constituents of which are previously adopted *goals.* This image represents what the decision maker hopes he, she, or the organization will become and achieve. Goals can be concrete, specific events (landing a contract) or abstract states (a successful career). The goal agendum is called the trajectory image to convey the idea of extension, the decision maker's vision of the ideal future.

The third image is the *strategic image,* the constituents of which are the various *plans* that have been adopted for achieving the goals on the trajectory image. Each plan is an abstract sequence of potential activities beginning with goal adoption and ending with goal attainment. One aspect of plans, their concrete behavioral components, are *tactics*. Tactics are specific, palpable actions that are intended to facilitate implementation of an abstract plan to further progress toward a goal. The second aspect of plans is *forecasts*. A plan is inherently an anticipation of the future, a forecast about what will happen if certain classes of tactics are executed in the course of plan implementation. However, it need not be inflexible—it can change in light of information about the changing environment in which implementation is (or might be) taking place. Therefore, it serves both to guide behavior and to forecast the results of that behavior. By monitoring these forecasts in relation to the goals on the trajectory image, the decision maker can evaluate his or her progress toward realization of the ideal agendum on the trajectory image.

Two Kinds of Decisions, Two Decision Tests

There are two kinds of decisions, *adoption decisions* and *progress decisions*. These decisions are made using either or both of two kinds of decision tests, the *compatibility test* or the *profitability test*.

Adoption decisions also can be divided into two, *screening* decisions and *choice* decisions. Adoption decisions are about adoption or rejection of candidate goals or plans as constituents of the trajectory or strategic images. Screening consists of eliminating unacceptable candidates. Choice consists of selecting the most promising from among the survivors of screening.

Progress decisions consist of assaying the fit between the forecasted future if implementation of a given plan is continued (or if a particular candidate plan were to be adopted and implemented) and the ideal future as defined by the trajectory image. Incompatibility triggers rejection of the plan and adoption of a substitute (often merely a revision of the old plan that takes into consideration feedback about the environment). Failure to find a promising substitute prompts reconsideration of the plan's goal.

The compatibility test makes adoption decisions on the basis of the compatibility between the candidate and the three images. Actually, the focus is upon *lack* of compatibility, in that a candidate's compatibility decreases as a function of the weighted sum of the number of its violations of the images, where the weights reflect the importance of the violation (Beach et al., 1988; Beach & Strom, 1989; van Zee et al., in press). Violations are defined as negations, contradictions, contraventions, preventions, retardations, or any similar form of interference with the actualization of one of the images' constituents. Each violation is all-or-none (−1 or 0). The decision rule is that, if the weighted sum of the violations exceeds some absolute *rejection threshold,* the candidate is rejected; otherwise it is adopted. The rejection threshold is that weighted sum above which the decision maker regards the candidate as incompatible with his, her, or the organization's principles, goals, and ongoing plans.

The compatibility test makes progress decisions by assaying compatibility between the trajectory and strategic images. In this case violations are of the trajectory image's constituents by the strategic image's constituents (its forecasts). The decision rule is that, when the weighted sum of violations exceeds the rejection threshold, reevaluation of the plan that generated the forecast is undertaken and the faulty plan is replaced. Note that the compatibility test serves both adoption and progress decisions.

The profitability test makes adoption choices from among the survivors of screening by the compatibility test. Unlike the compatibility test, the profitability test is not a single mechanism. Instead, it is a shorthand term for the unique repertory of choice strategies (Beach & Mitchell, 1978) that the individual decision maker possesses for adopting the potentially most profitable candidate from among a set of two or more candidates, all of which are at least minimally acceptable. The minimal acceptability of the adoption candidates from among which the choice is to be made is assured by the prior application of the compatibility test. In short, the profitability test is a "tie breaker" when more than one adoption candidate passes the compatibility test's screening. The compatibility test screens out the wholly unacceptable candidates, and the profitability test chooses the best from among the survivors. Of course, if only one candidate survives the compatibility test, there is no need to apply the profitability test—the candidate simply is adopted on the basis of compatibility. The profitability test serves adoption decisions but does not serve progress decisions.

Decision Framing

Both prescriptive and descriptive decision theories usually assume that the decision maker has identified the available courses of action and knows his or her preferences for the consequences of the actions. The theories then proceed to prescribe or describe the subsequent steps in the decision about which course of action to choose. From the decision maker's viewpoint this is the wrong emphasis—it usually is far more difficult to figure out what the decision is about, that is, what its goal is, than it is to make a decision about what to do once you know what is to be accomplished. Indeed, it often is the case that to have identified the goal is, effectively, to have decided on a course of action. This is because the decision maker can implement preformulated plans, called *policies,* for achieving goals of the class to which the current goal belongs. Indeed, much of what lay persons call "decision making" actually consists of identifying goals as having been successfully achieved in the past and applying the previously successful plan for achieving them, with appropriate modifications to fit the new circumstances (Klein & Calderwood, 1991). The process of identifying the goal, and the process of recalling a policy for it if one exists, is called *framing* the decision.

A frame is that portion of his or her store of knowledge that the decision maker brings to bear on a particular context in order to endow that context with meaning (Beach, 1990). As such it involves using information about the present context to probe memory (Beach, 1964; Hintzman, 1986). If the probe locates a contextual memory that has features that are virtually the same as those of the current context, particularly in regard to the goal that was predominant in both contexts, the current context is said to be *recognized.* Recognition serves two ends: first, it defines which image constituents are relevant to the situation at hand, and second, it provides information about goals that previously have been pursued in this situation and about the plans, both successes and failures, that have been used to pursue them.

That is, not all of the constituents of the images are relevant to the present situation, and in order to reduce cognitive load it is prudent to limit decision deliberation to those that are relevant—the relevant constituents of each of the three images constitute the *working images* for the decision at hand. (Of course, if for some reason the situation is misrecognized, misframed, the decision maker may later find that the working images did not contain the appropriate subsets of constituents. Thus, for example, principles that were deemed irrelevant to the decision may, in retrospect, turn out to have been relevant, and the goals and plans that seemed acceptable at the time should not in fact have been adopted.) In addition, part of the recognized contextual memory is the goal(s) that was pursued before, as well as the plan(s) that was used to pursue it; if a same or similar goal is being pursued this time, the plan that was used before may either be used again (in which case it constitutes a policy) or be used as the foundation for a new plan (which then must pass through the adoption process outlined above). Framing and its implications are an important part of image theory, but space precludes a more detailed discussion here. See Beach (1990) for more detail.

Research

Image theory draws upon a broad and varied conceptual and empirical literature (see Beach, 1990). However, because the theory is so new, the research that it has generated has necessarily been somewhat narrow in focus. Thus far the emphasis has been upon the compatibility and profitability tests.

Research on the compatibility test has examined the plausibility of the prediction that compatibility is determined primarily by violations. Studies have been conducted in both laboratory and nonlaboratory contexts. In one laboratory study, Beach and Strom (1989) had subjects screen potential jobs, the characteristics of which were or were not compatible with the decision maker's criteria for an ideal job. It was found that the threshold for jobs being rejected or accepted was based exclusively upon violations, and that the rejection threshold was constant across jobs. That is, the sole role of nonviolations in screening was to terminate information search when a job had too few violations to justify rejecting it—thus precluding an infinite search for flaws in near-perfect candidates.

In a nonlaboratory study of compatibility, Beach et al. (1988) examined the role of violations in executives' assessments of the compatibility of various plans for achieving a specified goal for their respective firms. There were three firms (two manufacturers of sports clothes and one manufacturer of alcoholic beverages). The guiding principles for each firm were ascertained through extensive interviews prior to the experiment. Then executives from each firm were presented with candidate plans for achieving the goal of successful introduction of a new product. The task was to assess the compatibility of each plan with the subject's own firm. It was found that the sum of weighted violations of the particular firm's principles accounted for the compatibility assessments made by the executives of that firm.

In a third study of the compatibility test, van Zee et al. (in press) examined the fate of information that is used in the compatibility test. It was found in a series of laboratory experiments that, when choices are made among the survivors of the compatibility test (screening), very little weight was accorded the information upon which compatibility had been assessed. It was as if the information in some way had been 'used up' during screening, and choice therefore was based almost entirely upon information acquired after screening had taken place. Because choice virtually ignores the prescreening information, it sometimes selects a different candidate than it would have if all of the available information had been taken into consideration.

Further research on compatibility, with emphasis upon the rejection threshold, currently is under way. One study in this series has found that, when told that none of the survivors of screening was still available for choice, 31 of 35 subjects (89%) opted to start all over again with entirely new candidates rather than go back and reconsider candidates that had been screened out earlier. This suggests that there is resistance to changing the rejection threshold unless the criteria (principles, existing goals, and ongoing plans) change. Apparently the unavailability of the survivors of screening is an insufficient reason to change the threshold.

Research on the profitability test is older than research on the compatibility test, because the former was motivated by Beach and Mitchell's earlier (1978) decision strategy selection model. As was stated above, the profitability test is a name for the decision maker's repertory of choice strategies. Image theory incorporates the Beach and Mitchell (1978) strategy selection model as the profitability test. Thus research on the profitability test, strategy selection, draws heavily from existing literature (e.g., Olshavsky, 1979; Payne, 1976; Payne, Bettman, & Johnson, 1988; Svenson, 1979) in addition to work done in our own laboratory (Christensen-Szalanski, 1978, 1980; Huffman, 1978; McAllister, Mitchell, & Beach, 1979; Nichols-Hoppe & Beach, 1990; Smith, Mitchell, & Beach, 1982; Waller & Mitchell, 1984). The results support the contention that decision makers possess repertories of choice strategies, and that their selection of which strategy to use in a particular decision is contingent upon specific characteristics of the decision problem, the decision environment, and of the decision maker himself or herself. In the context of image theory the profitability test specifies some of these contingencies (Beach, 1990).

SUMMARY

We briefly have examined a new descriptive theory of individual decision making for personal and organizational decisions. We began with an informal presentation of the general ideas. This was followed with a more formal presentation of the theory and a discussion of the research that has been done thusfar. Of course, in such a brief exposition it has been necessary to gloss over many of the details of the theory. For a fuller description the reader is directed to Beach (1990).

KEY POINTS

- Image theory is a descriptive theory of decision making, as opposed to a normative, prescriptive theory.

- Decision makers possess three decision-related images that constrain decisions they can make:
    — How things ought to be in terms of one's beliefs and values.
    — Goals toward which the decision maker is striving.
    — Plans for reaching the goals.
- Decision making consists of:
    — Adoption decisions, or deciding to accept or reject potential goals and plans.
    — Progress decisions, or monitoring progress towards implementation of plans.
- These decisions involve the use of the compatibility test and the profitability test.

Chapter 8

Deciding and Doing: Decision Making in Natural Contexts

Jens Rasmussen
Riso National Laboratory
Denmark

Several lines of academic research on decision making and judgment have concluded that decision makers are inconsistent, experts do not agree in judgment, and much less information is applied for judgment than the experts report as being significant. On the other hand, analyses have shown that decision making in actual work contexts is consistent and effective when judged against the pragmatic performance criteria that are actually governing work, and that very often are different from the criteria considered in research. This chapter presents a discussion of research on decision making within several domains, including political judgment, troubleshooting, diagnostic judgment, and decision biases. It offers the conclusion that practical decision making is not the resolution of separate conflicts, but a continuous control of the state of affairs in a dynamic environment. It is dependent on the tacit knowledge of context and cannot be separated from action planning.

A change in the research paradigm for analysis and modeling of decision making seems to be emerging. Classical decision theory has been focused on normative models, frequently derived from economic theories relevant to a management context. In general, normative models are well suited to teach novices rational decision strategies, which can introduce them to their profession and help them to be synchronized to the work content in order to prepare them for development of professional know-how and skill. However, for proper design of tools to support decision making of experts, understanding the nature of expert skill and decision strategies is necessary. Attempts to use computer-based decision support systems have created a new interest in modeling decision making in natural contexts. There has also been a parallel shift from behavioristic studies and well-controlled laboratory experiments toward studies of cognitive and mental phenomena in complex, real-life work contexts.

Academic research repeatedly has concluded that human decision makers are inconsistent and irrational, and that different expert decision makers will disagree in their judgment. However, studies of actual performance in work contexts seem to lead to another conclusion. A few examples are discussed here and compared to the recent findings in studies of actual decision making in complex work contexts.

SOME APPROACHES TO ANALYSIS OF DECISION MAKING

Electronic Troubleshooting

A series of analyses of diagnostic behavior of electronic troubleshooting in the U.S. Navy during the 1960s concluded that service technicians were inconsistent and unsystematic, and that they used many redundant observations, some of which could easily have been deduced from their prior knowledge (Rigney, Towne, & Mason, 1968). Such a conclusion, however, depends as much on the criteria for judgment as on the observed behavior. A closer look at the study cited will show that the reference to judgment was an information economic Bayesian decision model. The researchers assumed that, in "rational decision making," new observations are selected from a comprehensive evaluation of all the information already collected.

Whether this reference for judgment of actual performance is fair, depends on the performance criteria which are rational in the context. Rasmussen (1974) showed that expert troubleshooters have available several different strategies with very different properties regarding information economy, cognitive strain, time spent, prior knowledge about the failed system, and so on. In addition, it turns out that expert performance depends on the ability to match the properties of these different strategies to the performance criteria relevant in the actual work circumstances. For instance, experts would choose an information economic strategy only when the cost of observation was high, such as during work on live control systems when measurement and manipulation involve the risk of system alarms and shut-down. In general, the criterion would be time spent on repair, with no concern about whether observations were redundant, because positive feedback from 'customers' is related to speedy service and not to elegant thought processes. In consequence, given the actual circumstances and the great flexibility of experts with respect to mental strategies, our troubleshooters were judged to be very rational in their choice of procedures—although they frequently made judgment errors. This can, however, be taken to be a kind of speed–accuracy tradeoff and a sign of expertise. The mathematician Hadamard (1945) found that expert mathematicians make many more errors than students but perceived and corrected them much more effectively than students.

Political Judgments of the General Public

In the analysis of general election behavior by Philip Converse (see Nannestad, 1989), the political knowledge of the general public was analyzed by means of interviews repeated at different intervals, and the same persons were asked a number of political questions. Similarly to Rigney's studies of troubleshooting performance (Rigney et al., 1968), it was concluded that people are inconsistent and only few people know what they are talking about in terms of political issues. In general, people responded as if they picked answers by chance. The presumed explanation of why people appear to have a rather consistent political behavior was that they develop a "political habituation." In this way, behavior can be reasonably well structured, even if thought is chaotic.

Following David Robertson, Nannestad (1989) has applied multiple-scaling techniques to analyze and correlate peoples' political attitudes and opinions about political parties. The result has been compared to a similar analysis of the voting behavior of politicians in the Parliament. The conclusion has been that the general public actually has a pretty clear picture of the different political parties, a picture that is consistent with the behavior of politicians in Parliament. Furthermore, analysis of actual elections shows that the movement of votes among parties is consistent with the change in behavior of the politicians in Parliament. The conclusion in the present context is that people can act consistently and rationally, without being able to make explicit the underlying conceptual structure during controlled experimental sessions.

Medical Doctors and Stock Brokers

Diagnostic behavior has been studied extensively within the social judgment paradigm, which is based on regression analysis of the effect of available cues on the judgment of subjects in laboratory environments. This approach has been used to study diagnostic judgment in several professions, such as stockbrokers, clinical psychologists, and physicians (see, e.g., Brehmer, 1981). Cues identified as diagnostically relevant by expert judges are used to present subjects with trial cases, generally in the form of verbal descriptions on paper. Then, the statistical model describing diagnostic behavior is identified. The general result has been that a linear statistical model, such as multiple-regression analysis, has been adequate. Four general results are typical of such diagnostic experiments. First, the judgment process tends to be very simple. Even though experts identify up to 10 cues as relevant to diagnosis, they actually use very few—usually only 2 or 3—and the process tends to be purely additive. Second, the process tends to be inconsistent. Subjects do not use the same rule from case to case, and judgment in a second presentation of a case may differ considerably from what it was the first time. Third, there are wide individual differences even among subjects with years of experience. They differ with respect to the cues used and the weights they apply. The fourth general result is that people are not very good at describing how they make judgments (Brehmer, 1981).

Results from studies of diagnostic judgment in actual work contexts tend to paint a different picture. One reason derives from the fact that research on decision making and judgment in the social judgment paradigm has been focused on isolated diagnostic tasks in which subjects are asked to categorize and label a set of attributes. Compared to our analyses of diagnostic tasks in hospitals and repair shops, we can identify some important differences that will signal great caution for transfer of the results to actual professional work contexts. This statement does not imply that the results of laboratory experiments are not valid for multiple-attribute judgment tasks, but rather that isolated multiple-attribute judgment is not the characteristic feature of real-life diagnostic judgment. First, the experimental design suggests that decision makers are subject to an information input that they have to process. The task is isolated from its normal context, and, therefore, the 'tacit knowledge' of the subject has no opportunity to be "synchronized." In actual work, subjects are immersed in the contextual background, and they are, therefore, tuned to ask questions to the environment rather than to process multiple-attribute sets. The various features of the context through time serve to update the "attunement" of the organism (Gibson, 1966). Second, in actual work, a diagnostic judgment is not a separate decision task, but it is intimately connected with the subsequent choice of action. Diagnosis is not a theoretical categorization of the observed data, but a search for information, to select, among the perceived alternatives for action, the one matching the case in question. Models of decision making are normally structured as a sequence, including situation analysis, goal formulation and priority judgment, and planning. This normative sequence is the basis of the decision ladder in Figure 8.1. Experts in

Figure 8.1.   The figure illustrates the sequence of basic information processes in a decision task along with a number of heuristic short-cut paths. It serves to identify a number of basically different decision functions, which are used to connect different "states of knowledge" with respect to the activity in the work domain. The figure is used in our field studies as a sketch pad for representation of the interaction of situation analysis, goal evaluation, planning, and action, and for indication of "recognition-primed" short-cuts (see Figure 8.2).

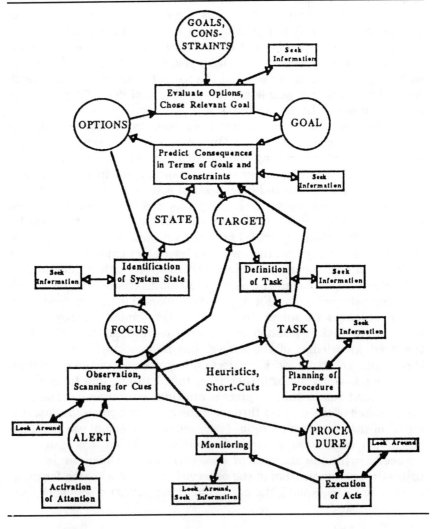

action, however, have a repertoire of heuristic short cuts bypassing the higher levels of the ladder. In any familiar situation, they perceive a small number of alternative plans and they only need enough information to resolve the choice among those plans. Therefore, diagnosis and action are intimately connected.

These two aspects of real-life diagnosis are illustrated in Figure 8.2, which represents the sequence of diagnostic judgments with respect to one patient's treatment in a hospital. It is clear that diagnosis is more of a dynamic control task than it is an isolated resolution of a multiattribute judgment problem. One important issue is that, irrespective of the stability of the patient's condition, the diagnosis has to be repeated many times, because the judgment is connected to different sets of action alternatives; therefore a diagnosis made in one situation might be unreliable for a later decision.

Statistical Intuition

Another line of research in human judgment is the psychological decision theory based on the work of Tversky and Kahneman's (1974) concepts of representativeness, availability, and other heuristics. Their approach rejects the use of normative decision models as a frame of reference for description. Their research is discussed in detail in other chapters of the book and will not be dealt with further here. One of their conclusions, however, should be related to analysis of the behavior of experts in work.

Discussing heuristic biases, the main cause for the failure to develop valid statistical intuitions is that events are normally not coded in terms of all the factors that are crucial to the learning of statistical rules (Tversky & Kahneman, 1974). As for diagnostic judgment, the question is whether expertise is related to learning statistical rules or to learning to act. Some research on human action in an uncertain environment, such as research on attention allocation, seems to demonstrate a pronounced human ability to adapt to a "statistical" environment without the need to form statistical inference rules. As already mentioned, humans do not constantly scan the environment and extract meaningful features from the available flux of information. Acting in a familiar dynamic environment, people sample the environment to update their world model, controlled by their expectation about where new information is likely to be present, that is, by their statistical intuition. This means that "statistical intuition" specifies *when* and/or update is needed, and *where* to look.

One family of models is based on *queueing theory*. The system considered in queueing theory is a person serving a number of tasks. The

Figure 8.2.   Represents a medical diagnosis in hospital context and illustrates several features of "naturalistic" decision making:

1. The different phases of decision making, such as situation analysis, goal evaluation, and planning are intimately connected. Diagnosis, therefore, cannot be separated as an isolated activity.

2. Diagnosis is repeated several times, and the process depends on the question asked, that is, whether to hospitalize and whether, when, and how to operate. Diagnosis is a choice among the perceived action alternatives, not an objective decision process.

3. The total process is not a linear sequence, but a complex communication network.

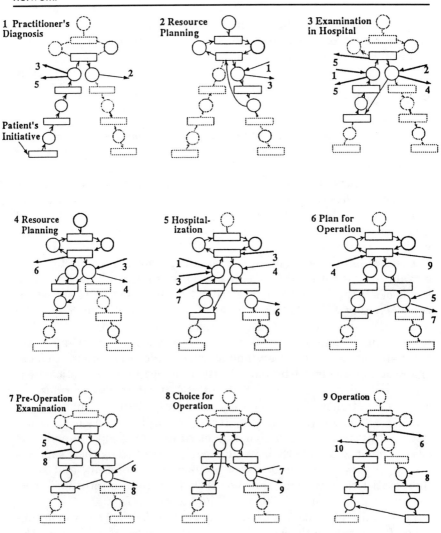

Figure 8.2.   Continued

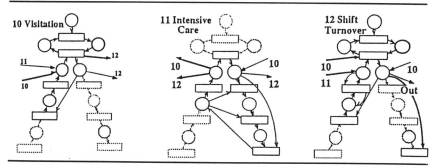

tasks cannot be attended to simultaneously but have to be considered on a time-sharing basis according to a service strategy which depends on the nature of the tasks. Many task demands, such as instrument reading during a monitoring task, arrive randomly. Typically, queueing theory considers demands with Poisson or exponential distributions. Queueing models of attention allocation postulate that humans optimize their performance according to a service strategy considering the arrival sequence and task priority. Queueing theoretic models have been used by Carbonell (1966) and Carbonell, Ward, and Senders (1968) for a study of instrument-scanning behavior of aircraft pilots to predict the fraction of time devoted to each instrument. Also, Senders and Posner (1976) have developed a queueing model for monitoring tasks. Queueing models basically represent the time distribution and priority characteristics of the task environment and can therefore be useful for analysis of workload posed in terms of time and scanning requirements in a monitoring task. Another approach in the frequency domain is based on Nyquist's *information-sampling theorem,* which states that the information from a source having spectral components with an upper limit frequency of w Hertz can be completely represented by an observer who samples 2w times per second. The sampling model has been validated by Senders (1964) in experiments where the subjects' task was to respond to a number of instruments fed by random signals of different bandwidth. Also, data from pilots in real-flight tasks support the view that actual behavior of experts is effectively adapted to temporal, statistical properties of the work environment (Senders, 1966).

The conclusion from this line of research on attention allocation and orientation behavior is that humans do have a 'statistical intuition' at the level-of-movement control, even if they are not able to express the related rules at the conscious, verbal level probed in most laboratory work on judgment.

LEVELS OF COGNITIVE CONTROL

The conclusions described above from studies of queueing theory and the information sampling model invite a discussion of the cognitive control of human activity in complex work domains. It is evident from the previous discussion that a model of cognitive control should include higher level analytical problem solving at one extreme, and also the control of actions at the other. A model including three levels of cognitive control has been proposed elsewhere (Rasmussen, 1983, 1986) and will be briefly reviewed as a basis for the final conclusion on decision making in natural contexts (see Figure 8.3).

Skill-based control is characterized by the ability to *subconsciously generate the movement patterns* required for interaction with a familiar environment by means of an internal, dynamic world model. This formulation of skilled performance is in line with Gibson's (1966) attunement of the neural system underlying direct perception of invariants of the environment in terms of *affordances*. The performance at this level is typical of the master, or expert; the smoothness and harmony of an expert craftsman has been fascinating philosophers and artists through ages.

At the next level is *rule-based behavior*. The composition of a sequence of subroutines in a familiar work situation is controlled consciously by a stored rule or procedure that may have been derived empirically during previous occasions or communicated from another person's know-how (e.g., an instruction or a cookbook recipe). An important point is that control of behavior at this level is goal oriented, but structured by "feed-forward control" through a stored rule. In other words, the person is aware that alternative actions are possible and has to make a choice. The choice is based on "signs" in the environment which have been found to be correlated to one of the alternative actions (cf. Klein's, 1989a, Recognition-Primed Decisions). Very often, the goal is not even explicitly formulated, but is found implicitly in the situation releasing the stored rules. The control is teleologic in the sense that the rule is selected from previous successful experiences. The control evolves by "survival of the fittest" rule. Humans typically seek the way of least effort. Therefore, it can be expected that no more cues will be used than are necessary for discrimination among the perceived alternatives for action in the particular situation.

During unfamiliar situations for which know-how and rules for control are not available from previous encounters, the control must move to a higher conceptual level in which performance is goal controlled and *knowledge based*. Here, knowledge is taken in a rather restricted

Figure 8.3.   Schematic map illustrating different levels in cognitive control of human behavior. The basic level represents the highly skilled sensorimotor performance controlled by automated patterns of movements. Sequences of such subroutines will be controlled by store rules, activated by signs. Problem solving in unfamiliar tasks will be based on conceptual models at the knowledge-based level that serve to generate the necessary rules ad hoc. The figure illustrates the flow of information, not the control of this flow. The figure is not meant to show humans as passive and subject to information "input." On the contrary, they actively seek information, guided by their dynamic "world model."

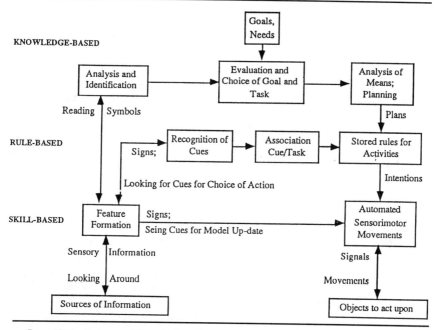

From "Skills, Rules, and Knowledge: Signals, Signs, and Symbols, and Other Distinctions in Human Performance Models," by J. Rasmussen, 1983. IEEE Transactions on Systems, Man and Cybernetics, SMC. 13(3), 257–266. Reprinted by permission of IEEE.

sense as possession of a conceptual, structural model or, in AI terminology, of deep knowledge. The level, therefore, might also be called *model based*. This level of control involves transformation of declarative knowledge into procedural knowledge, that is, what Anderson (1983) calls "compiling declarative knowledge." In this situation, the goal is explicitly formulated, based on an analysis of the environment and the overall aims of the person. Then, a useful plan is developed— by selection. Different plans are considered and their effect tested against the goal, physically by trial and error, or conceptually by means of "thought experiments." At this level of functional reasoning, the internal structure of the system is explicitly represented by a "mental model" that may take several different forms (Rasmussen, 1989). A major task in knowledge-based action planning is to transfer those properties of the environment that are related to the perceived problem to a proper symbolic representation. The information observed in the environment is then perceived as "symbols" with reference to this mental model.

COGNITIVE CONTROL AND LEARNING

It is clear from the discussion in the previous section that all the three levels of control (i.e., skill-based, rule-based, knowledge-based) can intimately interact in any given situation, and that the cognitive control of actions will be allocated dynamically to the three levels in a way closely related to the level of training.

During learning and adaptation to a work environment, the behavioral patterns of the higher levels are *not* becoming automated skills. Rather automated time–space behavioral patterns are evolving while behavior is controlled and supervised by the higher level activities—which will eventually deteriorate. In fact, the period when this is happening may lead to errors because of interference between a not fully developed sensory-motor skill and a gradually deteriorated rule system. Anderson (1983) describes the development of procedural knowledge during learning as a *compilation*. However, procedural knowledge derived by compilation of declarative mental models is a possible, but not inevitable, first phase of rule-based behavior. Actually, procedural knowledge is typically not derived from the basic, "deep" knowledge but has an empirical, heuristic basis, and compilation is not a suitable metaphor.

The transfer of control to new mental representation is a very complex process involving change along several different orthogonal dimensions. First, when trained responses evolve, the structure of the underlying representation shifts from a set of separate component models toward a more holistic representation. Typically, control by a structured, declarative model will also be replaced by an empirical, procedural representation concurrent with a shift from a symbolic to a stereotype sign interpretation of observations. This means that training involves at least three concurrent and structurally independent shifts, in terms of aggregation, declarative-procedural knowledge, and interpretation of information.

DECISION MAKING AND DOING

The complex interaction among the different levels of cognitive control of action in a dynamic environment leads to different kinds of decision making.

At the *skill-based level* which is active in familiar contexts, behavior unfolds as an integrated, continuous flow with no interruption and discrete decisions. Behavior relies on data-driven chaining of movement patterns generated by the "attuned" internal, dynamic world model. However, conscious mental operations (i.e., decisions) can play an important role by preconditioning the required dynamic model. A person can recall previous, similar activities and situations. Recall of analogues lets a person rehearse expected choice points and thereby become alerted to guideposts. In this way, the mental simulation of the internal world model prepares a decision maker for the proper cues for choice and for the events to come; the actual decision making can take the shape of Klein's Recognition-Primed Decisions, for occasions in which no alternatives are considered.

This mode of decision making has also been observed by Amalberti and Deblon (1989), studying the cognitive behavior of fighter pilots before and during attack missions. Expert pilots rehearsed a number of predictable circumstances and systematically prepared themselves for "automatic" response; a very effective strategy for high-speed scenarios. A similar strategy has been used for offline training of quick-draw skills of soldiers for commando-raids (Arnold, 1969). In hospital contexts, we have observed a related kind of natural decision making by not taking explicitly into consideration the available alternatives of action. Operation-theater planning is done during conferences, which include doctors and nurses. A typical feature of the hospital system seems to be a kind of collective memory. No one person has available all the relevant information about the individual patients, but the collective mind has this information. When treatment of an individual patient is planned, the context from previous considerations defines an elaborate knowledge background. If, at a meeting, an action is proposed which is not supported by the knowledge possessed by a member of the group, this will be voiced properly. If the situation is ambiguous, one member will very likely offer comments serving to better specify the context. This goes on until the context is properly established, and a decision can be concluded by the surgeon in charge without alternatives being explicitly mentioned. In other words, decisions emerge when the landscape is well enough shaped so the water flows in only one proper direction. One important aspect of this cooperative condi-

Figure 8.4. Illustrates the complex interaction between the different levels of cognitive control. Tasks are frequently analyzed in terms of sequences of separate decisions and acts. Typically, however, several activities are going on at the same time, and at the skilled level, activity is more like a contiguous, dynamic interaction with the work environment. Attention, on the other hand, is scanning across time and activities for analysis of the past performance, monitoring the current activity, and planning for foreseen future requirements. In this way, the dynamic world model is prepared for upcoming demands, rules are rehearsed and modified to fit predicted demands, and symbolic reasoning is used to understand responses from the environment and to prepare rules for foreseen but unfamiliar situations. Attention, decision, and acting may not always be focused on current activities, and different levels of control may be involved in different aspects, related to different time slots, in a time-sharing or a parallel mode of processing.

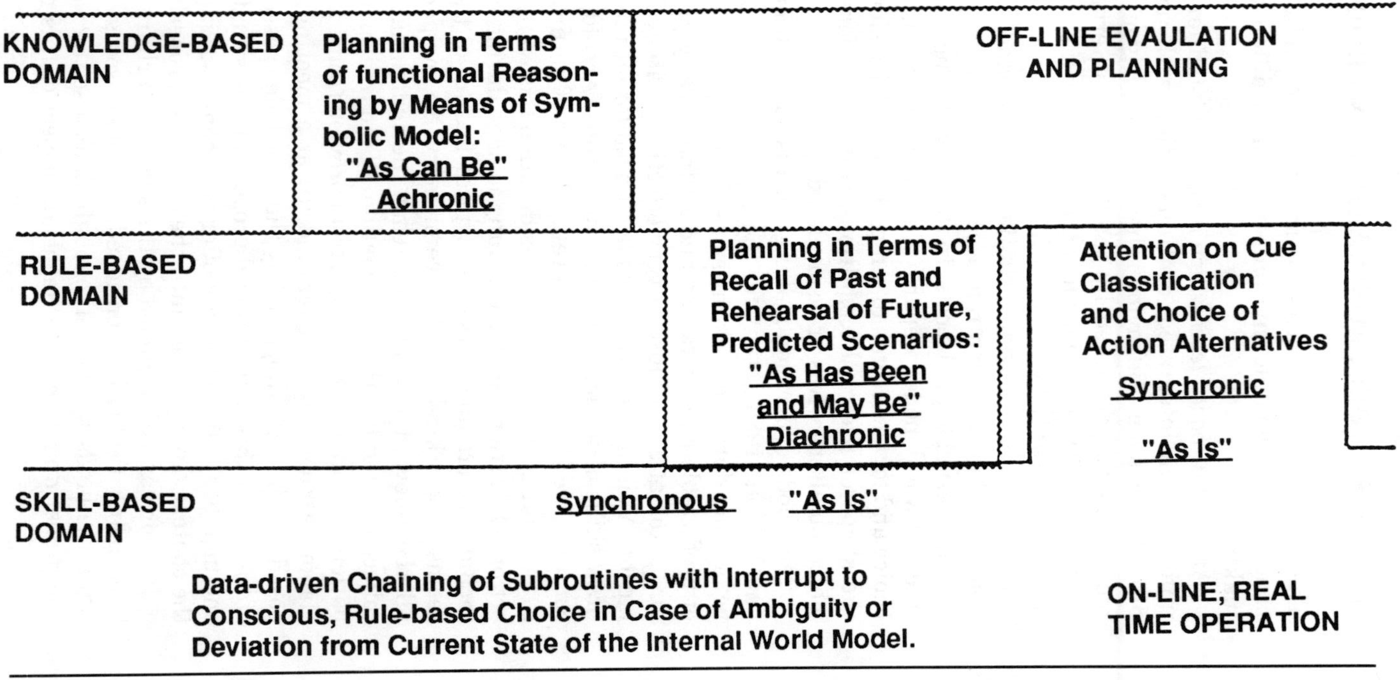

170

OFF-LINE EVALUATION
AND PLANNING

KNOWLEDGE-BASED DOMAIN

Planning in Terms of functional Reasoning by Means of Symbolic Model:
"As Can Be"
Achronic

Planning in Terms of Recall of Past and Rehearsal of Future, Predicted Scenarios:
"As Has Been and May Be"
Diachronic

Attention on Cue Classification and Choice of Action Alternatives
Synchronic
"As Is"

RULE-BASED DOMAIN

Synchronous   "As Is"

SKILL-BASED DOMAIN

Data-driven Chaining of Subroutines with Interrupt to Conscious, Rule-based Choice in Case of Ambiguity or Deviation from Current State of the Internal World Model.

ON-LINE, REAL TIME OPERATION

tioning model of decision making is the built-in redundancy. People with different perspectives on the patient's situation are evaluating the result of the negotiation. Another important aspect of this evolutionary completion of the context is that information is offered for resolution of ambiguities that could not be retrieved by an explicit question, because nobody would expect the information to be present, and, therefore, the question could not be phrased. Likewise, such important pieces of information would not be offered outside this face-to-face encounter (e.g., entered into a database), because only the specific context makes it worth mentioning.

This kind of high-skill decision making depends on conditioning in advance the internal world model which is required to generate automatically the proper behavioral patterns on occasion. The distinction between this kind of skill-based "decision making" and *rule-based action* is very fuzzy.

However, when this conditioning as described has not been effective, a mismatch between the state of affairs in the environment and the predictions by the internal world model can be experienced by the person. In this case, a number of alternatives for action may be perceived, and the environment will be consulted to read a sign which can resolve the ambiguity. If a relevant set of alternatives is not available, recall of prior similar cases can assist in identification of action alternatives and the related cues for selection.

If no resolution is found in this way, and only in this case, will resort be taken to an analytical, symbolic mode of *knowledge-based* decision making. In a complex, real-life situation, this leads to a very dynamic interaction between three different levels of cognitive control. The interaction is illustrated by Figure 8.4. One important feature of this interaction among levels of control is that the different levels may be applied to different activities simultaneously or in a timesharing mode, and they normally will have different time frames.

KEY POINTS

- These features of decision making in natural contexts make generalization from controlled laboratory experiments difficult:
  - Decision making is intimately connected to action.
  - Decision making is an activity through time, which depends on continuous updating of tacit knowledge.
  - Decision making has the character of a continuous control task, not the resolution of separate conflicts.

Chapter 9

Decision Making as Argument-Driven Action*

Raanan Lipshitz
University of Haifa

The decision to act is traditionally defined as choosing among alternative actions. *Behavioral decision theory* (BDT) assumes that decisions are made by consequential choice, that is, by choosing among alternatives "on the basis of expectations about the consequences of action for prior objectives" (March & Olsen, 1986, p. 1). Consistent with this assumption BDT "is concerned with *prescribing* courses of action that conform most closely to the decision-maker's beliefs and values . . . and *describing* these beliefs and values and the manner in which individuals incorporate them into their decisions" (Slovic, Fischhoff, & Lichtenstein, 1977, p. 1; emphasis added). This chapter presents a more inclusive conceptualization of decision making, which contains consequential choice as well as alternative ways of describing how decisions are made and prescribing for their improvement.

The search for an inclusive conceptualization of decision making is motivated by considerable evidence that real-world decisions are not made by consequential choice. Consider the following seven propositions:

P1. Real-world decisions are typically made without choosing among alternatives.
P2. The basic mechanism for making real-world decisions is situation assessment (sequential selection of action on the basis of a definition of the situation).
P3. Real-world decisions are typically made by a quick selection of a certain course of action followed by its further assessment.

* This chapter was supported by grant MDA-903-86-C-0146 from the U.S. Army Research Institute. The author thanks Chris Argyris, Victor Friedman, Gary Klein, Haim Omer, and Donald A. Schon for their help in writing the chapter.

P4. Real-world decisions are often determined prior to the (concurrent or sequential) evaluation of action.

P5. The uncertainty that affects real-world decisions is not limited to the nature, likelihood, or value of future consequences.

P6. Uncertainty affects real-world decisions by interrupting ongoing action, delaying intended action, and guiding the development of new alternatives.

P7. The critical element in real-world decision making is the framing of the decision problem.

The first five propositions have substantial empirical support; the last two are more conjectural. All seven are incompatible with consequential choice. In the following sections I will review the empirical support for each proposition, discuss its incompatibility with consequential choice, argue for the need to replace the conceptualization of decision making as choosing among alternatives with a more inclusive conceptualization, and propose such an alternative.

P1. REAL-WORLD DECISIONS ARE TYPICALLY MADE WITHOUT CHOOSING AMONG ALTERNATIVES

The absence of choice in real-world decisions has been noted by researchers using different methodologies in a wide variety of contexts: Isenberg (1985), who observed senior chief executive officers; Carroll (1980), who observed parole officers and conducted experiments to test his observations; Klein, Calderwood, and Clinton-Cirocco (1986), who conducted careful interviews of experienced fire fighters; Anderson (1983), who studied the minutes of the NSC meetings during the Cuban missile crisis; and Beach and Mitchell (Beach, 1990), who studied a variety of decision problems in both field and laboratory studies.

P2. THE BASIC MECHANISM FOR MAKING REAL-WORLD DECISIONS IS SITUATION ASSESSMENT (SEQUENTIAL SELECTION OF ACTION ON THE BASIS OF A DEFINITION OF THE SITUATION)

Proposition 2 is based on the heavy emphasis of situation assessment in descriptive models of decision making. In some models (e.g., Abelson, 1976; Klein, 1989a; March, 1978; Newell & Simon, 1972; Noble, 1989; Pennington & Hastie, 1988), situation assessment is a primary element; in others (e.g., Connolly & Wagner, 1988; Beach, 1990; Montgomery, 1989a), it plays a more secondary, but still important, role in setting the parameters of the decision problem. The principal difference between situation assessment and consequential choice is that the former does not require a comparison among alternatives or an *explicit* consideration of future consequences (e.g., script processing, Abelson, 1976; pure recognition-primed decisions, Klein, 1989a; rule-based decisions, Rasmussen, 1983).

P3. REAL-WORLD DECISIONS ARE TYPICALLY MADE BY A QUICK SELECTION OF A CERTAIN COURSE OF ACTION FOLLOWED BY ITS FURTHER ASSESSMENT

The notion that decisions are made by quick solutions tempered by arguments pro and con the intended action has been suggested by several researchers. De Groot noted that chess grandmasters "might discover the correct move in a complex position with 5 seconds or less of looking at the position for the first time, but might then spend 15 minutes verifying the correctness of the move" (Simon, 1978, p. 281). Klein (1989a) reports that fire-ground commanders make a quick selection based on situation recognition followed by mental simulation of its implementation. Beach and Mitchell (1987) suggest a similar combination, which they label *adoption and progress decisions*. Montgomery (1989a) suggests that decisions are made by the selection of a promising candidate followed by a search for dominance structure. Three features distinguish these processes from consequential choice: (a) action selection is sequential—that is, alternative courses of action are evaluated one at a time; (b) action development is intertwined with action selection—that is, the decision maker need not develop his or her alternative prior to beginning the evaluation; and (c) decisions may be made without the *explicit* consideration of future consequences, as, for example in pure recognition-primed decisions (Klein, 1989a) and the adoption of compatible or dominant alternatives (Beach & Mitchell, 1987, and Montgomery, 1989a, respectively).

P4. REAL-WORLD DECISIONS ARE OFTEN DETERMINED PRIOR TO THE (CONCURRENT OR SEQUENTIAL) EVALUATION OF ACTION

The influence of precommitment on decision making has been documented by Alexander (1979), Elster (1977), Hickson, Butler, Cray, Mallory, and Wilson (1986), Janis and Mann (1977), Soelberg (1967), Staw

(1981), and Teger (1980). The related tendency of decision makers to favor the status quo has been noted by Lindblom (1959) and Beach (1990). These findings are inconsistent with models of consequential choice that assume that commitment is *generated* by comparing alternatives in terms of future consequences. The implications for aiding decision makers are fundamental:

> If the choices which determine [the] outcomes [of decision processes] . . . are made informally and intuitively before the evaluation phase begins, then attempts at formalizing and rationalizing evaluation, however praiseworthy, are made in vain. . . . Perhaps all the efforts which are devoted to refining valuative methods and to applying ever more sophisticated techniques of valuative analysis are misdirected. (Alexander, 1979, p. 402)

The emphasis on valuative analysis is misdirected, because it is based on two unwarranted assumptions. The first assumption is that the decision maker's problem is how to choose from an available set of alternatives. The second assumption is that the decision maker can choose "objectively," that is, on the relative value of these alternatives. In contrast, propositions 3 and 4 suggest that the problem is how to generate such choice or, more broadly, how to avoid unreflective action, as both quick selection (proposition 3) and past decisions (proposition 4) tend to narrow decision makers' attention and effort on certain alternatives (Janis & Mann, 1977; Montgomery, 1989a; Staw, 1981).

P5. THE UNCERTAINTY THAT AFFECT REAL-WORLD DECISIONS IS NOT LIMITED TO THE IDENTITY, LIKELIHOOD, OR VALUE OF FUTURE CONSEQUENCES

By now it has been clearly recognized that the uncertainty that affects real-world decisions is more manifold than the identity, likelihood, or value of future outcomes as implied by consequential choice. Fischhoff, Goitein and Shapira (1982, p. 335) write that

> Many studies of how people estimate relative frequencies were conducted before researchers realized that whatever their intrinsic interest such tasks were not particularly relevant to the sort of uncertainty in most decision situations.

In a similar vein, Humphreys and Berkeley (1985) found that users of a multiattribute utility decision aid expressed seven different types of uncertainty, some of which were quite incompatible with consequential choice: (a) Uncertainty on act–event sequences; (b) uncertainty on event–event sequences; (c) uncertainty concerning the meaning of information; (d) uncertainty on the value of consequences; (e) uncertainty on the appropriate decision process; (f) uncertainty on future preferences and actions; and (g) uncertainty on their ability to affect future events.

Two types of uncertainty that affect real-world decisions can be derived from propositions 2, 3, and 4 above. Proposition 2, which suggests that decisions are based on situation assessment, implies that uncertainty pertains to the nature of the situation and the action that it requires. This has also been proposed by researchers of decision making in organizations (Duncan, 1972; Perrow, 1970). Propositions 3 and 4, which concern quick selection followed by reassessment and precommitment, imply that uncertainty is essentially retrospective: A decision has already been made, but the decision maker is not certain of its appropriateness, either because a quickly selected alternative is not dominant, or because something has changed since a past decision was originally made. As the next proposition claims, the impact of these uncertainties on the decision process is different from the role of uncertainty in models of consequential choice.

P6. UNCERTAINTY AFFECTS REAL-WORLD DECISIONS BY INTERRUPTING ONGOING ACTION, DELAYING INTENDED ACTION, AND GUIDING THE DEVELOPMENT OF NEW ALTERNATIVES

Proposition 6 follows Anderson (1983), Dewey (1933), and Cyert and March (1963), who describe uncertainty as doubts caused by a perception of a problem. The doubts sustain and guide a search for a solution and subside, either when a satisfactory solution is found or when the decision maker's attention is directed elsewhere. Four differences distinguish this conception of uncertainty from its conception in consequential choice models and methodologies (e.g., *subjective expected utility* and *decision analysis*):

1. Consequential choice models conceptualize uncertainty as an abstract element. Proposition 6 conceptualizes it as questions concerning concrete issues.
2. Consequential choice models conceptualize uncertainty as a quantitative factor in the evaluation of alternatives. Proposition 6 conceptualizes it as a causal factor in their development.
3. Consequential choice models suggest that uncertainty is handled

by preferring alternatives with low associated uncertainty. Proposition 6 suggests that uncertainty is handled by finding solutions to the problems that generate it.

4. Consequential choice models treat uncertainty as wholly detrimental to decision quality, because it handicaps the ability of formal models to identify optimal decisions (Collingridge, 1982), and because people are unable to assess its magnitude as they should according to formal probability theory (Kahneman, Slovic, & Tversky, 1982). In contrast, proposition 6 suggests that some uncertainty is essential to good-quality decisions, because it motivates decision makers to shift from automatic to reflective action, and guides their search for better solutions (Dewey, 1933).

P7. THE CRITICAL ELEMENT IN REAL-WORLD DECISION MAKING IS THE FRAMING OF THE DECISION PROBLEM

Tversky and Kahneman found that alternatives are evaluated differently if their consequences are framed as losses or gains (Tversky & Kahneman, 1981). The primacy of framing is even more pronounced if we take it to denote not only the wording of choice, but the substantive determination of what the decision is all about (Beach, 1990; Schon, 1983; Watzlawick, Weakland, & Fisch, 1974). This point was made by Dewey over 50 years ago as follows:

> The way in which the problem is conceived decides what specific suggestions are entertained and which are dismissed; what data are selected and which are rejected; it is the criterion for relevancy and irrelevancy of hypotheses and conceptual structures. . . . To find out what the problem and problems are which a problematic situation presents to be inquired into, is to be well along in inquiry. (Dewey, 1933, p. 108)

If decisions are not necessarily made by consequential choice, how are they made? Various models that are consistent with preceding propositions have been suggested by Beach and Mitchell (1987), Connolly and Wagner (1988), Klein (1989a), Montgomery (1989a), Pennington and Hastie (1988), Staw (1981), and others. These various models rely on two generic alternatives to consequential choice. *Matching* decisions are made by selecting an action on the basis of some rule, typically a rule that specifies which action is appropriate in a given situation (e.g., Klein, 1989a) or a rule that specifies which action is compatible with particular goals or values (e.g., Beach, 1990).

Reassessment decisions are made when the decision maker has to re-evaluate a decision, typically because of objections to its implementation or continuation (e.g., Anderson, 1983). The basic difference between models of consequential choice and matching, on the one hand, and reassessment on the other, concerns their treatment of commitment. Whereas the former assume that the decision maker begins the decision process uncommitted to a certain course of action, and that his or her task is to generate such commitment, the latter assume that the decision maker is already (albeit tentatively or unknowingly) committed, so that his or her task involves loosening as well as generating commitment.

It can be shown that consequential choice, matching, and reassessment are internally consistent and fundamentally different by comparing them on six parameters: *framing* (how problems are framed), *form* (how action is selected), the *uncertainty* that has to be resolved in order to act, *logic* (the type of underlying rationality), *handicaps* (which block high-quality decisions), and the *therapies* (which are entailed).

Consequential choice decisions take the form of comparing among alternatives in terms of future consequences. Thus, decisions are framed as problems of choice, and uncertainties concern the likelihood and attractiveness of future outcomes. The underlying logic is teleological, which means that the merit of an action is judged on the basis of its consequences (Boyce & Jensen, 1978). As people's ability to make high-quality decisions in this mode is handicapped by the limitations and biases that characterize human information processing, the therapies prescribed by proponents of consequential choice consist of decomposing complex problems, augmenting limited human capabilities, and correcting suboptimal biases and heuristics (Kahneman et al., 1982).

Matching: Matching decisions takes the form of defining the situation sequentially and selecting an appropriately matching action (March, 1978; Rasmussen, 1983). Thus, decision problems are framed as problematic situations, and uncertainties concern either the nature of the situation or the action for which it calls (Isenberg, 1986; Milliken, 1987). The underlying logic is deontological, which means that the merit of an action is judged by its compatibility with some value or rule of conduct (Boyce & Jensen, 1978). High-quality matching is handicapped by the inability either to identify the situation correctly or to produce the required action. Since these typically distinguish between novices and experts (Anderson, 1982; Calderwood, Crandall, & Klein, 1987), the corresponding therapies are training and use of expert systems (Anderson, 1982).

Reassessment: Reassessment takes the form of reevaluating an action to which one is at least tentatively committed. Decision problems are thus framed as objections to an intended or previously made decision, and uncertainty concerns the validity of these arguments. The nonjustificational logic appropriate for these situations has been provided by Popper (1969). He suggested that rational action does not mean following a model of optimal choice (as in consequential choice) or some other authority (as in matching) but rather criticizing the actions and beliefs to which one is committed and learning from errors. Thus, the principal handicap to high quality reassessment is unreflective action due to habit, past decisions and wishful thinking (Janis & Mann, 1977; Staw, 1981). The therapies called for consist of various methods of critical inquiry (Argyris, Putnam, & Smith, 1985; Collingridge, 1982; Mason & Mitroff, 1981; Schon, 1983).

A problem that presents itself given the differences between consequential choice, matching, and reassessment concerns the definition of *decision making.* Since decisions are not necessarily made by choosing among alternatives, what is a *decision?* For some reason the problem of definition has not received the attention it deserves. For example, Beach, Vlek, and Wagenaar (1988, p. 9) report that participants in a workshop on unique vs. repeated decision making

> expressed the opinion that the lack of a clear differentiation [between the two] reflects the lack of a clear definition of what a decision is, and that the word 'decision' has wrongly been restricted to gambling-like choices that fit the classical theory well.

However, no alternative definition is suggested. Another example is March (1978), who refers to "organizational choice" even while arguing that organizational decisions are not made by choosing but by "obligation and rule." Finally, Klein and Calderwood (1987) write that

> The FGCs [fire ground commanders] were clearly encountering choice points during the course of an incident. That is, there was *an awareness that alternative courses of action were possible.* However the FGCs insisted that they did not deliberate about the advantages and disadvantages of the different options. (p. 247; emphasis added)

The implicit use of choice as the definition of decisions allows for the argument that recognition-primed decisions are simply nondeliberate comparisons among alternatives. This is clearly contrary to the essence of the RPD model, which can be described, without recourse to choice, as matching (action selection on the basis of situation recognition) followed by reassessment (testing selected actions by mental simulation of their implementation).

The resilience of the notion that decisions are, and ought to be, made by consequential choice is truly amazing (Fishchhoff et al., 1982; March, 1978). Two factors can account for this resilience. The first is that decisions are still defined in terms of choice, and the second is the availability of numerous models of optimal choice (Lord & Maher, 1990). Firmer acceptance of alternative conceptualizations requires an explicit alternative definition coupled with convincing arguments that rational decision is not necessarily rational choice. Collingridge (1982), March (1978), and Quinn (1980), whose works are reflected in the different logics identified here for consequential choice, matching, and reassessment, contributed to the search for alternative rationalities. An alternative definition can be obtained by replacing *choice* with *argument* as the root metaphor for making decisions.

Consider the definition of a decision as the enactment of an action argument of the general form "Do 'A' because 'R'," where 'A' and 'R' denote an action and reasons for its implementation, respectively. The definition relates to a long tradition in ethics of discussing decisions in terms of arguments (Kattsoff, 1965). This particular definition is adapted from Toulmin (1958) and has three advantages:

1. The definition captures the essence of every discussion of decision making, namely, that decisions pertain to purposive action, even though the purpose may be implicit (Rasmussen, 1983) or discovered retrospectively (Weick, 1983).
2. The definition is inclusive, recognizing the variety of ways in which decisions are made and the different logics which they may obey. Every decision-making model corresponds to an action argument, and different models can be distinguished in terms of their underlying arguments. For example, consequential choice corresponds to the argument "do 'A' because it has better expected consequences than its alternatives," matching corresponds to the argument "do 'A' because it is appropriate given the situation or some social or professional code," and reassessment corresponds to the argument "do 'A' either because there are no objections to its implementation or because such objections can be rebutted."
3. Analyzing decisions as argument-driven action allows the analyst to enrich his or her repertoire of interpretation and suggestions for improvement, which brings the discussion to the problem of interpretation.

Decisions can always be interpreted as consequential choice because doing "A" implies choosing it over "Not-A" and because purposeful action implies working towards a desired future consequence. Though logically sound, these arguments do not allow that a decision was *actually* made by comparing among alternatives in terms of consequences. The facile applicability of consequential choice presents three dangers to analysts: (a) They may find a decision process to be faulty, assuming consequential choice, though it may be sensible, assuming, for example, matching or reassessment. (b) They may inappropriately prescribe consequential choice therapies for problems for which they are not designed (e.g., faulty situation assessment or misplaced commitment). (c) They may impair their ability to ask useful questions. As Fischhoff and Goitein (1984, p. 510) suggest,

> the role of formal analysis is to highlight the analyst's ability to ask penetrating questions that show ways to think about a problem that otherwise would not have occurred to the decision-maker.

Ignoring the plausibility of alternative interpretations clearly restricts analysts' ability to ask questions that are pertinent to matching and reassessment.

The advantage of analyzing decisions as argument driven is that it allows the decision makers to examine how they make their decisions and then use models of optimal choice to improve them, if that is their preference.

KEY POINTS

- There are three generic modes of making decisions:
  - Consequential choice, or comparing among alternatives in terms of future consequences.
  - Matching, that is, choosing an action based on its compatibility with some value or rule of conduct.
  - Reassessment, or reevaluating a prior choice.
- Most decision research presumes that decisions are and should be made from the first mode; much evidence contradicts this assumption.
- Decisions can be better conceptualized as argument-driven actions.

Chapter 10

The Search For a Dominance Structure in Decision Making: Examining the Evidence*

Henry Montgomery
Department of Psychology
University of Göteborg
Göteborg, Sweden

The dominance search model, which is excellently summarized by Lipshitz in Chapter 5 of this volume, largely grew out of observations of my own and others' decision-making behavior. In other words, the model aims at describing *real* decision making. Below, I will examine research carried out by myself and others bearing on the model's validity in realistic settings. Research on the dominance search model includes studies of postdecisional justification (e.g., Biel & Montgomery, 1989). However, in the following I will examine only research related to different predecisional processes and stages assumed by the dominance search model. This examination is the basis for a concluding discussion of limitations of the model and possibilities of developing it.

EVIDENCE FOR THE DOMINANCE SEARCH MODEL

Preediting

In the preediting phase the decision maker selects attributes (i.e., criteria) that are particularly relevant for his or her decision and screens alternatives that are unacceptable. An initial screening or preediting phase is not only associated with the dominance search model, but is often a part of descriptive accounts of decision processes (e.g., Kahne-

---

* This chapter was supported by a grant from the U.S. Army Research Institute.

man & Tversky, 1979; Montgomery & Svenson, 1976). The existence of a preediting phase is backed up by process-tracing data (e.g., think-aloud reports or search behavior on information boards) from several studies in laboratory settings (for a review see Svenson, 1979; see also Montgomery & Svenson, 1989b; Dahlstrand & Montgomery, 1984). Naturalistic data supporting an initial screening phase were presented in an early interview study of career decisions (Soelberg, 1967).

Finding a Promising Alternative

In this phase the decision maker finds an alternative that is a promising candidate for the final choice. Process tracing studies strongly support the existence of this phase, inasmuch as the finally chosen alternative tends to draw more attention than other alternatives quite early in the decision process (Dahlstrand & Montgomery, 1984; Montgomery & Svenson, 1989b). The promising alternative tends to be particularly attractive on some attribute (Dahlstrand & Montgomery, 1984). Naturalistic data suggesting that decision makers find a promising alternative long before the final choice were presented by Soelberg (1967) in his study of career decisions, and by Tyszka and Wielochowski (1991) in a study of boxing verdicts. The latter researchers found that boxing judges at an early stage of the match (typically at the first round of a three-rounds match) often pick one of the two contestants as their favorite, entailing an increased chance for this boxer to be judged as the winner of the match. Apparently, the assumption that decision makers often find a promising alternative long before their final choice rests on solid ground. However, recent think-aloud data (Montgomery, Selart, Gärling, & Lindberg, 1991) indicate that in simple decision problems (two alternatives × two attributes), the decision maker may go directly to a final choice of one of the alternatives.

Dominance Testing

At this stage the decision maker tests whether a promising alternative dominates the other alternatives. More precisely, he or she checks that the promising alternative is not (clearly) inferior to other alternatives on selected attributes. These tests can vary in how systematic and exhaustive they are. If a promising alternative is found to be dominant (i.e., no disadvantage and at least one advantage, as compared to other alternatives), it is chosen and the decision process is terminated. On the other hand, if the promising alternative falls short on the domi-

nance criterion, the decision maker proceeds to the dominance structuring phase.

The reality of a testing phase in the decision process is supported by
Montgomery and Svenson's (1989b) think-aloud study of housing
choices. Although the subjects in that study were presented with hypothetical alternatives, the choice task was very realistic, inasmuch as
the alternatives were descriptions of real houses and, moreover, the
subjects were actually searching for a new home. The data indicated
that 6 out of 12 subjects *abandoned* an initially selected, promising
alternative, since they found a better alternative. Since finding a
promising alternative does not determine the final choice, there is
probably a subsequent testing phase. However, the fact that the eligi-
bility of a promising alternative is tested does not necessarily imply
that the goal of such a test is to identify a dominant alternative.
Evidence related to that notion is discussed below in connection with a
description of the dominance structuring phase.

Dominance Structuring

The goal of this phase is to restructure or reinterpret given information in such a way that a promising alternative becomes dominant. To
achieve this end, the decision maker uses various methods to neutral-
ize or eliminate the disadvantage(s) associated with the promising
alternative. These methods include *deemphasizing* the likelihood or
value of such a disadvantage (or of an advantage associated with a
nonpromising alternative). Alternatively, the decision maker may *bolster* (i.e., enhance) the advantages of the promising alternative (or the
disadvantages of nonpromising alternatives). The result of bolstering
may be that the disadvantages of the promising alternatives are experienced as less important as compared to the enhanced value of the
bolstered information.

The combined effect of deemphasizing and bolstering is that the
difference between the decision maker's evaluations of the finally
chosen alternative and other alternatives will increase towards the
end of the decision process. Process tracing studies clearly show that
this indeed is the case, both for evaluations of single attributes
(Dahlstrand & Montgomery, 1984; Montgomery & Svenson, 1989b)
and for overall evaluations of alternatives (Lewicka, 1990; for an early
demonstration see Mann, Janis, & Chaplin, 1969). Montgomery and
Svenson's (1989b) housing choice data indicate that the tendency to an
increased differentiation across time between the chosen alternative
and its competitors may be explained primarily in terms of the de-

emphasizing operation. On the other hand, questionnaire data on choices among hypothetical housing alternatives showed that when information was missing about the alternatives, subjects tended to bolster (i.e., enhance) the value of inferred aspects of the finally chosen alternative (Lindberg, Gärling, & Montgomery, 1990a). However, questionnaire data on choices with no requirements to infer missing information have not consistently shown that subjects use the deemphasizing or bolstering operations in order to find a dominance structure (Lindberg, Gärling, & Montgomery, 1989; Garvill, Gärling, Lindberg, & Svenson, 1990).

The reality of deemphasizing and bolstering is also supported by naturalistic data. First, it may be noted that Tyszka and Wielochowski's (1991) finding that boxing judges tend to pick the winner long before the match is finished suggests that judges in later parts of the match deemphasize information supporting the other contestant and/or bolster information supporting the winner. More direct support for both deemphasizing and bolstering was found by McCoch (1990) who noted that bond traders use these operations by consulting appropriate colleagues and economic news in approaching a decision to switch between different bond investments. Further support for these operations were obtained in a longitudinal field study (interviews) of persons looking for a new home (Lindberg, Gärling, & Montgomery, 1990b). The data suggested that in order to facilitate a choice of a new home, attributes favoring the new dwelling were seen as more important (bolstering), whereas attributes favoring the old dwelling were perceived as less important (deemphasizing).

There are two additional operations associated with dominance structuring, namely: (a) *cancellation,* where the decision maker counterbalances a disadvantage by relating it to an advantage that has some natural connection to the advantage (e.g., in terms of tradeoff relationships or similarity), and (b) *collapsing,* where two or more attributes are collapsed into a more comprehensive attribute or into general life values, such as security, freedom, self-development. Think-aloud data on choices among hypothetical alternatives do not yield much evidence for the cancellation operation, whereas collapsing appears to be more common (Montgomery, Selart, Gärling, & Lindberg, 1991). The following two think-aloud statements illustrate the collapsing operation. "A skilled therapist works better" (choice between therapists varying in skill and available working hours; the collapsed attribute appears to be amount of good work). "Knowledge does not add to a teacher's qualifications if he cannot teach it" (choice between teachers varying in pedagogic skills and knowledge; the collapsed attribute appears to be amount of efficiently taught knowledge).

The realism of the collapsing operation is also supported in our studies of housing choices since we have found that these choices may be predicted from the respondents' beliefs about how housing alternatives relate to various life values (such as freedom and security). This is true for both hypothetical choices (e.g., Lindberg, Gärling, & Montgomery, 1988) and real choices (Lindberg, Gärling, & Montgomery, 1990b). We also found that at least 50 percent of the choice situations were associated with dominance structures on the level of life values (e.g., a chosen alternative is seen as better than or equal to its competitors with respect to freedom, security, family, etc.), whereas on the level of attributes (e.g., size, location, standard) pure dominance structures were very rare (Garvill, Gärling, Montgomery, & Svenson, 1990). The fact that subjects' choices appear to be guided by life values suggest that the dominance structures available on this level may have facilitated the respondents' choices.

CONCLUSIONS

The dominance search model seems consistent with data from both artificial and real-choice problems. The support for the model is least clear-cut in situations where subjects make many repeated choices among similar problems. Although these situations involved hypothetical choice problems, it is clear that repeated more or less automatized decision making is common in real life (e.g., when shopping). In such situations subjects' choices may be guided by various simplifying heuristics (such as using only the most important attribute as a basis for the choice), which will not lead to changes in the evaluations of attributes or values. Montgomery (1989b) distinguished between simplifying and elaboration in decision making. Simplifying heuristics may be consistent with dominance structuring (Montgomery, 1989b), but elaboration (changing or adding information) is more likely to lead to changes in subjects' evaluations of aspects of the decision situation, changes that may be used for testing the dominance structuring notion.

Decision making often is a very creative process, and not only a question of exploring and evaluating given information. It often involves *creation* or *modification* of alternatives (see Svenson's, 1990, classification of decision problems). Recently collected think-aloud data give several illustrations of how creative processes may lead to a dominance structure (Montgomery et al., 1991). As an example consider subjects facing a choice between buying a very entertaining but short book (few reading hours), and a slightly less entertaining but longer book (more reading hours), for a fairly long train ride. The subjects invented various modifications of the promising alternative (the more entertaining book) in order to reduce its disadvantage (few reading hours). For example, they stated "I may read the book twice;" "I may read another book;" "I'll read the book very slowly and meditate on it;" "I'll make breaks during the reading." Hence, the subjects did not accept the given information, but searched for ways of changing it. The goal of these activities was obvious, namely, to come closer to a dominance structure. The activities may be seen as examples of the deemphasizing operation, but they are also examples of creativity. In future developments of the dominance search model it may be interesting to delimit the role of creative activities in decision making.

KEY POINTS

- The dominance search model describes how people make decisions in real settings.
- Search for dominance structure includes these phases:
  — Preediting, or selecting relevant attributes and using them to screen alternatives.
  — Finding a promising alternatives.
  — Dominance testing, or insuring that the promising alternative is not inferior to any others.
  — Dominance structuring, or reinterpreting information to promote the dominance of the promising alternative.

Chapter 11

A Theory of Explanation-Based Decision Making

Nancy Pennington
Psychology Department
University of Colorado

Reid Hastie
Center for Research on Judgment and Policy
University of Colorado

Many important decisions in engineering, medical, legal, policy, and diplomatic domains are made under conditions where a large base of implication-rich, conditionally dependent pieces of evidence must be evaluated as a preliminary to choosing an alternative from a set of prospective courses of action. We propose that a general model of *explanation-based* decision making describes behavior under these conditions (Pennington, 1981; Pennington & Hastie, 1980, 1986, 1988, in press). According to the explanation-based model, decision makers begin their decision process by constructing a causal model to explain the available facts. Concommitant with, or subsequent to, the construction of a causal model of the evidence, the decision maker is engaged in a separate activity to learn or create a set of alternatives from which an action will be chosen. A decision is made when the causal model of the evidence is successfully matched to an alternative in the choice set. The three processing stages in the explanation-based decision model are shown in Figure 11.1.

The distinctive assumption in our explanation-based approach to decision making is the hypothesis that decision makers construct an intermediate summary representation of the evidence, and that this representation, rather than the original "raw" evidence, is the basis of the final decision. Interposition of this organization facilitates evidence comprehension, directs inferencing, enables the decision maker to reach a decision, and determines the confidence assigned to the

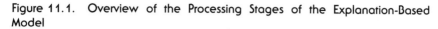

Figure 11.1.   Overview of the Processing Stages of the Explanation-Based Model

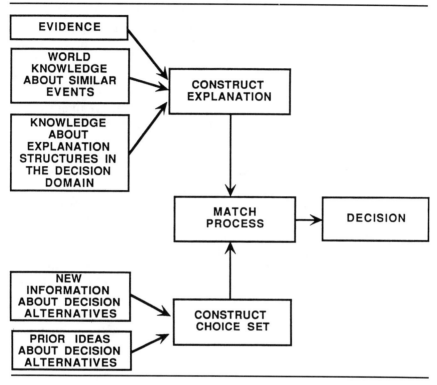

accuracy or success of the decision. This means that the locus of theoretical accounts for differences in decisions rendered by different individuals, systematic biases exhibited by many individuals, and the effects of most variations in decision task characteristics will usually lie in the evidence evaluation stage of the decision process.

The fundamental difference between our explanation-based approach and traditional algebraic approaches (e.g., cognitive algebra—Anderson, 1981; the lens model—Hammond, Stewart, Brehmer, & Steinman, 1975; utility theory—von Neumann & Morgenstern, 1947) is that we view *reasoning about the evidence* to be a central process in decision making, in contrast to an emphasis on the computation that occurs once evidence has been selected, augmented, and evaluated. Our direction in this regard parallels recent work demonstrating the role of explanation and the insufficiency of similarity computations to account for categorization behavior (Murphy & Medin, 1985; Rips, 1989), category learning (e.g., Schank, Collins, & Hunter, 1986), planning (Wilensky, 1983), and learning by generalization from examples (e.g., Lewis, 1988).

The structure of the causal model constructed to explain the evidence will be specific to the decision domain. For example, we have proposed that a juror uses narrative story structures to organize and interpret evidence in criminal trials. Different causal rules and structures will underlie an internist's causal model of a patient's condition and its precedents (Pople, 1982), an engineer's mental model of an electrical circuit (de Kleer & Brown, 1983), a merchant's image of the economic factors in a resort town (Hogarth, Michaud, & Mery, 1980), or a diplomat's causal map of the political forces in the Middle East (Axelrod, 1976); an operator's cognitive model of a nuclear power plant (Rasmusson, this volume; Woods, this volume); a military officer's image of a skirmish (Beach, this volume; Cohen, this volume; Orasanu, this volume), or a firefighter's mental model of the status of a conflagration (Klein, this volume). Thus, a primary task in research on explanation-based decision making is the identification of the type of intermediate summary structure that is imposed on evidence by decision makers in a specific domain of decision making. This is in contrast with earlier process-oriented calculational models where the theoretical focus was on attentional processes and the computations whereby separate sources of information were integrated into a unitary value or utility (Anderson, 1981; Edwards, 1954; Kahneman & Tversky, 1979).

EXPLANATION-BASED DECISION MAKING IN JUDICIAL DECISIONS

In the present chapter we concentrate on the example of juror decision making. The juror's decision task is a prototype of the tasks to which the explanation-based model should apply: First, a massive "database" of evidence is input at trial, frequently requiring several days to present. Second, the evidence comes in a scrambled sequence; usually several witnesses and exhibits convey pieces of a historical puzzle in a jumbled temporal sequence. Third, the evidence is piecemeal and gappy in its depiction of the historical events that are the focus of reconstruction: event descriptions are incomplete, usually some critical events were not observed by the available witnesses, and information about personal reactions and motivations is not present (often because of the rules of evidence). Finally, subparts of the evidence (e.g., individual sentences or statements) are interdependent in their probative implications for the verdict. The meaning of one statement cannot be assessed in isolation, because it depends on the meanings of several related statements. (See Figure 11.2.)

Evidence Summary

Empirical research has demonstrated that the juror's "explanation" of legal evidence takes the form of a "story" in which causal and intentional relations among events are prominent (Bennett & Feldman, 1981; Hutchins, 1980; Pennington, 1981; Pennington & Hastie, 1986). Because the explanation takes the form of a story, we call our applica-

Figure 11.2.   The "Story Model" for Juror Decision Making

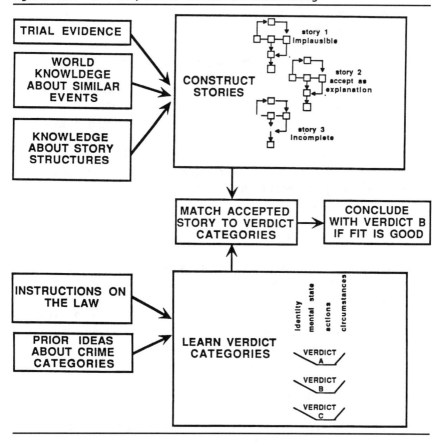

tion of the explanation-based decision-making framework to judicial decisions the Story Model (see Figure 11.2). The story is constructed from information explicitly presented at trial and knowledge possessed by the juror. Two kinds of knowledge are critical: (a) expectations about what makes a complete story, and (b) knowledge about events similar in content to those that are the topic of dispute.

General knowledge about the structure of human purposive action sequences, characterized as an *episode schema,* serves to organize events according to the causal and intentional relations among them as perceived by the juror. An episode schema specifies that a story should contain initiating events, goals, actions, consequences, and accompanying states, in a particular causal configuration (Mandler, 1980; Pennington & Hastie, 1986; Rumelhart, 1977; Stein & Glenn, 1979; Trabasso & van den Broek, 1985). Each component of an episode may also consist of an episode, so that the story the juror constructs can be represented as a hierarchy of embedded episodes. The highest level episode characterizes the most important features of "what happened." Knowledge about the structure of stories allows the juror to form an opinion concerning the *completeness* of the evidence, the extent to which a story has all its parts.

More than one story may be constructed by the juror; however, one story will usually be accepted as more coherent than the others. *Coherence* combines judgments of completeness, consistency, and plausibility. If more than one story is judged to be coherent, then the story will lack uniqueness and uncertainty will result. If there is one coherent story, this story will be accepted as the explanation of the evidence and will be instrumental in reaching a decision.

Choice Set

The decision maker's second major task is to learn or to create a set of potential solutions or action alternatives that constitute the choice set. In some decision tasks the potential actions are given to the decision maker (instructions from the trial judge on verdict alternatives) or known beforehand (treatment options available to a physician). In others, creation of alternatives is a major activity of the decision maker (for example, drafting alternate regulations for industrial waste disposal, planning alternate marketing strategies, or negotiating alternate acceptable trade contracts). These solution design tasks may invoke their own (embedded) decision tasks.

In criminal trials the information for this processing stage is given to jurors at the end of the trial in the judge's instructions on the law.

The process of learning the verdict categories is a one-trial learning task in which the material to be learned is very abstract. We hypothesize that the conceptual unit is a category (frame) defined by a list of criterial features referring to identity, mental state, circumstances, and actions linked conjunctively or disjunctively to the verdict alternative (Kaplan, 1978; Pennington & Hastie, 1981).

Match Process

The final stage in the global decision process involves matching solution alternatives to the summary evidence representation to find the most successful pairing. Confidence in the final decision will be partly determined by the goodness-of-fit of the evidence–solution pairing selected and the uniqueness of the winning combination when compared to alternative pairings. Because verdict categories are unfamiliar concepts, the classification of a story into an appropriate verdict category is likely to be a deliberate process. For example, a juror may have to decide whether a circumstance in the story such as "pinned against a wall" constitutes a good match to a required circumstance, "unable to escape," for a verdict of Not Guilty by Reason of Self-Defense.

The story classification stage involves the application of the judge's procedural instructions on the presumption of innocence and the standard of proof. That is, if not all of the verdict attributes for a given verdict category are satisfied "beyond a reasonable doubt," by events in the accepted story, then the juror should presume innocence and return a default verdict of not guilty.

Confidence in Decisions

Several aspects of the decision process influence the juror's level of certainty about the final decision. First, the accepted story is judged to be the most *coherent,* but the level of coherence will affect confidence. Thus, if the story lacks completeness, consistency, or plausibility, confidence in the story and therefore in the verdict will be diminished. Second, if a story lacks *uniqueness,* that is, there is more than one coherent story, then certainty concerning the accuracy of any one explanation will be lowered (Einhorn & Hogarth, 1986). Finally, the *goodness-of-fit* between the accepted story and the best-fitting verdict category will influence confidence in the verdict decision.

In summary, our application of the general explanation-based decision model to legal decisions is based on the hypothesis that jurors impose a narrative story organization on trial information, in which causal and intentional relations between events are central (Bennett & Feldman, 1981; Pennington, 1981; Pennington & Hastie, 1986). Meaning is assigned to trial evidence through the incorporation of that evidence into one or more plausible accounts or stories describing "what happened" during events testified to at the trial. The story organization facilitates evidence comprehension and enables jurors to reach a predeliberation verdict decision.

EMPIRICAL RESEARCH

Our initial research on the Story Model provided descriptions of mental representations of evidentiary information and verdict information at one point in time during the decision process (Pennington & Hastie, 1986). In that research we established that the evidence summaries constructed by jurors had story structure (and not other plausible structures); that verdict representations looked like feature lists (or simple frames); and that jurors who chose different verdicts had constructed different stories such that there was a distinct causal configuration of events that constituted a story corresponding to each verdict category. Moreover, jurors choosing different verdicts did not have systematically different verdict representations, nor did they apply different classification criteria. Thus verdict decisions covary with story structures but do not covary with verdict learning or story classification. However, the interview method used in this research precluded strong inferences concerning the spontaneity of story construction the functional role of stories in the decision phase.

In a second empirical study we established that decision makers spontaneously constructed causal accounts of the evidence in the legal decision task (Pennington & Hastie, 1988). In this study, subjects' responses to sentences presented in a recognition memory task were used to draw conclusions about subjects' postdecision representations of evidence. Subjects were expected to "recognize" as having been presented as trial evidence sentences from the story associated with their decision, with a higher probability than to recognize sentences from stories associated with other (rejected) decisions. This implies that hit rates (correct recognitions) and false alarm rates (false recognitions) for sentences from each story can be predicted from subjects' verdicts. These predictions were confirmed; verdict decisions predicted the high hit and false alarm rates found for sentences in the subjects' stories. Thus, a different method, subject population, and stimulus materials yielded results converging with the interview study conclusions about the correlation between memory structure and decision outcome. Even though we can conclude that story representations were constructed *spontaneously,* the causal role of stories in decisions is still not established because subjects could decide on a verdict and then (spontaneously) justify it to themselves by constructing a coherent story.

A third experiment was conducted to study the effects of variations in the order of evidence presentation on judgments. Our primary goal was to test the claim that the construction of stories in evidence evaluation *causes* decisions. A secondary goal was to determine whether story coherence and uniqueness influence judgments of confidence in the correctness of verdicts. The "logic" of the experiment was summarized in our hypothesis that (manipulated) ease of story construction would influence verdict decisions; easy-to-construct stories would result in more decisions in favor of the corresponding verdicts.

Stories were considered easy to construct when the evidence was ordered in a temporal and causal sequence that matched the occurrence of the original events (story order; Baker, 1978). Stories were considered difficult to construct when the presentation order did not match the sequence of the original events. We based the nonstory order on the sequence of evidence as conveyed by witnesses in the original trial (witness order). Mock-jurors listened to a tape recording of a 100-sentence summary of the trial evidence (50 prosecution statements and 50 defense statements), followed by a judge's charge to choose between a Murder verdict and a Not Guilty verdict. The 50 prosecution statements, constituting the First Degree Murder story identified in our initial interview study (Pennington & Hastie, 1986), were presented either in a story order or a witness order. Similarly, the defense statements, the Not Guilty story, were presented in one of the two orders creating a four-cell factorial design. In all four order conditions, the prosecution evidence preceded the defense evidence as per standard legal procedure. After listening to the tape recorded trial materials, the subjects completed a questionnaire indicating their verdict, confidence in the verdict, and their perceptions of the strengths of the prosecution and defense cases.

As predicted, subjects were likeliest to convict the defendant when the prosecution evidence was presented in story order and the defense evidence was presented in witness order (78% chose guilty), and they were least likely to convict when the prosecution evidence was in witness order and defense was in story order (31% chose guilty). Conviction rates were intermediate in conditions where both sides of the case were in story order (59% convictions) or both were in witness order (63% convictions). Furthermore, the perceived strength of one side of the case depended on both the order of evidence for that side *and for the other side* of the case. This finding supports our claim that the *uniqueness* of the best-fitting story is one important basis for confidence in the decision.

In our explanation-based model the decision process is divided into three stages: construction of a summary explanation, determination of decision alternatives, and mapping the explanation onto a best-fitting decision alternative. This subtask framework is in contrast to the uniform online updating computation or the unitary memory-based calculation hypothesized in most alternative approaches (cf. Hastie & Park, 1986). Furthermore, we diverge sharply from traditional approaches with our emphasis on the structure of memory representations as the key determinant of decisions. We also depart from the common assumption that, when causal reasoning is involved in judgment, it can be described by algebraic, stochastic, or logical computations that lead directly to a decision (e.g., Anderson, 1974; Einhorn & Hogarth, 1986; Kelley, 1973). In our model causal reasoning plays a subordinate but critical role by guiding inferences in evidence evaluation and construction of the intermediate explanation (Pennington & Hastie, in press).

EXPLANATION-BASED DECISION MAKING IN OTHER DOMAINS

The question of the generality of the explanation-based decision-making framework can be divided into two parts, one concerned with the pervasiveness of explanation-based decision strategies, and the other concerned with the extent to which story structures will serve as explanation frames in other explanation-based decision tasks. In the introduction to this chapter, we outlined the explanation-based decision strategy and suggested that it applied to several complex natural decision tasks from the domains of law, business, diplomacy, medicine, and engineering. To date we have only conducted research in the legal domain where we have shown it does apply. Evidence from other research programs in psychology and in artificial intelligence supports our claim for the generality of the explanation-based decision strategy, particularly in areas of medical diagnosis and economic reasoning.

Medical Diagnosis

Medical diagnosis was one of the earliest targets of expert systems research in artificial intelligence, which had the goal of reproducing expertise in subareas of medical diagnosis (Clancey & Shortliffe, 1984). In these systems (e.g., MYCIN) the patient was described as a list of findings (symptoms) about the patient's condition. A set of rules described known associations (with a particular degree of certainty) between findings and diseases. The diagnosis, or interpretation of the patient's condition was rendered in the form of a list of possible diseases ranked by a degree of belief in each. Although this conception of diagnosis captures some aspects of expert diagnosis on routine problems, it proved inadequate as a model of human reasoning for diagnosis over a large range of problems.

An important departure from MYCIN were systems (e.g., Patil, Szolovits, & Schwartz, 1981; Clancey & Letsinger, 1981; Weiss, Kulikowski, Amarel, & Safir, 1978) that viewed clinical problem solving as a process of constructing an explanation of the findings. In ABEL (Patil et al., 1981), this explanation is called a *patient-specific model,* and it includes data about the patient as well as the program's hypothetical interpretations of these data in a multilevel causal network. Clancey (1988) describes this view of diagnosis in detail:

> diagnosis is not just a label, but constitutes a *model of the patient.* This model is a causal story of what has happened to bring the patient to his current state of illness. The general questions of diagnosis regarding travel, job history, medications, etc., seek to circumscribe the external agents, or internal changes . . . that may have affected the patient's body. . . . In trying to establish a causal story of an infectious disease, the physician looks for general evidence of exposure, dissemination, and impaired immunoresponse—all of which are necessary for an infection to take place, regardless of the specific agent . . . Constructing a model of the patient is often described informally as forming a 'picture of the patient.' The physician establishes the sequence in which findings were manifested and factors this with information about prior problems and therapies, using their time relations to match possible causal connections . . . Thus a physician is not just matching a set of symptoms to a disease; he is matching the order in which the symptoms appeared and how they changed over time to his knowledge of disease processes. . . . We must have some way of viewing the competing diseases. In Neomycin, we call this the *disease process frame.* Its *slots* are the features of any disease—where it occurs, when it began, its first symptom, how the symptoms change over time, whether it is a local or 'systematic,' and so on. (pp. 359–361)

The correspondence between this description of medical diagnosis and the components of the explanation-based framework we have developed is quite close. The physician constructs an explanation of the patient findings in terms of one or more disease categories. Both the explanation and the diagnostic disease category have a well-specified causal structure. To some extent this is general across disease categories, as outlined above with the "who, what, when, where, how" components specified in Clancey's description. Some parts of this explanation structure (mainly the how) will apply only within particular subspecialties of medicine. For example, infectious disease diagnoses will have a form of exposure and a form of dissemination as integral parts of the explanation (Clancey, 1988) in contrast to reasoning about equilibrium processes in malfunctions of the kidney (Kuipers & Kassirer, 1984) where explanations involve reference to substances causing pressures which result in flows.

There is some empirical evidence for this view of medical diagnosis provided primarily by studies of physicians talking aloud while making a diagnosis or while explaining a diagnosis (Lesgold et al., 1988; Lesgold, 1989; Groen & Patel, 1988; Kassirer, 1989; Kassirer, Kuipers, & Gorry, 1982; Kassirer & Kopelman, 1987, 1989). The evidence supports the general claims that explanations are constructed in the course of diagnosis and that explanations have regular structures, at least within medical subspecialties.

Economic Reasoning

In the domain of economics, Riesbeck (1984) has modeled the reasoning of experts and novices in responding to an economic forecasting task (based on protocols collected by Salter, 1983). The experts' long-term knowledge structures are modeled as a graph of directed signed connections between economic quantities (see also Axelrod's, 1976, discussion of "cognitive maps," Jungermann & Thuring's, 1987, "mental models," and Hendrickx, Vlek, & Oppewal's, 1989, "causal scenarios" for related analyses). In responding to a prediction question such as "What happens to the federal deficit if interest rates increase?", the expert reasons by applying certain search heuristics to his or her long-term memory knowledge structure and constructing an explanation of the causal relations among the particular values of the economic quantities under discussion.

For the novice in economic reasoning, Riesbeck (1984) proposed that long-term knowledge structures take the form of assumptions about the hierarchies of goals and subgoals of economic actors. Riesbeck notes:

> The basic problem with novices' reasoning is that it is very much like the reasoning used in understanding stories or everyday life. Story under-

standing heuristics fail in economic reasoning, not because economic actors don't have goals, but because there are too many goals and too many interactions. (p. 58)

This analysis of economic reasoning is supported by data from a study of urban planning decisions by Hogarth et al. (1980) in which various actors concerned with the development of a French town were interviewed. The developers' cognitive maps of the situation were summarized as graphs of directed signed connections between economic quantities (similar to Reisbeck's "expert economists" described above). The homeowners' cognitive maps directly reflected their personal economic goals, such as getting a good price for their homes, and the opposing goals of the greedy developers, thus showing actor–goal relationships like those of the novice "economists" in the Reisbeck and Salter analysis.

In summary, these studies of diagnosis, prediction, and planning in the domains of medicine and economics show that decision makers construct causal explanations of the evidence, that these explanations have uniform structures for experts and novices, and the causal explanations constructed directly correspond to the judgments and actions of the decision makers.

CONCLUDING COMMENTS

Our approach to the problem of how to generalize conclusions from our research to new settings, tasks, and subject populations is to begin by assuming that the establishment of a phenomenon, such as a cause–effect relationship, in one setting is a prima facie argument for its generality. Then the projectability of the result should be evaluated by examining each conceptual dimension along which variation occurs from one setting to the other. Our program of empirical research relies on simulations of the juror's decision task in laboratory and field settings. We believe that this combination of low- and high-fidelity methods has yielded a stronger foundation for a theory of actual jurors' decisions that would have been possible with only one method.

It is *not* our claim that explanation-based decision making is the only decision-making strategy available to decision makers, nor do we claim it will be applied everywhere. For example, in the popular laboratory research tasks where subjects are asked to assess the attractiveness of lottery gambles, it is difficult to see why a subject would be motivated to construct a complex causal model of the evidence or to reason about causal relations concerning outcomes that are explicitly determined by mechanized random generators such as game spinners or bingo cages.

In other laboratory tasks where a decision is made on a relatively small set of independent evidence items, and where the required judgment dimension is unidimensional and known prior to hearing evidence, we believe that algebraic models such as those based on linear additive, anchor-and-adjust updating processes provide an adequate picture of the judgment strategy (Anderson, 1981; Einhorn & Hogarth, 1986; Hammond et al., 1975; Lopes, 1982b). Even in some complex judgments, such as diagnostic tasks that are made routinely, in which the configuration of evidence has been seen many times before, explanation-based decision making will not occur. For example, for certain instances of medical diagnosis a familiar pattern will be recognized immediately without need for intermediate reasoning or interpretation. We believe that this is also the case for "consumer" choice tasks in which a person chooses, for example, which car to buy or which apartment to rent. In such cases, where attributes of choice alternatives are explicit and unambiguous and the choice is one that has been made before, we would not expect interpretation of the evidence (attributes) to play a large role. However, for choices in which the person is a relative novice—the important dimensions are unknown and the choice is made for the first time (e.g., the first time a house is purchased, the first job selected after training)—we would expect that explanation-based strategies would come into play.

If there is one characteristic of our program of research that distinguishes it from the many recent efforts to study the manner in which complex knowledge structures serve as mediators for relationships among evidence, goals, and decisions, it is our intense focus on the specific (narrative) structures of the hypothesized mediating representation. Critics of the "mental models" approach to reasoning, planning, and decision-making processes have claimed that many theorists have failed to clearly specify the nature of these knowledge representations, and that, thus, their theories are vacuous and untestable (Rips, 1986; Rouse & Morris, 1986). We agree and hope that our research can provide one example of a rigorous approach to these issues that yields a useful theory of important decision-making phenomena.

KEY POINTS

- The model of explanation-based decision making applies to situations like juror reasoning and medical diagnosis, where a great deal of implication-rich information must be evaluated.

- In such situations, decision makers try to organize the information by arranging it into a story, which mediates all processes leading to a final decision.
- Decision makers also learn or create a set of alternatives from which they will select an action.
- Decision makers choose the alternative that best matches their explanation.
- The explanation-based model differs from traditional algebraic approaches in that reasoning about the evidence is the critical process, not performance of calculations on the evidence.

Section C

Methods of Naturalistic Decision Research

Chapter 12

Naturalistic Decision Making From a Brunswikian Viewpoint: Its Past, Present, Future*

Kenneth R. Hammond
Center for Research on Judgment and Policy
University of Colorado

There is ample ground for doubting the success and thus the appropriateness of conventional research doctrine in psychology, and naturalism may well be the road to follow. Indeed, a well-respected psychologist, speaking of research on memory, declared: "If X is an interesting or socially significant aspect of memory, then psychologists have hardly ever studied X" (Neisser, 1978, p. 4). Neisser also concluded that "the naturalistic [note parallel with the present volume] study of memory is an idea whose time has come" (1978, p. 3). And there are many efforts to implement the "naturalistic" approach in many areas of psychology (see Appendix for examples).

But conventional psychological research methods are strongly rooted in academia; it should not be expected that challenges to what is often one's strongest raison d'être will be gracefully received—and, in my experience, they are not. Although I have been—and remain—a dedicated critic of psychology's conventional methodological doctrine, it is practically useless (and methodologically vacuous) to argue that research should reflect the characteristics of the "real world." More-

* This work was supported in part by the Office of Basic Research, Army Research Institute, Contract MDA903-86-C-0142, Work Unit Number 2Q161102B74F. The views, opinions, and findings contained in this article are those of the author and should not be construed as an official Department of the Army position, policy, or decision, unless so designated by other official documentation. I thank Berndt Brehmer, Michael Doherty, Reid Hastie, C. R. B. Joyce, Cynthia Lusk, Kim Vicente, and the editors of this volume for their comments and criticism.

over, such expressions are unnecessary; as I will show, there *is* an alternative to conventional methodology; theory and method for addressing "interesting and socially significant" problems have been available and have been applied for decades.

In what follows I provide a broad historical context in which the topic of this volume—naturalistic decision making—is discussed from the point of view of a Brunswikian psychologist. I show how Wundt's choice of research methodology and that of his peers a century ago established the current research doctrine in psychology, indicate how that choice was challenged by Brunswik a half-century ago, and describe how the difference between Wundt and Brunswik has been brought into sharp focus by current theory and research in the field of judgment and decision making. Finally, I will indicate my expectations of how Brunswikian research will develop in the future.

PAST CHOICES FOR AND AGAINST NATURALISM

Wundt's Choice

Wundt is generally acknowledged to be the principal founder of scientific, that is, experimental, psychology. It is therefore instructive and interesting to note that, in his efforts to choose the proper methodological course for psychology, he described the issues in much the same way as they are described today. He drew a distinction between the exact, lawful nature of the hidden cause–effect relations to be discovered by psychologists and the chaotic surface circumstances that obscure such relations and thus confuse *both* the scientist and the behaving organism. Wundt argued that the obfuscating surface features of the environment should be eliminated through the use of *experiments;* Gillis and Schneider (1966) provide an eloquent, succinct description of Wundt's explanation for his choice.

> [Wundt recognized] that there existed both a regularity in nature that was inaccessible to the organism, and a complex, irregular pattern to which he was customarily exposed, [and thus] Wundt was faced with a methodological choice. He could choose to investigate the organism-environment relationship as the former actually experienced it, or he could choose to seek out those relationships that he believed obtained somewhere beyond the organism's ken. He chose, of course, the latter. And that choice required the use of an experimental technique that served to disentangle causal influences. (p. 218)

They then take note of one of Wundt's most significant remarks, quoted in Ribot (1886, p. 192): "By experiment . . . we strip the phenomenon of all its accessory conditions, which we can change at will, and measure."

Helmholtz, Wundt's contemporary, went further. Not only did he wish to avoid the confusion and complexity of cause–effect relations observed at the surface, he argued that: "It is just those cases that are *not* [emphasis added] in accordance with reality which are particularly instructive for discovering the laws of the processes by which normal perception originates." Lest readers think that such quotations are moldy methodological curiosities dug out of history books no one reads, they should know that I took this 1881 quotation from an article published in 1983 by Tversky and Kahneman (p. 313). It was used by them to defend their research methods, and their choice of tasks to present to their subjects, to uncover biases in judgment and decision making.

Thus, Wundt and Helmholtz chose to study those "deep" cause–effect relations between environment and organism that would not be apparent unless *"we strip the phenomenon of all its accessory conditions* [exactly what students are taught today], which we can change at will [through experiment in the laboratory], and measure" (Gillis & Schneider, 1966, p. 218). Wundt's argument is as modern and contemporary as today's instruction in introductory psychology and in the design of experiments.

Brunswik thought Wundt made the wrong choice, however. As a result, he devoted his life to arguing that to "strip the phenomenon of all its accessory conditions" (all those chaotic surface conditions) was to strip the research of its proper subject matter.

Brunswik's Choice

I have described elsewhere (Hammond, 1966, 1990; Hammond, McClelland, & Mumpower, 1980; Hammond & Wascoe, 1980), Brunswik's analytical treatment of the history of methodological doctrine in psychology, in which he directly challenged the wisdom of the choice made by Wundt, Helmholtz, and their many intellectual descendants (see Brunswik, 1943, 1952, 1956, for examples; see also Brehmer, 1984; Gigerenzer, 1987; Smith, 1986). Therefore, I will not repeat Brunswik's arguments here; rather, I will merely indicate through quotation and paraphrase his general argument that, since the behaving organism does not come in direct contact with the hidden (exact) laws controlling the environment, it must cope with the multiple, confusing, inexact "surface" events controlled by "many laws." This choice led to the development of a theory of *probabilistic functionalism*. The methodological counterpart to this theory is *representative design*. For only by presenting those irregular conditions to the behaving subject can we discover how the organism achieves a stable relation with its environment *despite* the uncertainty engendered by the irregular conditions at the surface. As Brunswik put it in 1954:

> So long as the organism does not develop, or fails in a given context to utilize completely, the powers of a full-fledged physicist observer and analyst, his environment remains for all practical purposes a semierratic medium; it is no more than partially controlled and no more than probabilistically predictable. The functionalistic approach in psychology must take cognizance of this basic limitation of the adjustive apparatus; it must link behavior and environment statistically. (Hammond, 1966, p. 509)

Thus, Brunswik agreed with Wundt that the behaving organism does not have access to the cause–effect laws controlling the organism's natural environment. In contradistinction to Wundt, however, it is precisely because that irregular, confusing concatenation of events provides the environment with which the organism must cope that we must not strip those irregular events away. *That* irregular, uncertain, confusing environment is the environment of interest, not the sanitized environment of the psychophysics laboratory or the perception laboratory of illusions and other "impoverished stimulus" conditions. And that is the type of environment that Brunswik and those who agreed with him attempt to employ, to simulate, to construct, and to present to human subjects. Wundt's choice led to the doctrine of the systematic, a priori decomposition design (hold all variables constant, that is, "strip away accessory conditions," except one), whereas Brunswik's choice led to a design that includes a *formal* representation of all those conditions toward which a generalization is intended; representative design thus refers to the logical requirement of representing in the experiment, or study, the conditions toward which the results are intended to generalize. Ecological situations, or ecological objects, should be specified, if not sampled, for the same reason subjects are specified or sampled—generalization beyond the circumstances studied, whether in the laboratory or outside of it, requires it.

Contemporary endorsement for the general principle of representative design can be found in a monograph by Paul Meehl, one of psychology's foremost methodologists, in which he states: "One badly neglected sampling problem, probably more important than the sampling of organisms to which such meticulous attention is conventionally paid, is the sampling of *situations,* which should be in some sense 'representative' of the statistical ecology of the species studied" (1990, p. 41).

Meehl's comment is virtually a paraphrase of Brunswik's (1956) remark that "proper sampling of situations and problems may in the end be more important than proper sampling of subjects, considering the fact that individuals are probably on the whole much more alike than are situations among one another" (p. 39). Further, "Each situation is a 'variate package,' that is, a more or less incidental combination of specific values along a large, and indeed unknown number of dimensions. Ecologies, and the situations that constitute them . . . exhibit consistencies and 'habits' all of their own . . . we may 'know' them and like or dislike them as we do our fellow men" (1956, p. 139).

In short, Wundt and Brunswik differed in their justification of the arrangement of variables in research at the most basic level. That difference is alive and pertinent today, as the publication of this book—and others—demonstrates. Not only did Wundt and Brunswik differ in their methodological premises, they differed in their metatheoretical premises. Wundt looked to physics for his model of the psychological science to be (thus *psychophysics*); Brunswik looked to Darwinian functionalism (thus *probabilistic functionalism*). (See Hammond, 1990, for contemporary consequences of these metatheoretical and methodological commitments.)

Brunswik Versus Wundt in the Study of Judgment and Decision Making

The study of human judgment and decision making brought the difference between Brunswik's choice and Wundt's choice into sharp focus. Early researchers studied "judgment" precisely as Wundt instructed them; as psychophysicists, they were to strip away all "accessory conditions," and they did. They measured, for example, "just noticeable differences" in various sensory domains under strictly controlled conditions. And much contemporary research in judgment and decision making continues to favor the basic feature of Wundt's choice. As pointed out by Hammond et al. (1980, pp. 21–29) in their review of the origins of judgment and decision research, the early work in decision theory by Edwards (as well as the contemporary widely read work by Tversky and Kahneman, Norman Anderson, and others) chose the psychophysics of judgment as a point of departure. (See, in particular, articles on "prospect theory" in which "psychophysical" functions are presented, e.g., Kahneman & Tversky, 1979.)

But those who were persuaded by Brunswik's criticism of Wundt's choice rejected psychophysics. As Darwinian functionalists, they approached the topic of judgment and decision making by attempting to *represent* the causal texture of the environment in the research circumstances presented to their subjects. In the formulation of *social judgment theory* (SJT), my colleagues and I (Hammond, Stewart, Brehmer, & Steinmann, 1975) described the new approach as follows:

> Knowledge of the environment is difficult to acquire because of causal ambiguity—because of the probabilistic, entangled relations among environmental variables. Tolman and Brunswik called attention to the critical role of causal ambiguity in their article, "The Organism and the Causal Texture of the Environment" (1935), in which they emphasized the fact that the organism in its normal intercourse with its environment must cope with *numerous, interdependent, multiformal relations* among variables which are *partly relevant* and *partly irrelevant* to its purpose, which carry only a *limited amount of dependability,* and which are *organized in a variety of ways.* The problem for the organism, therefore, is to know its environment under these complex circumstances. In the effort to do so, the organism brings a variety of processes (generally labeled *cognitive*), such as perception, learning, and thinking, to bear on the problem of reducing causal ambiguity. As a part of this effort, human beings often attempt to manipulate variables (by experiments, for example) and sometimes succeed—in such a manner as to eliminate ambiguity. But when the variables in question *cannot* be manipulated, human beings must use their cognitive resources unaided by manipulation or experiment. They must do the best they can by passive rather than active means to arrive at a conclusion regarding a state of affairs clouded by causal ambiguity. They must, in short, exercise their judgment. Human judgment is a cognitive activity of last resort.
>
> It may seem odd to remind the readers of this volume of the circumstances which require human judgment, yet it is essential that we do so, for it is precisely these circumstances which are so often omitted from studies of human judgment. If we are to understand how human beings cope with judgment tasks, however, not only must such ambiguity be present in the conditions under which human judgment is studied, but causal ambiguity must itself be represented within the framework of a theory of human judgment (Brunswik, 1952, 1956; Hammond, 1955). (p. 272)

Thus, the language of the above quotation urges the inclusion of the ambiguity of the environment unsanitized by the demands of Wundtian doctrine. But the ambiguous environment must somehow be described, and the quotation presents the pretheoretical concepts SJT theorists chose to use in their effort to describe such environments quantitatively, a matter to which we now turn.

SOME PRESENT CONSEQUENCES OF BRUNSWIK'S CHOICE

"Naturalism" demands a theory that will enable us to describe the confusing concatenation of events that disguise the regularities of our world and a methodology that will allow us to understand adaptation to them. Brunswik, of course, provided both: the theory was named *probabilistic functionalism* and the methodology was named *representative design* (Brunswik, 1955).

The Lens Model

In order to see why this model (see Figure 12.1) of the environment was chosen by SJT researchers, think of how an irregular, uncertain environment might be described. First, the problems must offer *many cues,* as there must not be one completely dependable, palpable, surface event (cue) from which one can infer with certainty the unseen, impalpable, depth event (Y_e). Second, the relations between cues and Y_e must be less than perfectly dependable. That circumstance is reflected in the uncertainty between cue and criterion shown in the lens model as r_e, the *ecological validity* of the cue. Specifically, the correla-

Figure 12.1.   Schematic illustration of the relation of achievement (r_a) and ecological validities; of cues ($r_{e,i}$) and cue utilization ($r_{s,i}$): an a posteriori decomposition of a person's judgment process.

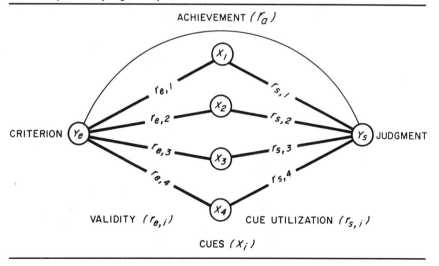

tion r_e must be less than unity. Third, there must be correlations—or at least the possibility of correlations—greater than zero between the cues. Fourth, irreducible uncertainty should exist—or at least be allowed to exist—between the cue data and the criterion (Y_e) data.

For example, in a study of highway engineers, experts were asked to judge the *safety* of 40 highway segments that were described/measured in 10 dimensions (e.g., lane width, shoulder width, curves per mile, etc.) which served as *cues* to the hidden (i.e., unknown to the engineers) *criterion* (safety of each segment measured in terms of accident rate averaged over seven years). The degree of certainty or *ecological validity* of each cue was measured in terms of the correlation between the cue and the safety criterion, and the intercorrelation among the cues was ascertained. The *uncertainty* of the system as a whole was measured in terms of the multiple correlation between the set of cues and the criterion. (See Hammond, 1988; Hammond, Hamm, Grassia, & Pearson, 1987; for a complete description.)

Substantive Versus Formal Descriptions of Environmental and Cognitive Systems

It is essential to note that, from its beginning, SJT intended to provide a *formal* theory of environmental tasks; it is not a *substantive* theory, nor does it wish to be (Hammond, 1966, pp. 68ff.). That is, SJT offers a general description that is independent of the substantive materials of any particular judgment task. SJT researchers never limit the description of a task to its content (e.g., fire-fighting, medical diagnosis, etc.), in contrast to research that centers on "knowledge-based" judgments. Content is of no interest to SJT researchers *except* for studies that examine the interaction between form and specific content (see, e.g., Adelman, 1981). Present naturalistic approaches err by emphasizing content over formal descriptions of the environment.

In addition to providing a quantitative *environmental* model, SJT provides a quantitative model of *cognitive* functioning, the form of which parallels the environmental model (see Figure 12.1). Both the properties of environmental systems and the properties of the cognitive systems of the subjects who must cope with them are linked by the *lens model equation* (LME) (see Hammond et al., 1975; Tucker, 1964). In short, the LME was constructed to fulfill the need for (a) a formal description of those environmental circumstances Wundt wished to be stripped away, (b) the cognitive system that is applied to them, and (c) the relation between the two.

These concepts (and others) were put forward in the 1960s (and earlier; see Hammond, 1955) and were found to be adequate for describing uncertain environments, not only in the laboratory, but outside the laboratory as well, some of which I now describe.

Multiple Cue Probability Learning and Cognitive Feedback

Brehmer and his colleagues (see especially Brehmer, 1979; Brehmer & Joyce, 1988), Doherty and his colleagues (York, Doherty, & Kamouri, 1987), my colleagues and I (see especially Hammond & Summers, 1972), and many others used these descriptors to study an entirely new problem in the psychology of learning, namely *multiple-cue probability learning* (MCPL). This topic was chosen because it represents in a *formal* manner some—but not all—of the properties of judgment tasks deemed to be representative of those encountered by human beings in their various habitats (e.g., many interdependent cues with ecological validities of less than one).

Studies of MCPL were productive in unexpected ways documented in Brehmer and Joyce (1988). Most significant, however, was the discovery that providing the learner with *cognitive feedback—* information about formal aspects of the task (e.g., cue validities, function forms, etc.)—resulted in rapid learning under conditions of uncertainty, whereas outcome feedback (providing the correct answer) resulted in slow, "stupid" learning (see Balzer, Doherty, & O'Connor, 1989, for a review of research on cognitive feedback). No other result from the SJT research illustrates so clearly the value of the representation of theoretically specified formal properties of task circumstances—in this case multiple (fallible) cues and irreducible uncertainty. For although the importance of cognitive feedback was discovered in laboratory circumstances, it has been put to good use in circumstances outside the laboratory (see Wigton, 1988; Wigton, Poses, Collins, & Cebul, 1990, for examples of teaching students and physicians to improve their diagnostic accuracy).

Thus SJT offers a theory that provides the measurable, quantitative terms that enable us to distinguish between various task circumstances, and thus enables us to make different predictions of cognitive activity for situations differentiated by the theory—irrespective of the substantive characteristics of the situation. In this way, SJT offers generalization to the naturalistic approach.

Policy Capturing

Another feature of laboratory research derived from the lens model that has been successfully applied to a wide variety of naturalistic situations is *policy capturing*. This term refers to "capturing"—that is, formally describing—the policy an individual uses to form a judgment regarding any object, event, or circumstance. The person's policy is described in terms parallel to those used to describe a task environment. Thus, the judgment policy used by a highway engineer (see above) to appraise the *safety* of a highway was described in terms of (a) the *cues* (lane width, shoulder width, etc.) he used, (b) the *weight* that he placed on each cue (measured in terms of the regression weights between each cue and his judgment), (c) the form (linear, nonlinear) of the relation between the cue and his judgment, and (d) the degree of uncertainty in his judgment system (measured in terms of the predictability of his judgments).

Policy capturing was demonstrated in 1955 in connection with studies of clinical psychologists and anesthesiologists and has been widely applied outside the laboratory ever since. (The studies are too numerous to cite here; I offer the following citations only to indicate the breadth of applications; see Cooksey, Freebody, & Bennett, 1991, for a clever innovation, the application of the lens model to a study of children's spelling problems; Dalgleish, 1988, for a study of social workers' judgments of child abuse; Fisch, Hammond, Joyce, & O'Reilly, 1981, for studies of judgments of depression; Kirwan, Chaput de Saintonge, Joyce, & Currey, 1984, for an analysis of rheumatologists' judgments; Stewart, Middleton, & Ely, 1983, for an application to an ecological problem; see also Brehmer & Joyce, 1988, and Hammond & Wascoe, 1980, for numerous other examples.)

Conflict Resolution

The results of research on the above three topics—MCPL, cognitive feedback, and policy capturing—were applied to laboratory studies of interpersonal conflict and interpersonal learning that began in 1966 (Hammond, 1966; Hammond & Grassia, 1985). Our most important naturalistic test involved reducing a bitter, public dispute among city councilmen and various interest groups (Hammond & Adelman, 1976). Success in this and subsequent studies (see Darling & Mumpower, 1990; McCartt & Rohrbaugh, 1989; Mumpower, Schuman, & Zumbolo, 1988; Rohrbaugh, 1984) have led to confidence that the laboratory research developed from the lens model framework and its concomitant quantitative expressions provide sufficient power for generalization to circumstances outside the laboratory. Indeed, cognitive feedback and policy capturing are regularly used at the Rockefeller Institute of Government for reducing policy disputes in the public sector (see Milter & Rohrbaugh, 1988; Reagan & Rohrbaugh, in press; see also Harmon & Rohrbaugh, 1990; Rohrbaugh, 1988). Analysis in terms of the formal properties of the task is the key element in such generalizations.

Cognitive Continuum Theory

It is essential to note that each parameter of the LME is a continuous variable. This means that conditions may vary yet remain within the capacity of the LME to describe them. And this means that the LME possesses the capacity to distinguish among, and provide exact descriptions of, *various* judgment tasks. Thus we may inquire into the effect of *experimentally* increasing or decreasing degrees of ambiguity, that is, the uncertainty between cue and criterion, amount of the entanglement (intercorrelation) among cues, as well as other changes in those task conditions Wundt wished to strip away. In addition, we may make post hoc, or retrospective, analyses of various judgment tasks that persons have encountered, or predictions about behavior in tasks persons will encounter. Indeed, it is now easy to see that task conditions can be located on a *continuum* that ranges from those that are highly intuition inducing to those that are highly analysis inducing by specifying values of the parameters of the LME. And once we have determined the location of a task on that continuum we shall be prepared to offer predictions of behavior in response to its location. That argument was followed up in what I have called *cognitive continuum theory*.

The concept of a cognitive continuum was introduced in 1973 (Hammond & Brehmer, 1973), further developed in 1980 (Hammond, 1980b), and first empirically employed by Hammond et al. (1987).

The utility of this premise was tested in the context of the study of expert highway engineers. Depth and surface features of three tasks were selected on a best guess basis for their ability to induce three different modes of cognition on the cognitive continuum mentioned above. The arrangement of task conditions was not left to guesswork, however; a quantitative method was used to *order* the tasks on a task continuum index from the intuitive to analytical pole of the index. (See Table 12.1 for a list of task properties inducing intuition and analysis.) At issue was the question of whether the tasks (at both depth and surface levels) induced the predicted type of cognitive activity measured by its location on the cognitive continuum index. (See Table 12.2 for a list of cognitive properties indicating intuitive and analytical cognition.) This hypothesis (and others) was tested for each engineer separately (each of whom spent roughly 20 hours in this

Table 12.1.   Inducement of Intuition and Analysis by Task Conditions

Task Characteristic	Intuition-Inducing State of Task Characteristic	Analysis-Inducing State of Task Characteristic
1. Number of cues	large (>5)	small
2. Measurement of cues	perceptual measurement	objective, reliable measurement
3. Distribution of cue values	continuous, highly variable distribution	unknown distribution; cues are dichotomous; values are discrete
4. Redundancy among cues	high redundancy	low redundancy
5. Decomposition of task	low	high
6. Degree of certainty in task	low certainty	high certainty
7. Relation between cues and criterion	linear	nonlinear
8. Weighting of cues in environmental model	equal	unequal
9. Availability of organizing principle	unavailable	available
10. Display of cues	simultaneous display	sequential display
11. Time period	brief	long

study) over nine task conditions: Results generally conformed with predictions (see Hammond et al., 1987, for details).

Thus, SJT researchers took both Wundt and Brunswik seriously; the unmanaged world does offer confusing uncertain events at the surface, as Wundt and Brunswik agreed. But we followed Brunswik's precept that, if we wish to generalize the results of our research beyond the conditions contained in our research situation, that situation must be formally representative of the circumstances to which we intend the results to apply. SJT researchers believed then, and believe now, that

Table 12.2.   Properties of Intuition and Analysis

	Intuition	Analysis
Cognitive Control	low	high
Rate of Data Processing	rapid	slow
Conscious Awareness	low	high
Organizing Principle	weighted average	task specific
Errors	normally distributed	few, but large
Confidence	high confidence in answer; low confidence in method	low confidence in answer; high confidence in method

they were, and are, studying judgment and decision making under exactly those circumstances the present proponents of naturalistic decision making wish to emphasize. And although the advocates of naturalism do not explicitly use the concept of representative design—and all that it implies—they should, because they cannot carry out their work otherwise.

FUTURE: COGNITIVE CONTINUUM THEORY EXTENDED

Applications of Brunswikian Principles to "Real Decisions" in the "Real World" by "Real People"

All of the expressions in quotations in the above heading should be proscribed, eliminated from the language of serious students of judgment and decision making; they merely reflect the emotional tones of a revolt against what many see as a sterile science. They should be replaced by theories that include terms necessary to describe (a) the properties of task environments, (b) the properties of cognitive systems, and (c) the relation between them. SJT and cognitive continuum theory provide the basic principles (derived from Brunswik) for doing this. Can these theories usefully address the kind of judgment and decision situations the advocates of "real-world" research have in mind?

In what follows I indicate how cognitive continuum theory and its extensions make possible both retrospective and prospective analyses of human judgment over a wide range of conditions without invoking such terms as "real world," "real decisions," or "real people."

Oscillation Between Intuition and Analysis

Once the researcher permits the element of *time* to enter his or her research situation, then it becomes possible to consider the idea that cognitive activity can *move* along the cognitive continuum. Indeed, cognitive activity may *oscillate* between intuition and analysis, an idea that was first introduced, so far as I know, by Stephen Pepper (1942). Pepper's argument was that analysis ("responsible cognition") became more precarious as it became more precise and found that it must return to the intuitively plausible for reassurance. But, of course, the "irresponsibility" of intuitive cognition leads us back to analysis.

My only attempt so far to quantify Pepper's proposition occurred in connection with a study of physicians teaching third- and fourth-year medical students one-on-one (Hammond, Frederick, Robillard, & Victor, 1989). This study entailed prodigious work on the analyses of student–teacher protocols, but we were gratified to find that we were largely successful in documenting Pepper's proposition. And in a follow-up article, Hamm (1988) also found support for the oscillation Pepper hypothesized.

Of course, the concept of oscillation raises interesting research questions. For example, (a) What effect does the differential use of each type of cognitive activity have on inferential accuracy? (b) What is the effect of different rates of oscillation? These and other questions are discussed in Hammond (1980); see also Hamm (1988).

Alternation Between Functional Relations and Pattern Recognition

The concept of pattern recognition was dismissed by almost all judgment researchers once it was discovered that virtually all judgments could be surprisingly well described by various linear models (Dawes, 1982; Dawes & Corrigan, 1974). But I have come, all too slowly I admit, to realize that all that is necessary to evoke pattern recognition is to provide the subject with materials that induce it. Thus, while subjects may oscillate from intuition through quasirationality to analysis (and vice versa), I argue that subjects' shift from the use of functional relations to patterns occurs in all-or-none form: One cannot, at the same moment, be a bit of functional relations user and a bit of a pattern recognizer. (Either functional relations or pattern recognition may be used intuitively or analytically.) Therefore, although *movement* on the cognitive continuum involves *oscillation,* the *shift* between the use of functional relations and pattern recognition involves *alternation.*

Together with my colleague, Cynthia Lusk, I have embarked on a research effort to inquire whether persons will *alternate* between the use of functional relations and the use of pattern matching when they have the opportunity to do so.

We have found that the radar displays used by weather forecasters do, in fact, present data in both forms, and that meteorologists can readily distinguish between displays that call for (induce) pattern recognition and those that call for (induce) analysis of functional relations. (See Schlatter, 1985, for a weather forecaster's detailed protocol that makes the alternation between these two types of cognitive activity obvious.) Because the call-up of the display is under the control of the forecaster (the forecaster may choose a display at any time from among the 1,000 available to him or her) it becomes possible for the forecaster to alternate at will between these two fundamental forms of cognition. Now we can—as always—raise a number of new and very interesting questions: What effect does the differential use of each type of cognitive activity—use of functional relations or use of pattern identification—have on accuracy of inference? What is the effect of different rates of alternation between them? (These considerations and others are described in Hammond, 1988.)

In order to show the ready application of cognitive continuum theory to decisions outside the laboratory, I turn now to a description of three hunters.

THREE HUNTERS AND THEIR TASK ENVIRONMENTS

The Task Environment of the Hunter-Gatherer

I begin with the natural environment of the prehistoric hunter-gatherer, because it marks one pole of the task continuum. For if archaeological and anthropological descriptions of primitive hunter-gatherer activities are correct, then the cognitive activity of these people must have been induced to be very near the intuitive pole of the cognitive continuum. Why? Because these people certainly lacked "the powers of a full-fledged physicist observer and analyst," and their environment was "no more than partially controlled and no more than probabilistically predictable" (Brunswik, quoted in Hammond, 1966, p. 509). Thus, their task environment can readily be assumed to have contained the task properties listed in the middle column of Table 12.1. That environment would induce—and select!—cognitive systems whose properties would be well described by a linear model.

This retrospective conjecture would be of little interest if it were not for the support it finds in the robust properties of the linear model. That robustness means that, even if the weights and function forms the hunter-gatherer attached to the variables in the equation were frequently wrong, the redundancy of environmental cues and irreducible uncertainty in a hunter-gatherer environment would allow them to be reasonably accurate in their judgments (see Dawes & Corrigan, 1974). No better cognitive system could be devised for hunter-gatherers in their natural environments.

But the environment has surely changed, and as a result, demands on cognitive activities have surely changed as well.

The Task Environments of Modern People

My evolutionary epistemology may be incomplete and even primitive, but it provides a useful point of departure for considering the natural habitats (note plural) of modern people. These habitats provide task environments that vary greatly; they run from those that are highly intuition inducing to those that are highly analysis inducing. Although the latter, of course, were almost completely absent from the hunter-gatherer's environment, today we all encounter highly engineered task environments (e.g., the freeway judgment task) that we had better treat analytically. Modern task environments also include tasks that induce elements of *both* intuition and analysis, and thus induce quasirational cognition. And there are the task environments such as those created for the modern forecasters, that encourage people to *alternate* between functional analysis and pattern recognition, as well as to *oscillate* between intuition and analysis.

Naturalists' theories must acknowledge this range in task variation if they are to take account of the wide variation in cognitive activity of which modern people are demonstrably capable. I now illustrate how this approach can lead to a far different retrospective analysis of the Israeli/Libyan plane incident than that proposed by Beach and Lipshitz (this volume).

The Task Environment of a Modern Hunter: General Hod

First it is essential to note that General Hod was able to solve his problem of determining whether the intruder was hostile or neutral through *action and outcome feedback,* as Beach and Lipshitz correctly observe. That is, his task environment enabled him to *manipulate* the critical objects, acquire feedback from each manipulation, and make new manipulations if necessary. These circumstances therefore make the general an active problem solver, not a passive observer, as, for example, a weather forecaster. That distinction is important, for it suggests that the problem-solving literature is also germane to this situation, perhaps even more so than the judgment and decision making literature. Recall that the vast majority of all the research on judgment and decision making is directed toward the passive cognizer who cannot manipulate objects in the environment. (See Brehmer, 1990, for a description of an extension of SJT to dynamic tasks that permit object manipulation.)[1]

---

[1] Integrating the currently disparate literatures of problem solving and judgment and decision making would be a worthy task, and the time may be ripe for this. Those advocating naturalistic decision making may take heart from observing that a promi-

Keeping in mind the above distinction, we now consider the proper-ties of the ground commander's information-presentation situation (the right-hand side of the lens model). We know that, at the outset, he was given only a few, highly reliable cues. The cues were discrete, offered low redundancy, and occurred sequentially; in fact, virtually all the task characteristics in the right hand column of Table 12.1 were present. Because cognitive continuum theory predicts that the ground commander will employ the form of cognition induced by the task, he should be analytical (see Table 12.2). And, indeed the story indicates that he *was* deliberate; he was highly aware of each step and con-sciously followed the rules; he could easily retrace his steps. The situa-tion provided for him was by no means "ill structured," nor was his cognitive activity.

Now contrast General Hod's hunting environment with the pre-historic hunter's environment in which little manipulation was avail-able. The latter had to use his or her eyes, ears, and nose to seek out a variety of cues presented simultaneously, or nearly so, measure them perceptually, take advantage of natural redundancy, combine the in-formation, and make instantaneous, nonretraceable decisions. Gener-al Hod's hunting, however, involved the opposite circumstances. All his information was presented in a form that was engineered to be highly reliable (e.g., perceptual measurement was eliminated); indeed, his situation was engineered to *prevent* him from using his personal judg-ment and, instead, to make him an analytical problem-solver.

As the General and back-up team review (analytically) all the new information (feedback) that their actions have produced, they again come to a rationally defensible conclusion. As he put it, "uncertainty gradually transformed to a certainty"; the information "convinced us absolutely"; and, he adds, "that's how all uncertainty dissipated." The General reached a new conclusion; the new information allowed him to become certain that the Libyan plane was a terrorist. He arrived at that conclusion analytically—he can retrace his steps, something the hunter-gatherer could not do—because the properties of the task situ-

---

nent cognitive psychologist, John Anderson, has recently published a new book, *The Adaptive Character of Thought* (1990), the title as well as the substance of which sig-nifies a recognition of the importance of the task environment as well as probabilism. Regrettably, however, Anderson ignores decades of relevant work. As a result there are curiously innocent pronouncements. For example, "the approach of this book . . . un-avoidably requires getting serious about the nature of the information-processing de-mands imposed on us by the environment, the statistical character of those demands, and doing a little mathematics" (p. 256). Equally startling is: "There should be empirical work on the actual structure of the environment" (p. 256). Of course, "getting serious about the nature of the . . . environment, the statistical character of those demands and doing a little mathematics" is exactly what Brunswikian psychologists have been doing for roughly half a century.

ation allowed him to do so. And note his final remark: "I confess that [if the same situation would occur again], I would react precisely in the same way." That is a mark of "high confidence in method" and "high awareness" (see Table 12.2). General Hod knows exactly what he did and why he did it, as well as what conclusions he reached and why he reached them.

Thus, my retrospective analysis is different from that offered by Beach and Lipshitz, not only in terms of the description of the task and the General's behavior, but also because it provides both a concrete, specific description of task circumstances (from Table 12.1), and a concrete, specific prediction (from Table 12.2) of the cognitive activity of the principal actor. I do not agree with their description of the General's situation; it is simply too vague to be of help, and it offers no useful prediction of cognitive activity. It is of no help to say that "this situation was ill-structured in that it was at first unknown whether the intruding aircraft was military or civilian." That simply tells us that the answer to the problem was unknown; it says nothing whatever about the "structure" of the situation. On the other hand, Table 12.1 does speak to the structure of the situation; it is in terms of such tables derived from theory that we should describe task environments, and their effects on cognition, as indicated in Table 12.2. Of course, I do not insist that the content of these tables represents ultimate truth; I do insist, however, that tables of this form, if not this content, replace such useless vagaries as "real world."

The Task Environment of the Microburst Hunter

Lusk and I recently studied aviation weather forecasters in their customary task environment—observing Doppler radar screen displays in an effort to detect microbursts (Lusk & Hammond, 1991; Lusk, Stewart, Hammond, & Potts, 1990). These forecasters are hunters in much the same way as General Hod was a hunter, and their prey is as dangerous as a terrorist aircraft. The properties of their task are such that analytical cognition is definitely induced ("What is the dew point? Are the winds divergent?"). They become "full-fledged physicist observer(s) and analyst(s)" *insofar as possible*. On the other hand, the forecasters make heavy use of visual perception applied to radar displays that to the untrained eye appear as hopeless confusion, and they face irreducible uncertainty. In short, because their task environment—the radar displays—induces elements of *both* intuition and analysis, the aviation weather forecaster-hunters are induced to be more analytical than their primitive forebears, but not induced to be—nor can they be—as analytical as General Hod. That is, they are in an environment that induces *quasirational* cognition, and suffer and enjoy the consequences thereof.

As part of our prospective analysis Lusk and I predicted that agreement among the forecasters would be *lower* in their forecasting-hunting habitat—with full information—than when offered objective cue data in which perceptual measurement of the cues was eliminated. The forecasters, like all experts in similar situations, thought the reverse would be the case. Our prediction was correct. It was based on the well-established generalization from SJT that perceptual observation would introduce error as well as induce intuitive (and thus less controlled) cognition (Lusk & Hammond, 1991).

We also learned that SJT is readily applicable to a complex dynamic task that involves the use of hierarchical inferences. We argued that agreement in forecasts would be modest, primarily because different forecasters would combine primary cue values into secondary cue values in different ways. Analytical thought would not be fully shared at this level. The results supported the argument. In short, because the task properties were both analysis inducing and intuition inducing, we predicted that agreement would be higher when the former were more salient and agreement would be lower when the latter were more salient.

To summarize, the task properties of the hunter gatherers' environment were analyzed, as were the task properties of General Hod's (hunting) environment, and the task properties of the forecasters' (hunting) environment. This step allowed a retrospective *conjecture* for the cognitive activity of the hunter-gatherer, a retrospective *analysis* that rests on a plausibility argument for the cognitive activity of General Hod, and testable *prediction* for the cognitive activity of the weather forecasters. Theory and method replaced the useless appeal to the need to study the "real world," "real decisions," or "real people."

HUMAN ERROR

One further aspect of cognitive continuum theory deserves separate emphasis. The Israeli/Libyan plan incident is attention getting, because it raises the question of *human error*. That topic attracts us for two reasons: (a) the fallibility of human judgment has occupied (perhaps preoccupied) researchers in this area for nearly two decades; (b) society is beginning to see that human error is now responsible for consequences of enormous proportions (not so in the days of the hunter-gatherer's cognitive activity).

Cognitive continuum theory (following Brunswik) offers important predictions concerning human error. It argues that analytical cognition—thinking—produces few errors, but that, when errors do occur they will be "catastrophic" (Brunswik, 1956, p. 93), in contrast to the errors produced by perception. Allow me to quote from my own text:

> Brunswik saw perception as a probabilistic, intuitive, continuous, highly adaptive and rapid process—though not without its occasional stupidities. In contrast, thinking is at the opposite pole—deterministic, analytic, discontinuous, with sudden attainment and lengthy pauses, and frequent maladaptive twists. Perception, in short, is "uncertainty-geared;" thinking is "certainty-geared." . . . the more perceptual-like the process, the greater the importance of empirical near-regularities, the greater the expectation of being right in the long run, and the more likely is the subject to achieve "smallness of error at the expense of the highest frequency of precision." Analytical thinking gains in rigor—but its errors are greater and more likely to be catastrophic. (Hammond, 1966, pp. 47–48)

(See Brunswik, 1956, pp. 89–99, for his development of the distinction between perception and thinking.)

The applicability of these remarks to the difference between the situation faced by the prehistoric hunter and that faced by General Hod is obvious. General Hod was using a highly engineered, highly analytical system that was designed to cope with anticipated circumstances, a system carefully considered, carefully thought through in advance. But when unimagined—better, unimaginable—events occur, such systems fail badly. When the contents of the "black box" revealed to the General the circumstances of the ecology, he found he was in error. His detection system was well designed to cope with well-planned, rational enemy action, but it was applied to semierratic, partly rational, partly irrational enemy action. Who would dream that an airliner would contain a wine-drinking crew whose captain and first officer could not communicate because they did not speak the same language? And who could imagine the consequences of the Israeli pilot's approach to the right—the first officer's side?

Application of analytical cognitive systems to erratic systems creates the strong likelihood of terrible mistakes, not through the intrinsic fallibility of human judgment, but through a gross mismatch of the two systems. (See Berliner, Goetsch, Campbell, & Ebeling, 1990, for a comparable example in computerized chess.)

In short, cognitive continuum theory explicitly includes a theory of how task conditions vary, and the consequences for cognitive activity; the method of representative design is responsive to that theory. Conventional research ignores task conditions and is responsive to statistical criteria alone, thus employing an implicit, highly oversimplified theory of the environment. The consequence is vast overgeneralization across conditions; as new conditions are brought under investigation, the generalization fails; psychology finds itself constantly starting over. Unless naturalism addresses task theory in terms of formal properties its future will remain in doubt as well.

CONCLUSIONS

If we reject Wundt's methodological admonition, and Helmholtz's dictum, and follow instead Brunswikian principles—if, that is, naturalism is to succeed—then naturalists must provide testable theories of the environment that describe its formal properties and their consequences for cognitive activity; otherwise results simply become retrospective products subject to multiple ad hoc interpretations that cannot be falsified. But when testable theories of the environment are developed, and when naturalists make use of the well worked-out precepts of representative design, they will be able to do the research that is so badly needed in a manner that will stand up to thoughtful criticism.

Of course, it won't be easy. As Gibson (1957) said of Brunswik's work: "He asks us, the experimenters in psychology, to revamp our fundamental thinking. . . . It is an onerous demand. Brunswik imposed it first on his own thinking and showed us how burdensome it can be. His work is an object lesson in theoretical integrity" (p. 35). In short, there is no easy way to reach the goals of those who would be naturalistic. But the path is well defined.

KEY POINTS

- The study of decision making and judgment highlights differences between Wundt's psychophysical approach and Brunswik's functional approach.
- Wundt's approach supposes that regularities in nature can be studied only by tightly controlling most variables, while manipulating a few others.
- Brunswik argues that removing ambiguity and complexity amounts to removal of the object of study.
- Naturalism demands a theory to describe events that are so complex that they can disguise the regularities in nature.
- Social judgment theory (SJT) is one such theory that is applicable to decision making and judgment.

- Many current naturalistic approaches err by emphasizing content over formal descriptions of the environment, and by proposing theories that are too vague to be tested.
- These problems are critical to resolve in future work on naturalistic decision making.

APPENDIX

Parallel Naturalistic Efforts

Because the current major dissidents seem to be best identified by use of the word *ecology* or *ecological* in the title of their articles or their (usually) edited volumes, I present in Figure 12.2 a graph of the appearance of the root term *ECOLOG* in the PSYCHOINFO database. Below I list some of the areas of research of authors who have used this term to describe their work, or who have tried to break with the Wundtian tradition.

Perception

- Brunswik (1934 f), (Introduces *ecological validity*), (1956), *Perception and the Representative Design of Psychological Experiments*
- Gibson (1979), *The Ecological Approach to Visual Perception*

Memory

- Bartlett (1932), *Remembering*
- Neisser (1978), In *Practical Aspects of Memory*

Figure 12.2.   Results of search of PSYCINFO database on the root "ECOLOG."

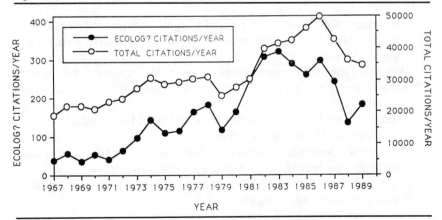

- Harris and Morris (1984), *Everyday Memory: Actions and Absentmindedness*

Child Development

- Barker (1968), *Ecological Psychology: Concepts and Methods for Studying the Environment of Human Behavior;* (1978), *Habitats, Environments, and Human Behavior*
- Bronfenbrenner (1974), *Ecology of Human Development*
- Pence (1988), *Ecological Research with Children and Families*
- Vygotsky (1978), *Mind in Society*
- Wertsch (1985), *Vygotsky and the Social Formation of Mind*

Cognitive Psychology

- Rogoff and Lave (1984), *Everyday Cognition: Its Development in Social Context*
- Poon, Rubin, and Wilson (1989), *Everyday Cognition in Adulthood and Late Life*
- Chi, Glaser, and Farr (1988), *The Nature of Expertise*
- Cooksey et al. (1991), *The Ecology of Spelling*

Ethology and Behavioral Biology

- Lorenz (1966), *On Aggression*
- Petrinovich (1989), In *Everyday Cognition in Adulthood and Late Life*

Judgment and Decision Making

- Social Judgment Theorists (1955 ff), Hammond, Brehmer, Stewart, Doherty, Mumpower, Rohrbaugh et al.
- Klein, Orasanu, & Calderwood (1991), *Naturalistic Decision Making*
- Wigton et al. (1990), *Teaching Old Dogs New Tricks*

Human Factors

- Vicente and Rasmussen (in press), *Ecological Interface Design*

General

- Willems and Rausch (1969), *Naturalistic Viewpoints in Psychological Research*

Chapter 13

Process-Tracing Methods for The Study of Cognition Outside of the Experimental Psychology Laboratory*

David D. Woods
Cognitive Systems Engineering Laboratory
The Ohio State University

> to be successful in unlocking the doors concealing nature's secrets, a person must have ingenuity. If he does not have the key for the lock, he must not hesitate to pick it, to climb in a window, or even kick in a panel. If he succeeds, it is more by ingenuity and determination than by method. (Hildebrand, 1957, p. 26)

STUDIES OF COMPLEX BEHAVIORAL SITUATIONS

I will approach the topic of research methods for the study of human decision making and problem solving outside the usual psychology laboratory, that is, human cognition as it occurs in its natural setting (or situated cognition), in terms of a dichotomy between studying human cognition in complex, rich, multifaceted settings versus simplified, spartan, single-factor settings. Each setting offers different potential for insight into human behavior, and each is subject to different kinds of biases or sources of uncertainty.[1]

---

* Research support was provided by the Aerospace Human Factors Research Division of the NASA Ames Research Center under Grant NCC2-592. Everett Palmer served as technical monitor. I would like to thank the many colleagues who provided many useful comments and critiques. There were too many to mention all by name, but I am extremely fortunate that so many would help so much to improve this work.

[1] This distinction, I hope, focuses attention on constructive debate about research methods rather than the destructive debates framed in terms of ecological versus laboratory, applied versus basic or other similar dichotomies (e.g., Banaji & Crowder, 1989). Similarly, I hope to avoid a mere sermon on virtues associated with more ecologically valid studies.

This distinction defines the challenge that I will examine—how does one achieve valid, generalizable results when examining complex behavioral situations.

Why Study Cognition Outside the Laboratory?

Studying human behavior in complex situations is extremely difficult. So a dominant tactic people use to manage complexity in this as is in other difficult tasks is to bound the situation under consideration by focusing on one isolated aspect, cut off from the simultaneous function of other aspects with which it is normally integrated (Bartlett, 1932). Thus, in this spartan or austere approach, one might address only a single time slice of a dynamic process, or only a subset of the interconnections between parts of a highly coupled world. The strategy is to understand one variable or one subprocess at a time and then to consider how to put the pieces back together again (e.g., tachistoscopic-based research in perception).

However, this spartan, elemental approach is just one research strategy, which has limits. It is not clear with the spartan strategy whether the relevant aspects of the whole target situation have been captured in a test situation that extirpates or paralyzes most aspects of the whole. The importance of various parts of the problem-solving process may be underestimated, for example, "predecisional processes" (e.g., Friedman, Howell, & Jensen, 1985). Some aspects of problem solving may emerge only when more complex situations are examined directly. For example, there has been a great deal of research on human fault diagnosis. However, this work has almost exclusively addressed static devices with single faults, which is an oversimplification of many diagnostic situations where human problem solvers must cope with the possibility of multiple failures, misleading signals, interacting disturbances (e.g., Woods, Roth, & Pople, 1987). The assumption of a static situation has resulted in the failure to see a critical part of dynamic problem solving—*the disturbance management* cognitive activity (Woods, 1988) where managing the process to cope with the consequences of faults, that is, disturbances, goes on in parallel with and interacts with fault diagnosis.

Results from previous research (much of it of the spartan variety, ironically) also point to the need to investigate more complex behavioral situations. If thinking is a skill, as the Bartlett/Craik tradition in information processing holds, then we can study it in those who possess the skill. If skilled thinking is grounded in particular contexts (fields of knowledge-in-use), then the phenomenon of interest exists to be studied in the exercise of the skill in these contexts. If, as a broad assessment of studies of judgment and decision making indicates (e.g., Hogarth, 1986), strategies for judgment and choice are task-contingent, then we need to understand the role of that context in information-processing strategies, rather than always eliminate it from the task as in the spartan strategy.

These examples show the danger of falling into the psychologist's fallacy described by William James (1890), where the psychologist's reality is confused with the psychological reality of the human practitioner in his or her problem-solving world. One cannot simply assume that the experimenter's representation of the task is the same as the participant's representation (Cole & Scribner, 1974; Hutchins, 1980; Lave, 1988). The burden is on the experimenter (of either the spartan or complex persuasion) to determine or measure the participant's representation of the task so as to be able to interpret and generalize the observed behavioral results.

In reducing the target behavioral situation to a tractable laboratory or desktop world in search of precise results, we run the risk of eliminating the critical features of the world that drive behavior. But there seems to be an implicit assumption that researchers must suffer this risk, because the alternative is to study complex situations directly, which means all experimental control or focusing is necessarily abandoned. The familiar story of the drunk searching for the lost keys where the streetlamp casts light, rather than where the keys were lost, points out that both sources of uncertainty need to be overcome for effective behavioral science research. This chapter explores some of the ways that methodological lamps can be directed at complex behavioral situations.

Representativeness and the Mapping between Test and Target Behavioral Situations

Instead of focusing on the elemental, spartan strategy of throwing away complexity to achieve tractability, the appropriate criterion for creating tractable study situations is establishing a *mapping* between the *test* behavioral situation (where one is observing and measuring behavior) and the *target* behavioral situation one wishes to understand or generalize to.

We are often stuck with the appellation *real world* to distinguish research directed at complex settings from more spartan laboratory work. However, this terminology obscures the more relevant concept of the *representativeness* of one's experimental situation, that is, the relationship between the specific situation that is under study with respect to the class of situations that is the target of the study (Brunswik, 1956; Hammond, 1986). It is this test behavioral situation/target behavioral situation relationship that is the critical prerequisite for building a generalizable behavioral science research base. This is true whether the generalization is from a spartan situation to a complex one or from one complex situation to another complex one.

This point of view has several implications for research methods. First, there is the need for a much better understanding of the kinds of problems to be solved. To achieve representativeness we need to be able to analyze the "formal" characteristics of the situations towards which we want to generalize and map those characteristics into specific features of the test situation where we will actually observe and measure behavior. "Without a theory of task systems, however, it is impossible to know how to apply or to generalize the results of any given study" (Hammond, 1988, p. 3; cf. also Hogarth, 1986). For example, research results on one-shot decisions (a test situation frequently used in the laboratory) are of limited relevance for dynamic situations where information comes in over time and the problem solver must also decide when to act (e..g, Kleinmuntz & Thomas, 1987; Woods, Roth, & Pople, 1987). However, the optional-stopping decision problem does capture some of the characteristics of dynamically evolving situations and therefore can provide results transportable to other situations that possess these characteristics (Schwartz & Howell, 1985).

When one studies complex behavioral situations, the multifaceted nature of the setting creates the methodological and theoretical problem of deciding what counts as effective stimuli out of the total array. Note how this is analogous to the development of the area of ecological perception, in contrast to the "minimalist" research strategy in perception, where the commitment to studying more complex perceptual situations led to the need for a better understanding of the stimulus world—ecological physics. The effective stimuli in a multifaceted situation can be characterized, and the means is a semantic and pragmatic analysis of environment–cognitive agent relationships with respect to the goals/resources of the agent and the demands/constraints in the environment. For example, Bartlett (1932, p. 4) comments:

We may consider the old and familiar illustration of the landscape artist, the naturalist and the geologist who walk in the country together. The one is said to notice and recall beauty of scenery, the other details of flora and fauna, and the third the formations of soils and rocks. In this case, no doubt, the stimuli being selected in each instance from what is present, are different for each observer, and obviously the records made in recall are different also. Nevertheless, the different reactions have a uniformity of determination, and in each case spring from established interests.

This type of model of the characteristics of the setting relative to a practitioner's interests is what the person–machine system community tends to call the cognitive task analysis or cognitive work analysis (Rasmussen, 1986; Woods, 1988; Mitchell & Miller, 1986), and it is critical for characterizing the demands of problem-solving worlds (e.g., Roth & Woods, 1989).

In addition, the concept of representativeness points to more perception-like research programs where discovery of phenomena and demonstration of control of phenomena is the primary goal, rather than hypothesis testing per se. This style of research is oriented to characterize phenomena, to explore the factors that produce and modify phenomena, and to develop models that may capture the underlying psychological mechanisms.

PROCESS-TRACING METHODOLOGIES

This part of the chapter addresses various techniques that have been used to study complex behavioral situations. This section necessarily covers broad categories of techniques because of the extreme diversity of methods used, and because virtually every new, major "naturalistic" study includes some methodological innovation. However, the main focus of the discussion here will be protocol analysis or process-tracing methods. Another class of techniques has been developed for measuring the organization of knowledge possessed by an individual, especially expert practitioners in some domain. These techniques use classification and scaling methods derived from theory and research on semantic memory and concept formation to assess the kinds of categories by which the practitioner parses the domain and the relationships between these categories (e.g., semantic networks). To begin to examine these techniques in more detail see Chi, Feltovich, and Glaser (1981) and Cooke and McDonald (1987), as well as the work based on the classic deGroot memory paradigm.

The term *protocol analysis* has been used in a variety of ways, creating some confusion. I prefer to use the label *process-tracing methodologies,* which is more descriptive of the basic character of a wide variety of techniques (e.g., Ford et al., 1989). The goal in these methods is to map out how the incident unfolded including available cues, those cues actually noted by participants, and participants' interpretation in both the immediate and in the larger institutional and professional contexts. This is called a process-tracing or protocol analysis method because it focuses on how a given outcome came about.[2]

The specific techniques within this family are all oriented towards *externalizing internal processes or producing external signs that support inferences about internal workings.* To this end there are innumerable techniques and variants that have been used and that will be invented for tomorrow's study (Kato, 1986). One common technique is to transform the target behavioral situation into one that requires cooperation between two people (for examples, see Miyake, 1986; Suchman, 1987). This manipulation generates protocols based on verbal behavior that occur as part of the natural task behavior, rather than having participants produce concurrent verbal reports as an additional task. Note how the choice of manipulation in the test situation— change the task to a cooperative one versus ask for concurrent verbal reports—represents a tradeoff in sources of uncertainty about how the externalized cues relate to internal processes.

Another technique has been called *withheld information* (cf., as examples, Duncan, 1981; Johnson, Payne & Bettman, 1988). This technique is designed to externalize data acquisition and monitoring behavior during a problem-solving episode. Rather than having the entire set of data or data channels available in parallel for the study participant to examine, the experimenter withholds state information until the problem solver explicitly requests a specific datum. This allows the experimenter to watch the evolving process of data search to characterize the state of the underlying process (variable x is not behaving as expected), what knowledge is activated based on each observation (e.g., generating an hypothesis which might account for observed anamolous behavior in a device), which in turn directs new explorations of the data field (Woods, Roth, & Pople, 1987). Thus, this technique is particularly suited for making portions of the perceptual cycle more observable. However, the manipulation which produces observable signs of internal cognitive processing also produces a mismatch between the test behavioral situation and the target situation, and a source of uncertainty in data interpretation. In this case, the withheld information technique is not capable of supporting insight into processes associated with data-driven monitoring for new events and changes in the state of the underlying device, and the role of physically parallel data representations in those processes.

Note how there is a tradeoff where techniques that help externalize

---

[2] The increasing interest in including process as well as outcome in studies of human decision making can be seen in the formation of the European Group for Process Tracing Studies of Decision Making; cf. Montgomery and Svenson (1989a).

and make observable internal processes also can introduce distortions that reduce the accuracy of the mapping between test and target behavioral situations. Basically, there are two challenges to validity that the investigator attempts to cope with in the design of a process-tracing study (Russo, Johnson, & Stephens, 1989): (a) does the assessment technique change the primary processes that are the target of study (and how does it change those), and (b) to what degree do the data accurately reflect the underlying cognitive activities minimizing omission of important aspects, intrusions of irrelevant features, or distortions of the actual processes (and what checks on these sources of invalidity are included in the design)?

Verbal Reports

Process-tracing techniques primarily use data from verbal reports or from records of problem-solver behavior to build protocols that describe the sequence of information flow and knowledge activation. In addition, process-tracing techniques can be used to address critical incidents that have already occurred in retrospective analyses.

One type of process tracing is based on data derived from verbal reports made by study participants *about their own* process of solving the problem posed. This is not to be confused with verbal behavior, that is, task-related behavior that happens to be verbal, such as verbal communication in multiperson situations.

The debate about the validity of verbal data or about the importance of unverbalizable components of performance is large and ongoing (cf., e.g., Nisbett & Wilson, 1977; Ericsson & Simon, 1980; Berry & Broadbent, 1984). Verbal reports are just another kind of data which can be interpreted to provide insight and are subject to a number of dangers (e.g., Bainbridge, 1979; Praetorius & Duncan, 1988; Russo et al., 1989). Overall, there is agreement that it is critical to avoid and guard against verbal reports as introspections where the study participants analyze their own processes or behavior.

Techniques for verbalization include:

- Thinking-aloud protocols, where participants are instructed to think aloud as they work on the problem, that is, externalize the contents of working memory in the Ericsson and Simon view (cf. Russo et al., 1989).
- Retrospective verbal reports where participants solve the problems posed and afterwards provide a commentary about what they were thinking about at various points, for example, debriefing sessions (cf. Fidler, 1983).

- Cued retrospective verbal reports where participants comment after the problem-solving session but where the verbal report is cued to a record of their behavior during the case, for example, videotape (cf. Leplat & Hoc, 1981; Hoc & Leplat, 1983).

Behavioral Protocols

This technique has been developed in the context of domains where there is some underlying engineered or physiological process (e.g., Hollnagel, Pederson, & Rasmussen, 1981; Woods, O'Brien, & Hanes, 1987; Johnson, Zualkernan, & Garber, 1987). The human role is to manage that process in the face of disturbances produced by faults (domains where this occurs include aircraft flightdecks, managing space missions, nuclear power plant control rooms, air traffic control, managing patient physiology during surgery).

Rather than focus exclusively on participant verbalizations, behavioral protocols are built from a variety of data sources about the behavior of the people in relation to changes in the underlying process over time. Data sources include (a) direct observation of participant behavior, (b) traces of data acquisition sequences, (c) traces of actions taken on the underlying process, (d) records of the dynamic behavior of critical process variables, (e) records of verbal communication among team members or via formal communication media, (f) verbal reports made following the performance, and (g) commentaries on their behavior made by other domain knowledgeable observers. Data from all of these sources are correlated and combined to produce a record of participant data acquisition, situation assessment, knowledge activation, expectations, intentions, and actions as the case unfolds over time (cf. Woods, O'Brien, & Hanes, 1987, for several examples from simulated and actual nuclear power incidents). Note how different types of verbal behavior and verbal reports may contribute to the available lines of evidence. In behavioral protocol analysis the experimenter actively cross references the different lines of evidence in order to establish a trace of participant behavior and cognitive activities. This cross-checking and integration can help support the validity of the data with respect to participant cognitive activities at some level of analysis.

Typically, a major activity in behavioral protocols (as in any protocol analysis) is using knowledge of the domain to fill in gaps between observables. The raw data records may establish what a person did and in what context (what actions and signals had preceeded it, what did the team say to each other before the action was taken, etc.); however, these observables do not directly establish the person's intentions or situation assessment. But in fact one can establish what these are likely to be in most cases for behavioral situations where the human role is supervisory control (Rubin, Jones, & Mitchell, 1988). This is because there is usually only one interpretation or very few possible alternatives, given domain knowledge and the assumption of limited rationality; that is, human behavior is assumed to be the result of limits on rationality—people behave reasonably given their knowledge, their objectives, their point of view, limited resources (e.g., time or workload), the demands of the situation (Reason & Mycielska, 1982; Rasmussen, 1986; Woods & Roth, 1988). The assumption of limited rationality is used to understand human behavior *from the point of view of the person in the situation* rather than from the point of view of an omniscient observer, in order to reduce difficulties caused by hindsight bias, including the psychologist's fallacy. This is a fundamental objective of a process-tracing analysis—to lay out the problem-solving episode from the point of view of the people in the problem. The methodological tactics are selected or created to understand and represent the point of view of practitioners in the problem (either the specific people in a specific incident or the general view of the practitioner population).

The basic target to be achieved in a behavioral protocol analysis is tracing/understanding the evolution of the state of the underlying process or device *in parallel with* the human agents' state of understanding (situation assessment), intentions, and activities in managing the process. This means understanding discourse and action, data gathering, and situation assessment in relation to an external device/process—the referent world—which is itself changing both as a function of new events (e.g., faults) and corrective actions. It also includes understanding how changes in the referent domain activate new knowledge and trigger/shift lines of reasoning in the agents managing the process. Of course, signals can be missed or misinterpreted, knowledge can be buggy, relevant knowledge may not be activated, all of which can lead to mismatches between the agents' perception of the situation and the actual state of affairs and to erroneous actions (Woods, Roth, & Pople, 1987). Identifying these mismatches, and the circumstances that led to them, is the goal of a successful behavioral protocol analysis.

One useful technique to support behavioral protocol analysis is to use domain experts other than the study participants to observe episodes or review data records to help establish the participant's intentions and interpretations. This domain knowledge functions as a background for interpreting the behavior of study participants and may need to be captured more completely and formally as a cognitive task and work analysis (this may be a prerequisite for being able to build behavioral protocols). Mitchell and her colleagues (Rubin et al., 1988) have taken the next step and used the results of a cognitive task analysis as the knowledge base for a cognitive simulation that can fill in or delimit the intentions that would account for observable practitioner behaviors as an incident unfolds.

Retrospective Analyses of Critical Incidents

Retrospective analyses refer to cases where the incident of interest has already occurred (i.e., the classic critical incident technique in human factors). However, some data are available about the incident itself— one can review flight recorder transcripts, interview the participants in the incident after the fact, explore the context prior to the incident. This type of study is particularly important in investigations of human error in rarely occurring but very high-consequence situations where it is difficult to create the situation of interest (cf. Pew, Miller, & Feehrer, 1981; Woods, O'Brien, & Hanes, 1987; Klein, 1989b, for examples of retrospective analyses of human problem solving). A broad assessment of the methodological status and challenges of retrospective analyses of decision making is needed, but I will be content to sketch out some of the important issues here.

The assumption of limited rationality is important in applying a process-tracing method to past incidents. The participant's reports and other data records specify a sequence of activities. Clearly definable events, such as specific observations and actions, are used as starting points. The investigators use the participant's reports and the knowledge of other domain experts to interpolate the kinds of knowledge activated and utilized that would make this sequence of cues and actions rational from the point of view of limited cognitive agents. In other words, one reconstructs the mental dynamics by determining the answers to such questions as—what did this signal indicate to the problem solver about process state? Given a particular action, in what perceived process state or context is this action reasonable? Errors are seen as the result of limited rationality—the people involved in the incident are doing reasonable things, given their knowledge, their objectives, their point of view and limited resources, for example, time or workload (Reason & Mycielska, 1982; Woods & Roth, 1988). Reconstructing a trace of the problem-solving process can identify points where limited knowledge and processing led to actions that are clearly erroneous from hindsight.

In the end, any reconstruction is a fictional story—it may have happened "as if . . ." A critical factor is identifying and resolving all anomalies in a potential interpretation. We have more confidence in, or are more willing to pretend that, the story may in fact have some relation to reality if all currently known data about the sequence of events and background are coherently accounted for by the reconstruction. However, any reconstruction is tentative, for a later investigator may turn up more evidence that creates anomalies in previous reconstructions and motivates the creation of a new or modified account.

There are a number of major outstanding questions about how to do this type of critical incident study so that meaningful interpretable results are generated and not just anecdotes (cf. Klein, 1989b, on the alternative interpretations of the psychological implications of the Vinncennes incident). For example, for retrospective studies to be meaningful, should the investigative team personally interview participants in the incident and related domain personnel, or can the analysis be carried out based on second-hand reports? When? Are there ways to do retrospective analyses of decision making that support constructive debate about alternative interpretations rather than ad hoc assertions (e.g., when is it meaningful to conclude that an incident contains an example of people committing a decision bias or some category of human error)?

FIELD OBSERVATION

Another source of techniques for the study of human cognition outside the laboratory is the tradition of field studies in industrial settings (primarily European; see De Keyser, 1990, for an excellent critical review) and of anthropological field research (e.g., Suchman, 1987; Lave, 1988; Hutchins, 1980, 1983).

A field research perspective raises questions about the relationship of the investigator to the domain of interest and the domain practitioners. Do you have to "go native" or "become an expert yourself" in order to do meaningful complex world research (Hutchins, 1980)? Does the researcher require a domain-knowledgeable guide or informant (a Virgil to guide the researcher cum Dante through the seven circles of naturalistic research hell) to help penetrate the surface veil of the domain and identify the deeper structure (e.g., Cook & Woods, 1990)?

Meaningful investigations of complex behavioral situations where the domain practitioner's performance and skill is the focus of the study will require a significant amount of personal knowledge acquisition and experience with the domain, and especially with the role and point of view of the practitioners within the domain. Some of this domain appreciation can be provided by domain-knowledgeable guides; for example, the earlier discussion of behavioral protocol analysis mentioned several ways that other practitioners can be harnessed to help in data collection and analysis. Very frequently, it may be critical to formalize this knowledge acquisition through in depth cognitive task analysis (Roth & Woods, 1989).

While immersion in the domain "culture" is an important contributor to doing complex world studies, it is not the end itself. The danger is that one can be drawn in too deeply and learn only about that specific context. In part this is due to referential transparency—what one sees with is seldom what one sees (Hutchins, 1980). The investigator must preserve some distance (while at the same time being intimate with the domain details) in order to be able to see what the domain practitioner sees with.

The field research tradition points out a variety of techniques and obstacles in the study of complex behavioral settings (cf. Roberts & Rousseau, 1989). For example, one important requirement is to live among the "natives" long enough to be confident that you are minimizing the distortion produced by your presence prior to collecting any data. On the other hand, the practitioners in the field are not and cannot be treated as "subjects" in a traditional laboratory experiment (hence, the use of the moniker *study participant* in this chapter). Frequently, the reason an investigator has access is to provide practical assistance in solving "applied" problems. Providing this assistance is the coin of the realm for the time and real cooperation of the practitioner.

Is the Choice Between Rich Field Work and Spartan Experiments?

One possible methodological conclusion for those interested in complex behavioral situations is that there is no relationship to spartan experimental psychology laboratory methods. Rather, one should learn, use, and advance the techniques worked out for anthropological field research in order to do a "cognitive anthropology" of work cultures (Hutchins, 1980). I do not believe that these two approaches exhaust our repertoire. I am convinced that there are techniques for examining complex settings that fall between descriptive field observation and narrow laboratory experimentation.

Field observation is a valid, meaningful technique that belongs in our research repertoire. For example, field observation is necessary to establish the mapping between target and test situation, to make decisions about what manipulations to use in the test situation to make observable the phenomenon of interest while preserving the basic character of the target situation. Bartlett's (1932) investigations of cognition began with observation of everyday activities, which formed the basis for experimental studies, which in turn informed further observation in the field.

There are a variety of major problems in field research oriented toward understanding human cognition (cf. De Keyser, 1990). One that occurs even with good field studies is the gap between data collection and interpretation. The problem is that a critical reader of a field study report cannot retrace the study and reinterpret the purported conclusions, as one in principle can do with archival reports of traditional laboratory studies. This is a major issue for complex-world research. There tends to be a great leap from the data collected to interpretative conclusions, with a vast wasteland in between. This forces other researchers either to accept or reject the investigator's interpretation rather than criticize, reinterpret, or build on the study. This is exacerbated because it is not standard practice of authors or journals to include all protocols, at some level of encoding, in the report of a study which used a process-tracing method (but cf. Roth, Bennett, & Woods, 1987, for one exception). Effective methodologies for studying complex behavioral situations must support this process of criticism, reinterpretation, and follow-ons to produce cumulation, generalization, and the growth of knowledge.

ISSUES IN USING PROCESS-TRACING METHODS

The driving assumption behind this chapter is that there are research methodologies, which fall between the poles of descriptive field observation techniques, which can investigate complex behavioral settings directly, and spartan laboratory research approaches, which are relevant only obliquely to complex settings. In this section I will try to outline an approach to process-tracing studies that falls between these two poles.

The Concept-Specificity/Context-Independence Tradeoff

One technique (Hollnagel et al., 1981) to deal with the above gap in studies of complex behavioral situations is derived from the idea that there is a tradeoff between concept-specificity and context-independence in analyses of human behavior. The technique Hollnagel et al. proposed is to use a succession of levels of analysis in a process-tracing study, which begin at a context-dependent, concept-independent level of analysis. Performance is first analyzed or described in the language of the domain/profession: this user, in this domain, in this simulated or actual context, in this scenario, did action x or made statement y at time z. Analysis at this level—what can be called a *description of actual performance*—is relatively concept free but highly context dependent; in other words, it is difficult to generalize the results to other users, tasks, or events.

In the Hollnagel et al. technique the description of actual performance is followed by successive stages of progressively more concept-dependent, context-independent levels of analysis. The use of a non-domain-specific concept language based on models of human performance allows one to produce a description of behavior that is context independent and therefore potentially generalizable to similar situations in different domain contexts (cf. Montgomery & Svenson, 1989a). Since concepts or models form a basis for succeeding levels of analysis, they can be called *formal performance descriptions*.

Take an example from studies of human error (Reason & Mycielska, 1982). Imagine a user executing action set Y (an infrequently performed task) who erroneously substitutes actions from set X (a frequently performed and closely related task). The actual performance description would state that the user committed an error in maneuver Y, executing an action from set X, rather than the correct action from the appropriate action set Y. The formal performance description would state that a "capture" error had occurred, because the action in its domain context meets the criteria for a capture error defined as one category of human error. In this example, concepts about human error have been used to encode the domain level view of user performance; as a result, the data can be combined with, and generalized to, other users in other events. However, note that, despite the shift in language of description, the result can be seen as data (i.e., a description of what happened), albeit filtered through a conceptual looking glass. Furthermore, the conceptual dependence that underlies the abstraction can be specified explicitly.

In process-tracing studies of human problem solving and decision making the concepts used to move beyond context-dependent descriptions come from human information processing defined very broadly (cf. Pew et al., 1981; Woods, O'Brien, & Hanes, 1987; Roth et al., 1987; Klein, Calderwood, & MacGregor, 1989). In other words, the formal description of performance marks a shift from a domain specific language to some type of a cognitive language. This shift is often referred to as the encoding stage of analysis. It is important to keep in mind that the two descriptions exist as parallel accounts of behavior in the episode (trial).

"Field Experiments"

One can use the process-tracing approach described above to produce behavioral protocols that address cognitive activities in the incidents in question. But what is the larger context of the study? Protocol analysis or process-tracing is just another measurement technique (like reaction time measures). What defines studies in a larger sense is the psychological topic or concept being investigated. In more descriptive research, the psychological topic may be the kind of cognitive situation selected or staged for investigation. For example, how do people solve garden path problems: where this class of problems is defined (i.e., problems where there is a highly plausible but in fact erroneous hypothesis), a set of problems that have these defining characteristics is identified or created, and results from this investigation can be compared critically to other studies on this cognitive topic, independent of the domain that generates the specific problem (e.g., Johnson et al., 1981).

Let us pick up again the capture error example discussed a little earlier. The details behind the concept of a capture error provide guidance about what kind of situation should be created in order to have the opportunity to observe capture errors or investigate underlying psychological mechanisms. The concept specifies the critical variables, or the effective stimuli, to be measured or controlled—that is, what are the aspects of the situation that really matter with respect to the behavior of interest. As a result, the domain description of an episode can be shifted to a cognitive description in terms of the concept of capture error and similar error forms (slips). For example, distractions and interruptions may be critical contributors to the occurrence of slip errors. Therefore, the test scenarios should include these elements (note that an *interruption* must be defined as a domain-specific event, for example, a call from air traffic control timed to occur during the execution of a checklist, if the domain is commercial aviation flightdecks). Also, a formal description of behavior can be developed in terms such as the called-for action sequence, the timing or form of the interruption, the action sequence that could take over (the potential capture sequence), the participant's behavior following the interruption (repeating actions, ommitting actions, reorienting behaviors, etc.), and the relation between the nominal and the capture action sequences (e.g., frequency of occurrence, task criticality, etc.). In this approach, the traditional problems of identifying evaluation criteria and selecting test scenarios are mitigated, because the explicit formulation of the detailed psychological question to be tested contains a measure of successful performance and the essential conditions that must be produced in any test scenario.

What is fundamental in a protocol analysis study is the psychological question under study. This question guides the construction of test scenarios, the raw data to be gathered, and the kind of concepts brought to bear to analyze human behavior. Therefore, one can think of studies designed in this approach as field experiments—*field* experiments, based on the use of complex behavioral situations (which could be the naturally occurring situation or practitioner behavior in simulations at various levels of fidelity); field *experiments,* in that the scenario, study participants and conditions of observation are focused in on some psychological question.[3] Hogarth (1986, p. 445) has remarked that the yield of this type of study "depends crucially upon whether the investigator adopts an 'experimental framework' in organizing observations." Adopting this experimental framework means conducting the study as an empirical confrontation, that is, a process of observation where doubts can be formulable in order to reappraise beliefs.

Because of pragmatic limitations on *access* when one wishes to study actual practitioners working with substantive tools and on substantive problems, coupled with challenges of experimental design, field experimentation involves an element of capitalizing on naturally occurring opportunities to pursue a cognitive issue. Upon recognizing that the opportunity for access is available under conditions that will allow some control/focusing, the investigators proceed to shape that naturally occurring situation into an experimental investigation. Roth et al. (1987) is an example of this occurring. Pragmatic and scale limitations may preclude individual studies from including a thorough sample over conditions (Hammond, 1986b), but the explicit mapping between the test situation being investigated and the psychological situations and issues of interest allows for a cumulation of results and knowledge across studies. This is critical in order to avoid an endless stream of studies with apparently conflicting or nongeneralizable results (deKeyser, 1990).

Finally, the idea of studying complex settings directly, through tech-

---

[3] I have adopted the term suggested by Jane Malin of NASA Johnson Space Center—*field experiments* or *experiments in the field*—to describe this type of focused field-oriented study. Others have suggested other terms; for example, Gentner and Stevens (1983, p. 2) used "designed field observation, in which an artificial domain is constructed that has interesting relevance to the real domain under consideration."

niques like field experiments, reveals a hidden bias in both the "basic" and "applied" psychological communities. It is accepted without quarrel that studies of spartan situations will eventually result in fundamental concepts, laws, and models of cognitive processing that will transfer eventually to real world, applied problems, at least in principle. Meanwhile, applied researchers, driven by pressing problems related to people in complex systems, undertake domain specific applied research, frequently with few ties to the spartan basic research going on in parallel (hence, we have the field of human factors divided up by domain boundaries—aviation human factors, nuclear power human factors, forensic human factors, etc.). However, there is another possibility, one that is not accepted as a viable approach by either the basic or applied communities. One can study complex worlds directly and produce results that add to the generic research base on human cognition, as well as produce results specific to the complex setting that served as the research vehicle. The results will cumulate and be transportable from one complex setting to another with similar "deep structure," or even to the next problem in the same domain. One can call this approach a complementarity assumption on the relation of "basic" and "applied" behavioral science research.

The complementarity assumption maintains that complex settings have a dual interpretation: one as an "applied" or local problem to be solved within some temporal and resource horizon, and another as a specific behavioral context that is an instance of some classes of behavior which can serve as a field laboratory for investigating that class of behavior. As a result, there is a natural complementarity between growing the research base and using the research base to develop pragmatic, though approximate, solutions to application problems.

One criterion for understanding of a phenomenon requires that the scientist demonstrate control of the phenomenon, that is, the ability to eliminate or create the phenomenon, to enlarge or diminish the effect. If we claim to understand decision making, planning, problem solving, etc., then we must be able to demonstrate control of these aspects of behavior even in complex "applied" settings. In other words, we must be able to improve human performance through a variety of means for supporting human problem solving and decision making. Thus, demonstrating fundamental understanding can, at the same time, help solve immediate problems such as the impact of new information technology on the flightdeck on aviation safety.

Similarly, the only path to get ahead of the pace of technology change and the progression of domain-specific "hot buttons" is to use a generic but relevant research base to go beyond technology-specific or completely domain-specific descriptions (e.g., Cook & Woods, 1990).

This research base has been lacking or remained impoverished because of the gulf between basic and applied research. As a result, human factors and person–machine system researchers have been reduced to chasing a rapidly changing series of locally defined and technology-driven problems.

Field Experimentation Using Process Tracing

This section outlines a basic set of steps to be followed in setting up a field experiment using the process-tracing methodology.

Step 1. The critical precursor for all of the steps is to define the psychological issue being studied.

This can be done in several directions, that is, starting with an issue and then searching for an accessible situation that is an instance of the class to be investigated, or starting with an accessible complex setting and defining the class of psychological concepts or models that are relevant to that situation. Field observation frequently is an important activity in this step.

One typical error in the design of field experiments is to mistake superficial labels (e.g., diagnosis, planning) for insight into psychological issues. The source of this flaw is a failure to build an adequate account of the task demands—a cognitive task or work analysis or a cognitive model based in part on field studies.

Step 2. Develop an explicit mapping between the psychological issue under study and the test situation, for example, how does the question under investigation (e.g., garden path problems or the disturbance management cognitive task) get translated into characteristics of a specific test situation. Note that the test situation has a dual interpretation—one, in terms of domain-specific features and events, and a second in terms of a cognitive or behavioral language, that is, a behavioral situation that possesses certain characteristics.

The design of the study as an experiment occurs at this stage. The experimenter takes steps to ensure that the data of interest will be in the protocols to be collected. To accomplish this, it also helps to define the protocol building process, that is, the raw data collection step, so that the investigators will be in a position to extract the data of interest from the raw protocols. The experimenter develops the study as a field experiment, primarily through manipulation of the set of scenarios and the detailed features of individual scenarios in relation to the psychological questions of interest. For example, Roth et al. (1987) developed a set of scenarios where the goal was to challenge straightforward fault diagnosis in order to learn about some issues in human–

intelligent computer cooperation. As a result, the problem set was selected to include cases with various kinds of complicating factors such as miscommunications, impasses, bugs in the knowledge base, and multiple faults.

At this stage the experimenter should develop the tactics to cope with the challenges to validity in process-tracing studies—tactics for generating observable data that will support inferences about the psychological topic of interest. How do the assessment techniques change the primary processes that are the target of study, and how can I eliminate, counterbalance, or estimate the effects of these changes? How can I minimize or place checks on omission of important aspects, intrusions of irrelevant features, or distortions of the actual processes in the data collection and analysis process? Consider a simple example of the tradeoffs the experimenter faces. In dynamic fault management situations the portions of a scenario that are of greatest interest are almost always high operator demand periods where any secondary task can interfere or interact with the primary task. Often in studying this type of situation the experimenter wants to understand how the problem solver copes with high workload. A thinking-aloud technique is not suited to these circumstances, as it constitutes a secondary task that may interfere with the phenomenon under study or that may be shed at exactly the time when the experimenter wants to focus his or her data collection efforts.

Step 2 is also important in avoiding the psychologist's fallacy. As mentioned earlier, one is not justified in *assuming* that the experimenter's representation of the problem is the same as the study participant's representation; that is, the problem representation is not inherent or given in the problem statement *outside any larger context*. The experimenter has the burden to include some manipulation or check that provides evidence about the participant's problem representation. For example, Maule (1989) combined a classic laboratory technique with protocol analysis to investigate the role of decision frames in choice problems. One of the advantages of process-tracing methodology is that the investigator directly focuses on determining the participant's representation of the problem.

A typical danger at this stage (besides failing to build any mapping between test and target behavioral situations) occurs in studies that use an experimenter-designed microworld as the test situation. The microworld may be related to the target situation, but only at a surface level, for example, cloaking the microworld in the language of the target situation, which masks the absence of any deeper relationship based on a cognitive model or task analysis (cf. Cook & Woods, 1990).

Step 3. Collect data; that is, run the study participants in the test scenarios.

Step 4. Construct a domain specific protocol from the raw data records for each episode (trial).

Process-tracing studies generate a very large amount of raw data. One frequent source of failure in studies of complex worlds is getting lost in the details of overwhelming amounts of raw data. A critical pragmatic issue is efficiency in processing of the raw data. Using the knowledge of the issues being investigated, and the encoding approach to be used in step 5 to focus the collection and handling of raw data, can greatly increase the efficiency of the process (Woods, O'Brien, & Hanes, 1987). However, note that, in this filtering process, one should not lose the base raw data, in part because interesting behaviors and findings that were not anticipated in detail in advance almost always occur in studies of complex settings.

Step 5. Construct a formal, cognitive, or psychological protocol for each episode.

The cognitive encoding of the description of actual performance is the critical step in producing general, transportable results. Note that, frequently, there should be several layers of these protocols. One can see this first layer as a translation or transformation of the raw domain data into a cognitive language. Successive levels of analysis can attempt to get more leverage through stronger conceptual dependencies. In this process it is critical to be able to separate uncertainties regarding what occurred from debates on interpretations about what the observed behavior means relative to some psychological issue.

Another issue in human performance studies that use process-tracing concerns the reporting of data. Process-tracing studies, like other studies, should be reported in a way that supports a critical reading. One limit on complex world studies is that other researchers need to understand the domain in detail in order to be able to examine the study critically. Obviously, reporting lengthy process tracings also presents difficulties. The cognitive description, or at least a schematized version that minimizes the need for extensive domain background knowledge, should be required for archival publication. See the protocols as published in Roth et al. (1987) for an example of the entire technique described here, especially as an example of cognitive, domain independent protocols.

A typical failure in studies of complex worlds is to get lost in the language of the domain, that is, to fail to move from a domain description of behavior to a psychological description. This is due often to a failure to specify the mapping between the test situation and the target situation of interest.

Another difficulty comes from the danger of excessive microencodings of participant information processing. The fundamental point of a protocol analysis is to specify the process an individual (or a team) used to solve a particular problem, for example, to extract their strategies. The investigator's first responsibility is to be able to report these strategies. These strategies are the critical unit of analysis on which other aggregations and analyses of data are based.

Finally, there is always the danger of the hindsight bias. As was mentioned earlier, the point of a process-tracing method is to establish how the incident unfolded from the point of view of the person in the problem.

Step 6. Analysis across protocols with respect to psychological questions of interest.

One way to assess the protocols is to generate measures of the problem-solving process by relating behavior against a background frame as a model of the task.

This can be done in a variety of ways. One is to build a problem space for each test scenario that captures the set of trajectories along which the incident may evolve from the point of view of the person in the situation, at each point in the evolving incident. This includes mapping the cues potentially available, their interpretation in context, the knowledge relevant to characterize the underlying problem state, the potentially relevant goals, and the set of plausible actions. This is built through a cognitive task analysis of the domain. For efficiency purposes this should be done prior to data collection and used during Step 3 as an aid to generate efficiently both the raw and the first-level encoded protocols.

Another is building a cognitive simulation as an explicit model to account for the observed behavior (Newell & Simon, 1972). The concepts at the formal level of description can be as strong as a cognitive model for the class of situations investigated. Expressing this model as a runnable symbolic-processing simulation allows one to test the ability of the concepts captured in the simulation to account for the observed behavior. When the cognitive simulation produces the same behavior as the human study participants, the model becomes a candidate hypothesis about the underlying cognitive activities or strategies people use in that situation (e.g., Woods, Roth, & Pople, 1987). Furthermore, the formalization required to produce a cognitive simulation introduces increased rigor into the interpretation of the protocol results.

In effect, the problem space and cognitive simulation techniques are ways that one uses psychological concepts and models as a language for the formal layers of analysis. In addition, the problem space and cognitive simulation techniques can be used as computer aids for protocol analysis (e.g., Kowalski & VanLehn, 1988; there is also work to develop concept-neutral computer aids that support more efficient encoding and manipulation of protocol data).

Another type of background frame for interpreting participant behavior comes from what other domain practitioners see as plausible activities. A basic defining characteristic of human information processing is that the immediate problem-solving context biases the problem solver. In naturally occurring problems, the context in which the incident occurs, and the way the incident evolves, activate certain kinds of knowledge as relevant to the evolving situation, which affects how new incoming information is interpreted. The investigator can gain insight into the observed behavior by comparing it to how other domain practitioners would interpret the situation. In one technique the investigator presents the evidence available at one point in the evolving incident to observers who have not undergone the incident evolution. This "neutral" observer then makes a judgment or interpretation about the state of the world, relevant possible future trajectories, and relevant courses of action. The question is whether the path taken by the actual problem solver is one that is plausible to the neutral observers (i.e., they entertain that path as a serious candidate).

Special issues of interpretation of behavior arise when the focus of the study includes human error. The main problem is definitional—there are various positions about how to define errors including both domain standards and psychological taxonomies (cf., e.g., Reason, 1990).

Special issues also arise with respect to tools for problem solving. Spartan research related to problem solving strips the participants of any tools. Yet in almost all naturally occurring situations people devise, adapt, or utilize tools to assist in accomplishing goals or reducing effort. Understanding how people adapt or create tools may be an important approach to a better understanding of human problem solving. Studying human performance with significant tools adds another set of factors to an already multifaceted stimulus situation (cf. Hutchins, 1989, and Cook et al., 1990, for examples of such studies; cf. Woods, O'Brien, & Hanes, 1987, for some of the methodological challenges in studying tool use). What role does the tool play in practitioner cognitive activities (e.g., does it function as an external memory)? How are practitioner strategies changed when the tools available change? In this case the difficulty is that questions about the cognitive role of problem-solving support systems and tools are framed too easily in terms of the technologies from which the systems are built (e.g., should I use tiled or overlapping windows?). But again we are led to the challenge of developing a cognitive language of description, not only independent of the domain language (i.e., the language of the complex setting itself), but also independent of the languages of tool creation (Woods & Roth, 1988).

Another challenge for process-tracing methods is describing activities involving distributed cognition (Hutchins, 1989), where the cognitive activities in monitoring, situation assessment, and corrective actions are distributed over several people. With the introduction of intelligent machine agents into systems, cognitive activities become distributed over people and machines (Woods & Roth, 1988).

DISCOVERY OR VERIFICATION?

Destructive debates arise from claims that one methodological strategy or another has priviledged access to fundamental results. The contrast between spartan laboratory situations and complex behavioral settings was used as a vehicle to point out the underutilization of direct investigations of complex settings. Convergence between studies of simple and complex behavioral situations is important—there is a tradeoff, with sources of uncertainty and error on both sides (Bartlett, 1932; Hogarth, 1986).

One strategy may be more appropriate for hypothesis generation or discovery as opposed to hypothesis testing or verification, especially in immature research areas such as person–machine interaction. For example, studying complex settings can help to focus spartan lab research in more productive directions; spartan lab research results can guide new ways to look at and parse complex settings (Bartlett, 1932, saw this as the proper relationship between behavioral science research directed at spartan and complex settings). One research problem is revealing the basic phenomena, given the richness of the phenomenal world—seeing beyond the "blooming, buzzing confusion." Before we can say what hypothesis accounts for some observed effect, we need to characterize what are the observed effects, especially in terms that are not test situation, tool, or domain specific. We need to develop new ways of seeing in these rich situations—rich in the knowledge of the participants, rich in the diversity of strategies by which one can achieve satisfactory performance, rich in the tools available to assist human performance. In many areas the current need is to generate meaningful, fruitful hypotheses that eventually may be testable under more targeted circumstances.

In a theory-testing approach to behavioral science research, the objective is to support the current model and extend it to new tasks/variables. The critical constraint in developing the experimental task is tractability within the theoretical paradigm. The emphasis on the mapping between target and test behavioral situations points to another valid research strategy—one that is task driven where a cognitive analysis of the task demands guides the specification of meaningful test situations and relevant psychological models and concepts (e.g., Sorkin & Woods, 1985; Kleinmuntz & Thomas, 1987). The cognitive analysis then guides how the pieces (existing data models or new results) are put back together to form a coherent picture of human behavior in that class of situations. In the task-driven strategy, there is a natural complementarity between growing the research base and using the research base to develop pragmatic, though approximate, solutions to application problems.

SUMMARY

Research on problem solving in more complex situations, where significant tools are available to support the human and where experienced domain knowledgeable people are the appropriate study participants, requires a shift in research methodology from typical laboratory studies. This does not mean that rigor or control or generalizability or theory must be sacrificed. Rather it means using a wide set of research tools to converge on an understanding of the phenomenon in question.

> The analyst's task is no more difficult in the field setting than in the laboratory. The impression that this cannot be so rests primarily on unjustified assumptions regarding the extent to which the behavior of subjects in experimental settings is directly revealing of cognitive processes. Whether the setting is experimental or natural, the investigator must be able to make and support assertions about the representation of the task that the subject brings to the task. The laboratory setting has its advantages, but so has a more naturalistic environment. (E. Hutchins, 1980, p. 125)

KEY POINTS

- It is not necessary to impose a spartan research methodology to achieve tractability in studying complex behaviors.
- Whether data are collected from laboratory or field studies, the concern should be representativeness and the mapping between test situations where one is observing behavior and target situations which one wishes to understand.
- One methodology available to study complex behavioral situations is process tracing (or protocol analysis).
- There are numerous types of process-tracing methodologies that can be imposed on various field study designs to yield reliable and generalizable results.

Chapter 14

A Comment on Applying Experimental Findings Of Cognitive Biases To Naturalistic Environments*

Jay J. J. Christensen-Szalanski
Department of Management and Organizations
the Center for Health Services Research
University of Iowa

Throughout this book authors cite the need to study decision making in naturalistic environments. Nonetheless, data from laboratory-based experiments will continue to be published. Hammond (this volume) has already discussed the necessity to use experimental tasks that are generalizable to naturalistic tasks. This chapter outlines additional concepts that researchers and practitioners can use to apply appropriately these experimental data to naturalistic decision making.

SEPARATING COGNITIVE PROCESSES FROM DECISION OUTCOMES

Costs/Benefit Constraints in Naturalistic Decision Making

One of the hindrances to effective applications of experimental results in decision making that is shared by many disciplines is the failure to maintain the distinction between *statistical significance* and *meaningfulness*. In the decision-making literature, this important distinction is often further blurred by experimenters mistakenly equating cognitive processes with decision outcomes.

*Work for this project was partly funded by a grant from the University House Summer fellowship program at the University of Iowa.

Much of the experimental work in decision making has focused on providing information about cognitive *processes,* that is, the mental processes associated with acquiring and applying knowledge (Brehmer, 1984). At the same time there has been little inquiry into the effects of different cognitive processes on the outcomes that result from a decision (Brehmer, 1984; Christensen-Szalanski, 1986). For example, while researchers have a good understanding about how people purchasing cars will use information presented to them (the cognitive process), researchers lack knowledge about how or whether people's satisfaction with a purchased car (an outcome) changes with different methods of processing the information to select a car. If different methods of processing the information result in buyers being equally satisfied with the car purchased, then, with respect to the outcome *satisfaction,* all the processes are equally good.

Consider the decision-making literature on cognitive biases (Kahneman, Slovic, & Tversky, 1982). This compilation of biased processes suggests that unaided decision outcomes may be compromised. While it identifies the need for practitioners to examine the merits of corrective interventions, it does not establish that such interventions should be carried out. The existence of a biased process may not merit correction.

Corrective interventions and changes in support systems require resources. For a practitioner to rectify a biased process, or for a decision support designer to alter the support system to compensate for the bias, invariably requires the investment of time, energy, and or money. To justify the expenditure of these costs, the practitioner or support designer needs to be confident that these costs will be exceeded by the benefits resulting from correcting the biased cognitive process.

While one would hope that the correction of a biased cognitive process would meaningfully improve the outcomes that result from a decision, such is not always the case in the natural environment (Christensen-Szalanski, 1986; Funder, 1987). The complexity of the natural environment as described in Chapter 1 of this volume can be very forgiving of biased processes. Sometimes this complexity results in the decision maker being exposed to a large amount of redundant information that does not have to be used efficiently (Einhorn, Kleinmuntz, & Kleinmuntz, 1979). For example, consider the redundancy of information on letters that are mailed. In the United States, people sending mail typically write on the envelope information about the receiver's street address, city, and state. They also write the receiver's nine-digit zip code, which conveys the same information. Because of this redundancy, it is not necessary that the mail sorter efficiently process all of the information in order to deliver the mail to the correct address.

The complexity of the natural environment can also generate forces external to the decision maker that can "wash out" the negative outcomes of the decision maker's biased processes. Consider the case of physicians processing probabilistic information. In a recent study of physicians estimating the risks associated with circumcising newborn sons, Christensen-Szalanski, Boyce, Hevrill, and Gardner (1987) observed that physicians overestimated rare risks and underestimated common risks. When researchers previously identified this type of bias in a laboratory setting, they concluded that it needed to corrected (Christensen-Szalanski, Beck, Christensen-Szalanski, & Koepsell, 1983; Manu, Runge, & Lee, 1984). Such an action would make sense if physicians solely determined the type of care given newborns, but in the natural environment physicians do not work in isolation. In this particular setting, parents of the children are also involved in the decision making process. Christensen-Szalanski et al. (1987) showed that the elimination of this processing bias in physicians had no effect on the parents' decision on whether to circumcise their newborn sons, the primary outcome of concern. At the same time, eliminating this bias did change other outcomes, but for the worse. Parents of the newborns felt less confident in the quality of their irreversible decision, which then led to their feeling more resentful towards the physicians. Some parents even threatened to take their children to different physicians in the future. Not surprisingly, the physicians soon informed the researchers that their "corrective intervention" was being terminated!

In light of the findings that correcting biased processes may not improve decision outcomes, and given the cost/benefit constraint on resource expenditures faced by people in naturalistic environments, it is clear that naturalistic decision-making researchers must consider more than just information about the presence of biased cognitive processes. They must also consider (a) the effect of the process on decision outcomes of importance, (b) the benefit associated with any improvement in the outcomes that might occur as a result of correcting for the biased process, and (c) the amount of resources that have to be expended to achieve this improvement in outcomes.

Selecting Outcomes of Importance

Identifying the impact of a cognitive process on the outcome of a decision is not always easy. Often a succession of outcomes can result from a person's cognitive process, and the effects of a cognitive inefficiency on one of the outcomes may not be passed on to ensuing outcomes. Thus, one needs to determine which of several decision outcomes merit optimizing, and then focus on the effects of the biased process on those specific outcomes.

Consider the case of a physician who is evaluating patients at risk for having pneumonia. There are several decision outcomes that a biased cognitive process might influence. These include: the physician's initial assessed probability that a patient has pneumonia, the selection of tests and procedures to make a diagnosis, the diagnosis assigned to the patient, the treatment given the patient, the quality of the patient's recovery, the cost of managing the patient, and the patient's satisfaction. A bias may affect some of these outcomes but not others. For example, a biased process that alters the physicians' probability assessment will not alter the physicians' diagnosis if the altered probability happens to fall on the same side of the threshold probability used to assign the diagnosis. Similarly, a biased process that alters the assigned diagnosis may not alter the quality of the patient's recovery if the treatment given the patient happens to be the same (Christensen-Szalanski, 1986; Reuben, 1984). Thus, if researchers are interested in assessing the effect of a biased cognitive process on a specific outcome, for example, the quality of the patients' recovery, they must directly examine the effect of the bias on that specific outcome.

EFFECT SIZE AND THE STATISTICAL SIGNIFICANCE OF AN EFFECT

Calculating Effect Sizes

When assessing the costs and benefits of changing the process by which decisions are made, researchers evaluating data on the harm of cognitive biases or the merit of debiasing techniques need information about the *magnitude* of the observed effect, that is, the *effect size* (Cohen, 1977). This information is usually omitted in many experimental studies. Instead, a review of the published experimental literature will reveal that the results are often evaluated exclusively in terms of their p-values, that is, their statistical significance. Once researchers cite a finding with a significant p-value, they attempt to address the meaningfulness of the findings by speculating about the possible consequences that such an effect will have without ever evaluating the actual magnitude of the observed effect.

Information about a result's p-value, or statistical significance, is useful for determining whether an effect "exists" according to a specified level of statistical probability. However, p-values are not as useful as effect size measures for naturalistic decision makers, because, unlike measures of effect size, the p-value of a finding depends upon the size of the sample that happened to be used in the study. Large effects may not be statistically significant, because too small a sample was used, while trivially sized effects may be statistically significant because an extremely large sample size was used.

Fortunately, one can often calculate a measure of effect size from the statistical information that is included in most experimental studies (Rosenthal, 1984). Equations 1–4 (Table 14.1), for example, show how results of frequently used statistical tests can be transformed into the Pearson product moment correlation coefficient (r), a commonly used measure of effect size. The square of the correlation coefficient indicates the proportion of the variance in the observed variable (e.g., probability assessments from a biased cognitive processes) that can be attributed to the suspected cause (e.g., the cognitive bias). The larger the R^2, the more of the outcome's observed variability can be accounted for by the suspected cause. Equation 5 provides a formula for calculating Cohen's d, another common measure of effect size.[1] Finally, equations 6 and 7 show how to transform the r and d measures of effect size into each other.

Application of Effect Size Information

Identification of moderator variables. Consider now how a decision support designer can apply the equations in Table 14.1 for calculating effect sizes. In a recent study, Bukszar and Connolly (1988) were examining the robustness of the hindsight bias—a bias that, depending upon the information given an individual, could inflate or reduce an individual's probability assessment of an event occurring. They examined whether an individual's participation in a group discussion after receiving the potentially biasing information, but before making a probability assessment, might alter the impact of the hindsight bias on the individual's probability assessments. The authors observed a *statistically significant* effect of the bias on probability assessments made by individuals, regardless of whether they were preceded by a group discussion. This led the authors to conclude that the group discussion had no effect. However, this conclusion is at

---

[1]This measure indicates the standardized difference between the control and treatment groups.

Table 14.1.   Relationships Between Effect Sizes and Tests of Significance*

(1) $$r = \sqrt{\frac{t^2}{t^2 + df}}$$

(2) $$r = \sqrt{\frac{F_{(1,-)}}{F_{(1,-)} + df_{error}}}$$

(3) $$r = \sqrt{\frac{X^2_{(1)}}{N}}$$

(4) $$r = \frac{Z}{\sqrt{N}} \; **$$

(5) $$d = \frac{X_1 - X_2}{\frac{sd_1 + sd_2}{2}} \; ***$$

(6) $$d = \frac{2r}{\sqrt{1 - r^2}} \; ***$$

(7) $$r = \frac{d}{\sqrt{d^2 + 4}} \; ***$$

*From *Meta-analytic Procedures for Social Research,* by R. Rosenthal, 1984. Copyright © 1984 by Sage. Reprinted by permission.

**Can also be used when only exact p-value is given by converting p-value into its standard normal equivalent

***When sample sizes for two groups can be viewed as equal

best premature, since the authors' analysis showed only that the bias still existed after a group discussion—it did not address whether the magnitude of the bias's effect was reduced. In fact, using equation 5 (Table 14.1) to transform the authors' results of their statistical significance tests into a measure of effect size reveals that the group discussion *did reduce* the impact of the bias to as little as one-sixth of its original size. Once a decision support designer was satisfied about the reliability of these effects and the generalizability of the study, he or she could begin to explore the benefits and costs of implementing appropriate changes into the support system that take advantage of the "group discussion" moderating factor.

Transforming changes in probabilities to changes in decisions. Many experimental studies focus on the effect of cognitive processes on individuals' probability assessments. While one can calculate the size of the effect on probability assessments from these studies, one needs to remember that the degree to which a bias changes a person's probability assessment is not always related to changes in decisions. For example, suppose the threshold probability for choosing an alternative was 60%. If a person normally estimated the probability to be 58%, but because of a bias, estimated it to be 62%, then, even though the effect of the bias on the probability assessment was small, it still would be of meaningful importance, since it would change the person's decision.

To assess the impact of a bias's change on probability assessments, one needs to examine the degree to which the bias causes people to cross a decision threshold. This can be accomplished by using the d measure of effect size (Christensen-Szalanski & Fobian, 1988; Christensen-Szalanski & Willham, 1991). As an example, suppose it was shown that the magnitude of the hindsight bias's effect on a person's probability assessments was $d = 0.46$. Since the variable of interest in the study was an individual's probability assessment, and since the d measure of effect size is measured in standard deviation units of the variable being examined (i.e., the persons' probability assessments), the effect "0.46" implies that the bias inflated the population's mean probability estimate 0.46 standard deviations above the mean foresight estimate. By assuming a normal distribution, one can graphically portray this effect of the bias on probability assessments by comparing the unbiased (foresight) and biased (hindsight) distributions in Figure 14.1. The vertical line intersecting the distributions represents the location of a hypothetical threshold probability for selecting an alternative. In this example, the threshold probability is rather high and represents a condition in which most of the people without the biasing information would not have chosen the particular alternative, because their estimated foresight probability was below the threshold probability. The shaded area to the right of the threshold line indicates the proportion of the population that would have selected the alternative after receiving the potentially biasing hindsight information. The darkly shaded portion indicates those people who would have also selected the alternative without the biasing information, while the lightly shaded portion indicates the "changers"—those who changed their decision because of the hindsight bias.

One can assess the degree to which decisions might be changed by the hindsight bias by measuring the proportion of changers, that is, the proportion of the population contained in the lightly shaded area for different threshold probabilities. This can be done by varying the threshold probability, using the normal probability distribution to determine the proportion of the hindsight bias curve that was shaded, and then subtracting from this amount the proportion contained in the

Figure 14.1.   Impact of the hindsight bias with an effect size of 0.46 on people's probability assessments and decisions. Darkly shaded area represents the people who would have chosen the alternative without the potentially biasing information. Lightly shaded area represents the people who changed their decision because of the hindsight bias.

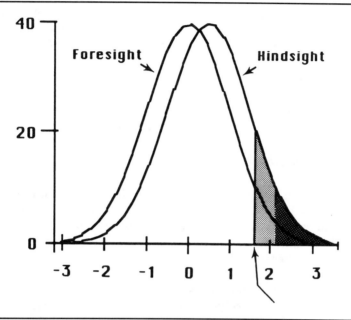

darkly shaded portion of the curve (see Christensen-Szalanski & Fobian, 1988; Christensen-Szalanski & Willham, 1991). The results of this analysis, for an effect size of 0.46, indicates that the maximum effect of the bias on individuals' *decisions* would occur when the threshold probability was near the population's mean probability assessment. At this point there is an 18% chance that an individual receiving the potentially biasing information would make a decision different from what would have been made without the information. The likelihood that the biasing information would alter a persons' decisions then drops rapidly to zero the further the threshold probability is from the population's mean probability estimate.

   Transforming measures of effect size into changes in success rates. For studies that examine the effect of a debiasing procedure (or a bias) on outcomes such as success rates or improvement rates, the *r* measure of effect size can be used to more easily appreciate the impact of the procedure on these rates. It can be shown (Rosenthal & Rubin, 1982) that the obtained *r* effect size in these type of studies is equivalent to the debiasing group having a success rate equal to ".50 + r/2" and the control group having a success rate equal to ".50 − r/2." Thus, the obtained r is equal to the difference between the two groups' success rates. An r equal to 0.50, implies that the debiasing procedure increases the success rate by 50%; an r equal to 0.25, implies that the debiasing procedure increases the success rate by 25%, and so on. Given this relationship, it becomes clear that even effect sizes as small as r = .05 can easily become meaningfully important when they are obtained from studies that examine changes in success rates, survival rates, or improvement rates, and so on.

III. CLOSING COMMENTS

Moderator Variables

A word of caution needs to be made regarding the use of effect size information to identify moderator variables. Nearly all decision-making studies are based on sample sizes of less than 1,000. Consequently, effect sizes calculated from these studies will depart from the "true" effect size because of sampling error (Hunter, Schmidt, & Jackson, 1982). The smaller the sample size, the more the observed effect size may depart from the true effect size, and the more likely an observed difference may reflect the impact of sampling error.

Researchers in decision making often misunderstand the effect of sampling error on effect sizes (Christensen-Szalanski & Fobian, 1989) and *erroneously* claim to have identified a moderator variable for a bias when they have observed that a particular group did not exhibit the bias (Dawson et al., 1988; Dawson, 1989; Norman & Brooks, 1989), or because there was a significant interaction between the effect of the bias upon different groups (Elstein, 1989). In fact, Hunter and Schmidt (1989) prove how these differences may be artifactual effects of sampling error. In their book they give several examples of significant interactions that disappear once the results have been corrected for sampling error. Therefore, before concluding that a moderating variable exists, one needs to correct for sampling error the results obtained from *independent replications* of the effect (Hunter et al., 1982).

Meaningful Significance

Throughout this commentary, I have avoided implying that a standard exists for evaluating the meaningful significance of an observed

effect. This is because there is no uniform index of meaningful significance. The utilities associated with the cost/benefit constraint faced by
practitioners and designers of decision support systems is, by definition, situation specific and subjective in nature (Feinstein, 1971). Even
a very large effect may not be meaningfully significant if (a) the
benefits associated with the corrected outcome are small, (b) the costs
needed to achieve the benefits substantially outweigh the benefits, or
(c) the experimental condition generating the effect is not generalizable to the naturalistic environment (Hammond, this volume).

Given the subjective nature of meaningful significance, neither the
effect size nor the p-value of a finding determines the meaningful
significance of an experimental finding. However, as discussed in this
chapter, effect size information can be combined with information
about the costs and benefits associated with outcomes of importance to
practitioners to help us better assess the meaningful importance of
experimental findings.

KEY POINTS

- Researchers' failure to distinguish *statistical significance* from
  meaningfulness, and *cognitive process* from *decision outcome,* hinder
  effective applications of experimental results.
- Before implementing corrective interventions, researchers must
  consider the cost of the intervention and the benefit associated with
  any improvement in the outcomes that might occur as a result of
  correcting for the biased process.
- A biased cognitive process might influence some decision outcomes
  while not affecting other, similar, outcomes.
- P-values are not as useful as *effect size* measures for naturalistic
  decision makers.
- There is no uniform index of meaningful significance.

Section D

Applications of Naturalistic Decision Models

Chapter 15

The Bottom Line: Naturalistic Decision Aiding

Marvin S. Cohen
Cognitive Technologies, Inc.
Arlington, VA

It is appealing to suppose that technology has the means for improving decisions. Computer-based systems to advise decision makers have incorporated decision analysis, expert knowledge, and/or mathematical optimization. Success, however, has been limited; the very features of real-world environments that are stressed in this volume, for example, their ill-structuredness, uncertainty, shifting goals, dynamic evolution, time stress, multiple players, and so on typically defeat the kinds of static, bounded models provided by all three technologies. Each decision involves a unique and complex combination of factors, which seldom fits easily into a standard decision analytic template, a previously collected body of expert knowledge, or a predefined set of linear constraints. Users are sometimes ahead of the aids in their ability to recognize and adapt to such complex patterns.

The literature on decision biases (as described in Chapter 3 and 4) has reinforced the tendency to regard users as passive recipients of assistance: unaided decision making is presumed to be subject to fundamental flaws, which can be corrected only by adoption of "normative" methods such as Bayesian decision analysis. The rationalist tradition has encouraged a sort of arrogance toward actual decision makers that can only make their acceptance of decision aids (and the aids' success if accepted) less likely (Berkeley & Humphreys, 1982; Lopes, 1988). Such an approach may force decision makers to adopt highly unfamiliar modes of reasoning; as a result, aids may not be used, or if used, may be poorly understood; worse yet, they may fail to exploit user knowledge or expertise that might facilitate adaptation to complex, novel situations. Although there is lip service to "supporting the user rather than replacing him," in technology-driven approaches (whether based on decision analysis, optimization, or expert systems) *the user's approach to the problem,* if not the user himself or herself, is replaced: at best, the user may provide probability and utility inputs for a standard decision analytic model.

Should we give up hope of advising decision makers? At the other extreme are less ambitious (and more organizationally acceptable) *status-quo-driven* approaches, which merely automate the more tedious aspects of a task without modifying it in any essential respect. Such aids do not correct any flaws in traditional procedures, fail to exploit potential synergies between humans and computers, and—ironically —may be just as unacceptable to users as technology-driven aids.

An alternative approach is to start with the user's preferred way of solving the problem and to examine its strengths and weaknesses carefully. Attention is paid to how decision makers actually solve problems (including consideration of individual differences and changes over time) and the cognitive strategies and knowledge representations underlying performance, as well as to normative models as sources of potential insight for improvements. Aids are then designed which support more optimal *variants* of the user-preferred strategy. We have called this methodology *personalized and prescriptive aiding* (Cohen, Bromage, Chinnis, Payne, & Ulvila, 1982; Cohen, Laskey, & Tolcott, 1987). The naturalistic framework encourages aiding that is *user driven* (or personalized)—that is, tailored to user knowledge representations and processing strategies, but not necessarily to the status-quo procedure—and simultaneously *problem driven* (or prescriptive)— that is, able to safeguard against errors and pitfalls to which the user-preferred approach is susceptible, but not necessarily wedded to traditional normative models.

The reader need not subscribe to non-Bayesian normative models [Chapter 4, Challenge (6)], or to alternative Bayesian models [Challenge (5)], to be persuaded about the value of a more adaptive approach to decision aiding. The reader need not even accept the claim that knowledge [Challenge (3)] and limited capacity [Challenge (4)] sometimes justify non-Bayesian decision processes. The case for adapting aids to users can be made purely in terms of outcomes [Challenges (1) and (2)]: by arguing, for example, that deviations from optimality often don't matter much (von Winterfeldt & Edwards, 1973), and that, where they do matter, specific safeguards can be provided. The argument, however, gets stronger, and the associated concept of aiding gets richer, as one's acceptance of the naturalistic point of view moves from outcomes to processes to decisions. Let us look briefly at the implications for aiding, together with some examples, from these different perspectives.

An aid developed for the command staff of an attack submarine illustrates the role of decision analytic models as advisors who step in only when the user's approach is likely to produce an unfavorable outcome (Cohen et al., 1982). As a "hunter-killer" submarine stalks an enemy submarine, the commander must balance competing goals of improving the accuracy of localization and probability of kill (thus taking time and getting closer), while minimizing the chances of being detected (thus shooting early and far away). A decision analytic model can integrate all the factors involved in the time-of-fire decision into a single aggregated figure of merit (subjectively expected utility) for each tactical option. Such a measure, however, requires highly ambiguous uncertainty estimates (e.g., the detection capabilities of the opposing submarine), difficult preference tradeoffs (e.g., the value of own ship versus the target), and numerous assumptions (e.g., about what each commander will do if the first shot misses). By contrast, the personalized and prescriptive aid allows the commander to evaluate options in terms of goals and constraints at whatever level of concreteness he or she chooses (e.g., achieve a particular probability of kill on the first shot; get within x yards of the target but no closer than y yards). At the same time, in the background, the aid creates a decision analytic model of the problem; it also creates a model of the user: inferring his or her decision strategy by monitoring his or her information requests and goal specifications. Finally, the aid compares the recommendations of its model with the implications of the user's strategy. The user is prompted if, and only if, they are significantly different (at a threshold set by the user): for example, the aid might point out that an option that has been rejected by the user because it just misses the desired 90% chance of kill achieves a far better chance of avoiding counterdetection. Prompts are framed in terms of the specific factors that cause the discrepancy, described at the level of concreteness the user prefers. As a result, the user can benefit from the decision analytic model without being forced to abandon his or her own way of thinking.

A dyed-in-the-wool Bayesian might accept such an aid (grudgingly), because the *outcomes* it leads to should not be significantly worse than those expected from a more orthodox aid. A naturalist is more likely to focus on the advantages of supporting the user's familiar decision processes: Those processes may produce outcomes that are not merely just as good as, but better than, Bayesian procedures—because they more effectively exploit the decision maker's knowledge and capacity. Traditional decision analysis takes knowledge for granted, assuming, in the extreme, that the required judgments of probability and preference preexist somehow in the decision maker's head and are accessible on demand; traditional decision analysis thus neglects the metacognitive processes of inquiry and reflection by means of which a problem-specific model is constructed (Levi, 1986). In response, new *formal* methods have been developed, including the assumption-based reasoning framework that I discussed in Chapter 4, that explicitly consider the amount of knowledge or ignorance underlying a decision and formally incorporate the dynamic processes by which beliefs and preferences are tentatively adopted and subsequently revised.

An aid has recently been developed that focuses directly on the dynamic aspects of crystallizing one's own knowledge. D-CIDER (Cohen et al., 1987) is based on the premise that users differ in how much they know about their preferences and in the way they know it, and that users' understanding may evolve as they work the problem. D-CIDER enables users to express preferences in a variety of qualitatively different formats, including direct judgments of a sample of options, setting goals on different dimensions, rank ordering dimensions, and assessments of exact or inexact importance weights. Implications of inputs in any one format are displayed in all the other formats, to prompt and constrain further judgments. D-CIDER also provides a choice of decision strategies: for example, elimination-by-aspects (which screens options by user-set goals in order of importance), dominance structuring (in which users work backwards from a tentative choice, determining whether the choice can be justified by comparison to other options), and maximization of utility (which takes whatever tradeoff information the user has provided, however partial and incomplete, and calculates which options could be best). Prompts help users shift strategies, and add, drop, strengthen, or weaken their goals, when the information provided is inadequate to make a choice from the available options.

Whether we focus on decision outcomes, decision processes, or the decisions themselves, then, the conclusion is that aiding should start with the user's preferred approach. Normative models are appropriate only when they fit the basic contours of the decision maker's knowledge and preferred method of problem solving. From the naturalistic point of view, the goal of aiding is not to radically alter an experienced decision maker's decision-making style, but to mitigate specific potential weaknesses, and to amplify his or her decision-making strengths.

KEY POINTS

- Most decisions involve unique and complex combinations of factors that seldom fit into standard decision analytic templates.

- Users are often ahead of their aids, because they can recognize and adapt to these novel and complex patterns.
- The naturalistic paradigm suggests that decision aids should
    — take advantage of users' knowledge
    — support the user's naturally preferred strategies
    — guard against errors associated with the user's preferred strategy

Chapter 16

Evolutionary Design of Systems to Support Decision Making

William B. Rouse
Search Technology, Inc.
Norcross, GA

John Valusek
Air Force Institute of Technology, WPAFB
Dayton, OH

INTRODUCTION

The design of systems to support decision making is an age-old pursuit. Pharaohs, kings, and generals for millennia have employed "experts" who have used various exotic means to forecast and evaluate options.

In recent centuries, much progress has been made in putting such advisory mechanisms on a more rational basis. Since Descartes's "age of reason," the model of *economic man* has continued to evolve, leading to Bayesian thinking in the 18th century and culminating in formal axioms of rationality by the middle of this century.

In the last two or three decades, the emergence of powerful and inexpensive computing has enabled the development of computer-based systems that explicitly incorporate the axioms of rationality and/or computational mechanisms based on these axioms. These systems have been designed to support decision makers to behave more like economic man (e.g., Andriole, 1986).

This need emerged when it was realized by behavioral scientists and others that humans have great difficulty behaving in accordance with the axioms of rationality, despite the *apparent* desire to behave in this manner. Particular difficulties humans encounter include estimating and updating probabilities, consistently weighting attributes of alternatives, and generating multiple viable alternatives. These types of difficulty, when combined with tendencies to seek only confirming information and attribute cause when only correlation is warranted, led to a picture of humans as being fundamentally flawed information processors, particularly for probabilistic information (Kahneman, Slovic, & Tversky, 1982).

The field of *decision analysis* emerged to assist humans to overcome their limitations and behave in accordance with the axioms of rationality. The humans' part of the decision analysis process is the contribution of utilities—the 18th-century construct of Bentham—or values to the analysis. *Multiattribute utility analysis* (MAUA) emerged in the 1970s with a powerful set of tools and methods for assessing, combining, and employing utility functions (e.g., Keeney & Raiffa, 1976).

Impressive applications of this approach included blood banking (Keeney & Raiffa, 1976), airport siting (Keeney, 1973), acquisition management (Rouse, 1974), and system staffing (Rouse, 1975). The common characteristics of these applications include well-defined alternatives, ample time for data collection and analysis, and situations where technical attributes primarily influence decisions. In situations with these characteristics, this type of analysis can be quite valuable.

However, as noted by many other authors in this book, there were numerous attempts to apply this approach to situations without these underlying characteristics. An example is military command and control, where the alternatives are not clear, time constraints are tight, and attributes can be vague and immeasurable (e.g., threat lethality). Such situations obviously do not allow for much analysis when the decisions are needed. Thus, if MAUA is to be used, it is necessary to formulate and, in effect, solve the problem in advance.

It should not be surprising that the expectations of success surrounding this endeavor were not met—predetermining the best choice among, as yet, unknown alternatives is a difficult problem. Actually the problem is a bit more subtle. One often can determine general classes of alternatives in advance. However, one cannot fully know the context within which these alternatives will emerge. To the extent that contextual factors should strongly influence choices, one finds that decision analysis tends to be much too narrow and rigid to provide the necessary support.

The recognition that context can dominate decision making, particularly expert decision making, led in the 1980s to the reemergence of *artificial intelligence*. Expert systems, which typically are very context sensitive, has been the most recent panaceas for providing less-than-expert decision makers with the "right" answers. This approach has merits, and important successes have been achieved in highly structured domains such as medical diagnosis (Shortliffe, 1976), configuring computer equipment (McDermott, 1982), and aircraft piloting (Rouse, Geddes, & Curry, 1988; Rouse, Geddes, & Hammer, 1990).

However, many domains are not highly structured—the "physics" of these domains does not constrain acceptable behaviors to enable prescriptions for decision-making behavior. In other words, most domains are loosely structured and allow decision makers substantial discretion in how they bring order to their world and produce acceptable results. Indeed, the ability to flexibly and successfully deal with a lack of structure is one of the primary reasons for utilizing human decision makers—if prescriptions were possible, automation would be likely.

To summarize our arguments thus far, the context-free equations of decision analysis and context-dependent rules of artificial intelligence provide powerful and valuable support for relatively small classes of decision-making situations. For the very large class of problems where it is not meaningful to formulate probability distributions for a fixed set of alternatives, or where structural constraints are weak, other approaches are needed. This chapter discusses alternative approaches.

It is important at the outset to recognize that we should not delude ourselves into thinking that what is needed is a different set of mathematics, something other than probability theory or the predicate calculus. Instead, what is needed is a different design philosophy, as well as methods and tools, that provide means for supporting decision making when we, as designers, do not know what decision makers should do or will do. Obviously, different types of design prescription are needed.

This chapter emphasizes supporting human performance. This is accomplished by first understanding the nature of humans' tasks, not just their decisions, and then determining the information necessary for supporting task performance. This includes tasks performed by both individuals and teams. The resulting supports do not, by definition, prescribe how tasks are to be performed. Instead, the emphasis is no providing the information decision makers want, in the ways that they want it. As might be expected, this strategy can result in requirements being a moving target. This chapter illustrates how this is much less of a problem if the design premises include the concept of an evolutionary design that is adapted to an evolving understanding of what supports are needed.

DECISION MAKERS' TASKS

Figure 16.1 depicts humans' tasks in complex systems. Three major classes of activity are shown. *Execution and monitoring* is the predominant class.

Figure 16.1.   Decision Makers' Tasks

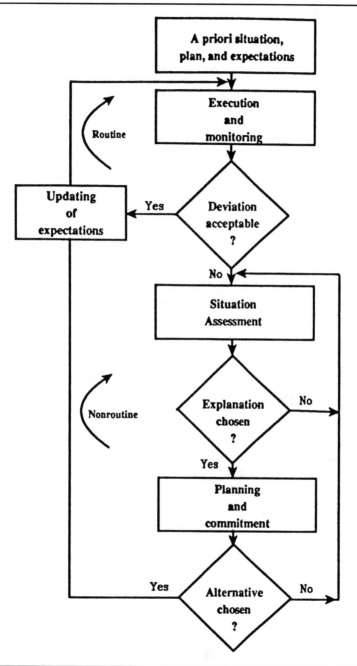

Despite the stereotypical view of humans proceeding from one decision event to another, most if not all humans spend the vast majority of their time doing things (e.g., moving control sticks and writing memoranda and letters) and observing results (e.g., watching displays and reading reports).

Most of these activities are quite routine, with actions following well-worn patterns and observations agreeing with expectations. For the most part, therefore, execution and monitoring continue uninterrupted.

However, occasionally, deviations from expectations are sufficiently large to cause activities to expand to include *situation assessment*. First, information may be sought as a basis for assessing the situation. Typically, alternative information sources are well defined and choices are obvious—information seeking is likely to be virtually automatic in such situations. Once in a while, the situation is sufficiently puzzling to cause humans to seek less familiar sources. In these less frequent situations, information seeking is likely to be a more conscious activity.

The information accessed, implicitly or explicitly, provides the basis for recognizing or devising an explanation that "fits" the observations and additional information. Quite often, information readily available will result in humans immediately recognizing the new situation. Much less frequently, more explicit analysis, if only "in the head," is required to devise a satisfactory explanation.

The assessed situation may or may not require a revised plan of action. In the minority of cases where a new or revised plan is needed, it is common for decision makers to resort to well-worn alternatives. In many cases, the choice is so obvious that plans need not be explicitly evaluated. Occasionally, however, explicit *planning and commitment* are necessary. This involves synthesizing a course of action for dealing with the assessed situation.

The three classes of activities in Figure 16.1 can also be viewed in terms of the objects of these activities. Execution and monitoring involve implementing a course of action, observing its consequences, evaluating deviations from expectations, and deciding whether or not deviations are sufficient to warrant anything beyond routine monitoring. For experienced decision makers, much if not most of this activity requires little deliberation, with the possible exception of the recognition of unacceptable deviations. In fact, it can be argued that information displays for supporting execution and monitoring should be such that humans need not consciously seek and utilize information.

The information-seeking aspects of situation assessment may occasionally involve consideration of alternative information sources. In such cases, selection among sources is often virtually automatic, particularly when the sources are all at hand. Selection in some situations may be preceded by evaluation of sources in terms of relevance, reliability, cost, and so on. On rare occasions, new sources will have to be identified or generated. These sources may subsequently be evaluated and, when multiple alternatives are deemed necessary, selected among.

The explanation aspects of situation assessment are concerned with alternative explanations. For experienced decision makers, selection among alternatives is usually rather simple—a satisfactory explanation is simply recognized. In some cases, explanations are evaluated in terms of fit, consequences of adoption, and so on. These evaluations are typically in the head, but can be supported with the appropriate information displays. Occasionally, a new or novel explanation must be generated, which leads to one or more alternatives which are evaluated, either subsequently or somewhat in parallel with being generated.

Planning and commitment focuses on alternative courses of action. In the vast majority of cases, selection among alternatives draws upon the repertoire accumulated by the decision maker during his or her many past experiences. Selection is often the process of choosing the first acceptable alternatives, rather than weighing multiple acceptable alternatives. In some cases, the decision maker will pause to consciously evaluate a course of action in terms of its consequences, costs, and so on. This evaluation is likely to occur as a mental simulation or accounting rather than an explicit analysis. Occasionally, a new course of action is needed, perhaps for unfamiliar and infrequent situations. In this case, one or more alternative courses of action will be generated by resorting to analogies, metaphors, or, typically in the last resort, explicit "ideation" techniques. These alternatives may be evaluated as described above.

This discussion of humans' tasks has repeatedly used the terms *selection, evaluation,* and *generation*—as will be seen, these terms facilitate discussion of support concepts. First, however, it is important to note the relative frequencies of these activities.

- Selection occurs frequently, usually involving unconscious retrieval of well-worn alternatives without any sense of "having selected."
- Evaluation occurs occasionally, typically via mental simulation or accounting of fit, consequences, costs, and so on.
- Generation occurs rarely, via analogy or metaphor if possible, or formal means if necessary.

SUPPORT CONCEPTS

This section considers alternative ways to support humans in the activities of implementation, observation, selection, evaluation, and generation. In general, support concepts do *not* involve automating these activities—recall the discussion in the Introduction about the prevalence of ill-defined and ill-structured tasks. Instead, the emphasis is on providing the types and forms of information that are likely to facilitate humans' pursuit of these activities.

Implementation

A support system can display plans and procedures chosen by the decision maker. To a limited extent, a system can monitor execution and "check off" completed steps, and perhaps highlight omitted steps (e.g., Rouse, Rouse & Hammer, 1982). Such omissions may or may not be errors—typically, humans will promptly correct any omissions that they judge to be erroneous.

Observation

This activity can be supported by modifying, filtering, interpolating, and extrapolating information. Scrolling, zooming, and branching among display pages can also be facilitated. The value of these types of support depends, of course, on satisfying humans' information requirements.

Beyond satisfying requirements, information must be displayed using formats that are compatible with humans' tasks. A common shortfall of support systems is to provide elegant color-graphic displays of information in a manner that conflicts with humans' views of their tasks—for example, presenting a matrix of resources vs. demands when the user actually thinks of the task in terms of the spatial arrangement of resources and demands. Various other chapters in this book discuss alternative ways of conceptualizing humans' tasks.

Selection

Since selection is frequently unconscious and automatic, it is important that supports for this activity foster such modes of choice. This requires that information regarding sources of information, explanations of situations, and courses of action be displayed in manner that is natural for the humans who are to be supported. Typically, this does *not* mean that the alternatives are displayed. Instead, appropriate cues are displayed that enable humans to recall the most appropriate alternative. In other words, the alternatives are in the decision maker, and the purpose of the support system is to prompt their retrieval.

To provide this type of support, it is *not* necessary for the support system to know about relevant alternatives. It is only necessary that sufficient front-end analysis be performed to identify cues used by decision makers, and displays for those cues be devised. Thus, for example, an appropriately designed map display can prompt a decision maker to choose useful routes even though the map display system has no explicit knowledge of the concept of routes.

Occasionally, alternatives will be explicitly compared. Often this is best supported by enabling decision makers to consider ordinal comparisons between pairs of alternatives along each decision-making attribute. The resulting *dominance structure* is usually sufficient for choosing among alternatives. In some cases, quantification such as provided by utility, value, or worth functions can be useful.

Evaluation

Supports for evaluation typically involve presentation and/or computation of the present or future characteristics of one or more alternatives—as noted earlier, a single alternative is the dominant situation. Present characteristics include relevance, information content, resource requirements, physical configuration, and linkages to other entities. These characteristics can be displayed automatically if one is aware of the attributes of interest to the decision makers. Alternatively, they can be retrieved via, for instance, menus or selectable tables.

Future characteristics include consequences such as expected performance impact and resource requirements. A classical approach to presenting such information is predictor displays, which have been in use for almost 40 years. Succinctly, a model of the phenomenon of interest, as well as the decision makers' expected course of action, are used to extrapolate the current state to the future, using calculation or simulation procedures. Using current modeling and display technologies, it is possible to enable decision makers to modify or even construct the models that underlie simulations.

It is important that evaluative information be displayed in a manner consistent with its likely use. Evaluation is not an end in itself. Instead is a means to improve alternatives and/or provide the basis for selection. Thus, it is important that evaluative results be integrated into displays suitable for modifying alternatives and, in some cases, selecting whether or not to proceed with the evaluated alternative. Otherwise, humans may find the information integration to be too difficult to justify using the evaluative support.

Generation

In rare, but nevertheless very important, situations, new alternatives may have to be generated. Alternatives are new to the extent that humans cannot simply retrieve them from memory based on salient cues. In such situations, a support system can help by retrieving previously relevant and useful alternatives.

Retrieval of alternatives can be based on humans' specification of situational characteristics, desired attributes of alternatives, possible analogies, or even metaphors. In virtually all situations, the human will have to recognize whether or not a retrieved alternative is truly relevant and useful. This is likely to involve evaluation, typically performed in the head, but occasionally using the types of evaluative support discussed earlier.

Summary

The types of support outlined in this section are appropriate for task situations that are not amenable to formal decision analysis, or sufficiently structured to be approached with artificial intelligence methods. Consequently, these types of support emphasize access, utilization, and management of information in ways that assist humans in performing their tasks in whatever ways they choose.

As noted earlier, many of the other chapters of this book provide alternative perspectives on the ways in which humans in realistically complex situations are likely to perform their tasks. Such descriptions are important inputs to the process of designing support systems. However, this information is not sufficient. One also needs a design process that enables production of appropriate support systems (Rouse, 1990). The remainder of this chapter focuses on the design process.

PERSPECTIVES ON DESIGN

It can be reasonably argued that one of the major reasons that many information-based support systems have failed to meet expectations is that there are flaws in the process of designing and building these systems. The process through which support systems are typically derived assumes that the end result will be stable. However, the product, the hardware and software, is the only stable component. The "user" is not and cannot be stable, due to the nature of human information processing as well as the nature of task environments. The typical design process does not facilitate adaptation of the support system to its changing environment. This problem in the way support systems are designed suggests a need to investigate system design and the roles of each of the participants in the design process.

Design in its verb form means "to plan creatively." In its noun form, it is a pattern from which something is created. The designer's role then becomes one of creating the pattern from which something will be delivered. In the case of support systems, the deliverable is the system specifications. The designer's role in creating support systems is to translate from the user's world to the builder's world.

Designer as Omniscient

Designers need a translation mechanism to allow these two diverse communities to communicate. However, in most instances designers have risen through the builder ranks. Consequently, rather than creating a language useful to the two parties for whom they are translating, designers have attempted to use the languages of the builder. These "foreign" languages (relative to users) have created a mystique surrounding the process. These languages have hindered rather than facilitated communication of needs.

The foreign languages came in two forms, each with its own dialects. Computer scientists approach the process from a variety of software languages. Operations researchers pursue the process with a range of modeling techniques. Use of these languages for communication initially overwhelms the user and continues to mystify, frustrate, and even anger many.

From the outset users are typically given at best an extremely limited role and/or responsibility in the design process and often become comfortable in their nonrole. As such, users have acquiesced to applications designers through nonparticipation—other than via perfunctory "reviews" of functional descriptions and system/subsystem specifications, a language that is supposed to be their means of communication. Thus, users have essentially been removed from the process. They certainly have not been given tools to assist them in problem formulation and communication.

Meanwhile designers and builders have continuously evolved their toolkit to include, for example, *computer-aided software engineering* (CASE) tools, which allow them to rapidly implement whatever the user says he or she needs. Armed with flow-charting templates, computer science languages, and the tools of operations research, there should be little wonder why the designer is treated as omniscient. Few users can understand the world at the other side of the designer's bridge, or the components of the bridge that is supposed to get them there.

The presumed omniscience of the designer has involved several major assumptions, including:

- There is such a thing as a "representative" user,
- The user's needs can be captured from representative users in interviewing sessions by merely asking them what they need,
- Users are willing to participate in the mystical world of computers, especially when done at the designer's and builder's convenience.

The support system design process has failed to question these assumptions.

Designer as Fallible

A major reason support systems have failed at the design level is that these systems have been treated like any other system. With the traditional approach, all that is needed is a statement of requirements, and like most industrial systems, a product can be designed and built against the set of requirements that are assumed to be stable. However, support systems are typically information based, and information is both a resource and a product, and not typical of other resources or products. Consequently, systems based on information supply and consumption require atypical considerations, including the notions that information:

- is nonexhaustive,
- is self-generating, and
- interacts with the cognitive processes of the system user.

The design process for information-based support systems should be different from that required to build a "stable" system that is based on industrial, assembly-line technologies (e.g., an automobile). Automobile manufacturing demands accurate specifications to permit tooling of the assembly line. Once established, changes are very expensive. In contrast, today's information system technology allows software to be changed virtually instantaneously and at relatively low labor cost and virtually no materials cost. Therefore, treating the design and development of information-based support systems the same as other systems has suffered a poor track record, because human information processing has not been considered within the system-design process.

Another reason designers have failed is because their translation responsibilities have been inappropriately divided across components (e.g., data, model, and dialogue). Each component has been treated as an independent entity. For example, the database aspects have been thoroughly covered by the *management information system* (MIS) community with little regard for models found in operations research or in decision analysis. Similarly, the operations research/management science community has continued to develop large prescriptive models while ignoring the human–machine interface and any concept of alternative descriptive decision models. This resistance on the part of the modeling community is due partially to inadequate technology, and partially to a reluctance to accept the current state of cognitive psychology as useful for engineering consideration.

The fact that most designers come from the system builder's world provides another explanation for designer fallibility. Their training and education results in their structuring of the solution, while requirements are still being formulated, too soon in the process to allow effective communication among users and builders. The system, then, not surprisingly, has the structure of the tools in the designer's toolkit (Gingras & McLean, 1982).

Another source of designer inadequacies has been the invalid assumption that "representative" users exist. The users "selected" to participate in support system design efforts are merely individuals with varying levels of expertise, varying levels of computer expertise, and varying amounts of time available to contribute to the task. The support system community is, however, beginning to recognize the need for adaptive systems that accommodate a wide variety of users.

Another aspect of the design problem arises because most design is done within the constraints of the designer/builder. The user's requirements are seldom really addressed. Instead, the designer responds with what can be done at the time. If the user is willing to "back off" to what is possible, this then becomes the design. Upon completion, the designer and builder can point to the system–subsystem specifications and say that requirements were met.

A final explanation for the fallibility in our approaches to support system design is that "freezing" the design from a builder's perspective (i.e., the structured components) is not conceptually separated from freezing requirements. Requirements are perceptions of need and are continuously evolving. Therefore, a means is needed to allow requirements to continually evolve independent of structural designs, which are frozen.

The above reasons for designer fallibility, coupled with the ever-present need for users to be more involved in support system development, point to the necessity for a significant change in the design process. The traditional design approach is slowly yielding to *rapid prototyping* as the preferred approach to building smaller systems. The establishment and maintenance of databases now permits concentration on the decision-making aspects of requirements. Even though the concept of decision support systems has been around since the early 1970s, the technical environment was insufficient until the mid 1980s to allow:

- adequate human–machine interfaces via networked workstations,
- databases maintained corporately as well as portions maintained individually,
- model support in versions that permit system evolution via more user involvement.

The technological support for all of the system components, especially the dialogue, has eliminated some of the technical barriers to adequate system design.

EVOLUTIONARY DESIGN

The foregoing section outlines a clear need to modify our approach to designing of information systems in general, and support systems in particular. What is needed is an approach to design that recognizes the evolutionary nature of requirements as typified by systems that are predominated by feedback rather than feedforward.

Rapid prototyping is a very popular approach to exploiting current technological advances. If the approach to rapid prototyping is evolutionary, it may provide a breakthrough necessary to designing support systems that are truly supportive. The basic premise of evolutionary design is that users can specify their own needs if given a methodology and tools to assist them in *their* process of design. In this approach, design is divided into two distinct processes: *information requirements determination* (IRD) and *information requirements analysis* (IRA).

IRD is a continuous process for which users have a primary responsibility. The goal of IRD is a product that communicates a pattern which builders can readily translate into structured components. IRA is the structuring process which converts users' stated requirements into system components. This process is often accomplished with CASE tools. To the extent possible, it is very useful to have IRD and IRA interact and involve much iteration.

The phrase commonly used to describe evolutionary design is to "start small and grow." Unfortunately, few authors provide any idea of how to accomplish this. Major questions are raised, such as "Where to start?" and then "How to let the system grow?" In essence this approach is merely an application of the way many solutions to problems are derived—iteratively starting with a *straw man* provided for comment. In the case of support system design, a key consideration for establishing the anchor, or *kernel,* is the importance of the decision elements of the problem and how they contribute to the solutions.

An approach to tackling the "start small" includes the following:

- Focus on critical decisions,
- Model the decision process descriptively,
- Determine *appropriate* places for prescriptive models in the process.

Typically, *decision support systems* (DSSs) have focused on the system, not the decision or support of the process. An approach that has worked well in both classroom and applied settings focuses first on the decision, then the decision process, then support to the process via the system. The builder is not even contacted until the first two steps of the three above have been accomplished (Valusek, 1988).

Focus on Critical Decisions

A decision generally involves a commitment of resources. It is a process and involves judgments and choices. Now that technology is available to monitor environments and detect potential problems, the emphasis in many domains is turning to identifying the decisions of importance within the environment. Emphasis then shifts to modeling to support those decisions. The critical incident technique, critical decision methodology, and case-based reasoning method discussed elsewhere in this volume support this identification task.

Another technique that has been enthusiastically accepted by user participants is *concept mapping* (Gowin & Novak, 1984). This technique, which originated in educational psychology as a communication tool, has been adapted by McFarren and Valusek as a user-oriented problem formulation technique (McFarren, 1987). It was found to be a suitable technique because large amounts of knowledge can be obtained in 1-hour sessions. Although the use of concept mapping was initially applied to DSS design, it was soon recognized as a means to capture a global picture of a problem/opportunity domain. This yields a sense of the problem boundaries and is useful in detecting key decisions within the problem environment.

Descriptive Model of the Decision Process

The concept map is also the first stage of a four-step user-oriented methodology for performing IRD and yielding a descriptive model. The decision process model can and should be assembled by the user to represent his or her needs. The four steps include:

- Concept Mapping
- Critical Decision Methodology
- Storyboarding
- User's "evaluation"

The concept map is the first communication tool in developing the model of the decision process. By collecting multiple maps across individuals and within an individual over time, a picture of important objects and events becomes apparent. These objects and events are useful for identifying the judgments and choices involved in making decisions. Figure 16.2 presents a concept map of design as presented in the preceding paragraphs.

An important aspect of the concept map is that it is an unstructured, unformatted free-flowing representation. However, the power of the concept map to communicate is apparent when builders look at it and immediately describe it as an entity relationship diagram, or a semantic net, or some other structuring representation they use for IRA. The difference is that the concept map is derived without structure imposed on the user. In fact, the user need only see the concept map and subsequent "storyboard." These are elements of his or her design. The builder can translate directly from these communication mechanisms into structured design components.

The next step in the methodology is to create storyboards. *Storyboarding* is the creation of scenarios via screen displays. Here again a typical builder response to the methodology is, "This is nothing more than what we done all along." However, storyboarding permits the

Figure 16.2.

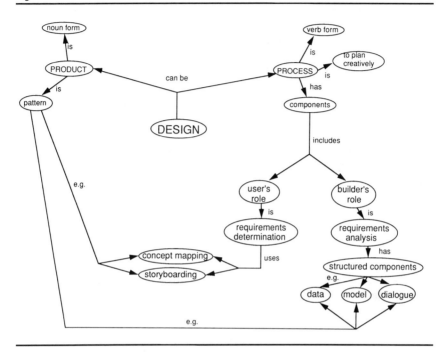

user and designer to think about and discuss information requirements, alternative support concepts, and salient contingencies.

The final step of this approach to user-oriented design is a mental exercise for the *users* to insure they are satisfied with their design *before* they contact the builder to begin structuring a solution (e.g., designing the databases, models, and dialogue components). The exercise is driven by thinking about measures they would use to evaluate the effectiveness of the support system. Thinking hard about how effectiveness will be measured has resulted in many users completely revising their storyboards *before* the requirements are presented to the builder.

CONCLUSIONS

This chapter has provided a broad view of supporting decision making and requirements for evolutionary design. A few key concepts are central to this panorama.

First, decision making occurs in a context and support is needed for the range of tasks that occurs in this context. The decision event is but one aspect of these tasks. Consequently, it is better to think of task support rather than decision support.

Second, very few situations are sufficiently well defined and crisp to allow straightforward application of prescriptive models from engineering, operations research, and computer science. Rather than prescribing and enforcing use of "the best," albeit ill-fitting, approach to task performance, support systems should enable users to use satisfactory approaches and achieve desired results.

Third, requirements for support continually evolve, partially in response to use of support systems. Consequently, the nature of the support systems should also evolve to meet requirements. This chapter has illustrated how evolutionary design can be pursued and, in itself, supported.

KEY POINTS

- It is better to think of task support than decision support because
  — decision making occurs in a context
  — support is needed for the range of tasks that occur in this context.
- Few situations permit use of prescriptive models of decision making.
- Support systems should allow users to rely on strategies with which they feel comfortable.
- In natural settings, requirements for support continually evolve.
- The nature of the support systems should evolve to meet these requirements.
- The result is evolutionary design.

Chapter 17

A Model to Support Development of Situation Assessment Aids*

David Noble
Engineering Research Associates
Vienna, VA

SITUATION ASSESSMENT AND DECISION MAKING

Recognition-primed decision making (Klein, Calderwood, & Clinton-Cirocco, 1986) is a theory which accounts for observed decision performance by proficient decision makers. In recognition-primed decision making, people identify, and sometimes select, promising alternatives because these alternatives seem to fit a particular type of situation. They assess the situation with respect to its possibilities for different types of actions, a process called *situation assessment.*

This chapter describes a cognitive model for the initial phases of the situation assessment, the phases which correspond to the recognition part of recognition-primed decision making. During these phases an experienced decision maker interprets the meaning of the situation. He or she infers the reasons why the situation appears as it does, assesses the risks and opportunities inherent in the situation, and identifies the actions to minimize the risks and exploit the opportunities.

Situation assessment is often the critical component of decision making. As described in Chapter 2, the Israeli general who decided to shoot down the Libyan airliner based his decision on an assessment of the aircraft pilot's intent. He inferred from the pilot's responses that the aircraft was on a terrorist mission. Similarly, the medical professionals selecting different treatments for the banker described in

*This research has been sponsored by the Office of Naval Research, contract N00014-84-0484 and the Naval Ocean Systems Center, contract 87-D-3439.

Chapter 1 based their decisions on their situation assessments, which in this case were the different diagnoses concerning the cause of the banker's facial pain. Likewise, the fire chief who ordered his men to drop their efforts at suppressing the fire and to concentrate instead on rescuing building occupants based his decision primarily on his assessment of the nature of the fire.

Because an accurate situation assessment can be so important to effective decision making, decision aids that improve the quality of the situation assessment may significantly improve decision quality. Such situation assessment aids will help less experienced decision makers interpret a situation more as an experienced decision maker would, and can help an experienced decision maker under stress interpret it more as he or she would when not under stress. These aids help the decision maker notice those aspects of the situation that are most significant for its correct interpretation and that help suggest effective courses of action.

Because computers can calculate aspects of a situation that cannot be directly observed and can emphasize selected situation features in ways that support selected types of judgments, situation assessment aids involving computers can depict situations in a manner that supports decision making much more effectively than would a literal, photograph-like depiction. In order to develop effective situation assessment aids, designers must be able to identify those situation features which should be computed and emphasized. The following cognitive model can guide this process.

A COGNITIVE MODEL FOR SITUATION ASSESSMENT

Experienced decision makers interpret a situation by augmenting what they observe with other general information acquired through experience and training. The Israeli general used his understanding of how pilots behave to infer the aircraft's likely mission, the physicians used their experience about the symptoms of diseases to infer the illness causing the banker's pain, and the fire chief applied his knowledge about different types of fires to select an effective course of action.

The cognitive model for situation assessment describes an organization of memory and an information-processing flow that explains how experienced decision makers use their previous experiences to assess a situation and identify promising actions. This model was developed as part of several research programs in decision making, man–machine interface design, and computer-based situation assessment (Noble, Truelove, Grosz, & Boehm-Davis, 1989). Like the Klein RPD model, this model also proposes that goals, expectancies, cues, and actions are important in recognition-based action identification. It is more specialized and detailed than that model, however, for it attempts to connect situation observables with assessment output.

We believe that this model is both a reasonable representation of human situation assessment processes and a useful guide for developing situation assessment aids, because:

- It was initially formulated from a literature review of data on memory organization, cognitive information processing, and expert problem-solving performance and was designed to be consistent with data in this literature. In particular, it is consistent with data supporting schema and exemplar theories of recognition matching (Rumelhart, 1980, 1984; Whittlesea, 1987), with data on exemplar models of classification (Kahneman & Miller, 1986; Hintzman, 1986), and with models of human expertize (Chi, Feltovich, & Glaser, 1981).
- It was formally evaluated as part of the Distributed Tactical Decision Making program of the Office of Naval Research (ONR) and, as described below, successfully accounted for subject's situation judgments in these tests (Noble, Boehm-Davis, & Grosz, 1986).
- It is the basis for a situation assessment computer system that has demonstrated many of the strengths of human situation assessment during operational tests.
- As described below, it was able to capture the expertise Navy operators use when they localize distant targets from ambiguous and uncertain target position and identity reports.

Laboratory Evaluation of the Model

In 1986, Engineering Research Associates (Noble, Boehm-Davis, & Grosz, 1986) performed several experiments to validate the model, which is summarized in Table 17.1. According to the model, people evaluate new situations by comparing them with previously experienced "reference" situations encoded in memory. These comparisons are not a rigid feature by feature similarity assessment, but instead make use of general world knowledge to interpret the significance of deviations between the new situation and the various stored reference situations. When applied to decision making, the reference situations are previously encountered decision problems.

Table 17.1.   Summary of Recognition Model

MEMORY ORGANIZATION

Memory stores examples of previously solved problems. The stored representation specifies the problem, the problem solution, and environmental indicators useful for predicting when that solution method will work. Each of these stored previously solved problems is called a "reference problem."

Each reference problem has three types of components: objective features, environment features, and action features. Objective features characterize the problem, including its objectives. Action features specify the steps in the action to solve the problem. Environment features are the cues that a solution method is likely to work.

Features may be represented at several levels of abstraction. Concrete features describe specific observable events or objects. Abstract features generalize the problem type, problem solution method and environmental indicators of the solution method's likely success. They allow recognition-based solution of new problems which resemble but are not identical to previously experienced problems.

The reference problems are organized as a part—whole hierarchy. Details of summarizing features higher in the hierarchy are represented by other detail features lower in the hierarchy.

INFORMATION PROCESSING

A promising problem solution method is identified when the environment and objective features of a stored reference problem match the environment and objective features of a new problem sufficiently well. Features able to suggest a problem solution method are the problem solution cues.

The initial evaluation of a potential solution method's applicability is an activation level. A candidate solution method is highly activated if all of its stored reference problem's environment features match those in the new problem. A possible solution method is less activated if some of these indicators of success are not present.

Matching observed and reference features may sometimes entail considerable sophisticated information processing requiring general world knowledge.

Often not all of the environment features in the reference problem can be observed in the new problem. This occurs when information is incomplete or when some of the events on which the solution method depends have not yet occurred. When the success of a potential solution method depends on them, unobserved environment features may define what new information is required.

The match evaluation may not occur all at once, but may take place over time using an interplay of top-down context-driven and bottom-up data-driven processes. In bottom up processing observed features cue promising solution methods and test problem expectations. Top-down processing guides the cognitive processes needed to determine whether problem expectations are being met.

Figure 17.1.   A barrier training picture. The barrier is the row of black ships and submarines at the top of the figure. The group of white ships and submarines will attempt to pass through or go around the barrier. Subjects shown this picture were told that "the barrier is both long and solid. The ships at the two ends are sufficiently far apart to make the barrier difficult to go around. The platforms are close enough together through its entire length to make passage through the barrier very difficult."

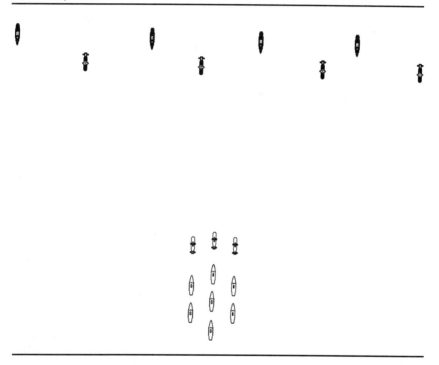

One phase of these experiments evaluated the model's ability to predict subjects' performance on barrier evaluation problems. Subjects (college undergraduates) were trained by being shown 10 different examples of stylized barriers. This training was intended to encode the required reference problems in each subject's memory. Figure 17.1 is an example of the training picture showing a "perfect" barrier, represented by the eight black enemy ships and submarines aligned along the top of the figure. The group of white ships and submarines in the center of the figure represents U.S. forces which will try to pass through or around this barrier. Each of the ships or submarines in this figure is a "platform." Subjects were told that this barrier has an effectiveness rating of 10. They were also told the reasons for that rating, expressed in terms of relevant barrier features. Some of these features are "physical" (platforms are close together), and some are "functional" (passage through the barrier is very difficult).

The other nine training pictures were similar to this one. Each picture depicted a different barrier composed of a row of ships and submarines. These barriers varied in the numbers and spacings of submarines and ships, but were otherwise the same. For each of these barriers subjects were given an effectiveness rating, expressed as a number between 1 and 10, and were told in what ways the barrier was strong or weak.

After training, the subjects were asked to rate some new barriers. The first 10 of these resembled the barriers seen in training, consisting entirely of a row of ships and submarines. The numbers and spacings of platforms in these barriers were new, however. Figure 17.2 is an example of one of these new barriers. The average subject rating for this barrier was 4.9.

To test the model, the subjects' actual ratings were compared to the ratings which the model predicted they would make. For the initial 10 test barriers, the average correlation between predicted and actual ratings was .86. One subject's correlation was only .43. The other 19 subjects' correlations ranged from .83 to .98.

The subjects also were shown five additional barriers that differed from any that were shown during training. These were identical to five of the previously shown barriers, except that they were augmented with islands or peninsula.

The model predicted that adding an island or peninsula to a barrier would significantly change the subjects' ratings of that barrier, because the model assumes that the subjects would use their knowledge about the general properties of barriers, ships, islands, and peninsula to adjust their estimates. The data confirmed this. In all cases, adding an island or peninsula to a barrier changed the subjects' ratings considerably. Filling the gap in the barrier shown in Figure 17.2, for example, increased the subjects' barrier effectiveness ratings from 4.9 to 7.0.

Furthermore, in four of five cases the model was able to *quantitatively* account for the subjects' responses by using the simple assumption that subjects would evaluate the new barriers by replacing the island or peninsula by a functionally equivalent row of ships, and then comparing this new barrier to the ones shown in training. In the one case in which this simple rule did not account for the subjects' ratings, the islands' strengthening of the barrier by increasing its solidness appeared to be offset by their ability to shelter the penetrating ships from the barrier ships' gunfire.

Figure 17.2.   A barrier test picture. The average subject effectiveness rating was 4.9.

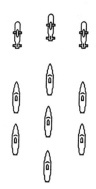

Modeling Decision Processes in a Military Decision Task

The laboratory tests validated the model's utility for explaining certain types of situation assessment judgments in a controlled experiment. Of course, a few successful laboratory tests are not sufficient to demonstrate the model's usefulness as a guide for situation assessment aids to be used for real problems in complex and uncertain environments. To determine whether the model might be useful for this purpose, the Navy sponsored research to determine whether it could capture situation and decision elements important in an actual operational decision task, the resolution of report-to-track ambiguities. The representation of knowledge used by experienced operators performing this task was developed by working closely with Navy experts. At the completion of this research, these Navy experts reviewed the model and agreed that it reflected much of the knowledge they use in resolving report-to-track ambiguities.

In this problem Navy operators attempt to localize and identify hostile ships from a sequence of situation reports. The data in many of these reports are incomplete and uncertain. Frequently, the names of the ships to be localized are unknown, though ambiguous ship identification data will often be available. In addition, the positions of the ships are uncertain. Each ship's location is reported as a 90% containment ellipse. There is a 90% chance that the ship is within the ellipse and a 10% probability that the ship is outside the ellipse.

The position history of each ship is represented by a track. The line which connects the four ellipses at the left in Figure 17.3, for example, represents a track. Although this line seems to imply that the location of the ship was known with certainty, this is actually not true. In fact, the position of the ship could be estimated only roughly. What is actually known is that at the ship had a 90% chance of being somewhere in each shaded ellipse at the time labeling that ellipse. For example, when the time was 5 o'clock, the ship had a 90% chance of being somewhere in the leftmost ellipse. It also had a 10% chance of being outside the ellipse, and mathematically it has essentially no chance of being at the exact center of the ellipse.

Although Figure 17.3 contains only a single track, normally several ships will be tracked at the same time. Each of these tracks summarizes a ship's position history and provides available ship identification data.

Figure 17.3 is an example of a report-to-track ambiguity resolution problem. In this problem there is one ship being tracked, which is represented by the line, and a new report being considered for association with an existing track, which is represented by the small dark ellipse. This ellipse is the 90% containment ellipse for a ship referenced by a new report. As in the other ellipses, there is a 90% chance that the ship is somewhere in this ellipse, and very little chance that it is exactly at its center.

The operator's problem is to decide what to do with this report.

Figure 17.3. An example of a report to track association problem. By drawing on similar previously solved problems, an experienced decision maker would not associate this report with this track. The proposed cognitive model explains such experience-based decisions.

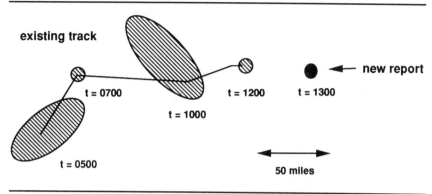

Because there is no ship identity information in the report, the operator cannot be sure that this new report is a continuation of the track shown on the left. If it is, then he or she can use the information in the report to extend the track line to the next position at "t = 1300." If it is not, however, he or she must not extend the track, because this will convey incorrect information about the location of the ship that actually belongs to the track. Instead, he or she should use the report to start a new track, delete the report if it is erroneous, or associate it with some other existing track.

In this case an experienced operator will decide not to associate this report with the existing track, because the position specified by the report looks too far from the last estimated position in the track. Although the operator may feel that his or her decision was "intuitive," it was actually supported by extensive data in memory and sophisticated cognitive information processing to make use of that data. The following model describes the content and organization of data in memory, and the information processing that supports experienced-based decisions such as this.

Memory Organization to Support Alternative Identification and Evaluation

A decision maker's previous experiences are encoded within memory in a way that enables these experiences to be applied to new similar situations. Because a new situation rarely occurs in exactly the same way as any of these old ones, this memory encoding must accommodate differences between a new situation and any of the previously experienced ones.

In this model, each type of previously experienced problem is treated as if it is stored in memory as a separate *reference problem*. We acknowledge that this is a simplification, and that memory is likely to use a more efficient storage scheme than this. For example, similar reference problems may be "averaged" into single representations. Nevertheless, because this simplified representation is functionally similar to other representations with more efficient storage schemes, we retain it as a useful framework for visualizing the cognitive processes underlying human alternatives identification and evaluation.

Each of these previously experienced reference problems is the mental representation of the problem that existed at the conclusion of the solution process. Thus, the reference problems in memory include more than just the situations or problem statements. They also include the contexts of the problems, the problems' objectives, their solution methods, and other information useful for adapting these solution methods to future problems. Among this other information are the situation features useful for a quick initial evaluation of how well a previously used solution method will work in new situations.

Figure 17.4 depicts three different previously experienced report-to-track association problems as encoded within memory. Each of these reference problems includes three types of data: action features, objective features, and environment features.

The action features specify one method for achieving the specific problem solution goal specified by the objective feature. Each of the three reference problems depicted in Figure 17.4 has an associated action: associate by position fit for problem "a," associate by identity fit for problem "b," and associate by overall fit for problem "c." These are general types of actions. By specifying actions at a general level, as illustrated in Figure 17.4, it is possible to represent all possible actions with relatively few stored reference problems.

Our representation of expert knowledge for report-to-track ambiguity resolution included only 15 to 20 general types of actions. Though more might be identified in the future, these 15 to 20 difference actions seem to represent *all* the possible general types of action which an expert can use to process an ambiguous platform position/identity report. Because these 15 to 20 actions constitute an exhaustive list of possible report-to-track ambiguity resolution actions, an experienced decision maker can easily identify all possible problem solution methods to consider. He or she just selects from this list.

Figure 17.4. Examples of high level reference problems which guide report-to-track association decisions.

Case a

OBJECTIVE	ENVIRONMENT FEATURES				ACTION
ASSOCIATE REPORT WITH TRACK		IDENTIFICATION FIT	EMITTER FIT	POSITION FIT	ASSOCIATE BY POSITION FIT
	BEST CANDIDATE	OK	OK	excellent	
	NEXT BEST CANDIDATE	OK or worse	OK or worse	poor	

Case b

OBJECTIVE	ENVIRONMENT FEATURES				ACTION
ASSOCIATE REPORT WITH TRACK		IDENTIFICATION FIT	EMITTER FIT	POSITION FIT	ASSOCIATE BY IDENTITY FIT
	BEST CANDIDATE	excellent	OK	OK	
	NEXT BEST CANDIDATE	poor	OK or worse	OK or worse	

Case c

OBJECTIVE	ENVIRONMENT FEATURES				ACTION
ASSOCIATE REPORT WITH TRACK		IDENTIFICATION FIT	EMITTER FIT	POSITION FIT	ASSOCIATE BY OVERALL FIT
	BEST CANDIDATE	good or better	good or better	good or better	
	CURRENT CANDIDATE	medium or worse	medium or worse	medium or worse	

The ability to represent all possible actions by a small number of basic different kinds of general actions is not unique to the report-to-track ambiguity association problem, but is characteristic of many different types of problems (see Chi et al., 1981, for another example).

Objective features represent the specialized low-level goals which the decision maker hoped to achieve using the solution method designated by the stored reference problem. They are generalized solution methods. Generally, there are associated with any given kind of problem only a few different types of objectives. An operator resolving a report-to-track ambiguity resolution problem will adopt one of four goals: associate the report with one of the old existing tracks, start a new track from the report, delete the report from the report data base, or defer action until additional information becomes available. Each of the reference problems in Figure 17.4 has the first of these as a goal: "associate report with track."

The environment features associated with each solution method specify criteria for adopting that solution method. These environment features are the situation characteristics whose presence indicate whether or not that method will likely work. There are three important environment features to consider when deciding whether or not to associate a report with a track: *identification fit, emitter fit,* and *position fit.* Identification fit measures the compatibility between the platform identity data contained in the report and track. Emitter data refer to characteristics of radar and communications signals intercepted from ships. Emitter fit measures the compatibility of the emitter characteristics intercepted from the ship represented by the track and the possibly different ship represented by the new report. Position fit is a measure of the geographic compatibility of the report and track.

As indicated by the "best candidate" row in Figure 17.4, the "associate by position fit" reference problem specifies that, in order to associate a report with a track on the basis of its position fit, the position of the platform specified in the report must closely match the position of the platform specified by the track. In addition, there must be no incompatibilities between the report and track estimates of platform identity and radars. An experienced operator whose memory contained this reference problem would know that reports can be associated with tracks on the basis of its position fit, what situation features are relevant for deciding whether to take this action, and what characteristics of these features would indicate that this would be a correct action to take.

The reference problems in Figure 17.4 have a second row in their environment features, "next best candidate." This row is needed because most report-to-track association problems are more complex than the one illustrated in Figure 17.3. When several different ships are being tracked, the operator has more choices about how to dispose of a report. Besides considering whether to delete the report or start a new track, he or she must also consider which, if any, of the existing tracks to associate with the report. According to case a in Figure 17.4, he or she would associate a report with a track on the basis of position fit only if that report fits that track very well *and* does not fit any other track adequately.

Abstract features. All of the features in Figure 17.4 are abstract. For example, the environment position fit feature shown in Figure 17.4 provide an abstract criterion but does not specify how close the report and track positions should be in order to merit a value of "excellent position fit," "OK identification fit," and "OK emitter fit." These values cannot be directly observed but must be estimated from more concrete "surface" features. Surface features are the measurable or countable physical properties of the situation. In contrast, abstract features may be a required capability of an object, or a broad class type, or a measure of how well an object can fill a role. Abstract features are very important in this model, for they enable each previous experience to be applied to many different new situations.

Evaluation of abstract features. A decision maker evaluates these abstract features by accessing other data in memory, possibly also encoded as reference problems. In this example, the decision maker would have reference problems whose objectives are "evaluate position fit," "evaluate emitter fit," and "evaluate identification fit." The stored reference problems for "evaluate position fit" enable an experienced decision maker to evaluate each of the situations depicted in Figure 17.5 by comparing each of these problems with a previously solved reference problem.

Like the reference problems in Figure 17.4, the reference problems used to evaluate position fit also have environment and action features. Their environment features include the report and track times, the size and overlap of the report and track 90 percent containment ellipses, and the pattern of platform movement suggested by the track. In Figure 17.5 case (a), for example, the reported platform position is so far from the track that the expert assigns the position fit to be "poor." In case (c), however, he or she assigns the fit to be "good" even though the centers of the reported containment ellipses in cases (a) and (c) are nearly the same. The difference, however, is that, in case (a) the ship's actual position is almost certainly inconsistent with the track, while in case (c), with its large uncertainty ellipse, the ship's actual position could easily be consistent with the track.

Embedded part-whole hierarchy. Because the reference problems used to evaluate the position fit environment features in Figure 17.5 feed into the environment features of the reference problems shown in Figure 17.4, the position fit reference problems and general report-to-track reference problems are organized as a part–whole hierarchy. Details of features higher in the hierarchy are represented in other reference problems lower in the hierarchy.

Information Processing for Alternative Identification and Evaluation

According to this model people identify promising solutions to problems by comparing the properties of a new problem with the properties of previously solved ones. This match process may be complex. It is characterized by an interplay between top-down context-driven and

Figure 17.5.   Four examples of position fit evaluations. The labels on the left indicate how an experienced decision maker would evaluate the position fit of the track (ellipses connected by solid line) with the ambiguous report on the right.

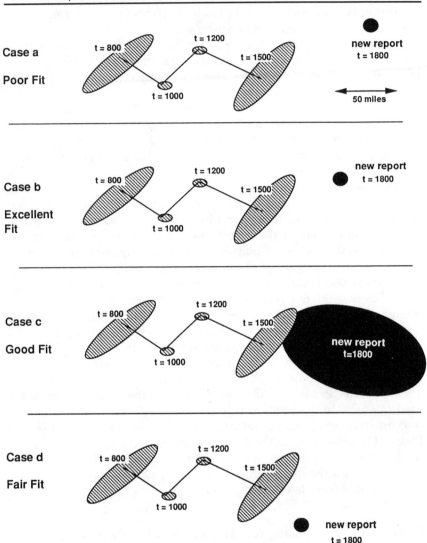

bottom-up data-driven processes, by interactions between feature representations at different levels of abstraction, and, when required, by use of general world knowledge. These comparison processes may be automatic, and an expert may not be consciously aware of them.

Reference problems whose properties match those of the new problem become "activated." If all of the properties of the reference problem match those of the new problem, then the reference problem becomes "strongly activated." In that case, the decision maker would identify the reference problem's solution method to be very promising. If any of the properties of the new problem fail to meet the criteria specified in the reference problem, the decision maker would assume that the reference problem's solution method either cannot be used to solve the new problem or must be modified before it can be used. Sometimes a new problem may be solved in different ways. In that case, the new problem may activate several different reference problems in memory.

The following discussion traces through the steps that an experienced decision maker might have used in evaluating the example shown in Figure 17.4.

Top-down processing. In that example, operators have been given the task of resolving report-to-track ambiguities. Because this task always has the same objective, resolving report-to-track ambiguities, giving operators this task will weakly activate all reference problems with this objective. Each of these reference problems will specify a problem solution method and a set of environment features useful for determining the applicability of that solution method.

The set of weekly activated reference problems identifies the associated set of possible solution methods. These methods will include those shown in Figure 17.4: "associate by position fit," "associate by identity fit," and "associate by overall fit." Other activated reference problems will suggest additional possible actions, such as "initiate a new track from this report," "defer action on this report," or "delete the report."

The environment features of each of these initially activated reference problems specify properties that the new problem should have in order for that reference problem's solution method to work. Because they define what is relevant for selecting a course of action, these features direct attention and define information requirements. In order to associate a report with a track on the basis of position fit, for example, the location of the track and platform must fit very well. Thus, when evaluating whether to adopt this method, a decision maker must determine the position fit of the report and track, a process that uses the position fit reference problems.

Several previously solved position fit problems are illustrated in Figure 17.5. For the problem illustrated in Figure 17.3, the decision maker would compare (in his or her mind) the position fit in Figure 17.3 with those in Figure 17.5, and would determine that the Figure

17.3 position fit most closely resembles the position fit illustrated in the top example in Figure 17.5. Because this reference problem identified that position fit to be "poor," the decision maker will conclude that the position fit in the new problem is also poor. Therefore, the position fit criteria for "associate by position fit" is violated, and the decision maker will decide that he or she cannot associate the report with the track by position fit.

This sequence of first identifying a potential general solution, then identifying problem features relevant to this general solution, and finally accessing other reference problems useful for evaluating these problem features is called *top-down* processing.

Use of general knowledge. Using the position fits in Figure 17.5 to evaluate the position fit of the problem shown in Figure 17.3 requires judgment and interpretation when the cases being compared do not match exactly. Consequently, the decision maker must evaluate the significance of the differences in these cases in order to decide whether the Figure 17.3 position fit should be evaluated to be "poor." The model for recognition assumes that such evaluations access relevant world knowledge, as described in Noble et al. (1989).

As in the case of the island and peninsula added to the barrier problems used in the model's laboratory validation tests, this access to world knowledge enables decision makers to evaluate problems that differ from any that were previously experienced. For example, an experienced operator who encounters a platform whole velocity is greater than the velocity of any previously encountered platform could adjust his or her position fit estimate to reflect this greater velocity. The knowledge used to handle this novel situation is assumed not to reside directly in any of the reference problems themselves, but instead to be in other knowledge structures easily accessed by these reference problems. This organization decouples specialized knowledge needed to solve a particular type of problem from more general knowledge useful in many different problem solving tasks.

Bottom-up processing complements top-down processing. Although not illustrated here, vivid observed features, such as nearly overlapping report and track locations, can activate reference problems whose environment features include them. Identifying relevant reference problems from vivid surface features would fall in the category of "bottom-up" processing. Environment features activated from bottom-up processing can serve as action cues because they identify the problem solution methods in the reference problems which they activate.

The situation assessment model assumes that both top-down and bottom-up processing usually occur simultaneously. This combination often strongly activates just one problem. In that case, the observed problem is assumed to be of the same type as the activated reference problem, the reference problem solution method is assumed to be applicable to the observed problem, and any unobserved environment features are assumed to have characteristics consistent with those specified in the reference problem. Thus, besides defining information requirements and cueing actions, environment features can also provide defaults for unobserved situation features.

Although this discussion is written as if an experienced decision maker deliberately and consciously follows a sequence of information retrieval and evaluation steps, the theory assumes that an expert often does this almost automatically. He or she may evaluate the identification, emitter, and position fit scores simultaneously, often without any conscious awareness of these judgments or of how he or she identified the promising problem solution methods that emerged from the process.

APPLYING THE THEORY TO HELP DEVELOP SITUATION ASSESSMENT AIDS

Decision aid interfaces that support situation assessment should help a less experienced decision maker to "see the problem through the eyes of an expert." They should help him or her to focus on the properties of a problem relevant for selecting problem solution methods and to evaluate these properties more like an expert would.

In order to design an aid that helps operators "see the problem through the eyes of an expert," the designer must determine how the expert sees the problem. According to the theory, when an expert sees the problem, he or she activates in memory reference problems that (a) identify promising courses of action, (b) indicate missing information that should be collected or situation ambiguities that should be resolved in order to select an action, and (c) provide action-related inferences and interpretations of the observed situation surface features. Consequently, if the aid designer could characterize an expert's reference problems, he or she could use this characterization to identify information that should be provided by the aid.

There are two steps in an interface design methodology based on the model described in this chapter: (a) characterizing the set of reference problems used by experienced decision makers to solve a type of problem, and (b) determining ways to depict situation features to help in their correct evaluation.

Characterizing the set of reference problems used by experts requires eliciting this knowledge from the experts. Because experts are sometimes not aware of the knowledge they use in solving a problem, structured knowledge elicitation techniques that help an expert identify this knowledge have been developed. In their 1981 paper, Chi, Feltovich, and Glaser described one such knowledge elicitation procedure useful for determining the set of reference problems. In this process the expert is first asked to list the basic possible goals to be attained by solving the problem. He or she is then asked to list for each of these goals the basic different methods that each can be achieved, and to list for each of these ways the different conditions that should be present in order for each of these methods to work. Finally, he or she is asked to identify concrete problem observables useful for inferring whether these conditions are actually present in any particular problem.

This process identifies the general problem solution methods and identifies the environment features relevant to selecting one of these methods. The next phase of knowledge elicitation seeks to represent on paper specific reference problems, such as were illustrated in Figure 17.4. Each of these reference problems specifies a problem objective, general solution method, and problem properties that indicate when that solution method should work.

The next part of the interface design methodology is determining how to depict features so that operators will evaluate them correctly. A cognitive theory, such as the one outlined in this chapter, cannot directly specify these methods, for feature evaluation depends on perceptual processing as well as cognitive processing. Nevertheless, the theory can guide this process.

Figure 17.3, for example, can easily be redrawn to emphasize the poor position fit between the report and track. The small black circle marked "$t = 1200$" represents the 12:00 P.M. estimate of the location of the platform being tracked. The time of the report, however, is 1:00 P.M. If an ellipse were added which displays the estimated platform location at at 1:00, then the drawing would convey position fit much better than Figure 17.3 does. In this case, the additional 1:00 P.M. gray track ellipse would not overlap with the small black report circle, thereby directly conveying a poor position fit.

This same technique, redrawing a picture to emphasize important features and relationships, should help less experienced problem solvers evaluate a problem more like an expert does. In each case, the interface developer uses the reference problems developed earlier to identify expert evaluations of key characteristics of a problem.

KEY POINTS

- Situation assessment aids support recognition-primed decision making by computing and depicting situation features important for selecting a course of action.
- A cognitive model for situation assessment describes an organization of knowledge and information processing used by experienced decision makers in their situation assessments.
- In this model various types of previously solved problems are organized as reference problems in memory. Each reference problem specifies the problem objective, general solution method, and situation conditions that indicate the applicability of the solution method.
- During an assessment those reference problems that match the current problem are activated, and the problem solution methods associated with these activated reference problems become candidate actions.
- A designer of situation assessment aids can identify information to be included in the aid by making explicit the reference problems which experts use to assess the problem situation and identify promising actions. He or she can evaluate the effectiveness of presented information by comparing novice operators' interpretations of the situation with the evaluations of experienced operators.

Chapter 18

Training Decision Makers for the Real World*

Barbara Means
SRI International

Eduardo Salas
Naval Training Systems Center

Beth Crandall
Klein Associates Inc.

T. Owen Jacobs
Army Research Institute

Classical decision theory, with its assumptions that there are "right" ways to make decisions and that these models or procedures can be applied over a wide range of decision situations, implies one view of decision-making training. From this standpoint, normative models and analytic techniques should be taught so that they can later be used in whatever decision-making situations the learner encounters. This line of reasoning has, in fact, had an influence on the training provided for fields such as military command, intelligence analysis, business management, and medical diagnosis.

In this chapter, we take a different stance toward decision-making training, motivated by the new view of natural decision making presented in the preceding chapters. After briefly examining the evidence regarding the trainability of formal decision-making models, we will move on to our primary purpose, which is to discuss the training implications of the broader view of decision making taken by the authors in this volume. In doing so, we find that one consequence of studying decision making in naturalistic settings is that the distinction between decision making and other types of problem-solving behavior quickly blurs. Decision making is no longer conceptualized as a separate form of cognitive activity, but is seen as falling within the general rubric of problem-structuring and problem-solving behavior. We gain insights for training from a research literature which has not been labelled

---

*The views expressed are those of the authors and do not necessarily reflect official positions of the organizations with which they are affiliated.

decision making but which clearly encompasses decision skills in natural tasks. We will summarize the implications of this literature concerning how to train decision skills, and try to highlight some critical issues and requirements for future research.

TRAINING BASED ON CLASSICAL DECISION THEORY

Training Normative Models

There have been many efforts to train decision-theory-based procedures both within the context of professional preparation (e.g., for business managers or military planners) and as part of less occupationally oriented courses in problem solving skills. Hayes (1980), for example, trained students in his problem-solving course to make choices among sets of apartments, constructed in such a way that each set contained several apartments that were actually identical in terms of features. Students were more consistent in their evaluation of identical apartments after being trained in decision-making procedures such as additive weighting. Similarly, Beatty (1988) found that an hour of instruction in how to construct decision matrices and apply decision rules led to more consistent performance on decision making cases by a sample of 100 undergraduates. Venezuelan seventh graders, given units on decision making as part of a year-long course in thinking skills, improved their performance on specially designed measures of the trained decision skills (Herrnstein, Nickerson, Sanchez, & Swets, 1986).

There is little doubt that normative procedures for use on specific types of problems can be trained (although some of them are quite complex and require extended periods of instruction). The more pertinent question regards the generality and durability of training effects—whether there are positive effects on subsequent decision making in natural tasks outside the classroom. We were unable to identify any studies in which the experimenter not only trained normative decision-making procedures but also tested their transfer to real-world decision tasks. Certainly, studies of decision makers in real-life settings suggest that the formal models taught in professional programs do not get used on the job by most business managers (Isenberg, 1984; Mintzberg, 1975), financial analysts (Paquette & Kida, 1988), or medical diagnosticians (Alemi, 1986; Elstein, Shulman, & Sprafka, 1978).

Although failure to find training transfer is hardly unusual, there are good reasons to suppose that transfer of such formal decision-making procedures will be especially problematic. Both the circumstances under which such models are taught and practiced, and the models' implicit view of the decision-making task, are inconsistent with much real-world decision making. As discussed by Orasanu and Connolly in Chapter 1, real-world decision tasks are typically much less well defined than laboratory and school decision tasks. In many cases, the decision maker does not conceive of his or her task as one of "choice." Even when the task does involve a selection, much effort may be required simply to identify the alternatives available. Information is likely to be partial, ambiguous, and require effort to obtain. Further, much of the information may resist the quantification required for implementing formal decision models. Rather than being an abstract, independent task, a real-life choice will be embedded in a web of cross-cutting activities, goals, and emotions. It is not that the normative models are incorrect, but just that they are far more limited in their applicability than many of their advocates seem to recognize.

A large part of the reason that training in normative decision-making models does not endure in practice is probably attributable to the fact that such models are not very usable if the decision must be made under the kind of time constraints found in many natural settings. Zakay and Wooler (1984) trained university students to apply multiattribute utility procedures to the task of selecting an appliance for purchase. The training led to more optimal decisions (according to the MAU model) when decisions were made with no time pressure, but produced no benefits for the conditions where decisions had to be made with either moderate or severe time constraints. Payne, Bettman, and Johnson (1988) found that, under time pressure, a number of heuristic choice strategies are more accurate than attempts to apply a truncated normative model, and subjects adapt their decision strategies in reasonable ways when placed under time constraints.

Finally, people appear to judge many of the formal models as requiring more effort than they are worth. After reading descriptions of five decision-making techniques, the majority of the graduate students studied by Means (1983) said that they would not use models based on multiattribute utility theory in making a real-life decision such as which car to buy. The chief criticism of multiattribute utility approaches was that they are too "complex, difficult, and time-consuming." Along similar lines, Elstein et al. (1978) and Simon (1976) attribute the failure of physicians and business managers, respectively, to use formal decision models to unwillingness to take on the required cognitive processing load. Lave, Murtaugh, and de la Roche (1984) document the variety of alternative strategies people develop for comparing the value of two substitutable products of different size and cost to avoid having to do formal arithmetic. If many people are unwilling to do division to make real-life decisions, how likely are they to apply multiattribute utility models?

Bias Reduction Training

A second thread of training research spawned by traditional decision theory studies is work aimed at reducing or eliminating decision biases such as overconfidence, representativeness, and hindsight (but see Cohen, Chapter 3, for a critique of this concept). In this case, rather than teaching a new set of procedures, the training designer is trying to extinguish natural or intuitive ways of thinking. As one might expect, this appears harder to accomplish.

Tolcott, Marvin, and Bresnick (1989) found that a combination of instruction and provision of a decision aid reduced but did not eliminate the confirmation bias of military intelligence analysts. Bukszar and Connolly (1988) provided training to overcome hindsight bias in students' analyses of business cases, but were unable to do so. Choo (1976) provided calibration training to assessors and obtained little improvement and no generalization. Lichtenstein and Fischhoff (1980) provided subjects with extensive calibration training. They obtained improvement between the first and second sessions of training but found only modest generalization to some external tasks and no generalization to others.

Although there is not an extensive literature systematically testing the effects of various training strategies on bias reduction, the available research does not inspire optimism about this kind of training. Most typically, bias reduction training produces some reduction but not an elimination of the bias within the experimental task and limited generalization to other experimental tasks. With such small effects within the experiment itself, it is unlikely that such training would have enduring effects on real-world tasks. Certainly, within the decision bias literature there is ample evidence of bias in experienced practitioners who have had plenty of practice (Fischhoff, 1982).

Summary

The training research stimulated by decision theory does not produce optimism about prospects for general training to make people into good decision makers. Although prescriptive models based on quantifying utilities can be trained, there is little indication that, when they are successfully taught within the classroom, they will have a positive impact on real decisions. Training aimed at eliminating decision biases has had mixed success, but again, when improvements are obtained, they tend to be of limited generality and duration.

However one assesses the track record of such training approaches, we would argue that this view of decision-making training is inappropriate if we want to understand and facilitate decision activities in natural settings. Decision making is a critical component within tasks such as diagnosis, negotiation, design, situation assessment, and command and control. In many cases, the context within which these tasks are performed precludes the use of formal models, no matter how well trained. This is not to say that there are not situations where the assumptions for a multiattribute utility approach are reasonably well satisfied, and conditions permit its use. However, our emphasis here is on exactly those tasks and situations that have not been conducive to the application of normative approaches. Our starting point is the tasks themselves and the study of how they are actually performed—rather than an a priori formal model of decision making. From this vantage point, we find that we know something about the nature of expertise in these domains, and how it can be acquired. As our view of what constitutes a *decision* has broadened, we can appreciate the relevance of the literature on the nature of expertise, and expert–novice differences in a wide range of cognitive tasks.

EXPERT–NOVICE DIFFERENCES

In cognitive psychology a whole research tradition has developed based on detailed comparisons of experts and novices in specific domains. The tradition began with deGroot's classic study of chess masters. In trying to understand the basis for the masters' ability, deGroot (1965/1978) and later Chase and Simon (1973) compared the masters to less expert players in terms of their memory abilities, the depth of their planning (number of moves ahead), and so on. None of these characteristics accounted for the chess masters' expertise. More than anything else, what set them apart was their ability to look at the complex display provided by dozens of pieces on a chess board and to see it in terms of a few meaningful chunks. In contrast, if the chess board contained a random array of pieces, chess masters were no better able than other subjects to reconstruct the configuration after a brief viewing. Chase and Simon (1973) attributed the masters' skill at reconstructing meaningful chess configurations to the fact that, through experience, they have come to perceive the display in terms of highly familiar patterns. Also through experience, the master comes to associate a few moves with each pattern, so that these come rapidly to mind and the master does not need to go through a random search-and-test process for all possible moves.

This line of research has been replicated and extended in fields as diverse as physics (Chi, Feltovich, & Glaser, 1981; Larkin, 1983), statistics (Schoenfeld & Herrmann, 1982; Xu, 1987), computer programming (Adelson, 1981), music (Sloboda, 1976), baseball (Chiesi, Spilich, & Voss, 1979), radiology (Lesgold, Feltovich, Glaser, & Wang, 1981), and basketball (Allard & Burnett, 1985). A common theme in this work has been the importance of the expert's knowledge base. This goes beyond the obvious fact that experts "know more" than novices do. As expertise grows, individuals come to know things differently. Thus, an expert and a novice radiologist confronted with an x-ray do not *see* the same event. Often much of the expert's knowledge is tacit; the expert sees the world through these categories without necessarily being aware of them. Associated with the problem categories are specific problem-solving procedures or strategies. Thus, when the category is perceived, the expert is predisposed to act in a certain way.

As individuals gain in knowledge, their abilities to chunk information, to recognize a familiar pattern, and to attend to critical indicators while ignoring less important features all become increasingly fine tuned. Cognitive psychologists tend to think of this process in terms of the proceduralization of declarative knowledge (Anderson, 1985). That is, in the first stage of acquiring expertise, an individual acquires factual knowledge about the domain. If confronted with a problem, the learner attempts to apply general, "weak" strategies, such as means–ends analysis, to the knowledge available. Through repeated attempts of this nature, general strategies become particularized to fit the domain, and production rules linking actions to specific situations become compiled into larger and larger units.

This theoretical model of skill acquisition has several important implications. First, expertise is domain specific. Although we have often tended to think of general skills as "higher," experts do not use general problem-solving procedures (i.e., means–ends analysis) when dealing with the content customary to their work. Instead, they employ more powerful domain-specific methods tailored to their field. Second, the expert's knowledge is highly proceduralized—it is linked to action and conditions of applicability. It is difficult to separate *what* an expert knows from how he or she uses that knowledge.

Studies of expert and novice performance in field settings corroborate the position that the two groups are distinguished by how they use their domain knowledge rather than by the ability to use general or weak problem-solving methods. For example, in a study of Air Force avionics technicians, Glaser et al. (1985) found that skilled and less skilled troubleshooters do not differ in terms of planning or systematicity per se. Large differences do appear, however, in the ability to relate symptom information to a representation of the problem that can then guide the selection of specific troubleshooting actions. Lesgold et al. (1981) compared the performance of 5 expert radiologists to that of 18 radiology residents as they examined X-rays and made diagnoses. Differences between the two groups lay more in pattern recognition and the ability to build a rich mental representation of a particular patient's anatomy based upon the x-ray than in the decision processes that were imposed.

A recurring theme of the detailed analyses in specific domains is that the effective decision maker is distinguished by an ability to frame the problem well. Recent research on decision making in operational settings (Calderwood, Crandall, & Baynes, 1988; Crandall & Calderwood, 1989; Lipshitz, 1989) comes to the same conclusion. Klein, Calderwood, and Clinton-Cirocco (1986) report that their fire ground commanders, rather than generating multiple options and weighing their attributes, react to a situation in terms of highly familiar patterns associated with certain actions. If time permits, commanders used an apparently imagery-based consideration of the implications of the planned action, "watching" it unfold in the present context to watch for any complications. The explicit consideration of more than one alternative at a time was more characteristic of novices than of experts. Similarly, Lipshitz (1989) concludes that the Israeli army officers he studied make decisions by matching a situation to an associated action, considering whether there are any problems with the anticipated action, and executing it if there are not. Decision making in these environments appears to be determined by the nature of the individual's experience, the patterns that are recognized, and associations between patterns and actions.

When we move to a consideration of decision making within natural contexts of the sorts described above, it becomes apparent that the decision itself is only one part of task performance. Given the limited processing capacity of humans and the complexity of these real-world tasks, it is clear that a person's ability to make and execute good decisions is going to be affected by his or her ability to execute the other components of the task.

The deleterious effects that incompletely acquired supporting skills can have on decision making in a complex task have been observed many times. For example, in studies of avionics technicians of varying degrees of experience and expertise (Means & Gott, 1988), it appears that expert and less-than-expert technicians use the same decision rules, but less-expert technicians often end up applying the rules to the wrong content because of difficulties they have in executing other aspects of the task. Given a component that is not producing the expected signal, for example, both the expert and the less-expert technician might want to find out whether the component is getting a control signal from the computer. If not, both would reason that the component itself is not at fault. But tracing electronics schematics is a very complicated, painstaking process. And it was common for less expert technicians to get so caught up in trying to trace data or signals through page after page of detailed schematics that they forgot what inference they were going to make once they got the desired information. This problem of cognitive overload is a critical issue in many of the real-world tasks involving decision making.

IMPLICATIONS FOR TRAINING NATURAL DECISION TASKS

Real-world tasks differ from the one-step choice decisions connoted by classical decision models along many dimensions. First and foremost, decision making is not a task. The fireground commander does not set out to "make a decision," he sets out to control a fire. Obtaining this goal requires making many decisions, but decision making is part of a larger activity, not an end in itself. Thus, the commander must make a whole string of decisions, each of which is part of a decision–action–feedback loop. This means that the decision-making process requires flexibility because the situation, or the decision maker's understanding of it, can change dramatically as events evolve.

In such complex task contexts, problems are ill structured. The decision maker will typically have multiple goals (e.g., "save the building," "protect my men") which may or may not be mutually compatible. Multiple problems are likely to compete for the decision maker's attention. There may be time pressure and stress related, not only to the workload, but also to knowledge of the magnitude of harm associated with a negative outcome. In most cases, execution of the action will involve multiple people, who may also be involved in providing feedback and in making decisions.

In this section, we consider these features of naturalistic decision-making tasks and draw implications for decision-making training.

Ill-Structured Problems

In contrast to the laboratory study of decision-making processes, decisions in natural contexts are embedded in a wider context. There are often one or more problems within this task context, and recognizing and defining those problems can be far from trivial. We have argued above that the literature on expertise suggests that, through years of experience and thousands of trials, experts build up a set of patterns for organizing information in their domain. The expert comes to see the world in terms of these patterns. This not only reduces the workload required to get information from the environment and store it in memory, but also facilitates rapid action, because certain plans or procedures have become strongly associated with certain patterns.

Given that pattern recognition is important, the training issue is, How do we build up such patterns? The main thing we know about doing this is that it appears to take many practice trials (Lesgold et al., 1981; Schneider, 1982). This does not mean that training cannot be designed to facilitate and speed up the process (Vidulich, Yeh, & Schneider, 1983). Simulation offers great advantages here, because it can (a) present problems that are designed around patterns that are common and useful in expert reasoning, and (b) provide many more trials than would occur naturally. Although we may agree with the old saw that "experience is the best teacher," the real world is not necessarily the best source of learning experience.

This can be illustrated by examples from any number of real-world training programs. For example, it takes nearly 3 years to train an air traffic controller, largely because there has been little or no simulator practice available to students, so they must acquire and practice skills in on-the-job training (as they are controlling real aircraft). Since they are dependent on the real world for their training experience, at air traffic control facilities with low amounts of traffic for large periods of the day, a student may go for weeks before encountering enough traffic to get any meaningful training. On the other hand, the student may be assigned to control a sector of airspace that undergoes such an increase in the quantity and complexity of air traffic that it is far above a difficulty level where he or she can be acquiring new skills. Simulation offers the attractive alternative of being able to provide many, many practice problems, designed to build up recognition of patterns, and consistently adapted to the student in terms of difficulty level and instructional purpose.

An additional advantage of simulation is that it makes it possible to provide more practice trials in a fixed amount of time. One method of doing this is by artificially compressing time. Vidulich et al. (1983) did this for an air intercept control task and demonstrated both that they could increase the number of trials provided within a given time period by many fold, and that the compressed-time training led to superior task performance.

Another way in which simulation can provide more practice trials is by eliminating aspects of the task that are time consuming but of little instructional value. For example, Lesgold, LaJoie, Bunzo, and Eggan (1988) argue that they can provide as much troubleshooting training in 25 hours on their automated training system (SHERLOCK) as an Air Force technician would encounter in 4 years on the job. This is because on the job (a) the equipment to be maintained doesn't fail all that often; (b) when the equipment does fail, there are thousands of ways in which it could happen, so any one type of failure is relatively rare; and (c) when a technician does get involved in diagnosing and repairing one of these difficult problems, much time is spent in mechanical actions and waiting for test results. On the automated tutor, the student can be exposed to dozens of difficult problems in a week, because solving the diagnostic problem does not require task components such as having to attach 15 cables and wait for 4 hours for a set of automated tests to run to find out whether this action had any effect on the fault. Thus, much more of the student's time can be spent in the process of diagnostic decision making, and he or she can get many more practice trials designed to build up recognition of problem patterns.

In addition to the need to provide lots of practice, a training program for decision making in ill-structured problem domains often faces the additional complication that many natural decision tasks do not offer clear, timely feedback. As described in Chapter 1, there is no single correct decision in many situations. Nor is there any way for the decision maker to know whether a better outcome would have resulted from an alternative choice. For such cases, the training designer will have to seek reasonable criteria for judging whether a decision is acceptable. One strategy is to allow student decision makers to compare their solutions to those of one or more recognized experts. In other decision-making tasks, there are easily specified criteria for decision quality (e.g., mortality rates) but the consequences of a decision are either so slow in being felt or are affected by so many external factors that they do not function effectively as instructional feedback. For example, in the air intercept task studied by Schneider and his associates (Schneider, 1985), the natural feedback is the distance by which the aircraft misses its target. However, in real time, this feedback is not available until 5 minutes after the trainee has issued the command for a turn. Moreover, errors could be caused by misjudging the wind velocity, misjudging the initial heading, or misjudging the rollout for the turn. Instructional interventions can be designed to address this problem by decomposing the task and giving explicit feedback on individual components in a timely fashion. Schneider (1985) used computer graphics and time compression to give prompt feedback for each task component and eliminate time when the trainee would be passively watching the screen as the aircraft moves through its trajectory.

Action/Feedback Loops

Natural decision making is not an isolated activity but occurs in the context of complex diagnostic, command and control, design, and planning tasks. As described in Chapter 1, the decision task is not a matter of making a single choice at one point in time but rather involves a whole series of actions or decisions, each of which affects the external environment (or the decision maker's understanding of it) in ways that influence the decisions that are made subsequently. The quality of performance will depend, not just on the procedures used to integrate information or the nature of the decision rule, but also on the decision maker's ability to execute other components of the task and to coordinate the entire process. Because human processing resources are limited, poor performance on one aspect of task performance can disrupt the outcome, no matter how well the decision rule or decision process is mastered. Task performance requires, not just mastery of individual task components, but also the ability to orchestrate those components into a smooth performance.

The training implication is that the decision component of these tasks should not be taught just in isolation. It needs to be trained within a meaningful (but not necessarily whole) task context, so that the student can learn to make decisions at the same time that he or she is executing other components of the task. In this way, the student gets practice combining decision making with the other required task components and learns more about the domain at the same time that decision skills are being exercised.

Complex Tasks, Multiple Goals, and Uncertain Environment→ Heavy Workload

Like the fire command task described by Orasanu and Connolly in Chapter 1, many natural decisions occur in the context of complex tasks that feature, not only the kind of series of action/feedback loops described above, but also multiple goals and dynamically evolving environments. All of these features increase the mental workload experienced by the task performer. A pilot has to maintain control of the airplane, monitor instruments, and handle ongoing radio and cockpit communication. Conditions can and do arise under which each of these activities becomes problematic, demanding a large share of the pilot's attention. If the pilot is to have adequate resources for identifying problems and evaluating alternatives, none of these subtasks can be allowed to consume all of his or her attention.

During early stages of learning, this level of task complexity can be too much for trainees. At a time when they are having difficulty discerning any meaningful patterns in the data presented, they can feel bombarded by a bewildering array of information, goals, and uncertainties. An instructional technique for reducing mental workload during early portions of training is *scaffolding*. This involves having the instructor or instructional system take over portions of the task— for example, keeping track of information obtained thus far and actions that have been tried—while the learner works on the rest of the task. In this way, the trainee is able to practice the whole task with assistance at a much earlier stage than would be possible without the scaffolding. As the trainee acquires competence, the scaffolding is gradually removed.

An important theoretical concept for the design of training for tasks that must be performed under high workload is the distinction between automatic and controlled processing (Schneider & Shiffrin, 1977). Controlled processing is slow, usually serial, under the subject's conscious control, and requires attentional resources, thus reducing the resources available for any other activity. Automatic processing is rapid, relatively effortless, and can occur without conscious attention. Automatic processing thus can be done in parallel with other activities with no detriment to them, an important advantage in complex, high-workload tasks.

Achieving automatic performance on a task component requires hundreds or even thousands of practice trials and means training far beyond the level that is generally accepted as mastery. Moreover, automatic processing is possible only for task components for which the subject's response to a class of stimuli is consistent from trial to trial. It is not possible where no consistent relation exists, excluding those task components that involve problem solving or novel decision making.

We are not arguing that decision making per se should be trained to automaticity—this would be counterproductive, since there will always be variations among situations, and the decision maker must attend to them. Rather, we are recommending that task components that must be performed synchronously with making decisions should be automated wherever possible. Automating these components will reserve limited mental resources for the decision-making portions of the task that require flexibility.

The recommendation to provide many practice trials on task components that can be automated should not be construed as implying that most training should be on single task components. Rather, we recommend that part-task training be alternated with training within a wider task context, so that the student does not lose sight of the relationship between the component and the task as a whole. Schneider and Detweiler (1988) have demonstrated that there is an advantage to providing practice on at least two task components at a time rather than practicing each alone. Transfer from this kind of training to the full task is better than transfer from training of each individual component to the full task. In their view, this is because practice with multiple task components requires the student to learn and practice strategies for task shedding, delay, shortening task components, chunking components, and so on. If students practice only one task component at a time, they may learn to perform components by using strategies that are easy to acquire but involve high workload to execute. Training that requires simultaneous performance of multiple task components forces students to abandon these strategies for less resource-intensive ones.

A similar argument is made by Gopher and his colleagues (Gopher, Weil, Bareket, & Caspi, 1988a). Based on their work training high-workload tasks, they conclude that (a) mere experience on complex tasks is insufficient to produce effective performance, because many performers hit upon suboptimal strategies that permit survival but fall short of the performance of which they're capable; (b) subjects can be taught better attention allocation; and (c) this capability will transfer to new situations.

In research on students in the Israeli air force flight school, Gopher et al. sought to teach attention allocation skills through a microcomputer game. The game was designed to include decision making and resource management in a complex task context, including complex visual scanning, manual control, and short- and long-term memory requirements. Students who received just 10 hours of practice on this game subsequently had a 30% higher probability of successfully completing flight school than those with no game experience. Gopher et al. attribute the success of the computer game to its ability to teach time-sharing and workload management skills.

Time Stress and High Stakes

Numerous studies show that, under time pressure, people use less information in making choice decisions (Wallsten & Barton, 1982; Wright, 1974; Rothstein, 1986). Decision making under these conditions can be shown to be suboptimal in the sense that choices do not correspond to the outcomes of multiattribute utility models. The answer to this problem does not appear to be more training in MAU models, however. The Zakay and Wooler (1984) study cited above showed that training in MAU methods does not increase the quality of subject decisions if they must be made under time stress. Moreover, if decisions made under time pressure with alternate decision heuristics are compared, not to the outcome of a perfectly executed MAU procedure (the theoretically optimal choice), but to the actual outcome of an MAU procedure executed under time limits, it turns out that an MAU approach is not ideal under time stress. Payne et al. (1988) showed in a set of Monte Carlo task simulations that alternative models, using less information, produce better results than a truncated multiattribute utility approach when time is limited. Moreover, when Payne et al. had human subjects choose gambles under the same conditions tested in the simulations, they found that subject behavior corresponded quite well to the optimal strategies identified by the simulations. Under moderate time pressure, subjects used the same decision strategies they had employed when given unlimited time, but accelerated the procedures. Under severe time pressure, they changed strategies and focused on a subset of the information provided. The strategies they used were generally among the best for those task conditions (according to the Monte Carlo simulations).

In many natural decision-making tasks, the degree of time pressure varies. Thus, there will be periods where more deliberate decision processes and more elaborate analyses are possible. At other times, the decision maker must be able to act quickly. It seems reasonable to suppose that there may be advantages to normative approaches and more analysis of alternatives when time is available (provided that the information requirements of the models are met), but the decision maker needs to know when to abandon time-consuming strategies in favor of more expedient decision making. Training can explicitly address the speed/accuracy tradeoff issue, providing practice and feedback in adapting to changing time pressure.

Other types of stress, such as concern about the high stakes riding on the decision outcome, potential emergency conditions, fatigue, or physical discomfort, can affect decision-making performance as well (see Driskell & Salas, 1991). Under stress, the likelihood of making serious errors increases. People ignore relevant information, make risky decisions and perform with less skill (Foushee, 1984; Keinan, 1987).

An implication of the fact that many decisions involve high stakes and must be made under stress is that training should include extensive practice to overlearn key behaviors, as demonstrated by Driskell and his colleagues (Driskell, 1984; Driskell, Hogan, & Salas, 1987; Driskell & Salas, 1991). However, the Zakay and Wooler (1984) finding that practice without time pressure did not enhance decision making under time constraints, suggests that, if decision making is likely to be required under time pressure or other stressful conditions, practice should include task performance under those conditions (or their simulation). Adding time pressure is usually quite easy. It is more difficult to simulate the sense of life and death involved when one is deciding whether or not to shoot down an aircraft that could be either an F-16 attack mission or a confused civilian airliner. Although it may never duplicate the real experience, simulation can provide reasonable approximations of this kind of stress and has been successful in a variety of military applications. For example, Krahenbuhl, Marett, and Reid (1978) found that simulator pretraining reduced the in-flight stress experienced by student pilots.

Caution should be maintained, however, in introducing stress into training programs. Submitting the student to an excessively stressful environment is not only questionable on ethical grounds but is also ineffective in that it disrupts learning, particularly during stages when new concepts or strategies are supposed to be acquired. Determining when to introduce stress, and how much stress training is necessary, is still an art.

Another complication is the difficult of defining *stress* objectively. Fitts and Posner (1967) equate stress with information overload. There have been ample demonstrations that a person's sense of information load depends on the number of separate pieces of information to be dealt with, not the amount of information per se. Thus, the same input seems much more manageable to an expert who perceives it in terms of meaningful patterns than to a novice who has no organizing structure. The implication is that stress is a subjective variable, and that the same task conditions may stress some students but not others. So, if we are training students to perform under stressful conditions, we want to insure that stress and workload are neither too high nor too low for each student individually.

Multiple Players

Many real-world decisions are made in the context of tasks performed by a group or team of people. Resnick (1987) describes a nice example supplied by Ed Hutchins from his work for the Navy. When a ship is piloted into or out of San Diego harbor, six different seamen are involved. Two stand on deck and take visual sightings of designated landmarks, using devices that give exact headings. These readings are called out to two other sailors, who telephone them to someone on the bridge. That person repeats them for confirmation and records them in the ship's log. Another seaman uses the headings, along with navigational tools, to plot the ship's position on the chart and project where the ship will be at the next fix. These computations are used to decide what landmarks should be sighted by those on deck, starting another cycle. Thus, the decision making uses information provided by many people and also sets up their next actions, which will in turn feed into subsequent decisions.

Individual skill proficiency appears to be a necessary but not a sufficient condition for effective teamwork. McIntyre, Morgan, Salas, and Glickman (1988) argue that teamwork is something more than work accomplished by a group. Team members must interact, work toward shared goals, and adapt to environmental demands to meet those goals. Teamwork involves the behaviors of monitoring, feedback, communication, and backing each other up (Salas & Morgan, 1989).

Research on team decision making is described in Chapters 19 and 20. Although teamwork is widely acknowledged to be important, questions remain regarding how to obtain it. There have been few empirical studies of team training strategies or design (Salas et al., 1991). Studies that are available generally describe what happens in a team or report correlations between performance level and selected variables such as team size. The work has not generated a set of findings that can be used to design training for team performance (Dyer, 1984; Hall & Rizzo, 1975). However, interest in this topic is on the rise, and some new work is analyzing the functioning of more and less effective teams in great detail. For example, analyses of recordings of commercial airline cockpit crew interactions suggest that crews that make few errors spend more time framing problems and justifying their decisions, engage in more contingency planning, and manage time and human resources better (Orasanu, 1990). Such findings have implications for skills that should be included in training for tasks involving team decision making.

Organizational Goals and Norms

Orasanu and Connolly point out in Chapter 1 that much decision making occurs in an organizational context, and that the organization influences decisions both directly, by stipulating standard operating procedures, and indirectly, through the organization's norms and culture. While incorporating standard operating procedures into a job training program is straightforward, the more elusive norms and values of the organization are normally acquired through incidental learning. In a study of Xerox maintenance technicians, for example, Orr (1985) concluded that technicians value the informal learning they obtain through swapping "war stories" with other technicians more than the explicit instruction provided at the training center. A way to inject this kind of learning into a training program for new entrants into a field is to provide them with opportunities to interact frequently and informally with current job incumbents. Involving representatives of the organization in the design and delivery of training will help guard against a training program that is incompatible with the "unwritten rules" of the organization.

Summary

Table 18.1 summarizes the training guidelines discussed above, relating each to the task features that make it relevant. As a group, these task features set natural decision tasks off from the kind of experimental tasks studied in much of the decision literature. However, natural decision-making tasks vary in the extent to which they exhibit these task features. Electronics diagnosis, for example, is usually done without a great deal of time stress. The diagnoses performed in emergency rooms, on the other hand, are typically extremely time sensitive. The table is designed to be a tool for thinking about training for specific types of natural decision-making tasks once their characteristics have been identified.

IS THERE A ROLE FOR TRAINING GENERAL DECISION SKILLS?

We have tried to make the case that appropriate domain-related training will facilitate acquisition of decision making within the domain. At this point, the reader may be wondering whether there is anything

Table 18.1.   Training for Decision Making in Natural Tasks

Task Features	Desirable Training Practices
Ill-Structured Problems	• Provide many trials in problem recognition and representation, using a wide variety of problem types. • For tasks with time-consuming components other than problem formulation and decision making, use simulation to more efficiently train on the latter. • Provide timely, informative feedback; simulation can help accomplish this.
Action/Feedback Loops	• Train decision making along with other task components in a meaningful task context.
Heavy Workload	• Employ techniques such as "scaffolding" to reduce workload in early stages of training. • Introduce "dual-task" training early in the instructional program. • Train constant-mapping task components to automaticity. • Model and train experts' strategies for minimizing workload. • Train students to monitor their workload.
Time Stress and High Stakes	• Introduce "dual-task" training early in the instructional program. • Train constant-mapping task components to automaticity. • Provide some training under speed stress. • Provide practice and feedback on making speed/accuracy tradeoffs. • Train with simulated stressful conditions. • Require overlearning of emergency procedures.
Multiple Players	• Train procedures for monitoring, agenda setting, and communicating. • Provide training and feedback on teamwork behaviors.
Organizational Goals and Norms	• Involve organization members in the design and delivery of training. • Allow for informal contact between trainees and experienced job incumbents.

left to train after providing the instruction described above in recognizing important patterns and problem types, automating constant mapping task components, and making speed–accuracy tradeoffs under different conditions.

Based both on the traditional decision-making literature and the record of generalized training of problem solving, we are skeptical about the likelihood that domain-independent training in decision strategies will have much effect on subsequent performance within a range of task domains. Our sense is that most of the decision rules used in these natural tasks are tailored to a particular domain.

Metacognitive skills may well constitute the best candidates for generalizable skills that will aid decision making across domains. These skills involve both reflection upon, and regulation of, one's own thinking. Thus, the term has come to be used both to describe awareness of the cognitive demands associated with different task conditions and specific strategies for improving memory, comprehension, and performance. Some of the specific metacognitive skills that have been studied are predicting the outcome of learning activities, apportioning time across components of a task, and implementing strategies such as summarizing and self-questioning to aid learning and memory. The importance of such skills in memory tasks (Lodico, Ghatala, Levin, Pressley, & Bell, 1983), reading comprehension (Palincsar & Brown, 1984), mathematics (Schoenfeld, 1985), flight training (Gopher et al., 1988b), and writing (Scardamalia & Bereiter, 1985; Flower & Hayes, 1980) has been amply demonstrated. Better performers employ metacognitive strategies, and teaching the strategies to poorer performers leads to improvement on the task.

Although we are not aware of a literature on "metadecision making," it seems reasonable to propose that analogies to the organizing and checking routines employed in reading, writing, and mathematical problem solving would prove useful to the decision maker. Laskey, Leddo, and Bresnick (1989) reached a similar conclusion in their study on the cognitive structures needed by military executive-level decision makers (i.e., three-star generals and above). They suggest training the planning skills that individuals who eventually reach executive-level positions appear to develop on their own—planning, not just for the immediate objective, but also for long-term goals, looking for indirect consequences of a proposed action, and taking the perspective of the "other guy." Other decision-making tasks, depending on their features, would call upon additional metacognitive skills. Training decision makers to search for alternative problem representations and consider their implications would be sensible for tasks that are not time stressed. Training in monitoring one's workload, and flexibly changing procedures when it becomes too great, is an important metacognitive skill for a wide range of operational decision-making tasks. These ideas appear promising but need to be tried out and evaluated for various kinds of natural decision tasks.

If programs to train metadecision skills are developed, we recommend that the skills be taught in the context of practicing domain-relevant decisions. The danger in trying to teach metacognitive skills in isolation is that they can become verbal exercises: Students learn to describe the principles without ever necessarily incorporating them into their task performance. Schoenfeld (1985) describes how this has often happened with efforts to teach general mathematical problem solving. Students come to understand the general idea of the various heuristics but lack enough mathematical knowledge to apply them successfully in specific contexts. When the goal is to train metadecision skills that can be applied in multiple contexts, our recommendation is to train those skills in a series of concrete, relevant domains rather than with abstract, "content-free" material (cf. Perkins & Salomon, 1989). After students have learned to apply the skills in several domains, instruction can highlight the essence of the skill that applies across domains and can address the issue of the range of tasks to which the skill can be applied.

There is a sizeable literature on training metacognitive skills (Bransford et al., 1986). The lesson to be drawn from this literature is that we must first establish that the metacognitive skills or strategies we propose teaching do in fact improve task performance. Once we have done this, we can design instruction such that the student not only sees models of skill execution and practices the skill in a task context but also is provided with evidence of its efficacy (Brown, Campione, & Day, 1981). Finally, training on when to use the skill (conditions of applicability), giving students both positive and negative examples, is required as well (Gagne, Weidmann, Bell, & Anders, 1984).

A corollary to this emphasis on metacognitive skills in the individual decision maker is the need to teach "group" metadecision skills if the task is one that must be performed by a team. Although there is little guidance available from research in this area, we can envision a group monitoring and agenda-setting process very much akin to the self-regulatory processes observed in individuals. The lessons learned from the metacognitive skills training research could then be applied to the design of training for group decision-making skills, as suggested above when we discussed the training implications of the fact that decision tasks involve multiple players.

CONCLUDING REMARKS

Our general theme in this chapter is that the move toward considering decision making within the context of real-world tasks brings with it a new set of implications regarding how decision-making skill should be trained. Just as ideas about training problem solving moved from an emphasis on working with abstract puzzles to training problem-solving skills within specific task domains, so too our ideas about training decision making are being changed by research on how decisions are actually made in natural settings. When decision making is considered in a task context rather than as an isolated activity, we realize that our training needs to take into account the specific characteristics of the task and of the social and organizational context within which it is performed.

KEY POINTS

- Decision training based on classical decision theory has not been shown to transfer to natural tasks outside the classroom.
- Bias reduction training transfers only marginally to natural settings.
- In real settings, experts and novices differ in how they use their domain knowledge, not in their ability to use particular problem-solving methods or decision rules.
- Decision-making training needs to address characteristics of the task and the context within which it is performed.

Chapter 19

Team Decision Making in Complex Environments

Judith Orasanu
NASA Ames Research Center

Eduardo Salas
Naval Training Systems Center

Team decision making invades the public consciousness most often when it fails. An Air Florida flight crashed on take-off from Washington's National Airport on a snowy January day after the copilot recognized a problem with engine power but the crew failed to decide to abort the take-off. The USS Vincennes shot down an Iranian airliner carrying 382 passengers, mistaking it for an attacking military plane, because the crew misinterpreted data from electronic sensors.

In many everyday situations, important decisions affecting the lives of many people are made by groups rather than by individuals. Even if a single individual bears responsibility for the decision, many participants contribute to the final product. Decision problems in business, military, health care policy, and other settings are often so complex that multiple experts and sources of information are essential to reach a satisfactory solution.

This chapter is motivated by three questions about team decision making, which we will address in turn: (1) What theories account for team decision performance in everyday situations? New concepts of shared mental models and team mind will be offered as organizing frameworks for emerging findings. (2) What factors influence the effectiveness of decision making and broader problem solving performance by teams? (3) What can be done to improve team decision making?

Before addressing the above questions, we will define what we mean by team decision making, identify the features of teams in which we are interested, and distinguish between teams and groups in terms of the tasks they perform. These distinctions will be important as we consider contributions from the literature on group decision making to our present concerns.

First, we define team decision making as the process of reaching a decision undertaken by interdependent individuals to achieve a common goal. What distinguishes team decision making from individual decision making is the existence of more than one information source and task perspective that must be combined to reach a decision. While ostensibly working toward the same goal, participants may have differing agendas, motives, perceptions, and opinions that must be melded into the shared product.

In keeping with the theme of this book, our chapter focuses on decision making by teams with certain characteristics performing in selected types of environments. These special conditions include the following:

1. Decision making is part of a larger task performed by the group in a meaningful environment. The group exists to perform a common task; it has not come together simply for the purpose of making a decision.
2. Participants possess knowledge and skills relevant to the task and the decision.
3. Task conditions may change dynamically, decision time may be limited, workload may be high, and information ambiguous.

We use the term *team* quite deliberately, in contrast to collections of people we will call *groups*. Following Dyer (1984b) and Morgan, Glickman, Woodard, Blaiwes, and Salas (1986), team characteristics include:

- set of two or more individuals
- more than one information source
- interdependence and coordination among members
- adaptive management of internal resources
- common valued goals
- defined roles and responsibilities
- task relevant knowledge

Most critical for distinguishing teams from groups is the degree of differentiation of roles or knowledge relevant to the task, and the degree of member interdependence. Teams consist of highly differentiated and interdependent members; groups, on the other hand, consist of homogeneous and interchangable members, like juries. This chapter is primarily concerned with teams, although we will draw from the literature on group decision making, as it is much more extensive. Unfortunately, the bulk of that research is based on ad hoc groups of college students.

The above distinction rests on differences in the *tasks* usually performed by teams versus groups. A critical feature of team tasks is that they require multiple, interdependent participants for successful accomplishment. For some tasks, tight coordination and collaboration among participants is required. Examples include operating a tank, conducting surgery, playing a string quartet, or operating within military command and control. Other tasks, like deciding where to situate a nuclear power plant, hypothetically could be accomplished by an individual, but a team is preferred because the task itself is extremely complex, and no single individual possesses all of the relevant knowledge or perspectives.

The range of team tasks described above differ in the centrality of decision making in their activities. For some teams, making decisions is their primary activity, such as military command and control, policy making (e.g., siting a waste dump), or management of new product development. For other teams, decisions are embedded in performance. For example, a tank crew must identify and select targets and choose local tactics. Cockpit crews must decide how to deal with system malfunctions in flight. Engineering teams must decide which design to adopt. Still other teams make few decisions, and are more performance oriented. For sports teams or musical ensembles coordination is most important. The coach or conductor may make most decisions, but the team implicitly decides how to implement them. The important point is that in all the above cases, decisions are part of an ongoing larger activity in which the team engages. For recent discussions of work teams see Hackman (1985, 1990) and Sundstrom, DeMeuse, and Futrell (1990).

THEORIES OF TEAM DECISION MAKING

When we look to the literature for theory that accounts for team decision making in complex environments, we find the shelves to be practically bare. As Davis (1986) notes, "A listing of the major research efforts addressing group performance phenomena of the last 25 years documents the tendency for research activity to cluster around particular problems, common discoveries, effects, or practical concerns—but not approaches, schools, or grand theoretical orientations" (p. 9). Most of the research literature deals with what we are calling groups. As Steiner (1972) points out, social psychologists over the past 50 years have studied groups, alternating their focus on group *product* and group *process*. Prior to World War II psychologists studied productivity in ad hoc groups, attempting to demonstrate the superiority of group effort to individual performance. Following World War II the emphasis shifted to laboratory studies of group process and new methods were adopted: researchers created "synthetic" groups to gain experimental control.

Group decision-making research examined the effects of group size, composition, structure, cohesion, member status, and influence patterns. One theory that dealt specifically with group decision making is Davis' (1973) Decision Schemes theory. It tried to account for group decisions on the basis of the distribution of votes (pro/con) on an issue and a combination rule for reaching the decision (truth wins, majority wins, plurality wins, etc.). While Davis' approach showed systematic relations between the task, group variables, and decision rules, its applicability to team decision making is not clear. The problem stems from the types of groups and tasks that were studied by Davis. McGrath (1991) captures this problem with respect to group performance research broadly defined:

> There are some serious limitations to much of that earlier work, especially regarding the degree to which it reflects the structures and processes of naturally occurring groups as we meet them in our everyday lives. In part those limits reflect features of the methodological and conceptual paradigms that have dominated the group research field, along with most of social psychology, within that same period of time: An analytic paradigm that presumes directional causal relations among isolated factors with little regard for physical, temporal, or social context. Much of the empirical foundation of group theory derives from study of a limited range of types of ad hoc groups under controlled experimental conditions.
>
> Most of that work involves very small groups (2 to 4 members) with constant membership arbitrarily assigned by an experimenter, that exist only for a limited period of time without past or future as a group, isolated rather than embedded in any larger social units (organizations, communities). These groups are studied while performing single and relatively simple tasks arbitrarily assigned to them by the experimenter (i.e., not tasks indigenous to those groups) under "context stripped" conditions. . . . The theories do not purport to be about ad hoc, laboratory groups of limited mission and under limited conditions. To the contrary; most group theories purport to be about groups in general, and by implication, about naturally occurring groups. But the groups we meet in those theories, like the groups used in most studies, differ markedly from the kind of groups we meet in everyday affairs. (1991, pp. 3–5)

McGrath points out recent research on small groups that is beginning to address some of these criticisms, such as time-linked transitions in work groups (Gersick, 1988, 1989), group development (Levine & Moreland, 1985, 1990), and adaptive structuration theory (Poole & DeSanctis, 1990). Research on decision making by teams is just beginning to emerge. It consists mainly of descriptive studies of complex task performance in natural environments, with decisions embedded in those tasks, or analysis of communication in teams performing natural tasks.

Two major impediments to research on real teams or groups have been limitations of method and technology. Both of these are being overcome, however. Videorecorders are now making it possible to record interactions for future and repeated analysis. Use of computers for distributed decision making also preserves interactions for subsequent analysis. And new analytical methods with roots in anthropology, linguistics, and cognitive science are yielding new findings and theories. For example, Wellens (1990a) has developed a theory of distributed decision making via computer communication. And Hutchins and Klausen (1991) have used ethnographic methods to study cockpit crews communicating with ground controllers.

Shared Mental Models and Team Mind

These new technologies and analytical methods have spawned new conceptual frameworks for team decision making. We offer here a sketch of two related theoretical frameworks that have emerged from recent investigations of team decision making in natural environments: shared mental models (Cannon-Bowers, Salas, & Converse, 1990; Orasanu, 1990) and team mind (Klein & Thordsen, 1989b). While these are not fully developed theories, they account for certain team phenomena and provide direction for future research. After a brief description of these notions, we will describe some of the research findings that led to their development and some older data that are consistent with them. To date these theories have not been tested experimentally, but serve as conceptual frameworks for thinking about the problems of teams making decisions.

Shared mental models refer to organized knowledge shared by team members. Some of this knowledge is broadly shared by members of a culture; some is limited to members of a restricted group, such as a profession; and some is particular to a situation. For example, airline cockpit crews know the principles of how airplanes fly and how the

systems in their planes function. This knowledge facilitates communication about systems, providing ready terms of reference. They
also know standard operating procedures and company-specific policies. Furthermore, they know the norms of behavior and roles of each
member of the crew (Cannon-Bowers & Salas, 1990). Such knowledge
enables each person to carry out his or her role in a timely and coordinated fashion, helping the team to function as a single unit with little
negotiation of what to do and when to do it.

But what about making decisions when faced with novel situations
or emergencies? Orasanu (1990) has suggested that crews must develop shared situation models for the specific problem, which are
grounded in the crew's stable models of the system, task, and team, but
go beyond them. These situation models include shared understanding
of the problem, goals, information cues, strategies, and member roles.
Communication is used to build shared situation models when conditions demand nonhabitual responses. Once shared models have been
created, they provide a context for interpreting commands or information requests, and allow for volunteering of information or actions at
appropriate times. They also provide a basis for predicting behavior or
needs of other crew members.

What evidence supports the existence of shared mental models? And
how do they contribute to team decision making behavior? Hints in
several early studies suggest that shared models may have contributed
to observed behavior. First was Torrance's (1953) report of World War II
military units downed behind enemy lines. Retrospective accounts by
survivors indicated that survival itself depended on the leader quickly
and accurately assessing the situation, providing frequent status up-
dates, maintaining a goal orientation, and making sure each member
knew what had to be done in order to survive. In other words, the
leader built and maintained a shared situation model.

In a laboratory study of group problem solving, Lanzetta and Roby
(1960) used a continuous task that required induction of condition-
action rules and development of a "jurisdictional structure" for dis-
tributing responsibility and authority. They found that the way the
group utilized its resources and communicated essential information
were critical factors determining group performance. Specifically, the
best performance was observed in groups that volunteered information
when it was needed, suggesting that those groups had developed
shared task and team models.

Unfortunately, those older accounts do not provide unambiguous
data in support of the shared models construct. More recent studies
provide more convincing evidence. One set of studies supports development of shared models of the team—that is, knowledge about the

knowledge, skills, anticipated behavior, and anticipated needs of team members. Several studies of cockpit crews suggest how communication in the cockpit serves to build shared team models. In a study of fatigue effects on crew coordination and performance, Foushee, Lauber, Baetge, and Acomb (1986) found that familiarity among members of a crew based on shared experience was so powerful it overcame effects of fatigue. Superior performance was associated with more task relevant talk: more commands and suggestions by both the captain and first officer, more statements of intent, more exchanges of information, more acknowledgements, and more disagreements. Foushee et al. interpreted this pattern to mean that flying together enabled crews to develop interaction patterns that contributed to coordination and decision making performance. We might say they developed shared team models that supported building of shared situation models.

In a different analysis of the same data set, Kanki, Lozito, and Foushee (1989) found that high performing crews' conversations were characterized by great homogeneity: they adopted a conventionalized speech pattern that facilitated coordination, because crew members interacted in predictable ways. In contrast, low performing crews' conversational patterns were heterogeneous and less predictable. Thus, more work was required of poor crews to interact, which may have lowered their coordination scores. Kanki et al. concluded that flying together enabled crews to learn common terms of reference, conventional means of communication, and what to expect of each other. Again, we conclude that the good crews developed better shared team models.

The notion of shared team models is related to Wegner's (1987) concept of *transactive memory systems.* These systems pertain to *group mind,* which is analogous to individual mind in its information processing capabilities, especially memory encoding, storage, and retrieval. The critical components include labels that signify particular information and knowledge about which group member has what information. Transactive memory results in expansion of personal memory through interdependence on other members of the group. The concept does not mean that everyone shares all the stored knowledge, but that they share knowledge of the labels (which may be idiosyncratic to the group) and knowledge of who possesses specialized information.

Observations from a completely different domain support the notion of shared team and task models and the role of communication in developing them. Heath (1991) described the language used by a little league coach and his rag-tag team as he tried to give them the skills and coordination to function as a team. At the beginning of the season their utterances were lengthy and explicit. As the season wore on the utterances shortened, so that by the end of the season, the team, which had evolved into a winning team, communicated in brief cryptic utterances, more like signals than language. We conclude that the team members had developed shared models of the game and their roles in it so that much of their teamwork was habitual and that minimal language served a guiding or correcting role.

Distinctive communication patterns have also been found in laboratory studies. Using a simulated military command and control scenario, Kleinman and Serfaty (1989) examined the effects of workload, overlap of functional responsibility, and distribution of knowledge resources on communication and performance. As the tempo of the task increased from low to moderate, explicit verbal coordination increased. But as workload became high, the amount of communication went down. Virtually all resource transfers were unsolicited, resulting in implicit coordination. Kleinman and Serfaty interpreted this pattern as exercise of mutual mental models that allowed participants to anticipate each other's resource needs and actions.

However, implicit coordination does not always yield adequate performance. Given that Kleinman and Serfaty's task could be performed successfully by novices without any specialized knowledge, the task was probably not particularly difficult. Novel responses did not seem to be required in the high workload situation. However, other tasks may require nonroutine responses. When such conditions arise, teams may need to develop specialized situation models to cope with the crisis.

In her analysis of cockpit crews faced with in-flight emergencies, Orasanu (1990) found that good and poor crews differed in their communication patterns. Specifically, good crews were much more explicit in defining the problem, articulating plans and strategies for coping with it, obtaining relevant information, explaining the rationale, and allocating and coordinating responsibilities among the crew. Orasanu claimed that this pattern reflected their building of shared models for the specific problem, which enabled the crew to make situation-appropriate decisions and carry them out in an efficient and timely manner. Crews that relied on implicit coordination found themselves overwhelmed by the problems (a missed approach and hydraulic system failure), a situation from which many of them never quite recovered, resulting in potentially dangerous conditions.

Orasanu (1990) suggested that developing shared mental models for a problem creates a context within which decisions can be made, exploiting the cognitive resources of the entire group. Explicit shared models assure that everyone is solving the same problem, a critical issue given what is known about framing effects (Tversky & Kahneman, 1981). When all team members share the same problem definition, they can volunteer relevant information or strategies from their specialized perspectives, and can interpret requests and commands unambiguously.

While the concept of shared mental models provides a framework for interpreting team phenomena, it pertains only to certain team functions. A more encompassing notion of *team mind* has been proposed by Klein and Thordsen (1989a). Klein and Thordsen draw an analogy between team mind and individual mind, which allows introduction of concepts from cognitive psychology as sources of hypotheses about team performance. Three levels of team mind are proposed: the *behavioral level* (overt actions), *collective consciousness* (reflected in communication), and *preconscious* (individual knowledge or interpretations that are not shared with the group). The collective consciousness level maps most closely to Orasanu's notion of shared mental models. In trying to understand how teams perform and make decisions, Klein and Thordsen draw on concepts of limited attentional resources, working memory, workload, automaticity, and metacognition.

Indirect support for the notion of team mind comes from Klein and Thordsen's (1989b) observation that four different types of teams (military command and control, crisis management, firefighting, and cockpit crews) used the same decision strategy as individual decision makers when making decisions typical of those required in their jobs. Teams, like individuals, used what Klein (this volume) calls recognition-primed decision making. That is, rather than generating all possible options and concurrently evaluating them to choose the optimal alternative, decision makers used their experience to assess the situation, classifying it as an instance of a familiar type. Then they retrieved the most plausible response to the interpreted situation and evaluated its adequacy by using mental simulation of its outcome. If the outcome was adequate, they implemented the response. If not, they generated a second option and evaluated it, or reassessed the situation, until a satisfactory solution was found. The important point here is that experienced crews performed like individuals, lending support to the notion of a team mind. Most significantly, the teams did not adopt a more analytic strategy than individual decision makers in similar situations, as might have been expected on the basis of expanded cognitive resources.

TEAM DECISION MAKING EFFECTIVENESS

Before we can begin to consider variables that affect team decision making effectiveness, we must define the criterion by which performance is to be judged. Social psychologists studying small group performance in the laboratory used measures such as productivity, accuracy or efficiency of task solution, consensus, or member satisfaction. But what constitutes good team decision making in natural environments? In laboratory studies of individual decision making, criteria of rationality, optimality, consistency, and adherence to logical assumptions have been adopted. The problem with using these criteria for judging decision making in natural situations is that the features of the task and conditions under which the decisions are made do not correspond well to those assumed by normative models. These include stable goals and values, accessible and meaningful likelihoods of outcomes, and full information.

Performance-oriented teams exist to accomplish a task. Their ultimate criterion is how well they perform the task. To our knowledge, no one has systematically examined whether task performance depends on the optimality of embedded decisions. Presumably, a decision needs to be good enough for the task to be accomplished at some specified level of proficiency. Does improving the quality of a decision improve task performance? The little evidence available yields conflicting conclusions. Christensen-Szalanski (1986, this volume) has shown that in medical decision making situations, improving the quality of the decision does not necessarily change the diagnosis or treatment (unless it shifts the decision across a choice threshold).

The opposite conclusion was reached in a study of decision making and performance conducted by Murphy and Awe (1985). Using a full mission cockpit simulation, 6 check pilots rated the performance of 16 professional airline crews. Step-wise multiple regression was used to explore the relations between safety performance, decision making, communication, crew coordination, and leadership. They found that 46 percent of the variance on Safety was predicted by Decision Efficiency, Command Reversal, and Decision Quality. Sixty percent of the Decision Quality variance was predicted by Decision Efficiency and Captain Communication Quality. These positive correlations, of course, do not imply a causal relation between decision quality and task performance (Safety). In fact, based on a different flight simulation study, Orasanu (1990) found no relation between actual decisions and task performance (as measured by procedural and aircraft control errors). No relation was found because all crews made exactly the same ultimate decisions (to abort a landing due to bad weather and choice of an alternate landing site). However, Orasanu did find a positive relation between decision strategies and overall task performance. More effective crews showed greater situation awareness, obtained decision-relevant information in time to use it, adopted a resource-conserving strategy while they acquired needed information, and factored in more constraints on their decisions. All crews adopted an elimination by aspects strategy for the choice of an alternate landing site (six possible options were available).

These findings suggest that no general conclusions can be drawn at this time about the relation between decision quality and performance; any such conclusions will have to wait for analyses of the relation between embedded decisions and overall tasks, and experimental manipulations of factors that influence decision and task performance.

An innovative approach to applying mathematical models to team decision making can be seen in the work of Kleinman and his associates (Kleinman, Luh, Pattipati, & Serfaty, in press). They have taken a normative (prescriptive) or optimal mathematical model and appropriately degraded it with descriptive (data-oriented) information on biases in cognitive information processing, which they capture mathematically and integrate into the optimal model. Working with tasks for which it is possible to calculate "optimal" performance, they can predict how different types of biases will degrade performance. Then, by creating the conditions for those biases, they can test the predictions by measuring subjects' actual performance.

Working with a low-fidelity simulation of a military command and control task, Kleinman and his associates are currently investigating effects of centralization of information sources, (whether information is universally accessible or restricted to certain members), overlap of functional responsibility, task pacing, information load, differing values and priorities. While Kleinman et al. have found some interesting patterns of results, their findings are limited to greatly simplified tasks. They have shown how utility models can provide microlevel and analyses at critical decision points, a precision lacking in most process models. However, their approach runs into difficulty when stretched beyond its assumptions of stable mathematical weighting of decision components and its focus on a controlled, measurable environment. The work by Kleinman et al. stands out as an exciting exception in the active TDM research arena.

Group Communication and Performance Research

Following McGrath's (1964) model of examining process variables in order to understand the relation between input and outcome variables, several related findings in the literature suggest themes that may be productive to explore. Studies from several different disciplines, using diverse methods, implicate communication strategies in reasoning outcomes.

Two studies of cockpit crew communication (in addition to the Murphy & Awe, 1985, study cited above) show positive relations between features of crew discourse and decision making. Pepitone, King and Murphy (1988) found that crews that engaged in contingency planning during simulated flight were the ones that made more effective decisions when emergencies were encountered. Presumably those crews built shared models of potential problems so that when they actually encountered emergencies, they did not have to commit cognitive resources to beginning to figure out what to do (further increasing already high workload).

Orasanu (1990) analyzed the cognitive functions of crew utterances in a cockpit simulation study. Captains of high performing crews (defined by procedural and control errors) explicitly stated more plans, strategies, and intentions, considered more options, provided more explanations, and sounded more warnings or predictions. As in the Pepitone, King, and Murphy (1988) study, good crews used their low workload periods to plan for contingencies. What is important here is not just that one member of the crew had these thoughts in his head, but that they were articulated so that the entire crew shared them. Crews that exhibited higher levels of problem-related talk were the same ones who were more constraint-sensitive and planful in making their decisions.

An important aspect of Orasanu's findings is that the relation between these problem-related utterances and performance held only for the captain, not for the first officer. This probably says more about current culture and practice in the airline industry than about communication, reasoning, and performance in general, but the finding fits with earlier reports on status and contributions to team decision making. Torrance's (1954) study of problem solving by B-52 crews showed the power of status in quality of outcomes. Crews comprised of pilot, navigator, and gunner solved four different types of problems. In all cases the pilot's views carried more weight than the other crew members', regardless of whether he was correct or not. In fact, even when the navigator or gunner suggested the correct answer, it was not always accepted by the group.

High status can be used effectively to manage a team or it can lead a team to disaster. In a study of airline captains' personality types and crew performance, Chidester et al. (1990) found that crews led by captains who were both highly task-oriented and had good interpersonal skills consistently performed well. They made few operational errors and were highly coordinated. Consistently poor coordination and high performance errors were found in crews led by captains with negative expressive styles and low task motivation. Subsequent analyses of these crews' conversations showed that the effective captains created more democratic cockpits in which all crew members' contributions were valued.

Several studies of decision making by groups (as opposed to teams) support the critical role of communication in decision making. In comparing groups engaged in a problem solving task, Poole and Doelger (1986) show how different solution paths depend on how the group represents the task through their talk. When members' individual task representations differ, a group will recycle through old material, have several breakpoints, and make slow progress. However, when members' representations are compatible, the common representation dictates a straightforward agenda, and progress is rapid. Likewise, Hirokawa (1983) found that groups that spend time jointly analyzing the assigned problem prior to trying to solve it were much more successful than groups that jumped directly to solutions. Again, a shared problem model created the context for efficient problem solving.

Other group decision making research has examined consensus rather than problem solution as the relevant outcome. Using groups that had worked together over a school term, DeStephan (1983) analyzed the interaction patterns of high- and low-consensus groups in their final meeting. High-consensus groups required greater amounts of substantiation and clarification of positions before a proposal was accepted as a solution. Low-consensus groups, on the other hand, contributed many more undeveloped statements about the decision proposals. These statements tended to be accepted without demands for further substantiation. We interpret these findings as indicating that the high consensus groups were more cognitively demanding, seeking to assure that they understood each other's proposals before making decisions on them. They monitored the degree to which they had established shared models and took action to reach understanding.

In several experiments that manipulated communication adequacy, Leathers (1969, 1970, 1972) studied the relation between communication quality and decision quality. What he called "high-quality" communication can be glossed as "considerate" text (Anderson & Armbruster, 1986). It is highly coherent text, well organized, with clear relations expressed between ideas, and useful summaries. "Low quality" text included many high-level abstractions, implicit inferences, and irrelevant information. Confederates were trained to use high- or low-quality communication in group problem solving. Not surprisingly, high-quality text was associated with higher quality solutions. Presumably, high-quality communication made it easier for those groups to build shared problem models than low-quality communication did. Then they could get on with solving the problem.

Summary

1. Real teams, those with a history of working together, interact differently than ad hoc teams. This finding has two implications:
    a. Researchers will not obtain the same findings from ad hoc and established teams. Whichever one chooses depends on whether one is interested in the early acquisition phase or asymptotic phase of team performance. If one is interested in the behavior of strangers getting organized to perform a task, ad hoc groups are appropriate. If one is interested in learning about teams that have gotten beyond "getting acquainted," then real teams are desirable.
    b. Experience working together leads members to build a shared mental model for the team, which allows members to predict each other's behavior and needs. It also allows for development of a shared task model for routine team tasks (cf. Gersick & Hackman, 1990). Team member predictability in a stable task environment leads to better team coordination and performance.
2. Communication is central to team and group performance in nonroutine tasks. Individual skills and knowledge are not sufficient for successful team performance; individual resources must be appropriately utilized through interaction processes.
3. Building shared problem models prior to trying to solve a problem or make a decision enhances performance. Shared problem models are necessary for teams to make decisions in nonroutine or emergency situations.
4. High-status team members exert strong influence on team performance, often positively, but sometimes negatively.

CAN TEAM DECISION MAKING BE IMPROVED?

Before considering how team decision making can be improved, we should consider how teams can go wrong. Given that teams represent increased cognitive resources compared to individuals, we might expect teams to perform better than individuals. Teams represent multiple eyes, ears, and heads. To list just a few advantages, team members can monitor each other's performance, pool their knowledge or observations, suggest strategies or options, provide alternate viewpoints, reduce workload by sharing tasks, provide feedback, and critique each other. Yet this increased cognitive power sometimes leads to a whole that is less than the sum of its parts.

Sources of Failure in Team Decision Making

Social psychologists have identified many ways in which teams can go wrong. Perhaps most well known is *groupthink* (Janis, 1972), in which a group suspends its rational judgment in order to maintain group cohesion. Usually it involves the unchallenged acceptance of a proposal advocated by a powerful and respected leader, as in the Bay of Pigs invasion planning during the Kennedy administration. Social cohesion factors can also inhibit individual contribution of information relevant to a decision. Stasser and Titus (1987) have found that group members tend to offer information already shared by the group rather than novel information, thereby preserving group cohesion.

Another way in which teams can go wrong is failure to challenge assumptions about goals or values. In the Abilene Paradox (Harvey, 1988), members assume they know each others' goals and operate on that assumption. *False consensus* arises when one believes that others share one's opinions, and *pluralistic ignorance* results when one thinks that one is the odd person out. In all of these cases, status or conformity pressures may mitigate against checking one's assumptions.

Even when social pressures do not work to maintain ignorance, groups may make poor decisions because of shared misconceptions or poor communication. Shared experience may lead team members to think similarly—but incorrectly—while bolstering their confidence in their positions. Shared experience may also lead members to assume shared understanding of words like *risk, threat, likely,* when in fact they mean these differently. Finally, teams may make poor decisions due to outright hostility, lack of cooperation, or lack of motivation. Obviously, different remedies are warranted for the various sources of difficulty.

Another powerful social factor that contributes to faulty decision making is rejection by a high status team member of relevant information offered by a lower status team member. Transcripts from numerous black box recordings following airline crashes indicate that the captain failed to heed warnings or attend to information offered by crew members. Goguen, Linde, and Murphy's (1986) analyses of several transcripts show that linguistic factors play a role in whether captains "hear" the message. Utterances that are very polite and indirect are less likely to be "heard" than more direct utterances.

Klein and Thordsen (1989b) identified potential barriers to team decision making in command environments. They point out that elements of decision making like situation assessment and understanding of the commander's intention (which shapes and gives direction to decisions) are fraught with potential difficulties. Situation complexity exceeds individual expertise, thus requiring several specialists to communicate in order to understand the entire situation. Processed and interpreted information must be shared—much like the children's game of telephone. Distortions can enter into this process, and the receiver must evaluate the validity of the received information. Intentions must often be inferred.

A final but certainly not least important contributor to faulty team decision making is organizational policy. As Hackman (1988) pointed out, the organizational context in which real teams perform may be the most significant factor governing their performance. For example, an analysis of 23 fatal jet accidents showed 15 of them to be influenced by policy factors (Bruggink, 1985). One of the most prevalent policies stresses on-time performance. Braniff Airlines' "fast buck" program, instituted in 1968, promised to pay each passenger one dollar if a flight failed to reach its destination within 15 minutes of its scheduled arrival time. This policy was implicated in one crash when the pilot tried to fly through instead of around a line of thunderstorms near his destination airport, in hindsight a faulty decision (Nance, 1984).

Training for Improved Team Decision Making

Team decision making may be improved via organizational design, system design or aids, or team training. Organizational and system design issues will be addressed by Duffy (this volume); this chapter will deal only with improving performance through training. The first problem we must confront when considering how to devise training to improve decision making is: What to train? The literature reviewed in this chapter is notably silent on specific recommendations for training (see also Means, this volume). While many of the studies identified factors associated with more or less successful team performance, few of them dealt with decision making per se. Perhaps more significantly, none of them identified problems in team decision making stemming from heuristics, biases, or other logical flaws.

A search for research on training teams to make better decisions turns up many recommendations in the business management literature, but little in the way of empirical support (Swezey & Salas, in press). The problem is twofold: empirical research on groups has been quiescent for many years, yielding little in the way of new concepts or approaches. The second is that new models of decision making for action, by individuals or teams, are just emerging. These theories are too new for a substantial body of knowledge to have accumulated.

Salas, Dickinson, Tannenbaum, and Converse (1991), in their meta-analysis of the team-training and performance literature, have con-

cluded that there are few empirical studies that apply learning principles to teams, and those that do exist are difficult to interpret. In fact,
many evaluate a single training device or system because of problems
associated with a lack of an adequate terminology and the inadequacy
of available task analysis methods for describing team activities
(Modrick, 1986). Therefore, little is known about what actually constitutes *team* training, much less team training for decision making.

Nevertheless, we suggest two approaches to training teams for better decision making. The first is to use emerging theory as a guide and
train the skills prescribed by theory. See Means (this volume) for a
thorough discussion of training suggested by new models of decision
making, such as Klein's Recognition-Primed Decision (RPD) theory.
The second approach is to identify features of successful and less successful teams and use that information as a guide to training.

One of the few examples of a theory-based approach is Klein's RPD
model, which stresses the importance of situation assessment in decision making. Therefore, we might train teams in situation assessment,
particularly in ways to rapidly combine information and interpretations from a number of participants. Or, we might train teams to
evaluate options by using mental simulation: What will happen if we
do X? The concept of shared mental models suggests that we train
teams to use communication to develop shared problem models for
nonroutine situations (Orasanu, 1990). The feasibility of this approach
is supported by Lassiter, Vaughn, Smaltz, Morgan, and Salas' (1990)
demonstration that it is possible to train team communication skills
using modeling.

Two examples of the empirically based approach are already available, although both involve team training on a broader range of skills
than decision making. The first example is the work of Morgan, Glickman, and colleagues. They have begun to identify the behavioral constituents of optimal team performance in tactical decision-making
teams (Glickman et al., 1987; Morgan et al., 1986). Skills identified to
date fall into two categories: *taskwork* (situation awareness, mission
analysis, and decision making) and *teamwork* (leadership, adaptation,
assertiveness, communication). Specific behaviors include (a) identification and resolution of errors, (b) coordinated information exchange, and (c) team reinforcement.

The second example is the implementation by several commercial
airline companies of *cockpit resource management* (CRM) training programs (see Helmreich, Chidester, Foushee, Gregorich, & Wilhelm,
1989) or aircrew coordination training (see Prince, Chidester, Cannon-
Bowers, & Bowers, in press) to develop the kinds of team skills found
lacking when air accidents and mishaps occurred. Based in part on

research conducted at NASA (Foushee et al., 1986), CRM programs train crews to manage their information resources and workload, coordinate their actions, and communicate more effectively. Ongoing evaluations of training programs will indicate what works and what doesn't (Cannon-Bowers et al., 1989). A major problem is determining an appropriate criterion by which to evaluate the programs. Crashes or other severe incidents are infrequent, making them insensitive indicators.

Both the military and airline companies are heeding Hackman's (1988) admonition: If we want teams to perform effectively as teams, they must be trained as teams. Traditional approaches have trained individual skills, after which people were thrown together and expected to perform as a unit. Current empirical research should tell us how best to train various kinds of team decision making skills.

Helmreich (1990) has pointed out two special problems that should be addressed by future research: How do we train the "wrong stuff" kind of person (such as the negative-expressive captains identified by Chidester et al., 1990)? Certain individuals reject training on team skills, yet they tend to be the people who need it the most (Helmreich, 1990). How do we train people to make decisions and perform effectively in high-stress environments? Most current team training aims at developing habits for routine situations. A footnote in the training manual may provide guidance on what to do in an emergency, but these receive short shrift. Habit and implicit coordination will carry people a long way in routine situations; we need to prepare them for the unusual.

FINAL THOUGHTS

A word about methods: No longer are studies of team decision making restricted to simplified laboratory experiments. Methods are expanding beyond the traditional laboratory tasks to include microanalyses of behavior in natural settings. Simulators are making it possible to create experimental environments that are safe and controlled to observe "natural" behavior. Video recorders make it possible to capture behavior for leisurely analysis. New observational tools are emerging that provide reliable and valid means of describing behaviors. No longer are we bound by Davis and Stasson's (1988) complaint that real teams in natural environments are not a realistic alternative to the laboratory. They are.

That is not to say that we should give up laboratory research. As Driskell and Salas (in press) point out, laboratory research is a valuable tool for testing theory. Unfortunately, there has been precious little theory to test until now. We will see what kinds of laboratory research will emerge in the coming years.

KEY POINTS

- Effective teams appear to share a mental model of their members' knowledge, skill, anticipated behavior, and needs.
- Few studies have examined team decision making; of several reviewed, shared problem models based on explicit communication differentiated good from poor teams.
- Sources of failure in team decision making include poor communication, logical errors, inadequate situation assessment, and pressures to conform.
- More studies are needed to identify features that distinguish good from poor teams, so that training can address these features.

Chapter 20

Team Decision-Making Biases: An Information-Processing Perspective

LorRaine Duffy*
Air Force Human Resources Laboratory
Wright Patterson Air Force Base

INTRODUCTION

Decision problems in business, military, health care, and other settings are often so complex that multiple experts and sources of information are essential to reach a solution. The complexity grows when expert systems, decision aids, and other support technologies are included in the process. How are we to understand this phenomenon? How do we improve it?

The intent of this chapter is to introduce: (a) the concept of a *team* as the information-processing unit, (b) the specialized problems that teams can encounter when making group decisions, and (c) the methods that are developing to improve team process and outcome while attempting to resolve a decision problem.

The focus will be on a specialized collection of individuals (i.e., a team or group) who must coordinate their thoughts and actions to reach a desired state from their initial state (i.e., the resolution of the decision problem—MacCrimmon & Taylor, 1976). Teams,[1] as defined

---

* Currently located at the Naval Command Control and Ocean Surveillance Center, Research, Development, Test and Evaluation Division. The views expressed in this chapter are solely those of the author and should not be construed as an official position of the U.S. Government.

[1] The terms *teams* and *groups* have traditionally been used interchangeably (as in Sundstrom, DeMeuse, & Futrell, 1990), as will be the case in this chapter. The referent here, beyond the characteristics listed, is to a group of individuals, with each member having useful, specialized knowledge, interacting to some end (a decision resolution). This is also a broader definition than is being used in the chapter by Orasanu and Salas (this volume). As Seeger (1983) points out (with Orasanu and Salas concurring), the area

by Beer (1976), Dyer (1984), Morgan, Glickman, Woodard, Blaiwes, and Salas (1986), and Eddy (1989), are generally characterized by: more than one information source with defined roles and responsibilities; tasks that require interdependence and coordination of knowledge and actions among its members; an ability to adapt and manage internal resources; having a common and valued goal(s). Their process may include several decision-making processes: autocratic, consultative, and participative decision making (Vroom & Yetton, 1973; Vroom, 1976). For example, *autocratic decision making* can be defined by a team leader who would obtain all necessary information from team members, then decide on the solution alone, without sharing the problem. *Consultative decision making* would require the team leader to share the problem with the team members and then gather ideas and suggestions before making the decision alone. *Participative decision making* would require the team members to share the problem and the generation and evaluation of alternatives, in order to reach mutual agreement on the solution. Although participative decision making is most closely aligned with the concept of team decision making, all of the above strategies are used by teams at various times, depending on the task requirements, time pressure, and the need for acceptance of the decision. Team performance, on the other hand, accounts for far greater activity than just decision making. It implies coordination of information, resources, time, and actions. This will not be the focus of this chapter. See Dyer (1984), McGrath (1984), Modrick (1986), and Eddy (1989) for reviews.

Sundstrom et al. (1990) have conceptualized teams in organizations using two dimensions: differentiation of members, and integration within the organizational structure. *Differentiation* refers to the degree of task specialization, independence, and autonomy of team members. In this chapter, highly differentiated teams are the focus. These teams require expert, role-differentiated specialists, often in specialized facilities. *Organizational integration* refers to the degree to which the team activities are linked with other aspects of the larger organization. Teams with either high or low integration are the focus here. Action and negotiation teams, such as cockpit crews, medical emergency teams, or expeditionary forces, are generally highly integrated into the larger organizational system, indicated by perfor-

---

of group decision making is confused by the preponderance of academic literature that uses artificial groups brought together in a laboratory setting to finish some arbitrary task. These are not the same as "real teams" and, therefore, not the referent of this chapter. One variable that may serve to better define *artificial* versus *real* teams or groups is the accountability of each individual to the team (Tetlock, 1985).

mance that is closely synchronized with organizational counterparts and support units. Project and development teams are defined by specialized experts and are generally low in their organizational integration: They are often internally paced, with less synchronization within the organization (although there may be a requirement for much external communication). Sundstrom et al. (1990) portray two other teams in their team typology: advice/involvement and production/service work teams. Both are low in member differentiation and vary in organizational integration. Advice/involvement teams are low in integration, depicted by few demands for synchronization with other work units and often minimal external exchange; production/service teams are highly integrated, depicted by externally paced work which is usually synchronized within and outside the organization.

Teams may cycle through each of these types across time, as a function of task requirements. And task requirements engage different levels of psychomotor and task coordination, as well as different levels of intellectual teamwork (Galegher, 1990). Highly differentiated teams imply information-intensive environments (such as military intelligence units or system design teams) in which the participants (as specialists) are working together to produce or manipulate information in order to reach judgements and decisions. Team productivity may be more difficult to improve in these information-intensive environments. How do we support intellectual teamwork? An information-processing perspective facilitates understanding of this process and may suggest ways to improve it.

TEAMS AS INFORMATION PROCESSORS

In recent research, Hinsz (1990a) has outlined a framework from which to study team decision making. He implies that team decision making may be described as an information-processing process, as do others (Lord, 1985; Baron & Byrne, 1987; Wegner, 1987; Klein & Thordsen, 1989a apply it to a "team" description). Groups that make decisions must process information, and, therefore, can be considered information processors (Hinsz, 1990a). This approach suggests that "the same set of processes that occur for individuals are conceptually involved in the information processing by a group" (Hinsz, 1990a, p. 12). General information-processing categories that may serve to better describe the intellectual teamwork process are: attention, acquisition, encoding, storage/retention, retrieval, and judgement/response (Hinsz, 1990a). These represent the major points where information is filtered or changed

(Lord, 1985). These categories may also help us understand where and how team decision making biases occur. Team activities at each stage are represented next.

The processing objective. The team's task or the team's goal can be the processing objective and serves to define the context in which the activities take place (Mackie & Goethals, 1987). Or the team goal may be a more external and broader goal, such as a military commander's intent (Klein & Thordsen, 1989b). The processing objective provides a context in which the team acquires information to process. And it defines the processing domain for the researcher. For example, flight crews process information in order to ensure a successful flight, command and control teams process information in order to ensure predictive ability about the enemy, and medical teams process information in order to provide the correct treatment plan. The "end" goal provides the very different context of each of these examples.

Attention/perception. The information perceived depends upon individual attentional resources and *schemas*. Individuals have limited attentional capacity (Posner, 1982); however, can teams have a greater capacity for attention due to the additive effect of many individuals who are attending to a large body of information? Common sense dictates that this leads to a greater chance of object detection and problem resolution. Internal schemas (defined as preexisting cognitive structures that direct perceptual activity, Neisser, 1976, p. 14) can guide attention. (See Johnson-Laird, 1983; Thorndyke, 1984; and Gentner & Stevens, 1983, for a fuller explanation of schemas and mental models. They will be used interchangeably and in their general sense in this chapter.) If this is true, then the concept of shared schemas becomes one way to depict the "determinant" of team attentional capacity. If team members have consonant schemas (or mental models), then team attentional capacity should be enhanced because there will be less process loss (Steiner, 1972; 1976). If schemas are inconsonant, then misunderstandings and team failures can occur (Cannon-Bowers & Salas, 1990).

This raises two basic issues that are currently unresolved. (a) What do schemas refer to beyond similar understanding: schema of the problem, schema of the threat, schema of the overall situation, some sense of the predictability of the situation or some combination (Hinsz, 1990b; Noble, 1989)? (b) Second, at what point do you have an optimally "consonant" schema? If all the team members operate with very similar schemas, then why bother having multiple people? That is, what constitutes optimality in individual differences regarding these schemas? In other words, when do you need consonant schemas and what aspects of schemas are or need to be consonant (Rentsch & Duffy, 1990)?

Acquisition. Once information has been attended to, the team must acquire it in order to use it. Team acquisition of information is the most complex component of the team information-processing model (relative to individual processing). It is not necessary for all the members to have acquired the information for the *team* to have acquired it. Laboratory research indicates that, in order for a group to have acquired the information, at least two members of the group need to have received the information. If only one individual has the information, it is treated as an individual's opinion about that information (Hinsz, 1990a; Stasser & Titus, 1985, 1987; Stasser, Taylor, & Hanna, 1989). However, in highly differentiated teams, an individual member may be the only source for a piece of critical information, and the team has no choice but to consider that information. Laboratory research must be extended to these applied problems, where a member is held accountable for specific information and it is considered a team acquisition.

Encoding. The next step is encoding. Encoding is the process by which information is translated into an internal symbolic code (Lord, 1985). "Encoding is important because it reflects the question of how the separate individual representations of the information by each group member are combined in a meaningful representation by the group" (Hinsz, 1990a, p. 14). Encoding information by a team may result in a shared mental model or a shared representation and understanding of the decision problem, as well as the context of that problem (Zimmerman, Ono, Stasson, & Davis, 1985; Cannon-Bowers & Salas, 1990; Orasanu & Salas, this volume).

Storage. Once information has been encoded, it is then stored. Storage implies what is captured in group memory (Hinsz, 1990c), which is a function of the group process (Wegner, 1987). *Transactive memory,* as defined by Wegner, results in the expansion of personal memory through communication with the other members of the group. One could use a metaphor of "group mind," analogous to the individual mind. The critical components include labels for information and knowing where the information is located. In a group this means knowing who has what information. This does not mean that everyone shares all the stored knowledge, but that they share knowledge of the information category labels (which may be idiosyncratic to the group) and knowledge of who possesses specialized information. Hinsz (1990c) notes that the storage capacity of a group is "group size" times larger than individuals; however, groups are not as efficient as they should be because of the process losses incurred from the collaboration required to remember at the group level. Good teams may overcome this through extensive training or experience together (e.g., Navy Combat

Information Center teams, as described by Morgan et al., 1986), or through highly prescribed roles for interaction (e.g., ground control operators interacting with flight crews).

Retrieval. Retrieving the information from memory is different for a team, as opposed to individual retrieval. Retrieving information from group memory results in superior remembering than from individuals. Hinsz (1990c) suggests that this is because groups are more accurate at pointing out whether retrieved information is correct or not. And group members can correct faulty retrievals. Retrieving information is susceptible to point-of-view errors. An individual recalls information based on the point of view that one has chosen for the retrieval search (Lord, 1985; Hastie, 1981), which may or may not coincide with the group's point of view.

Judgement/decision. Finally, all this information processing results in a judgement or decision response. There is an extensive research history regarding individual decision making and judgements (see Abelson & Levi, 1985, for a review). To understand team decision making, one should understand the difference between a collective response and team decision making as a coordinated series of innumerable small decisions and actions resulting in a team product. An example of the former is a military command and control plan. An example of the latter is a high-performance flight by a cockpit crew. Whichever view you have determines the nature of the analysis. This results in a research literature divided into "problem camps," based on the task under study, not on a larger theoretical process. (See Davis & Stasson, 1988, for a discussion.)

In sum, the idea of the team as an information-processing unit has utility because it constrains a remarkably complex phenomenon. This framework will be used as a basis from which to analyze both biases and errors that teams commit in their information processing. It will provide a framework for addressing how we can go about improving the team decision-making process.

TYPES OF BIASES AND ERRORS IN TEAMS AS INFORMATION PROCESSORS

Although team decision making is similar to the individual process, it is susceptible to different types of errors and biases. Research has shown, and common sense dictates, that teams can make better (more informed, less biased) decisions than an individual (Hill, 1982; Michaelson, Watson, & Black, 1989), under certain conditions. However, when teams do go wrong, spectacular and devastating consequences can occur. For example, over 60 percent of airline accidents have been attributed to poor crew coordination and decision making (Foushee & Helmreich, 1988). The 1989 Valdez oil spill has been linked to a crew that decided not to intervene in the decision making of a drunken captain. The 1990 misfiring of a Martin Marietta satellite into the wrong orbit has been attributed to a misunderstanding between engineers and computer programmers (AP, 1990). Recent military incidents in the Persian Gulf (involving the USS Stark and the USS Vincennes) illustrate that the failure in team decision making can compromise safety and national security. The challenge is to understand what constitutes effective team decision-making performance and to determine interventions that can reduce potential errors in this process.

At this time, studies in team decision-making errors are productions of laboratory research. One taxonomy of errors that occur in team decision making consists of three categories: informational, normative, and structural (Duffy, 1990a). Informational errors occur as a result of misinterpretation of content and presentation of information (Sage, 1981). They are similar to Janis's (1989) and Kahneman, Tversky, and Slovic's (1982) depiction of cognitive errors. These are a function of cognitive "framing" effects and can result from the reliance on *supposedly* shared mental models, schemas, or scripts. They can occur at every stage of team information processing. For example, selective attention can be affected by a narrowing of attention and rigidity of thinking under stress, priming effects, vividness of object, confirmation bias (Taylor & Crocker, 1982; Tolcott, Marvin, & Bresnick, 1989), and illusory correlation (Chapman & Chapman, 1969). Encoding can be affected by coding information in a "story told" format or using inappropriate analogies to encode information (Janis, 1989). Retrieval can be affected by many biases: satisficing (Cascio, 1978) (i.e., retrieving the first alternative that meets minimal standards of acceptance, but that may not be the optimal solution); simply forgetting; the base rate fallacy (Kahneman & Tversky, 1973; Hinsz, Tindale, Nagao, Davis, & Robertson, 1988); the availability heuristic (i.e., remembering what's most easily retrievable in memory, Gabrielcik & Fazio, 1983), theory perseverance (i.e., remembering that which preserves one's implicit theory, Anderson, Lepper, & Ross, 1980); and group shifts (Myers & Lamm, 1976). These may most severely impact action and project teams, those that are highly differentiated, since there is a greater need to coordinate information. However, any team may succumb to these types of biases.

Normative influences are derived from interaction with significant others or the expectation of interaction with others, for example, social pressure. Janis (1989) refers to these as *affiliative influences*. They could impact multiple levels of team information processing at any point in time. They include such decision-making dysfunctions as groupthink (small group consensus to preserve group harmony; Janis, 1972; Janis & Mann, 1977); Harvey's (1974, 1988) "Abilene Paradox" (outward group acceptance of a proposal, which is, in reality, supported by no one, or false concensus effect, Sanders & Mullen, 1983); conflict or mismatch in member's goals (Klein & Thordsen, 1989); confusing decision quality with decision acceptance; unresolved personality and ideological conflicts; coordination errors (e.g., passing information to the wrong member, Klein & Thordsen, 1989a); bias towards turn taking by group members (Galegher, 1990); misunderstanding and language ambiguities; dominant personality usurping the team decision-making process; incremental decision making (Janis, 1989); or the inability to make quick, nonhabitual decisions. These errors tend to be a function of social influences and are unique to group decision making. They may more severely impact teams that are low in organizational integration, such as project and advice teams, because of their greater reliance on internal group process (see Sundstrom et al., 1990).

Structural effects on team decision-making errors result from larger, more global organizational processes and context (Cohen, March, & Olsen, 1972; Hackman, 1990), and are most relevant at the information acquisition stage of information processing. Structural effects include the organizational "meaning" (Rentsch, 1990) imbued in common organizational events experienced by each team member. Errors in team decision making can result from mismatches in teams and their organizational environment (March & Weissenger-Baylor, 1986), task circumstances, spatial arrangement in organizations (local or distributed settings), degree of technological support, degree of informational support, reward structure, inappropriate lines of authority (Rochlin, La Porte, & Roberts, 1987); or socially distributed cognition that is not taken into account (participants who vary in the knowledge they possess about a decision problem, Cicourel, 1990; Hutchins, 1990). The structural level of analysis gives one a "higher order" view of analysis; any given team error may still be described at the informational and normative level. Team type, by definition, is a structural variable. However, how team type interacts with structurally determined biases/errors is unclear.

IMPROVING TEAM DECISION MAKING

If teams engage in information processing, as described earlier, and teams are susceptible to unique errors, how is the process to be improved? There are three areas in which advances have steadily influenced improvement in team decision making. The most important, and the one with the longest research history, is team training. Organizational design to support team decision making and group support technologies are relative newcomers, with little empirical evidence to guide them. Team training is covered by others in this volume (both Orasanu and Means). The other two areas are described below.

Organizational design. Team decision making can be impacted by organizational design elements (Hughes, 1986), summarized by the following components: team size, member proximity, task type, centralization of control, temporal distance, and degree of cooperation (Dierolf, 1990; Huber, 1990). All these elements work in concert. However, empirical evidence comes in the form of laboratory experiments that manipulate any one or only a few of these variables. There is increasing evidence in applied research indicating that organizational structure and setting influences team cognitive strategies (Cicourel, 1990). A new perspective is to look at the organizational elements and see how they may enhance or constrain the way teams operate.

There is a relatively new point of view coming from in-depth analysis of several industries that operate in complex, inherently hazardous, and highly technical task situations, under conditions of tight coupling and severe time pressure: en route air traffic control, utility grid management by electrical companies, and Navy air operations (Rochlin, 1986). The most informative has been a study of naval flight operations on U.S. Navy carriers. These flight operations are executed successfully in a very complex environment, without adhering to the accepted requirements of long training, careful selection, task and team stability, and cumulative experience. The Navy has a young and largely inexperienced crew, with a management staff of officers that turns over about half of its number each year, and an environment which is rebuilt from scratch every 18 months (Rochlin, La Porte, & Roberts, 1987). Rochlin and his colleagues have examined the positive effects of high turnover, authority overlays (even the lowest ranking member has the authority to suspend flight operations immediately, under the proper circumstances), and redundancy in the form of technical, supply and decision/management redundancy (the latter is the internal cross-checks on decisions and fail-safe decision redundancy in the event of an organizational unit failure). These organizational design elements coalesce into a remarkably low error rate. They note that these elements in an "ordinary" organization would be characterized in negative terms. In other words, the Navy has back-up systems that are different in pattern and structure from the primary systems. There is constant critical monitoring of staff with task responsibilities. Authority and responsibility are distributed in different patterns and can shift in a contingency situation. As Rochlin defines it, these are examples of "organizational self-design, in which modes and modalities of adaptive response are created, within and by the operating organization, to deal with the recognized range and variance of contingencies and errors that they have observed" (1988, p. 2).

The above is an example of how teams as decision making units are impacted by their organizational context. This level of analysis highlights structural and some normative errors and biases that may afflict the team. It gives us less insight into informational sources of team errors. How the information-processing perspective impacts our understanding from this level is still uncertain. Team types, however, may provide a vehicle for better understanding. Would highly integrated teams be most impacted by organizational design, since they must coordinate intensely with their organizational counterparts? Future research may be able to answer this query.

Group support technologies. A second area of improvement involves "computerizing" the team. Earlier, a question was raised regarding the problem of increasing technological support of teams. On the positive side, greater emphasis has been placed on technological support of group activities (Galegher, 1990). On the negative side, we are unclear about the effects of this support (Duffy, 1990b). The issues are numerous: local versus distributed teams (National Research Council, 1990), computers as team members, task allocation among man and machine (Stammers & Hallum, 1985), and electronic meeting management and collaboration management by computer support. The latter area has the most complete research evidence. However, the question underlying all these new advances is: Will the technology improve team decision making? The answer is, of course, "It depends."

The areas that are encompassed by the computerization of decision support of groups comes under the title of *group decision support systems* (GDSS) and *computer support of collaborative work* (CSCW). A group decision support system is "an interactive computer-based system that facilitates the solution of unstructured problems by a set of decision makers working together as a group" (DeSanctis & Gallupe, 1985). These systems are designed to support planning and problem-solving functions (Morrison, Morrison, Sheng, Vogel, & Nunamaker, 1990). The hardware that supports these systems consists of some common elements. There is usually a meeting room with a large conference table situated in it. There are individualized personal computers at each work station, networked with each other, and large or multiple screen displays for common reference. Sometimes there are breakout rooms with more personal computers available, such as those described by Nunamaker, Applegate, and Kosynski (1988). Pinsonneault and Kraemer (1990) note that, in evaluating the empirical research in this area, one finds that the use of GDSS does have several positive impacts. It increases the depth of analysis of groups, participation, decision quality, consensus reaching, the confidence of group members in the group decision, and satisfaction with group process and the decision. It decreases domination by a few members and the decision time.[2]

A more software- and video-focused approach involves computer-supported cooperative work, which focuses on the joint creation of documents and design projects, the integration of teams to information support systems, and cooperative work systems (Morrison et al., 1990; CSCW, 1990). There is a greater emphasis on collaborative intellectual work and the technological advances developed to improve the quality and efficiency of collaborative work (Galegher & Kraut, 1990). Many of the latest advances involve common scripting environments and video linkages for distributed groups working in synchronous and asynchronous environments (CSCW, 1990).

The hardware and software of GDSS and CSCW have the following objectives: (a) to provide information more accurately, more completely, and in faster accession time; (b) to reduce coordination effort; (c) to reduce the negative group influence effects (and move from a normative influence to an informational influence); and (d) to increase wider audience view of the same material, with the assumption that this leads to faster common understanding (Kraemer & King, 1988).

In order to accomplish this with the systems that are available, some assumptions about group decision making had to be made. These include (a) rationality of group decision makers; (b) the structure of the decision making process; (c) use of anonymity as a process controller; (d) use of a "facilitator" as a process controller (whether it be a computer or a human); and (e) the attempt to replicate as much as possible the richness of the communication environment that occurs in a face-to-face environment (Kraemer & King, 1988).

These assumptions are still to be defended. First, March and his associates have questioned the rationality of group decision making in their depiction of organizational decision making and the "garbage can theory." It clearly depicts incidences of fortuitous interactions of problem, solution, participants, and choice opportunities (March & Weissinger-Baylor, 1986). Second, the team decision-making process is now redefined as an information-processing one. This is dissimilar in

---

[2] For further clarification, see reviews by Kraemer and King (1988), McDonald (1990), and Duffy (1990a).

some ways to the approach depicted by multiattribute utility theorists (Abelson & Levi, 1985). Third, anonymity as a process controller has had limited support from the empirical literature (Connolly, Jessup, & Valacich, 1990), but is less relevant in the team decision-making environment where one must know who one's sources of information are (Cicourel, 1990). Fourth, the issue of the facilitator is almost a complete unknown. The final assumption, the richness of the information communicated, is of particular interest in this arena.

Two types of communication requirements are influential in computer-mediated communication. Social presence (Short, Williams, & Christie, 1976) is the degree to which a medium communicates the actual physical presence of the participants. The second is *information richness,* which is defined by Daft and Lengel (1986) as a proposition that communication channels differ in their ability to convey the richness of information needed for a task. Simply increasing bandwidth of communication (providing more information for the participants via video and audio capabilities in a synchronous environment) has been the traditional tactic for improving team decision making, as suggested from empirical research by Williges, Johnston, and Briggs (1966). However, contradictory research by Wellens (1989) using a psychological distancing model of telecommunication, found that increasing communication richness did not always lead to increased team situation awareness or task performance (Wellens, 1990a). His use of an interactive resource allocation task (Wellens & Ergener, 1988) allowed him to manipulate bandwidth across keyboard, audio, and video dimensions. He found that there was a tradeoff between maintaining communication with remote team mates and completing local task responsibilities (Wellens, 1990a). This has important implications on the issue of presenting feedback from distributed team members to ensure a shared situational understanding, as Chapanis, Ochsman, Parrish, and Weeks (1972) and Galegher (1990) advise. One must also weigh the impact of "firehosing" team members in the context of complex individual tasks with too rich an information environment regarding their team members' decisions (Wellens, 1990b).

How team types interact in the context of group decision support systems is an unanswered question. Advice/involvement teams have been the focus of much of the group support technology, particularly since their process is more concensus dependent. However, negotiation teams fall into this category for the same reason. In fact, to pursue this typology proves confusing, since some other underlying—and unknown at this point—dimension may be operating. Research into the answer is sorely needed.

SUMMARY

There is evidence that team decision making is on the increase. Through technological innovation, we have begun to support their process with greater success (Galegher & Kraut, 1990). Although great attention was paid to this process in the 1960s (Parsons, 1972), few significant advances in understanding or predicting the process had been made until the 1980s. (See reviews by Davis & Stasson, 1988, and Levine & Moreland, 1990). With new perspectives on the phenomenon (as depicted here by the information-processing approach), greater emphasis on the team's system qualities (an individual within a team within an organization within an environment), and advancements in the support technology by system designers, we are on the verge of altering the way we do business. What does that mean?

There will be an increasing focus on mental models or schemas as the criterion of exchange among team members (Thorndyke, 1984; Cannon-Bowers & Salas, 1990; Orasanu & Salas, this volume) and the effect of team member relationships on that exchange (group process variables, as discussed by Foushee & Helmreich, 1988). The computerization of that exchange process will focus on concepts of group/team memory (Wegner, 1987), information richness (Daft & Lengel, 1986), and psychological distance (Wellens, 1989; 1990a), especially in distributed environments (Fischhoff & Johnson, 1990). As we understand what it is that teams do to make them so much better than individuals in certain situations (Hill, 1982), we will become better at building support systems to enhance their functioning. By using an information processing approach, we can break down what they do in complex environments into the observable pieces of what they *are* doing. This is contrasted by traditional approaches (e.g., multiattribute utility theory) which focus on what we would *like* decision makers to do. To paraphrase Tetlock (1985), a new research program, with an emphasis on understanding the *social* context, needs to be developed in order to provide us with a greater understanding of the team-technology fit.

KEY POINTS

- The complexity of studying team decision making can be handled by using an information-processing approach.
- The stages of information processing relevant to team decision making are:

— attention/perception
— acquisition
— encoding
— storage
— retrieval
— judgment/decision

- Certain biases and errors are unique to these stages.
- Improvements in organizational design and group support technologies are new to team decision-making support.
- An information-processing analysis of team decision making would help in improving the design of new supports.

Section E

Review of Current Progress

Chapter 21

A Laboratory Scientist's View of Naturalistic Decision Making*

Michael E. Doherty
Bowling Green State University

The editors have invited me to write a commentary, from the point of view of an "outsider" and a laboratory scientist, on the naturalistic decision making chapters in this book. It might be appropriate to note at the outset that I came to the study of judgment and decision making from outside the JDM fold; hence, the comments in this chapter can be attributed neither to loyalty to some former mentor nor animus toward some former mentor's antagonist. The comments are certainly not unbiased, as I think that I have been deeply influenced by probabilistic functionalism, especially as articulated and extended by Hammond. But I still have the deep intellectual and emotional attachment of the experimental psychologist to the simple, single variable experiment.

This chapter is in two rather distinct parts. The first, "Overview of Judgment and Decision Making," is an attempt to present the reader with a broad sketch of the entire field. It is included primarily to provide a relatively broad context into which to locate naturalistic decision making. The second part, "Naturalistic Decision Making," is a commentary on the above chapters. It is largely independent of the first.

* Written while the author was a visiting professor at University College, Dublin. The author expresses his appreciation to the Council for the International Exchange of Scholars for Fulbright support, to his home university for generous sabbatical support, and to University College Dublin for providing a home away from home.

OVERVIEW OF JUDGMENT AND DECISION MAKING

Historical Note

The field can best be traced, I believe, by simply noting some landmark publications. The roots may go back to antiquity; perhaps Adam performed a decision analysis before making the choice of whether or not to take that first bite. If so, his tech report is lost, probably in a flood, and probably uninsured. But for present purposes it might be more prudent to eschew the form of history that seeks the seeds of all knowledge in the wisdom, or folly, of the ancients.

The first landmark papers were in the mid-1950s, with the publication of two papers in the *Psychological Review,* "The theory of decision making" (Edwards, 1954) and "Probabilistic functionalism and the clinical method" (Hammond, 1955). These two seminal papers led to two significant programs of research, *decision theory* and *social judgment theory,* respectively, that progressed essentially independently of one another until the publication of the tour-de-force that many consider to have established the field of JDM, Slovic and Lichtenstein's (1971) "Comparison of Bayesian and regression approaches to the study of human information processing in judgment." I cannot pass the 1960s, however, without mentioning several other significant publications. Two, Hoffman's (1960) "Paramorphic representation of clinical judgment" and Goldberg's (1968) "Simple models or simple processes? Some research on clinical judgment" triggered much interest in the statistical modeling of judgment. Another was Coombs's "Theory of Data" (1964), which made theoretical and methodological contributions to the study of utility. Peterson and Beach's (1967) "Man as an intuitive statistician" was a high water mark for the conception of decision theory as a valid descriptive model, one that needed but minor parameter adjustments to make precise fits to behavior. That conception was already under fire, but the flush of enthusiasm reflected by *an intuitive statistician* provided a backdrop that made the next development dramatic.

The publication of "Judgment under uncertainty—heuristics and biases" In *Science* (Tversky & Kahneman, 1974) and the subsequent book of the same name (Kahneman, Slovic, & Tversky, 1982) introduced some radically new concepts which were then and are still extraordinarily resistant to incorporation into formal models. The heuristics and biases research sought to explain "both correct and erroneous judgments in terms of the same psychological processes" (Kahneman et al., 1982, p. xii). It had a major impact on cognitive social psychology (Nisbett & Ross, 1980), and as Hammond (1990) noted in his paper in the memorial tribute to the late Hillel Einhorn, it brought the whole JDM field into much more prominence in psychology in general. A consequence of this research was the conclusion that traditional decision theoretic models were of dubious validity as descriptive models, and that there were formidable measurement difficulties to be overcome when using decision analysis prescriptively, that is, as a decision aid. These messages were fully consonant with Herbert Simon's then already well-known assessment of decision theory, but which was stated especially forcefully in his 1983, *Reason in Human Affairs.*

Other traditions of decision research were also developing, more or less independently of those just noted. One that has been largely outside the JDM mainstream is the conflict theory of Janis and Mann (1977). Their book, *Decision Making: A Psychological Analysis of Conflict, Choice and Commitment,* seems to me to be a major, insightful effort at understanding decision making, but is cited neither Hammond, McClelland, and Mumpower's (1980) attempt at integration nor in the recent book by von Winterfeldt and Edwards (1986), and is cited in but one of the 43 readings in the recent compilation by Arkes and Hammond (1986). Janis and Mann's (1977) book cites Hammond not at all, and Edwards only in passing. I suspect that one reason that it has been essentially ignored by mainstream decision theorists is its nonquantitative character, for JDM has from its earliest wellsprings in statistical decision theory and economic theory (Edwards, Lindmann, & Savage, 1963) and in correlation and regression (Hammond, Hursch, & Todd, 1964; Tucker, 1964) been centrally concerned with quantitative modeling.

Much more in the mainstream has been the work of Norman Anderson (1981, 1982), and his students, Martin Kaplan, Lola Lopes, Irwin Levin, and Jim Shanteau. Shanteau's long interest in experts, dating to his work with expert judges in agriculture (Shanteau & Phelps, 1977), may be of considerable potential relevance to the content of the present volume. Perhaps the seminal Anderson paper from a historical perspective, one that links him firmly to what Hammond in this volume called Wundt's choice, was his 1970 *Psychological Review* paper, "Functional Measurement and Psychophysical Judgment" (Anderson, 1970).

A final major strain of decision research, more closely linked to the rich literature in problem solving than those already mentioned, is process tracing, with John Payne being a prominent representative. Although it is not a decision-making work per se, the classic and certainly seminal publication in this field has to be Newell and Simon's

(1972) *Human Problem Solving*. It is to be hoped that ties between the decision-making and the problem-solving literatures deepen and broaden; Hammond's chapter suggests that such an outcome might be one result of the work in naturalistic decision making.

Ten years after the publication of Slovic and Lichtenstein's (1971) "founding" review, another influential review appeared, this time in the *Annual Review of Psychology*. That was Einhorn and Hogarth's (1981) "Behavioral Decision Theory: Processes of Judgment and Choice." Now, 10 years later again, it appears that what Klein, Orasanu, Calderwood, and Zsambok hope to accomplish with this volume is to introduce into what I see as the young and remarkably vital field of JDM another strain, the study of complex, consequential decisions that must be made *rapidly*. JDM is far from a unified area of scholarship; it is still quite heterogeneous, as at this stage of our knowledge it ought to be. Despite this heterogeneity, the next section is an attempt to provide a characterization of the current state of the field, with respect to the general methodological predilections of the principal players, and to locate naturalistic decision making therein.

JDM Circa 1990

There are a number of ways to classify the various approaches to studying judgment and decision. One useful way is to consider them according to a set of characteristics of the methods chosen, for as Hammond (1966, 1990) insists, the commitment to a method implies a commitment to a theory, whether the theoretical commitment is implicit or explicit. The present selection of the characteristics by which to categorize the approaches was influenced by Ward Edwards' description of two basic processes of decision analysis as decomposition and externalization, but these processes do not neatly divide the approaches. Many important distinctions, such as that between static and dynamic decision making (Brehmer, 1990; Hogarth, 1981), have not been included as defining characteristics, mainly because of the paucity of research.

Three characteristics will be used to describe the field. Two are presented as though they represent clean dichotomies, but of course reality is much messier. The three are (a) whether the response required of the subject is holistic or decomposed, (b) whether the investigation calls for the subject to make responses to one problem or to many, and (c) a less clean dichotomy, if the judgment is holistic, then whether the subsequent decomposition (which is required to externalize the process) is via intuition or algorithm; if the judgment is already a decomposed one, then whether the subsequent aggregation (which is required to translate the process into judgment or choice) is via intuition or algorithm. If the subsequent aggregation is via intuition, it may be by either the subject or the investigator depending upon the purpose of the study. Figure 21.1 shows the eight resulting categories, with eight (even though there are nine acronyms shown on the figure!) major approaches to judgment and decision making classified into one or more of these categories. Let the reader be forewarned that some of the approaches described are primarily descriptive methods aimed at understanding decision processes, whereas others, while based on research, serve as decision aids.

The first methodological distinction is whether the investigator requires the subjects to make holistic judgments, that is, to integrate multiple information inputs and to process that information into a

Figure 21.1.   A classification of approaches to JDM according to three aspects of the methods used in each: (a) whether the response used by the subject is holistic or decomposed, (b) whether the subject response to one problem or many, and (c) whether the subsequent processing is intuitive or algorithmic. The acronyms are fully explained in the text. Briefly, they are: SW—subjective weights, SJT—social judgment theory, IIT—information integration theory, H&B—heuristics and biases, NDM—naturalistic decision making, J&M—Janis and Mann, PT—process tracing, SEU—subjectively expected utility theory, and MAUT—multiattribute utility theory.

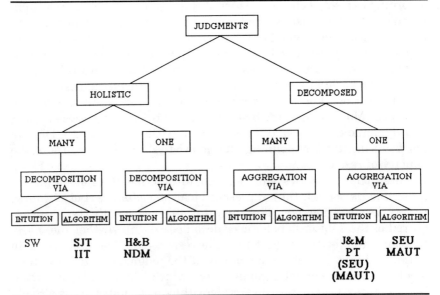

single output. This is contrasted with the decomposed judgment, wherein the investigator has the subject, often with extensive guidance from the investigator or consultant and from the structure imposed by the paradigm, break a complex problem down into its component parts.

The second refers to whether a given subject will see and respond to one or to many problems. If many problems are presented then they are typically problems of exactly the same type with the same set of characteristics, with from one to all of the characteristics varying from trial to trial. A holistic response is made to each problem, and decomposition (the third distinction) into the components of the subject's integration strategy is typically via statistical means, such as analysis of variance or multiple regression. If the subject responds holistically to but one problem, then decomposition via some computer algorithm does not appear to be a meaningful option, but that may simply reflect my lack of imagination.

Given that the person has decomposed the problem, the remaining role available to an algorithm is to put it back together. This approach is predicated on the logic that people are better at making judgments of the parts than of complex wholes. That is, the argument is that cognitive limitations prevent us from doing an adequate job of making complex judgments, or judgments with many component parts. For pragmatic rather than theoretical reasons, investigators rarely elicit large numbers of decomposed judgments from a single subject; hence, the node at Many on the Decomposed judgments side of the figure has no representatives.

There are, as noted, other category schemes, such as the classification into normative (ideal), prescriptive (pertaining to teaching or decision aiding), or descriptive models. However, some of the standard approaches might, depending on the purpose of the investigator or practitioner, serve any one or even more than one of these purposes in a given implementation. While this distinction is not criterial for the category system, it is a most useful one and will be brought to bear in the description of the models as circumstances warrant. Another characteristic that will not be used here as a classificatory feature is whether the paradigm calls for an action to be selected or calls for some judgment short of action. The same paradigm may call for an action in one implementation and a judgment in another, although there has been a tendency for holistic approaches to use judgments and decompositional approaches actions as dependent variables.

Let us briefly characterize each of the approaches so classified.

Social Judgment Theory (SJT). In a typical social judgment theory study the investigator, after consulting experts and relevant literature in the content area, decides upon a set of cues, often to some environmental object that is not directly knowable, and decides upon the levels appropriate to each of these cues. The number of cues may vary from one to a large number; as many as 66 have been used (Roose & Doherty, 1976). A large number of multicue or multiattribute objects, or cases, are then composed by having all of the cues present on each one, with the values of the cues varying. The subject inspects each multicue case and assigns a single value to it, the value representing a holistic judgment about some characteristic of the environmental object represented by that case. The availability of a substantial number of quantitatively described cases for each subject permits the investigator to gain insight into and describe the subject's judgment policy via an analytic procedure, multiple regression analysis (hence, the term *policy capturing*). The result is a quantitative expression that represents the subject's judgment policy by a set of weights and function forms (hence the term *policy equation*).

For example, Ullman and Doherty (1984, Study 1) had clinical psychologists and other subjects each inspect a large number (52) of clinical cases of actual children, each child being described by the values of seven attributes relevant to the diagnosis of hyperactivity. The subjects made a blind diagnosis on each case and provided a numerical confidence judgment of whether or not the child was hyperactive. Each clinician's judgments were regressed on the cues, with the resulting policy equations providing measures of the extent to which each attribute had influenced the diagnoses.

Brunswik's principle of representative design, discussed in some detail by Hammond in this volume, calls for the formal characteristics of the task to be maintained in the formal structure of the set of cases presented to the subjects. If the true value of the environment is available for each case, the subject's responses can be compared to the true values and the full analytical power of the lens model equation brought to bear on the job of interpreting how the subject knows the world. Notice that the singular "subject" has been used above. An important characteristic of much of JDM research in general and of social judgment theory in particular is the focus on the individual, and the intensive statistical analysis of the individual case has led Hammond to label social judgment theory as an "idiographic/statistical" approach (Hammond, 1980). In many investigations those individual subjects have been highly experienced practitioners (Ullman & Doherty, 1984; Wigton, 1988).

Social judgment theory normally serves as a descriptive model, but in some applications the subject is expected to learn a set of environmental relationships, perhaps via cognitive feedback (Balzer, Doherty,

& O'Connor, 1989). Cognitive feedback refers to the procedure of describing to the subject the actual relationships among the elements in the environment and in the subject's cognitive system. This form of feedback is contrasted with *outcome feedback,* which entails merely giving the subject the "right answer" on each trial. When the subject is expected to learn about an environment there is a normative aspect to the enterprise, with the environment serving as the normative standard and the degree of correspondence between the subject and the environment serving as an index of normativity. For a proper introduction to social judgment theory, consult the recent volume edited by Brehmer and Joyce (1988).

Subjective Weights (SW). The reason that SW is not in bold face in Figure 21.1 is that it is not really a judgment and decision approach on its own hook. Often, after a subject has completed the judgments on the set of cases, the investigator will ask the subject to assign to each cue the weight that he or she believes best describes how important that cue was to his or her judgments. It was the repeated finding of a rather dramatic mismatch between the subjectively assigned and statistically captured weights that led to the conclusion that people had poor insight into their policies (Balke, Hammond, & Meyer, 1973). In two recent investigations (Reilly & Doherty, 1989, in press), we have provided evidence that the mismatch may be due to subjects' inability to express the insight that they have rather than to the absence thereof (or, pointing the finger in the other direction, the researchers' inability to measure subjects' insight). I believe that the issue of the degree to which people know themselves or can express what they know (Nisbett & Wilson, 1977) is critical for some of the types of data gathering that are emerging as dominant methodologies in naturalistic decision making (for example, Klein, this volume).

Information Integration Theory (IIT). Like social judgment theory, information integration theory involves presenting the subject with a number of multiattribute bundles, to each of which the subject makes a holistic, quantitative response. The arrangement of variables in an information integration theory investigation is according to a factorial design, and decomposition of the individual's judgment strategy is via analysis of variance. The advantages of the factorial design are that the techniques of functional measurement allow the simultaneous assessment of the composition rule used by the subject (additive, averaging, multiplicative, etc.) and the subjective scale values of the levels of the variables: Model testing is not divorced from measurement. The analysis of variance of the factorial design permits much neater apportionment of variance to the interaction term than does the regression analysis. A disadvantage of the requirement of factorial design, mitigated partly by the use of fractional factorial designs, is that relatively few levels of relatively few attributes can be used. This is because of the exponential explosion of the number of cases required; four factors each with five levels would require, for a full factorial design, $5^4 = 625$ observations per subject, without provision for replication.

Hammond (1966) has referred to traditional Wundtian research design as the "rule-of-one-variable;" Anderson's methodological reliance on the factorial design in the study of judgment would suggest that in his case that be modified to the "rule-of-at-least-two-variables." Information integration theory has functioned primarily if not exclusively as a descriptive and theory testing approach, but its application has been to an astonishingly wide variety of issues. For a proper introduction, the reader is referred to Anderson (1981, 1982).

Janis and Mann (J&M). At the other end of the spectrum described in Figure 21.1 we have the decisional balance sheet method of decision aiding which forms a central part of Janis and Mann's work, although in adducing evidence for their larger theory of conflicted decision making they draw evidence from perhaps the widest variety of investigations of any approach represented in this brief survey. This description focuses on the "decisional balance sheet," which is a decision aid whereby the person decomposes and externalizes an important decision problem by listing the possible options for choice along one axis of a matrix, and listing four categories of anticipated consequences along the other. The four categories are determined by whether the consequences are relevant to oneself or to significant others, and whether the consequences involve utilitarian considerations or one's own self-esteem.

The decision maker fills in the matrix with the anticipated consequences, positive and negative, doing so over a period of time sufficient to allow reflection on the implications of the decision, to allow search for information about the consequences, and perhaps the generation of new options that may be facilitated by the processes of decomposing and externalizing the problem. At some point, the decision has to be made, and this is done intuitively by the decision maker, that is, the reaggregation of the information for purposes of action is done by the person without further decision aiding. Janis and Mann do provide some grading and counting procedures for the consequences, but it seems to me that their heart wasn't in it, and that they preferred the intuitive aggregation. It is my experience with graduate students who have done a decisional balance sheet as a course exercise that they, too, preferred intuitive aggregation. The best introduction remains Janis and Mann (1977), and there is a version for the nonspecialist (Wheeler & Janis, 1980).

Process Tracing (PT). The term *process tracing* refers to an attempt on the part of the investigator to arrange the situation so that the person reveals aspects of the psychological process as that person engages in the process of decision making or problem solving. One typical method, borrowed directly from the influential work of Newell and Simon (1972) involves the recording of think-aloud protocols that are taken as the subject goes through some complex task. Whereas Newell and Simon used problem-solving tasks such as cryptarithmetic, an investigator studying decision making might use a diagnostic problem (Dowie & Elstein, 1988; Elstein, Shulman, & Sprafka, 1978) or the selection of an apartment (Payne, 1976). The approach has been extended to still less well-defined problems, such as reasoning in social science, by Voss and his colleagues (Voss, Tyler, & Yengo, 1983) and scientific creativity by Tweney (1985). Process tracing approaches to the investigation of decision making blur the distinction between problem solving and decision making (Einhorn, Kleinmuntz, & Kleinmuntz, 1979), which is a good thing to the extent that the two traditions of research can begin to inform one another more than has been the case in the past. It is not a good thing if essential distinctions will be lost. This will come up again, in the discussion of actions vs. inferences.

Process tracing appears to me to be a purely descriptive approach, but as such, it has implications for the validity of normative models and for the potential utility of prescriptive models. For a recent review, see the article by Ford, Schmitt, Schechtman, Hults, and Doherty (1989).

Subjectively Expected Utility Theory (SEU). This, along with multiattribute utility theory, is the theoretical orientation with which much of the present book is contrasted. In its baldest form, it holds that decisions are or ought to be made according to a value maximizing principle. The procedure for doing so entails assigning values to a set of outcomes, the outcomes being conjunctions of options for action and the possible states of the world. There are always at least two options, even if only "act" vs. "do nothing." Each outcome is assessed according to its probability of occurrence and according to how much one would like the outcome should it occur, that is, its utility. The probabilities and utilities are assumptively independent, which means that you should not let your expectation of peace be influenced by how much you'd like there to be peace. The assumption of independence allows the product of the probabilities and utilities for each outcome to be taken. Those products are then summed across the outcomes associated with each option, those sums being the subjectively expected utilities of the options. The rational decision rule is simple; take the action with the highest subjectively expected utility. The typical decision theorist believes as most of us do that the computational requirements of the model exceed human capabilities. Hence, the decision maker, with guidance from a decision analyst and within the structural constraints of the model, first sets up, or *scaffolds,* the problem, that is, decides what the actions, states, outcomes, and dimensions of utility are. Then the decision analyst obtains the necessary values of the probabilities and utilities from the decision maker via one or more elicitation methods. The calculations necessary to aggregate the component information are then carried out according to an appropriate algorithm, which for a very complex, highly uncertain decision may require a computer.

Why is SEU represented twice, once under aggregation by algorithm, and again, in parentheses, under aggregation by intuition? A complex problem may well require extensive computation and computer support, but a simple SEU problem may be such that the process of structuring the problem clarifies it to such an extent that the decision is made intuitively in the course of the analysis. Many graduate students have performed SEU analyses over the years in my JDM course. Their reports have been virtually uniform, with comments such as "I have never thought too clearly about an important problem, but I made up my mind before I did any calculations." I recall Edwards making a similar comment, that for many decisions the scaffolding of the problem was the most important part.

SEU theory is an elegant formulation, which has resisted the most powerful attempts to bury it. It remains an influential model in JDM and in economics (Hogarth & Reder, 1986). It is, in the formulation just provided, clearly a normative model, the word *rational* being placed in front of *decision rule* above to emphasize that role. In the hands of applied decision analysts, it is a prescriptive model, a tool to aid decision makers to make better decisions. When some investigator compares behavior in a specific situation, such as gambling, with the output of an SEU analysis, then the model may be being used as a potential descriptive model. For a proper introduction an excellent source is von Winterfeldt and Edwards (1986).

Since this is the model that has provided the contrast for many chapters in this book, I will return to it briefly below, in the section "An amateur's view of decision theory."

Multiattribute Utility Theory (MAUT). In some decision situations, the decision will essentially determine the outcome, as there is relatively little uncertainty that can be usefully encoded. An example is the choice by a doctoral student in clinical psychology who is trying to decide which of a number of distant internships to select. There are many differences among internship stations, and while there are uncertain aspects, the difficulty of obtaining information relevant to the uncertainty seems to make exclusive attention to the dimensions of utility a reasonable decision strategy.

The MAUT procedure is straightforward. Each possible outcome, that is, being at the chosen station for the ensuing year, is listed. The decision maker is then required to decompose and externalize those aspects of his or her own value system, that is, to develop the dimensions of utility to which the decision is relevant, and to assign importance weights to those utilities. This may be done by a process, first, of ranking the dimensions, then of assigning an arbitrary value of, say, 10, to the least important one. Then, by analogy to the psychophysical method of ratio production, the decision maker assigns a set of numerical values to the set of utilities. Each possible outcome, which is assumed to be determined with certainty by the option selected, is then assigned a scale value that is supposed to represent the degree to which that option would satisfy the decision maker on each dimension of utility. The aggregation is then algorithmic, with the products of the importance weights and scale values being summed, and the rational decision maker opting for the action with the highest multiattribute utility.

As with SEU theory, multiattribute utility theory can function as a normative, prescriptive, or descriptive model, though it seems to me to be essentially prescriptive in nature. It appears twice in Figure 21.1 for exactly the same reason: self-reports have been that the decision became obvious as a result of the hard thinking that went into the decomposition and externalization of the problem, and into the very difficult intellectual work of dimensionalizing one's utilities and assigning explicit importance weights to those dimensions. The arithmetic was, according to the self-reports, superfluous for the relatively small-scale individual problems so decomposed. This would obviously not be so for complex, organizational applications. Edwards and Newman (1982) provides an introductory treatment.

Heuristics and Biases (H&B). A typical heuristics and biases investigation involves presenting the subject with a single scenario, a verbal description of some event or situation, and having that subject make a single response that will be an indicant either of how likely the subject thinks some aspect of that scenario is or what the subject's preferences are. This is done for a substantial number of subjects, and the data are presented as frequencies or means. Perhaps the word *typical* is less appropriate to the body of heuristics and biases literature than to others represented in this brief survey, given that there is no methodological core to heuristics and biases as there is to social judgment theory and information integration theory. There is a reliance on what Kahneman and Tversky (1982) call the *conversational* *paradigm,* which was just described, but in fact, *any* research method is appropriate that the investigator believes will provide insight into the ways people assess probabilities and preferences, and, depending on how broadly one defines heuristics and biases, into other psychological phenomena such as inferences concerning correlation or the psychology of planning. Often the investigations are stunningly—and beautifully—simple.

The references to probabilities and utilities indicate that one of the sources of interest in heuristics and biases is the reaction against the hypothesis of "rational man" embodied in normative models of decision. The research also demonstrates that the assessment of the quantities required by the employment of decision theory as a prescriptive decision aid is fraught with pitfalls. The heuristics and biases literature is purely descriptive, although, as just implied, it bears directly on both normative and prescriptive issues. For a proper introduction, see the volume by Kahneman et al. (1982).

Naturalistic Decision Making (NDM). The reader who has read to this point is already well aware of the nature of naturalistic decision making, so I need not describe it save to indicate why I locate it where I do in Figure 21.1. Taking Gary Klein's fireground commander as an exemplar, the decision is one shot and holistic, and the decomposition is via an intuitive reconstruction of the event, some time after it happened. Naturalistic decision making appears to me to be purely descriptive at this point, despite use of terms like *normative-descriptive* and expressions of hope that prescriptive models will soon emerge in the form of decision support systems based on the research described.

The reader who is interested in a more comprehensive history of JDM and a much more comprehensive comparison of the various approaches to JDM is referred to the book by Hammond et al. (1980).

An Amateur's View of "Decision Theory"

As noted above, I teach the elements of SEU theory and MAUT to doctoral students in psychology at Bowling Green, and have done so now for about 20 years. The course also covers social judgment theory, and heuristics and biases, in some detail, but due to time constraints I unfortunately give rather short shrift to Janis and Mann's conflict theory and to information integration theory. The point is that I do not *practice* "decision theory" for a living. So I speak as an amateur when it comes to decision theory, and there are plenty of professionals around, both in the sense of experts and of people who actually do decision analysis for a living. My view is quite different from some of those evidenced in several chapters in this volume.

Decision theory comes in many versions. No one in the field of JDM that I know takes the most extreme normative model, the maximization of expected value where the expected value is determined by objective probabilities and actual dollar values, as anything but an abstraction that not only fails as a descriptive model but isn't even a very good normative model from a human perspective. It is a good normative model from an axiomatic point of view, in that it is coherent. But then so would a normative model that entailed the maximization of doughnuts be a coherent, hence "rational" model. Some of the most powerful of intellects have leveled damning criticisms against a simple form of SEU theory as a descriptive theory and shown that it simply cannot be correct in its particulars (Coombs, 1975; Simon, 1983), yet it persists. There are more subtle versions of decision theory qua descriptive model, Kahneman and Tversky's (1979) prospect theory being the most prominent. Rather than reach beyond my grasp and attempt to *evaluate* prospect theory, I mention it only to point out that it is a full decision theory, in that, like SEU theory, it is concerned both with whether some outcome would occur and how much one would like that outcome should it occur. Prospect theory adds an editing phase and the concept of decision weights to the usual conceptual structure of decision theory, in an effort to bring theory into line with behavior. This reminder that decision theory incorporates both probabilities and utilities is worth emphasizing, since many commentaries on decision theory have failed to distinguish between normative rules for updating probabilities or making other statements about the state of the world on the one hand, and normative rules for making action decisions on the other. An example of the former is Bayes' theorem, while the latter is typically in the form of some maximization principle, with the quantity being maximized being a function of both probabilities and utilities, as in SEU theory or prospect theory, or utilities alone, as in MAUT.

What about decision analysis as employed by practitioners? That is, what about decision analysis as a prescriptive decision aid? I do not know the utility of decision analysis. I believe that it is applicable to a limited but important set of problems, but again I do not know if it, in some ultimate sense, "works." Worse, I do not know how to find out. One criterion for the utility of decision analysis appears to be consumer satisfaction, that is, it appears to me to be the same as the criterion for the success of such ventures as psychoanalysis. That is not a very serious criticism. It's just the way the world is. I think I'm a pretty good teacher, but do not ask me for ultimate criteria for teaching that would satisfy me as a laboratory scientist.

But, given that reservation, I think that decision analysis is very likely pretty good stuff for some problems. One feature that would define a problem for which it might be useful is that sufficient time and resources are available. Given these, the decision maker is forced to think hard about the problem facing him or her. Perhaps the most important step is the clarification or even creation of one's goals, that is, the goals to which the decision is meant to be relevant. The decision maker has to generate a reasonable set of possible actions—they are not there waiting to be selected from. Options for action may in some situations be hard to generate (Gettys, Fisher, & Mehle, 1978), since option generation is a creative act in itself, and creativity is mostly hard work. Thought must be addressed to the impossible but nonetheless necessary task of forecasting the future, another creative step. The decision maker then has to assign, with help to be sure, values for the probabilities and utilities. There is a search for information at each step, and the new data or simply a new idea may lead to a reconceptualization of the problem, and a new iteration of the whole process may be called for. Then the analyst does a preliminary aggregation, and there ensues give-and-take between the analyst and the client— the decision maker—with new insights being added as sensitivity analyses reveal what the key determinants of the decision are, and perhaps point the way toward more data collection. For some decisions, the decision may be essentially irrevocable, such as where to build a new facility. For others, such as some career choices, early consequences of the decision may function as data to update probabilities or change utilities, and a reanalysis undertaken.

It may be that prescriptive applications of decision theory are more appropriate to proactive decisions, such as planning, than to the sort of reactive decisions described above by Gary Klein. Clearly, this model as described is not the sort of decision aid that the officer who decided to fire on the KAL 007 would have found useful in deciding whether or not to down that aircraft of uncertain origin. Nor would it be appropriate to a fireground commander. But it might well be useful in making national policy decisions as to whether to have ground-to-air missile bases which automatically shoot down any airplane that overflies the nation's territory, or to decide where in a city to locate a fire station. There were a number of assertions in the above chapters that decision theory had been tried and found wanting. But the variety of decision situations that we face as individuals and organizations defies description: no adequate taxonomy of decision situations yet exists (I say this in spite of my admiration for Hammond's cognitive continuum theory), and I believe that there are many decision situations in the world for which decision theoretic decision aids would be of great value.

With this too brief and admittedly incomplete survey of the field of JDM as a backdrop, it is time to address naturalistic decision making.

NATURALISTIC DECISION MAKING

The commentary on naturalistic decision making will be divided into three sections, Methodology, Theory, and Practice, artificial though such separations may be. The first two will be fairly extensive, dealing with issues that cut across many chapters. The third will be brief.

Methodology

The methodological issues raised by the naturalistic decision making enterprise are profound and fascinating. There seem to me to be three major methodological issues that require comment: (a) What are the measurement methods? Are they valid? Reliable? Objective? (b) What are the criteria for good decisions and good performance? For error? The issues relating to criteria for subjects' performance are in some ways different from the more global issue of the degree to which naturalistic decision making meets the reasonably well-established criteria for the goodness of a scientific theory, and (c) What is the grain of analysis, or level of molecularity, in naturalistic decision making studies?

Measurement methods. The descriptions in the above chapters do not describe the measurement methods in nearly enough detail to permit full understanding, but it is clear that two of the major methods are (a) the case study, and (b) retrospective self-report in an interview setting. These often appear to be used together, with the latter being used as the database for the former. From the three scenarios at the very beginning of the first chapter right throughout the book, case studies and self-report have been used in two ways, both central to the structure of the book, as evidence *against* the validity of "the classical model of decision theory" and as evidence *for* models of naturalistic decision making.

There is, of course, a long tradition of debate about the use of case studies as evidence for or against a theory, and the battle lines are not at all clearly drawn in terms of James' "tender-minded" vs. "tough-minded" distinction. A common view, one that I share, is that the individual case study approach, even when applied to a substantial number of individuals, may be a rich source of hypotheses, but it has enormous potential to mislead theorists when it is taken as a serious source of evidence for most sorts of psychological theories. There is a famous aphorism that I might not have just exactly right, but it is worth noting anyway, *There are three kinds of lies: lies, damn lies, and case studies.* The problems typically associated with the individual case study approach are exacerbated by the basing of the case study data on postexperiential self-reports, taken either in writing as it appears to have been done in the "missing soldier" scenario, or orally, as it appears to have been done with the FGCs. This method of verbal report is decidedly not the same as that defended so powerfully by Ericsson and Simon (1984), and there is reason to believe that, under some circumstances, retrospective verbal report is unrelated to the actual sources of one's actions, constructed post hoc to make sense out of those actions. Jonathan Evans' (1989) *Bias in Human Reasoning* is especially apropos here:

> There are in fact—as Ericsson and Simon recognise—two different types of processes that are not reflected in verbalisable knowledge. The first is what Evans . . . calls heuristic processes and what Ericsson and Simon call recognition processes. These are the preconscious and inaccessible processes by which the subject and focus of our attention is determined. Such processes are equally involved whether attention is directed towards sensory input or information retrieved from memory. . . . One is not entitled to assume that because reasoning is successful, then any verbal account offered by the subject must be accurate. (p. 108)

Self reports, interviews and case studies have a role to play, but those methods will, I believe, only contribute to the development of a cumulative science if they are embedded in a complex of other methods all designed to converge on the central concepts of the theory under test. Garner, Hake, and Eriksen (1956), and Campbell and Fiske (1959), on converging operations and the multitrait-multimethod approach, respectively, may be old papers, but the ideas in them are not old hat. In our effort to describe a methodology for a scientific psychology of the cognitive processes of scientists (Tweney, Doherty, & Mynatt, 1981), interviews and case studies played a role, but only in the context of a wide-ranging set of converging operations. The multiple case study approach, wherein many of the conditions of investigation are standardized but there is detailed attention to the behavior of the individual and reporting of data across individuals, is a considerable improvement over the individual case study in many respects. It appears that some of the NDM investigators are moving in that direction.

I do not know the extent to which the other methods mentioned in the various chapters are being used by the emerging community of investigators of naturalistic decision making, but the faith of those investigators in the ones just criticized, reflected primarily in the numerous uses of self report to deny the validity of decision theory, is misplaced. I think that the arguments against decision theory based on self-reports are literally irrelevant to its status as a scientific theory.

This criticism can be framed in a positive light. The methods just criticized will, and perhaps must continue to, be used. But the very nature of the naturalistic decision making enterprise is such that other methods will also be used, especially simulation exercises such as those described by Duffy and Salas and by Klein, or the "field experiments" described by Woods. These methods appear to have some of the qualities of multiple case studies. The proponents of naturalistic decision making have probably the greatest chance of any research community to contribute basic knowledge about the situations in which postexperiential self-report can be taken to be indicative of the cognitive processes involved. There is no doubt that many aspects of cognitive process are opaque, but it seems self-evident that *some* aspects of cognitive processes are transparent under *some* circumstances. Hard data on those circumstances that allow self-report to be interpreted as reliable and valid indicators of process would be an invaluable contribution to theory and practice.

Performance criteria. This is a critical issue that must be faced if naturalistic decision making is to fulfill its promise, as Orasanu and Connolly implied when they said that previous work has chronicled the many ways in which reasoners can go wrong; now we need to balance that work with an account of how they can go right. That is a hard problem; it was Brunswik's goal in his life's work. When one uses a decision theoretic framework, or some other normative framework such as the correlation coefficient as the norm in an illusory correlation study or the syllogism as a norm in logical reasoning research, the investigator has a standard against which to compare the subject's performance. In a social judgment theoretic study the investigator has the environment against which to assess the subject's performance, and the lens model equation provides an elegant analytical tool to accomplish that assessment. What standard does the naturalistic decision making investigator have to know whether an FGC made a good decision? By what criterion did Rasmussen conclude that the troubleshooters were very rational?

The investigator using a normative model has what Hammond (1986) called the coherence criterion for truth, that is, whether the behavior is internally consistent according to the set of axioms embodied in the normative model. The lens modeler, at least in some investigations, assesses the correspondence between the behavior and the environment in correlational terms, since each subject makes a large number of judgments and the investigator has the environmental values. In a study based on information integration theory, the investigator can determine the internal consistency of the multiple responses, and see to what extent a model of those responses conforms to some conceptual model such as averaging or multiplying. Putting this another way, naturalistic decision making is simply silent on what constitutes an error. This is a serious issue.

I would like to put another twist on the same topic, since there is an interesting issue concerning statistical hypothesis testing issue lurking in here. Note that a normative theory that is masquerading as a descriptive theory is "falsified" (the quotes are in recognition of the role of auxiliaries in protecting core assumptions from what would otherwise be falsifying observations) by a single observation that does not conform to the normative standard. Conversely, a theory that is assessed by whether or not some observation departs sufficiently from some mean of a sampling distribution under the null hypothesis can be corroborated relatively easily and, as we all know, for a variety of reasons other than that embodied in the substantive hypothesis. Hence a theory that specifies ideal behavior faces an infinitely more rigorous test than one that is assessed by predicting an effect of unspecified size. Meehl (1978) pointed this out eloquently. He did not discuss normative models in so many words, but his discussion of the role of point estimates and consistency tests in other sciences is highly apropos.

To clarify the point, let me take two theories for which the critical test data are sample correlation coefficients. Consider a theory that, like a normative theory, propounds a canon of perfection, and asserts that a population correlation is 1.0, that is, $H_0: \rho = 1$. The sampling distribution of r when $\rho = 1.0$ has, of course, a zero standard error, and the slightest deviation of any sample from r = 1.0 gives a z of ∞ and a p value (for the sample statistic under the Null hypothesis) of 0.

Now consider a typical psychological theory for which the Null hypothesis is $H_0: \rho = 0$. That H_0 may, of course, be falsified for any number of reasons other than that specified by the theory, but since the investigator's interest is in supporting H_A, which is accomplished by rejection of the Null, then the data taken as "support" for the theory can also be explained by any of a potentially infinitely large number of alternative hypotheses. This problem is attenuated by exquisite experimental control, but is acute in less well-controlled situations.

More troubling still, failure to reject the Null hypothesis leads to no conclusion, since failure to reject may be attributed to poor measurement, inadequate sample sizes, and so forth. So the theorist who propounds such a theory is in, statistically speaking only, a "heads I win, tails I don't lose" situation; if $p < \alpha$, the theorist wins; if $p > \alpha$, the results don't count. Hence there is a logical asymmetry of enormous theoretical consequence for normative theories as contrasted with typical psychological theories; a precise theory faces an infinitely greater risk, and hence, in this one respect is a better scientific theory than one which predicts a nonzero correlation, or one that predicts a nonzero difference between means. None of this is new, but it is directly relevant to the comparison between decision theory and naturalistic decision making. Decision theory is criticized severely in some of the above chapters in light of deviations from the norm, while the several naturalistic decision making approaches are being supported by significance tests, that is, by deviations from chance, or by other means that have the analogous property of basing support for the theory on some degree of consistency with theoretical predictions. This is not a reflex call for "a level playing field," to use a sports metaphor bandied about a great deal these days, but rather a call for the proponents of naturalistic decision making to examine closely the logic of their criticisms of decision theory, and to consider the implications of that logic for the hoped for and highly desirable ultimate development of normative theories of naturalistic decision making. It is also an intrinsically interesting issue.

The grain of analysis. There is a theme that runs throughout the chapters that is best characterized by the use of the word *actually*. *Every* author has said or implied strongly that he or she was interested in how decisions were *actually* made in the world. That is undoubtedly an interest of every person who identifies with JDM and many besides, but the implication virtually every time it was used was that decision theorists are *not* interested in how decisions are *actually* made. The issue is not a them vs. us issue at all, but rather the grain of analysis with which one chooses to investigate and understand the world. You cannot play the science game without narrowing the focus of investigation. We have the same cognitive limitations as our subjects, and that means that we simply cannot study everything at once. Orasanu and Connolly, in a quotation that is representative of many similar sentiments throughout the book, express their dissatisfaction with what they term "decision event" thinking thusly:

> The Alphadrive CEO in Scenario 3 shows some of the "decision event" activities, in that she finally made the go/no go decision. But we find ourselves as interested in how the Marketing and Development people tried to control the CEO's information, and in the cunning effort by Betamem to trick them into a premature product launch. . . . The real-world processes have a number of features not explicitly considered by the basic decision event model.

Of course they are interested in those other things. Of course the explicit model does not have all the features of the world. That is the nature of scientific models. That is the nature of human knowledge. It is incumbent on the proponents of naturalistic decision making, or perhaps on the proponents of specific models, to be more explicit about the level of analysis that they are adopting, and to describe the grain at which they are investigating the processes of interest. In no chapter in the book was there a report of the research at a descriptive, operational level that would permit the sine qua non of scientific work, independent replication.

Finally, a comment is in order about what appears to be a growing tendency in psychology, exemplified in this book, to dismiss research methods on the grounds of artificiality. If one insists on studying interesting processes only in vivo and in all their full-blown complexity, then one cannot profit from possible lessons of other sciences. Mendel cross-bred peas, and Watson and Crick built models of chemicals. They thought they were studying something relevant to life in the real world. They were. This is no criticism of naturalistic decision making, but rather a strong statement that other people's research, artificial though it may appear, may be a search for elements, a search for order underlying apparent chaos. The psychologist investigating base rate neglect or illusory correlation in the laboratory is, in my judgment, investigating phenomena that characterize judgment and influence lives in many situations outside the laboratory. I close this comment with a quote from Francis Crick (1988), who cautioned that "it is important not to believe too strongly in one's own arguments. This particularly applies to *negative* arguments, arguments that suggest that a particular approach should certainly not be tried since it is bound to fail" (p. 112).

Before leaving the discussion of methodology, I would like to try to reduce, at least in part, the cognitive dissonance created by labeling myself an adherent of probabilistic functionalism, with its call for representative design, and at the same time admitting an attachment to the beautiful, simple experiment. Accepted wisdom is that one may get one's hypotheses anywhere, but that those hypotheses are submitted to rigorous test in the experimental laboratory. Perhaps that accepted wisdom should be turned on its head? Perhaps in psychology the most important role of the laboratory will turn out in the long run to be the place where we get our hypotheses, which are then tested in more naturalistic, representative designs.

Theory

The essential characteristic of a good scientific theory is that it must help make sense out of the world. To do so it must (a) explain existing data; (b) make predictions of new phenomena, ideally surprising ones that are not made by competing theories; (c) and it must do so economically, that is, without needlessly multiplying concepts. This latter criterion is called by various names, including parsimony, Occam's razor, Lloyd Morgan's canon, and simplicity. It is, at root, an aesthetic criterion (Wechsler, 1978). As Popper (1962) argued, the fundamental feature of the first two characteristics is that the explanations and predictions be falsifiable by objective (that is, public) observation. The first two criteria could be treated as one, since explanation and prediction are not, from a philosophical standpoint, that different, but for expository purposes it is useful to separate them. And the prediction of new phenomena is psychologically much more powerful than explanation of old data!

The contrast between naturalistic and traditional approaches to decision making. In contrasting naturalistic decision making with decision theory many of the chapter authors were quite dismissive of the older approaches. Orasanu and Connolly spoke of "the reinvention of decision making." Cohen referred to the nonlinearity of utility in money as a "technical thread." Beach and Lipshitz likened the continuing interest in decision theory to the "overlong retention of the Ptolemaic theory." (Would that we had a theory anywhere in psychology as good at making predictions as the Ptolemaic theory! Would that we had as useful a decision aid as those that Ptolemaic theory provided navigators!) But Ptolemaic theory was not overthrown by having its putative deficiencies pointed out. It was overthrown, or rather replaced, by a theory that ultimately explained the same data that it did, that predicted observations that it did not, and was simpler. The theory of relativity did not dismiss Newtonian mechanics, it included it as a special case. Watson and Crick did not dismiss Mendelian genetics as outdated, they discovered the mechanism that explains it. I think it not unreasonable to ask of theorists of a more complex form of decision making to explain the data generated by experimentalists who have investigated the simple forms.

There is another theme that runs through many of the chapters, perhaps most vividly in Cohen's, to the effect that the older approaches cannot be right because after all decision making in the world is pretty good, "People tend to use decision making strategies that make effective use of their substantive knowledge and processing capacity; such strategies are generally subject to incremental revision and improvement in dynamic environments; *the net result is performance that is generally adequate,* though subject to improvement in specific respects" (emphasis added). I agree with much of that, but I must express profound reservations about the *italicized* part. I recall Pearl Harbor, the holocaust, Joe McCarthy, Korea, and Vietnam. I see people sleeping in the streets and read about the S & L debacle and about people sharing needles. I see young people starting to smoke, and sober people young and old setting out in their cars to get drunk. People vote for presidential candidates based on acting ability, women stay with men who abuse them, and people in flood plains don't buy insurance. While it is hard to believe, I have read that there have been, even in this century, heads of state who govern their countries with the advice of astrologers. I'm writing this in a small country in which, just 145 years ago, there was a famine in which 1,000,000 people starved to death while food grown in abundance was exported under the protection of gunboats, and while salmon filled the sea but the shore was the exclusive province of the landowners. Now I do not pretend to explain these things (with the possible exception of belief in astrology) via principles such as the heuristics and biases, but I do not think that one can evaluate theories of decision making by asserting that performance is *in general adequate.*

Decision theory was criticized also for failing to square with everyday decision making as experienced. But the Aristotelian stricture that scientific knowledge should "save the appearances" of reality is no longer a sufficient or even terribly relevant criterion for science, though psychology *may* be an exception (Tweney, Doherty, & Mynatt, 1981). Surely the world *looks* flat and I *feel* solid, but geography and chemistry tell me otherwise. It has been argued that since people think fast, then decision theory's postulate that people select from among alternative options for action is, on the face of it, wrong. As the above quote from Evans suggests, there are many processes, recognitional and otherwise, that are preattentive, or inaccessible to verbalizable awareness. Scientific theories are supposed to reveal the order and simplicity that underly the appearances, hence one simply ought not adduce appearances as evidence against a scientific theory. The rapidity of complex decisions cannot be taken as convincing evidence against a theory that is silent about decision times. The fire-ground commander's assertion that he only thought of one way to put out a fire cannot be taken as evidence against the hypothesis that alternatives were weighed and dismissed by unverbalizable, preattentive processes. The weighing and comparing may occur just as rapidly and as automatically as processes that sort through the multitude of faces that we recognize and produce, unbidden, a recognitional response. Nor does their unverbalizability mean that people's speech is not governed by formal grammatical rules.

Naturalistic decision making, for example Klein's RPD, is silent on the process by which the expert arrives at the one option that the expert is hypothesized to select. Perhaps that expert has 50,000 patterns available in long-term memory, as chess masters are supposed to. Yet an action option is often taken seemingly instantaneously. Is there time for the expert to sort through all those templates in memory? Since we don't know how the hardware works, I think that the question is not appropriate. RPD seems to me to have considerable promise as a theory of action. It needs elaboration, as Klein himself notes. That elaboration seems to me to be most needed in the development of a theory of recognitional processes, perhaps along the lines of social judgment theory with pattern perception built in, to which past actions may be linked, perhaps by principles of reinforcement. If the theory were to call for the sorting through of 50 or 50,000 templates, so be it. Let the theory be evaluated by the extent to which it handles extant data, by whether it makes interesting new predictions, and by its conceptual simplicity. Let decision theory be similarly evaluated, and not by the intuition of the investigators or of the subjects. I say all of this, fully aware that I said above that the *ultimate* criterion of the goodness of a theory is going to be human judgment. But that judgment must be informed by experiment.

Naturalistic Decision Making as Science. JDM is younger than most of the people who study it. At this stage of its development I believe that a wide variety of approaches and methods is fully appropriate, and I applaud the effort to tackle complex problems. As I read the book, there were a few substantive issues that cut across many chapters, that may repay brief attention.

There is an important distinction to be maintained between actions and inferences. One of the fundamental distinctions made by decision theorists is between what is out there in the world and what action should be taken. For decision theorists the independence of probability and utility is axiomatic, what you *want* the world to be like ought not influence your assessment of what it *is* like. Both should, of course, influence your actions, since the very purpose of decision making is to exercise some control over the way the world will be, contingent on the consequences of the selected action. Clearly, in RPD and in other models, and also in decision theory, situation assessment is part of and propaedeutic to action selection. But often in the above chapters decision theory, unmodified, was labeled the normative standard for inferences as well as actions, for statements about the world as well as for action selections.

It is critical to keep the processes of recognition and action theoretically separate, even if the theory postulates that, under certain conditions, such as firefighting, recognition may directly trigger action. One of the hypotheses that has prompted much experimental work in our laboratory is that strategies of data selection differ, depending on whether the data are to be used for inference (diagnosis, recognition) or for actions, with subjects in inference tasks systematically seeking information sequentially about the same hypothesis and subjects in a choice task varying considerably in their information selection strategies (Doherty & Mynatt, 1986).

Are there testable consequences of naturalistic decision making models? It seems that Beach's image theory is furthest along in this regard, but too few of the other authors made explicit statements about testable consequences. The theorists have advanced many hypothetical constructs, but in the absence of details of the procedures of manipulation and measurement, I did not get the urge to sit down and design studies that I get when I read papers by Hammond, Kahneman and Tversky, Anderson, and so on.

One example of the use of a construct without apparent testable consequences is Rasmussen's use of the term *rational* absent a definition, either in terms of correspondence or coherence criteria, of rationality. Perhaps the most vivid example of the use of a hypothetical construct that appears to me to have no testable implications is *collective mind,* or in Orasanu and Salas' words, *team mind.* I do not readily see what hypotheses can be deduced from such a construct that could not equally be deduced more parsimoniously from traditional conceptions of interacting groups, yet it is attributed the status of a "unifying concept" by Duffy and Salas. If naturalistic decision making is to have the impact that these investigators hope, and that it should, the presentations of the models will have to be made in much more operational terms, terms that leave the readers with ideas for investigations that would be tests or extensions of the theories and models, and with the compelling urge to carry them out. If *collective mind* is to be used as a metaphor to aid in the generation of new hypotheses, then the hypotheses so generated should be stated in sufficiently precise terms that the reader can conceptualize the operations entailed in the test of those hypotheses.

Is naturalistic decision making "schema-driven" rather than "computational?" At a number of places in the book this or a similar contrast is drawn. Theorizing along these lines will likely lead to a blind alley, unless there are clear empirical consequences of the distinction. I think that there is a direct parallel with a theoretical dispute that is now generally considered unresolvable, about whether the behavior in so-called imagery research is mediated by actual images or by list-like computational routines. There is probably no operation that can distinguish the two explanations.

Practice

The pragmatic goal of naturalistic decision making is the development of interventions, either in education for better decision making or in the design of usable online decision aids. I think that the most acute need for the successful development of such interventions is a better understanding of the task environment that decision makers face. The psychological systems of Egon Brunswik, Herbert Simon, and B. F. Skinner may appear to be worlds apart, but Brunswik's *The Conceptual Framework of Psychology* (1952) and Simon's *The Sciences of the Artificial* (1969) agree on the primacy of understanding the environment to which our cognitive systems have adapted for a proper understanding of those cognitive systems. And Skinner argued throughout his career that to change the behavior we had to change the environment.

Hammond's (1986) Cognitive Continuum Theory, which as this volume shows is undergoing modification even now as ideas concerning pattern perception are added, provides explicit description of task characteristics and the cognitive activities they induce. Such a theory may provide a foundation for a still more articulated theory of tasks, which I believe to be necessary (Doherty, 1990). Clearly, one thing needed for a cumulative science of judgment and decision making is a taxonomy of tasks that will permit us to predict what tasks a finding will generalize across, and when to expect task specificity.

In the meantime, my image of JDM is that it is one of the most vital areas of research in psychology, one with a nice admixture of theory, experiment and practice. A new strain of research dedicated to complex problems requiring rapid action can only enrich the field.

KEY POINTS

- JDM is a young and vital area within psychology, with a variety of theories and a variety of methods.
- Decision theory provides a useful decision aid for situations for which there are adequate time and resources.
- In the investigation of NDM and decision making in general the use of multiple, converging operations is essential to ultimate progress in understanding decision processes.
- Many decision models have a standard for what is a good decision

process; the development of a similar standard is an important challenge to NDM.

- One's own experience of one's psychological processes is not a reliable guide to the truth status of a scientific theory of those processes. The testing of theoretically coherent propositions in the fire of "public knowledge" is the sine qua non of science.
- The seemingly inexhaustible variety of decision situations makes a taxonomy of decision tasks imperative.

Chapter 22

Twenty Questions—Suggestions for Research in Naturalistic Decision Making*

Gary A. Klein
Klein Associates Inc.
Fairborn, OH

The previous chapters have presented a wide array of models, methods, and applications, and have identified a number of gaps in our knowledge of naturalistic decision making. Knowledge can be in the form of questions as well as answers. This chapter attempts to integrate the questions into a research agenda.

Questions must be formulated carefully if they are to yield meaningful lines of investigation. For instance, we don't want to ask "Is recognitional or analytical decision making better?" This question creates an artificial controversy, since we haven't defined what 'better' means and we haven't specified the conditions we are interested in. What are the tasks? How will performance be measured? Will the decision makers be experienced or inexperienced? What about time pressure, and other contextual factors? As Greenwald, Pratkanis, Leippe, and Baumgardner (1986) have pointed out, after researchers wrestle with such questions they usually come to realize that each alternative has validity, under different conditions. So we can ask a more productive question: Under what conditions is it more efficient to use recognitional versus analytical strategies?

The questions in this chapter are organized into five topic areas.

1. Learning more about naturalistic decision strategies
2. Learning how the decision process can become degraded
3. Learning how teams make decisions

*I wish to thank Roberta Calderwood, Susan Chipman, Beth Crandall, Jeff Grossman, Ken Hammond, Helen Klein, Buzz Reed, and David Woods for their helpful suggestions for improving this chapter.

4. Improving decision making in operational contexts
5. Developing methods for better field experiments

At the end of each section a set of questions summarizes the issues raised. It is important to understand how a phenomenon varies across different conditions, and so for each question we can ask additional questions about the effects of different levels of experience, different tasks, different contexts, and so on until the reader is drowned in a sea of curiosity. To avoid this problem I will let these additional questions be understood rather than expressing them explicitly.

SECTION A. LEARNING MORE ABOUT NATURALISTIC DECISION STRATEGIES

In Chapter 5, Lipshitz describes five process models of naturalistic decision making: image theory (Beach & Mitchell), Recognition-Primed Decisions (RPDs) (Klein, and also Noble), dominance structuring (Montgomery), decision hierarchy of skills/rules/knowledge (Rasmussen), and explanation-based decisions (Pennington & Hastie). Will it be possible to synthesize all of these process models into one general account? Are there differences between the models that can be empirically tested?

Figure 22.1 presents an attempt to synthesize the five process models along with analytical strategies. Experience is interpreted in accord with the decision maker's own value images (Beach). Situation assessment may rely on pattern-matching processes (Noble), or be a more deliberate attempt to fuse events into a story that synthesizes different causes (Pennington & Hastie). For unfamiliar cases, situation assessment may require knowledge-based analysis (Rasmussen).

Situation assessment includes images about feasible goals (Beach's trajectory image) and plausible courses of action (Rasmussen's rule-based performance and Beach's strategic image). The decision maker may evaluate a course of action using mental stimulation, or he or she might focus on a course of action and try to reformulate the situation assessment to show the advantages of this course of action (Montgomery). If it was necessary to contrast different courses of action, the decision maker would use analytical decision methods. The decision maker also would have the option of implementing a course of action in its entirety, or implementing a portion of it in order to use feedback to guide the rest of the process (Connolly & Wagner's idea of hedge-trimming).

It is important to try to synthesize these models. Otherwise, the

Figure 22.1.   Synthesized Process Model of Naturalistic Decision Making

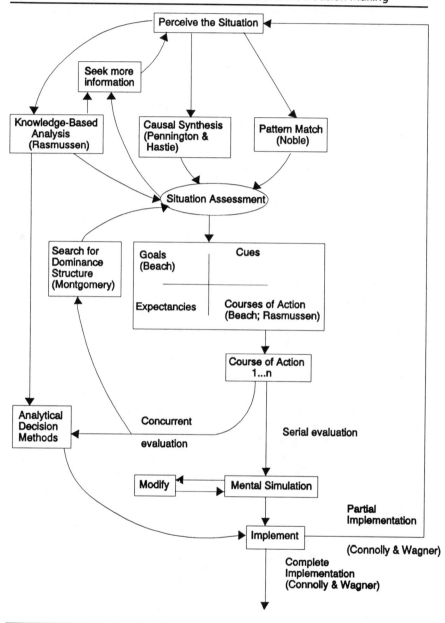

impression is created that there exists a disjointed set of strategies, without any understanding of when one strategy might be used instead of another.

In an operational situation, the simplest case is where a skilled decision maker recognizes a situation as typical in some sense. The RPD model asserts that situation assessment can occur quickly, without any need for analysis.

In a more complex case, there are competing ways to understand the situation. Here, the Explanation-Based Decision model would be needed, to judge which account to accept and which to reject. Even when there is a single way to understand a situation, by fitting the facts into a story, a decision maker can use mental simulation to derive additional implications.

Once situation assessment is achieved, in most cases it is obvious how to proceed, and here again the RPD strategy comes into play, enabling the skilled decision maker to generate and evaluate a single course of action.

If the decision maker is forced to contrast several alternative options, one easy approach is to use an Elimination-by-Aspects (EBA) strategy (Tversky, 1972), in which options are compared, dimension by dimension, until one of them is rejected. The decision maker is simply looking for a basis for rejecting one of the options. This EBA strategy requires that the task be fairly well structured, so that the evaluation dimensions are understood, and so that the options can be easily appraised on each dimension.

If the decision maker has to contrast several alternative options, and the situation is not well structured, then we might expect the use of the Search for Dominance Structure (SDS) approach, in order to find a structure that can make the choice clear-cut.

Finally, if the decision maker has to compare several options, and the task is well defined, and the time is unlimited, and so forth, we would arrive at the conditions needed to use a more formal, compensatory strategy such as multiattribute utility analysis.

Experience affects this synthesized decision model in several ways. We can speculate that experience affects decision making by improving the ease and accuracy of situation assessment, by increasing the quality of the courses of action considered by the decision maker, and by enabling the decision maker to construct and use a mental simulation. In contrast to naturalistic models, classical decision theories have not paid much attention to the role of expertise. Therefore, we may be able to make progress by studying these three processes: situation assessment, identifying plausible courses of action, and mental simulation.

Situation Assessment

Many of the naturalistic decision models described in Chapter 5 emphasize the importance of the way a situation is diagnosed, in terms of difficulties and imbalances that need to be corrected. Rasmussen makes perhaps the clearest distinction between situations that are completely typical and stereotyped (calling for skill-based responses), situations that are generally typical (rule-based responses), and situations that have not been encountered before and require knowledge-based responses. Judgments of typicality are also central to the models presented by Lipshitz, by Klein, and by Noble. They would also seem basic to the intuitive decision-making strategies addressed by Hammond.

There is a fair literature on judging objects and physical features as typical (e.g., Rosch & Mervis, 1975; Smith & Medin, 1981). But what about judging situations such as buildings on fire? How does a fire-ground commander recognize that one situation calls for immediate search and rescue, whereas another allows the commander a chance to try to put out the fire before it spreads? There has been very little research on how people use their experience to make and use judgments of typicality in order to perform dynamic tasks. I am not suggesting that the decision maker starts by making a conscious judgment of typicality, but rather that such judgments appear to be made as a byproduct of solving a problem or making a decision.

It is not enough to recognize a situation as typical. In the Recognition-Primed Decision model, sizing up a situation as familiar and representative of a certain type of incident carries with it some guidance about realistic goals, relevant cues, expectancies, and feasible courses of action. Models of how people judge prototypicality primarily focus on the *detection* of familiarity. Can we expand these models to describe how the detection of familiarity is linked to action?

Identifying Plausible Courses of Action

Classical decision theory has concentrated on powerful techniques for selecting the best option. Less attention has been given to the process of generating the options. Traditional advice (e.g., Gettys, 1983) is to generate many options to ensure that at least one of the options will be acceptable. The problem is that it takes time and effort to evaluate a large set of options, so this advice isn't always practical.

In contrast, a number of the models described in Chapter 5 (e.g., Rasmussen, Noble, Klein, and Lipshitz) claim that an experienced decision maker can come up with a satisfactory course of action as the first one considered. If this is possible, how is it done? Presumably it is based on some blend of recency, availability, and representativeness. How do decision makers use prior experience to generate options? Can we show that the order in which options are generated is related to their quality? Such a finding would strengthen our confidence in recognitional models of decision making. The contrast between analytical and recognitional strategies may boil down to issues such as this: Does a decision maker have enough expertise to make it likely that the first course of action considered will be feasible?

Mental Simulation

Mental simulation plays an important role in the process models of decision making presented by Beach, by Pennington and Hastie, and by Klein—the decision maker imagines how a sequence of events might unfold within a given context. Mental simulation lets decision makers assess whether their understanding of a situation makes sense, in part by imagining how the situation arose. Decision makers also use mental simulation to evaluate options without having to apply abstract evaluation dimensions. Instead, they imagine what could go wrong if a course of action was actually carried out in a situational context.

Thus far, there has been little work on the role of mental simulation in decision making. De Groot's (1965/1978) study of progressive deepening in chess grandmasters is one exception. Grandmasters imagine what will happen if they make a specific move, reacting positively or negatively depending on whether the imagined outcome exceeds their expectations. The next challenge is to find out more about where these expectations come from. Another approach to mental simulation is the work of Kahneman and Tversky (1982b) on the simulation heuristic. Kahneman and Tversky speculated about the types of errors (e.g., biases due to recency, availability, anchoring, and adjustment) that could arise from the simulation heuristic. It could be fruitful to study whether these errors arise in naturalistic settings. Another line of inquiry is to study whether people differ in their readiness to use mental simulations. And how much domain knowledge is needed in order to formulate useful mental simulations?

Research Questions

1. Under what conditions is it better to expend conscious energy in identifying and comparing alternative options, as opposed to imagining more clearly the process of carrying out a favorite option?

2. How do experienced decision makers judge what outcomes are feasible in a situation?
3. For experienced decision makers, are the first options they think of more likely to be successful than subsequent options?
4. As people gain experience, when do expectancies help them notice when their situation assessment is wrong, and when do expectancies blind them to mistakes?
5. As people become more experienced how do their mental simulations change?
6. As a person grows in domain knowledge, how does that affect the decision strategies used?
7. What strategies do people use in diagnosing a situation?

SECTION B. LEARNING HOW THE DECISION PROCESS CAN BECOME DEGRADED

The naturalistic decision strategies described in Chapter 5 enable people to use experience, but the strategies do not ensure perfect choices. Many things can go wrong. Sometimes people make errors in reasoning, sometimes conditions such as stress can disrupt the performance, and sometimes the task conditions themselves are to blame. Can we learn to anticipate and reduce human errors?

Sources of Decision Errors

We need to find some way to explain the reason for consistently poor decision making, when it arises. What regular patterns of mistaken thinking and appraisal arise from analytical and recognitional decision strategies? Callan, Gwynne, Kelly, and Feher (1990), for example, have studied Navy officers conducting simulated exercises in an aircraft carrier group. One scenario indicates that a massive enemy attack has been spotted in a certain quadrant. There is also the possibility of enemy attacks from other directions, but no sightings have been reported. Some officers launch most of their aircraft but hold some reserves. In these scenarios, the Navy officers are barely able to thwart the enemy attack, and afterwards they admit that it was foolish to hold back any reserves. If the officers failed to stop the enemy they knew about, then most of their group would be destroyed. Yet on the next simulation trial some of the same officers repeat the same mistake, holding back reserves and risking an enemy breakthrough. When we see stable patterns of admittedly defective decision making, we have to wonder what is going wrong.

The emphasis has to be on performance, and not simply on judgment. Christensen-Szalanski has demonstrated that in applied settings, judgment errors don't necessarily lead to worse performance. And Cohen pointed out in Chapters 3 and 4 that we have to be careful about how we use the concept of decision biases. Cohen argued that many decision biases could be traced to the laboratory paradigms used to conduct the research. Context is stripped away, task experience is minimized, and other precautions are taken to avoid contaminating the data. In naturalistic settings, these decision biases may not substantially affect performance.

What types of decision errors lead to degraded performance in naturalistic settings? One hypothesis is that recognitional decision strategies provide greater speed and flexibility at the cost of errors such as failing to think out a course of action far enough ahead, or being mistaken about feasible goals, or failing to notice that a situation assessment was incorrect. In my own research, decision makers have sometimes convinced themselves that a course of action was feasible because they could conduct a mental simulation that led to success; they failed to conduct evaluative mental simulations to identify potential breakdowns in their plans. Are there other types of limitations?

Effects of Stress on Decision Making

Stress can affect a person's ability to execute decision strategies. Time pressure is a good example. It makes little sense to learn elaborate analytical methods for making emergency decisions if the time stress won't permit you to perform the analyses. If time runs out, there isn't a clear basis for making a choice.

We would expect recognitional decision strategies to be less vulnerable to time pressure, but there is one process in the Recognition-Primed Decision model that is time sensitive—the use of mental simulation for evaluating potential courses of action. What is the relative amount of decision time needed to run a mental simulation? And how do experts differ from nonexperts in the efficiency of their mental simulations.

Stressors include psychological factors (e.g., unavailability of resources, as happens under time pressure; frustration with task barriers such as unreliable communications; fear of looking incompetent; worries that team members will prove unreliable; exposure to threat) and physiological factors (adrenaline reactions such as increased blood pressure and heart rate, startle reflexes that can interfere with performance; degraded performance due to physical dysfunctions, as with heat, cold, and sleep deprivation).

All three examples in Chapter 1 include psychological stress. The fireground commander was risking the lives of his crews, and of the people living in the apartment building. The physicians were risking the health of their patient, and the business executives were risking their reputations and jobs. The stress included fear of being caught making a mistake, and concern about the high stakes.

We can speculate how time stress affects decision making by adding distracting subtasks (e.g., attending to the stress itself) or changing speed–accuracy tradeoffs. As we learn more about naturalistic decision strategies we will find out how the strategies can be disrupted.

Effects of Dynamic Conditions on Decision Making

How do experienced decision makers use their knowledge and experience to make difficult decisions under challenging conditions? Most decision research to date has examined the inadequacies of human subjects in coping with laboratory tasks. But, with a few important exceptions, researchers rarely use experienced decision makers and even more rarely does a research task replicate the types of constraints found in dynamic environments: uncertainty, changing information about conditions, shifting goals, and so on. What strategies and tricks do people develop to cope with uncooperative environments? The appeal of the strategies described in Chapter 5 is that they should enable the decision maker to handle ambiguity and confusion and to quickly readjust to change in the environment. Are there other tricks of the trade that people use?

Research Questions

8. What types of errors would we expect from the use of different decision strategies?
9. In what ways do stressors such as time pressure affect the use of different decision strategies?
10. How do experienced decision makers work around problems such as missing and uncertain information?

SECTION C. LEARNING HOW TEAMS MAKE DECISIONS

Can we identify different team decision strategies? For individuals, we can distinguish multiattribute utility analyses from elimination-by-aspects, recognitional decisions, and search for a dominance structure. Do teams use the same types of strategies as individuals, or are there unique strategies that we wouldn't observe at the individual level? If we are able to describe a team's strategy, is it affected by conditions such as the makeup of the team, and the nature of the task? Can we compare an airplane cockpit crew with a command-and-control staff working on military maneuvers or to a team of business executives faced with a tough marketing decision? Are special strategies used when a team is faced with an intelligent adversary? What is the effect on team decision strategies of geographical separation of team members, or time pressure, or conflict about objectives?

If unique decision strategies emerge at the team level, what about unique types of decision errors? When a person makes a poor decision because he or she misread a dial, it doesn't matter whether a team is involved. But certain types of errors will only be found in a team. For example, Foushee and Helmreich (1988) have shown how personality traits of team leaders (e.g., commercial airline pilots) affect the team's willingness to question orders or suggest options. Other errors at the team level might include mistakes in interpreting someone else's situation assessment or orders, inability to get critical information from those who have been monitoring the situation, inability to see a pattern when different people have the pieces, and confusion about how to coordinate a plan with everyone involved. These types of errors involve situation assessment, planning, and coordination.

What enables a team to improvise? The ability of a team to understand *why* it is carrying out given actions will affect the team's readiness to adjust to dynamic conditions. For example, if a battalion is sent to prevent the enemy from crossing a bridge, and they arrive to find that the bridge is undefended, what should they do—take up a position, occupy the bridge itself, or move on across the bridge to another objective? It depends on the way the battalion commander understands the goals of the brigade commander. The need for improvisation is a continual aspect of team decision making. There can be errors of rigidly adhering to someone else's plan as well as inappropriately departing from the plan.

Chapter 5 covered process models of individual decision making. Chapters 19 (Orasanu & Salas) and 20 (Duffy) offer frameworks for developing process models of team decision making. Both chapters seem to view teams as cognitive systems, which is a useful point of departure. We can then look at the extent to which team members share a mental model, and we should be able to derive hypotheses about the way experience affects a team's decisions.

Research Questions

11. What enables a team to successfully improvise?
12. Can we chart the developmental sequence of a team's decision-making skills?
13. What unique types of errors and dysfunctions emerge at the team level?

SECTION D. IMPROVING DECISION MAKING IN OPERATIONAL CONTEXTS

One major reason to study naturalistic decision making is to increase the efficiency and quality of decision making through training and decision support systems.

Can we understand the strengths and weaknesses of the different decision strategies in order to develop guidelines about when each strategy should be used? For example, analytical decision strategies require effort in terms of contrasting different options, whereas recognitional decision strategies require effort to perform mental simulations. We can determine when it pays to exert effort in laying out and evaluating different alternatives, and when it is preferable to think through a single option. To the extent that we can differentiate the benefits of broad versus deep searches, we will be able to offer guidance about where to apply limited cognitive resources.

Chapter 5 presented typological models (Hammond, Rasmussen, Connolly and Wagner, and Lipshitz) of how people shift from one class of strategies to another. The typological models assert that it is rare to find a complex, naturalistic task that can be accomplished using only one strategy. Hammond, Hamm, Grassia, and Pearson (1987) have explicitly used the term *quasirational decision making* to refer to the need for both intuitive and analytical strategies. How are skilled decision makers able to determine which strategy to use at different points in a decision cycle, and how do they move back and forth? Is it harder to rely on pattern recognition after you have divided a problem into components? Is it confusing to work out abstract evaluations of options after you have been using mental simulation for one of those options?

Training

Years ago decision researchers had hoped that general training in formal methods such as multiattribute utility analysis, decision analysis, and Bayesian statistics would be so powerful that the trainees would naturally apply the methods in domain after domain. If the analytical methods had been more robust and generalizable, the effort may have been more successful. Even so, researchers such as Fischhoff, Slovic, and Lichtenstein (1979) have demonstrated some benefits from training in statistics and probability theory. Unfortunately, the payoff has not been as great as we had hoped. In Chapter 18, Means et al. questioned the effectiveness of general decision training. Such training is labor intensive and does not often generalize or have long-lasting effects. This is discouraging.

We might hope for more success in training the process decision strategies described in Chapter 5, but this may not be a useful idea either. The process models such as recognitional decision making, image theory, and dominance structuring describe what people ordinarily do, regardless of whether they are experts or novices. There is little point in training these strategies, since there is nothing new to train.

Means et al. suggest that it may be fruitful to provide instruction on metacognitive skills—training people to monitor their own decision making so they can better manage time stress, high workload, and so forth. Other than that, Means et al. argue that we will have to rely on specific skill training in each area, rather than trying to train generic decision strategies. If this is true, can we find ways to identify expertise needed to make critical decisions? Perhaps there are aspects of naturalistic decision strategies that can be trained, such as the ability to rapidly size up situations in a given domain, and the more careful use of mental simulation to search for pitfalls in a favored course of action.

There may be more promise for training strategies for team decision making than for individual decision training. Team decision training might make sense for the following skills: focusing the attention of the team further into the future, communicating the commander's intent, mentally rehearsing a complex plan, avoidance of problems such as micromanagement, and coordinating the actions of different team members. It takes a lot of training for teams to be able to coordinate efforts at all. What training strategies can be used to speed up the acquisition of team decision skills?

Tools for Decision Support

In the past, when it was thought that decision makers could benefit from applying general analytical methods, decision aids were designed to guide operators to structure the problem and derive the necessary calculations. Those analytical decision aids were not very successful, because they were inappropriate for many operational tasks.

As we learn to differentiate decision strategies, and as we learn the boundary conditions for each of these strategies, the challenge will be to develop guidelines for developing human–computer interfaces and decision support systems. If we are successful, we will be able to help system operators use the decision strategies with which they are most comfortable. We will know we are on the path to success if we can show that changes in the interface alter the decision strategy used, and also affect the level of task performance. The next step would be to develop guidelines about which interface features to use for different tasks.

It is important not to get fixated at the level of the individual work station, because team interaction is critical for most tasks. Segal (1989) has drawn on his experience as a helicopter pilot to illustrate this problem. The old-fashioned (e.g., 1970s) equipment let a helicopter co-pilot see what the pilot was looking at, and to note quickly what control actions the pilot took. Advanced helicopter cockpits are being designed to eliminate mechanical components and to allow the pilot and co-pilot to use computer-based displays and controls. Unfortunately, the newer equipment makes it hard for the co-pilot to keep track of the pilot's attention, intentions, and actions. Therefore team coordination may be degraded. We need to help system designers understand the teamwork requirements for operational tasks.

Research Questions

14. What methods are effective for training situation assessment skills?
15. What kinds of difficulty do decision makers have in shifting between analytical and recognitional strategies?
16. What techniques might speed up the acquisition of team decision skills in a training program?
17. How can we design decision support systems and computer interfaces to support naturalistic decision strategies?
18. What kinds of decision support systems and human–computer interface features will help decision makers handle physiological and psychological stress?

SECTION E. DEVELOPING METHODS FOR
PERFORMING BETTER FIELD EXPERIMENTS

A major reason for the interest in naturalistic decision making is that some researchers feel that laboratory paradigms are so limited that the findings will not generalize to operational settings. Certain phenomena, such as chemical interactions, can be examined in the laboratory without distortion. Other phenomena such as those encountered in political science have little meaning inside the laboratory. Psychology is a hybrid. Physiological psychology and the study of sensory mechanisms are nicely suited to laboratory research. The study of a large class of decision-making phenomena may not be suited to the laboratory (see Hammond, Chapter 12, and Woods, Chapter 13). Sometimes laboratory studies will provide useful hypotheses, but too often the artificial control of conditions and subjects renders the findings uninteresting to people working in an operational environment.

Unfortunately, naturalistic research will not necessarily generalize either. If an experimenter collects observations without being able to specify the environmental conditions, or the type of decision makers, then it will still be hard to know whether the findings will apply in a different setting. Will models of the decision strategies used by fireground commanders generalize to battle commanders who have to face an intelligent and deceptive adversary? Will the lessons learned from medical decision making apply to business settings?

David Woods (Chapter 13) describes a paradigm that can allow us to draw general conclusions from field experiments. Ken Hammond (Chapter 12) describes a research approach that has been oriented towards naturalistic decision making. Jay Christensen-Szalanski, in Chapter 14, provides guidance on how to focus research and analysis on findings that have impact, rather than on findings that are merely statistically significant. Additionally, we should remember that observational studies can be a valuable source of hypotheses, and we can try to identify better methods for collecting and analyzing observational data. LeCompte and Goetz (1982) have analyzed strategies for increasing the validity and reliability of ethnographic data.

In time, as more studies are performed of operational decision making, we will learn what can go wrong with different paradigms, and what safeguards to include for designing, conducting, analyzing, and reporting the results of naturalistic studies.

Research Questions

19. In performing a cognitive task analysis, what counts as a satisfactory story or account when we try to explain the strategy a person used to make a decision?
20. What features of methodology and analysis are necessary to increase our confidence in generalizing from a field experiment?

KEY POINTS

- The focus of NDM is to open up a range of new research questions so that we can:
  — Learn more about naturalistic decision strategies.
  — Learn how the quality of the decision process can become degraded.
  — Learn how teams make decisions.
  — Learn how to improve decision making in operational context.
  — Develop methods for performing better field experiments.

Chapter 23

CONCLUSIONS: DECISION MAKING IN ACTION

Gary A. Klein
Klein Associates Inc.
Fairborn, OH

David D. Woods
Cognitive Systems Engineering Laboratory
The Ohio State University

> Operations of thought are like cavalry charges in a battle—they are strictly limited in number, they require fresh horses, and must only be made at decisive moments. (Alfred North Whitehead)

The purpose of this chapter is to take stock of what studies of naturalistic decision making have accomplished, and what remains to be done. We want to review the major contributions of the research and observations that have been described, and we also want to identify what we perceive as some of the important weaknesses of this work to date. In addition we want to highlight linkages to other areas of cognitive science.

RESEARCH ACCOMPLISHMENTS

Studies of naturalistic decision making are, for the most part, very recent, with much of the important work being done after 1985. What have we learned so far?

Perhaps the most important finding has been that people are typically able to use their experience to adopt successful courses of action even without applying rigorous analytical strategies. One vivid way to make this point is to look back at an article published in 1978 by Beach and Mitchell. They presented a contingency model which asserted that there is no one best way to make decisions. Instead, the costs and benefits of each different decision strategy determine whether a person will use an analytical or a nonanalytic strategy in a given situation. This position is entirely consistent with the models presented in Section B of this book. Beach and Mitchell described several forms of analytical decision strategies, but when it came time for them to identify nonanalytic decision strategies, they were stuck. In 1978, the best they could do was to suggest simple rules like "Eeny, meeny, miney, mo . . . ," flipping a coin, or remembering homilies. So the decision models presented in Section B are not as obvious as they may seem. They are a radical departure from the state of knowledge of only a few years earlier.

A second contribution has been to broaden the field of inquiry from the decision event to the larger processes of situation assessment. Wohl (1981) was one of the earliest decision researchers to try to include situational understanding into decision making, and the models in Section B have more to say about situation assessment than about the so-called moment of choice. We believe that this expanded inquiry will have important implications for applied work. Except in limited settings, there is little need to help people handle the moment of choice, and a much greater need to help people size up situations rapidly and also to detect when their situation assessment is no longer accurate.

A third contribution has been the models of decision making described in Section B. Several themes recur when considering behavior in more complex decision situations. Models of naturalistic decision behavior tend (a) to emphasize how temporally evolving situations (as compared to static one-shot decision situations) create different cognitive demands and provide opportunities for different cognitive strategies; (b) to emphasize the role of action in cognition; (c) to emphasize the contribution of perceptual processing to cognition rather than seeing cognition as decoupled from perception; (d) to treat effort or cognitive cost as a significant factor which acknowledges the limited resources of human decision makers; (e) to describe how people can use their experience along with formal and informal reasoning strategies to adopt satisfactory courses of action; and (f) to emphasize competencies of decision makers rather than describing dysfunctions.

A fourth accomplishment is the development of methods to increase the representativeness of findings and descriptive accounts. These methods include ethnographic techniques, process tracing procedures, and attempts to perform interventions to test hypotheses.

WEAKNESSES OF NATURALISTIC DECISION-
MAKING RESEARCH

The models and research in naturalistic decision making have clear limitations, a number of which have been discussed by Hammond and by Doherty.

The major problem is that the models presented in Section B are not easily testable. There are a lot of statements about what goes on (at a very high level), but very little about how it goes on (especially in detail). While terms such as *recognize* occur frequently, testable models need to specify the detailed classes of events that experts detect and discriminate, the kinds of knowledge and processing that support recognition and discrimination of these categories of events, how recognition of these classes of events triggers follow-up lines of reasoning, and how these lines of reasoning are intertwined and shift as new events occur.

How would one formalize these models to put them in a rigorous form? One approach could be to use cognitive simulation where psychological concepts about decision behavior are expressed as a runnable computer program, either through symbolic processing or more conventional techniques (e.g., Kirlik, Miller, & Jagacinski, 1989; Payne, Johnson, Bettman, & Coupey, 1990; Thompson, Johnson, & Moen, 1983; Woods, Roth, & Pople, 1987). The cognitive simulation can be stimulated by inputs from a domain scenario to generate model behavior which can be compared to observed human behavior for the same scenario. While cognitive simulation has a number of problematic features, it does provide rigor by having specific processing mechanisms and by producing the model behavior which can be compared/tested against empirical data in specific cases. Cognitive simulation technique is only a tool to help elucidate the nature and basis for information-processing strategies that are relevant to the demands and resources available in naturally occurring decision situations. The importance of context and tacit knowledge in these situations is a challenge to this technique for formalizing models.

A second weakness is that the research base is limited. Many of the studies depend on ethnographic designs, which are less accepted in behavioral research than more rigorous laboratory designs. Moreover, the cost of these ethnographic studies is considerably greater than most laboratory studies. It seems likely that both the distrust of the methods and the difficulty of conducting the studies will restrict future research. But these barriers are eroding as more researchers innovate methodologically to make progress on the interesting and hard questions of decision behavior.

Third, we have not yet seen much in the way of application of these models to improve decision support or decision training. It seems as if the models should lead to successful applications—we will have to see if these emerge.

COMPARISONS BETWEEN NATURALISTIC DECISION-MAKING STRATEGIES AND COGNITIVE PROCESSES

It is essential that the strategies described in this book be tied in to advances in different areas of cognitive science. In this section we identify some of these linkages.

Situated Cognition

This modeling trend (Agre, 1988; Brown, Collins, & Duguid, 1989; Clancey, 1989; Suchman, 1987; Winograd, 1987) also recognizes the power of action in cognition and goes on to consider both the role of cognitive artifacts and the distribution of cognition across multiple people and machines which occur in everyday situations.

Problem Solving

The models in Section B are related as closely to problem solving as to classical decision theory. One avenue that has opened up involves research in artificial intelligence, where researchers have discovered that dynamic situations and the other factors on Orasanu's and Connolly's list require a shift in reasoning capabilities in order to achieve adequate autonomous machine performance. As a result, they have begun to develop specific reasoning mechanisms that function in evolving situations, that adapt/repair plans, and that reason in disturbance management situations (e.g., Dvorak & Kuipers, 1989; Marks, Hammond, & Converse, 1989). This work, while not directly psychological, may suggest modeling concepts for human decision behavior. Intelligent systems have inherent limitations, but if this work generates useful findings we want to take advantage of them.

There is a large body of work derived from a memory and problem-solving point of view which would claim to model the observed behavior in everyday settings, most notably, production system-based models such as John Anderson's model of skill acquisition (Anderson, 1987) and Allen Newell's (Laird, Rosenbloom, & Newell, 1987) unified theory of cognition as defined in the Space Operations Automation and Robotics (SOAR) system architecture.

First, both of these models feature a pattern recognition process within the cognitive architecture. That is, they can be seen as "recognition-driven." The SOAR architecture includes specification of how processing is driven by aspects of the situation. Impasses in the recognition process trigger the creation of a new subgoal and problem space search relative to that subgoal. Thus, SOAR can be thought of as an "impasse-driven" model of cognitive activities. Second, both models attempt to deal with the retrieval/control problem that derives from having large numbers of potentially recognizable patterns. Third, they both provide mechanisms for switching from a more pattern-driven "proceduralized" or "compiled" mode of cognition to a more deliberative mode.

Expertise

Changing views on the important properties of decision situations and on the activities of people in those situations should lead us to approach expertise and skill acquisition in new ways which emphasize perceptual learning, the acquisition of perceptual skills, and knowledge structures that support the observed flexibility of experts (cf., e.g., Spiro, Coulson, Feltovich, & Anderson, 1988). There has also been interesting recent work on informal reasoning (e.g., Voss, Perkins, & Segal, 1990). Collins and Michalski (1989) studied strategies people use to draw inferences in areas where their knowledge is incomplete.

Use of Cognitive Tools

Future model development will include as a fundamental element an account of how cognitive tools or artifacts affect information-processing strategies and performance. As a result, models of naturalistic decision making will need to develop a theoretical framework or language for describing cognitive tools independent of the languages of implementation technologies (e.g., tiled versus overlapping windows). People in naturally occurring settings fundamentally use, adapt, and create information processing and decision tools to get their job accomplished (e.g., Cook, Woods, & Howie, 1990; Hutchins, 1989). Thus, a fundamental part of understanding decision making is understanding the role cognitive tools and artifacts play in cognitive work (Norman, 1990).

Classical Decision Theory

Some of the authors of chapters in this book treat naturalistic and classical decision theories as antagonistic, criticizing the limits of classical decision theory and showing little interest in the research generated by the classical tradition. Other authors are more conciliatory, appreciating the effort that has gone into classical decision theory over the past few decades and recognizing the value of this research within the boundaries where it is relevant.

Reviewers of this book have also been divided. Some have criticized the chapters for beating a dead horse, since "everyone knows that subjective expected utilities and the like have been abandoned as serious topics for a long time." Other reviewers took the opposite position, that a vital field of research was being unnecessarily pilloried. To these reviewers, the criticism of classical decision making was a radical and unjustified step, and that it made little sense to abandon a research path that showed steady progress in favor of a different approach that seems to be far out of the mainstream.

To us, it is classical decision theory that is radical, not models of naturalistic decision making. Our position is that people use their experience when they can, don't do more work than they have to, and so forth. In contrast, classical decision theory has made daring assertions about human fallibility, about ways of developing normative models, about exciting techniques for prescriptive guidance. If these approaches had been able to develop wider applications, the potential power was enormous. The decision strategies described in Section B may represent a kind of backtracking from the ambitious position of classical decision theory to find new avenues forward. As we learn more about the boundary conditions for different decision strategies, it will become clearer how to interrelate the two approaches.

Another criticism directed at some chapters has been that the authors collapse together concepts of decision analysis, multiattribute utility theory, and Bayesian statistics into the category "classical decision theory." To researchers in these traditions, the distinctions between them are very clear. However, to people outside this tradition, the different approaches bear a strong family resemblance in terms of being reductionist, componential, highly analytical prescriptive methods of decision making.

Still another issue is whether this research in naturalistic decision making is actually very different from prior work. As we discussed earlier, in comparison to the ideas about nonanalytic decision making presented by Beach and Mitchell (1978), the work described in this book is quite different. But at the same time, Beach and Mitchell were sensitive to how limited their understanding of nonanalytic strategies was. In the same article, Beach and Mitchell noted that "habit" was a nonanalytic strategy that offered some clear advantages in enabling decision makers to use experience. So Beach and Mitchell did have a sense of what was needed even if they weren't able to provide a description. The contingency model presented by Beach and Mitchell and by Payne (1976, 1982) was a useful perspective that helped researchers to formulate noncompensatory decision models as an alternative to the classical compensatory models. Unfortunately, even these noncompensatory models have been primarily studied in laboratory situations, and have generally ignored the role of experience. Therefore, there are ways that the naturalistic decision research does follow from earlier lines of inquiries, and ways in which it departs from those lines.

NEXT STEPS

It appears that naturalistic decision research has good potential for building on its accomplishments. We look for progress in three areas.

First, the decision models must develop sufficient structure to allow hypothesis testing. This may require expansion in several ways—more carefully worked out models of the internal psychological processes, and more clearly worked out models of the environments that constrain the psychological processes. At the current stage of development, our models of decision making in natural settings are as much about developing a cognitive language for describing the task environment as about specific internal psychological mechanisms. Models of decision tasks cannot be pursued independent from understanding the psychological processes that occur in those tasks; the two are mutually constrained (Woods, 1988).

Second, researchers must develop improved methods. This will include better procedures for collecting and analyzing field observations to provide evidence of reliability and validity. We must learn how to define the environmental conditions to allow interpretation of the data. It will also include strategies for more controlled observations using simulations. The most important criterion for simulation research would be whether experienced decision makers take the simulation scenarios seriously. If so, then such research can be an effective extension of field observation studies.

Third, attempts are needed to apply the findings of naturalistic studies. Can we define strategies for training decision making, and will these differ from traditional training requirements? Can the research generate concepts of decision support that have not already been considered and examined? It is easy to say that this approach seems useful, but the hard task is to demonstrate applications. We have been studying and modeling decision making in action. The challenge is to put our models and methods into action as well.

KEY POINTS

- NDM can point to several accomplishments:
  — Highlighting the role of experience in decision making
  — Placing emphasis on situation assessment as part of decision processes
  — Formulating a set of descriptive models emphasizing competency rather than dysfunctions
  — Developing ethnographic methods for field research
- Weaknesses of NDM include:
  — Difficulty of testing the models
  — Limited rigor of the supporting research
  — Need to demonstrate applied value
- Linkages between NDM and topics in cognitive psychology:
  — Situated cognition
  — Problem solving
  — Expertise
  — Use of cognitive tools
  — Classical decision theory

References

Abelson, R. P. (1976). Script processing in attitude formation and decision-making. In S. J. Carrol & J. W. Paine (Eds.), *Cognition and social behavior*. Hillsdale, NJ: Erlbaum.

Abelson, R. P., & Levi, A. (1985). Decision making and decision theory. In G. Lindzey & E. Aronson (Eds.), *Handbook of social psychology* (3rd ed., Vol. 1, pp. 231–309). New York: Random House.

Adelman, L. (1981). The influence of formal, substantive and contextual task properties on the relative effectiveness of different forms of feedback in multiple-cue probability learning tasks. *Organizational Behavior and Human Performance, 27*, 423–442.

Adelson, B. (1981). Problem solving and the development of abstract categories in programming languages. *Memory and Cognition, 9*, 422–433.

Agre, P. (1988). *The dynamic structure of everyday life* (Tech. Rep.). Unpublished doctoral dissertation. Michigan Institute of Technology, Detroit, MI.

Alemi, F. (1986). Explicated models constructed under time pressure: Utility modeling versus process tracing. *Organizational Behavior & Human Decision Processes, 38*, 133–140.

Alexander, E. R. (1979). The design of alternatives in organizational contexts: A pilot study. *Administration Science Quarterly, 24*, 382–404.

Allais, M. (1953). Le comportment de l'homme rationnel devant le risque: Critique des postulats et axioms de l'écol américaine. *Econometrica, 21*, 503–546.

Allais, M. (1979). The foundations of a positive theory of choice involving risk and a criticism of the postulates and axioms of the American School. In M. Allais & O. Hagen (Eds.), *Expected utility hypothesis and the Allais paradox*. Dordrecht: Reidel. (Original work published 1953).

Allard, F., & Burnett, N. (1985). Skill in sport. *Canadian Journal of Psychology, 39*, 294–312.

Amalberti, R., & Deblon, F. (1989). Cognitive modelling of fighter aircraft's process control: A step towards an intelligent on-board assistance system. *International Journal of Man-Machine Studies*.

Anderson, C. A., Lepper, M. R., & Ross, L. (1980). Perseverance of social theories: The role of explanation in the persistence of discredited information. *Journal of Personality and Social Psychology, 39*, 1037–1049.

Anderson, J. R. (1982). Acquisition of cognitive skill. *Psychological Review*, *89*(4), 364–406.

Anderson, J. R. (1983). *The architecture of cognition*. Cambridge, MA: Harvard University Press.

Anderson, J. R. (1985). *Skill acquisition: Compilation of weak-method solutions* (Tech. Rep. No. ONR-85–1). Pittsburgh, PA: Carnegie-Mellon University.

Anderson, J. R. (1987). Skill acquisition: Compilation of weak-method problem solutions. *Psychological Review*, *94*, 192–210.

Anderson, J. R. (1990). *The adaptive character of thought*. Hillsdale, NJ: Erlbaum.

Anderson, N. H. (1970). Functional measurement and psychophysical judgment. *Psychological Review*, 77, 153–170.

Anderson, N. H. (1974). Cognitive algebra: Integration theory applied to social attribution. In L. Berkowitz (Ed.), *Advances in experimental social psychology* (Vol. 7). New York: Academic Press.

Anderson, N. H. (1981). *Foundations of information integration theory*. New York: Academic Press.

Anderson, N. H. (1982). *Methods of information integration theory*. New York: Academic Press.

Anderson, N. H. (1986). A cognitive theory of judgment and decision. In B. Brehmer, H. Jungermann, P. Lourens, & G. Sevón (Eds.), *New directions in research on decision making*. Amsterdam: Elsevier.

Anderson, P. A. (1983). Decision-making by objection and the Cuban Missile Crisis. *Administrative Science Quarterly*, *28*, 201–222.

Anderson, T. H., & Armbruster, B. B. (1986). Readable textbooks, or, Selecting a textbook is not like buying a pair of shoes. In J. Orasanu (Ed.), *Reading comprehension: From research to practice* (pp. 151–162). Hillsdale, NJ: Erlbaum.

Andriole, S. J. (Ed.). (1986). *Microcomputer decision support systems*. Wellesley, MA: QED Information Systems.

Andriole, S., Ehrhart, L., & Aiken, P. (1989). Group decision support system prototypes for army theater planning and counter-terrorism crisis management. *Symposium on Command-and-Control Research Proceedings*, pp. 272–284.

AP (Associated Press). (1990, March 21). Miscommunication puts satellite adrift in low, useless orbit. *Dayton Daily News*, p. 12-A.

Argyris, C., Putnam, R., & Smith, D. M. (1985). *Action science*. San Francisco: Jossey-Bass.

Arkes, H. R., & Hammond, K. R. (1986). *Judgment and decision making: An interdisciplinary reader*. Cambridge, UK: Cambridge University Press.

Arnold, M. B. (1969). Human emotion and action. In T. Mischel (Ed.), *Human action*. New York: Academic Press.

Axelrod, R. (Ed.). (1976). *Structure of decision: The cognitive maps of political elites*. Princeton, NJ: Princeton University Press.

Bainbridge, L. (1979). Verbal reports as evidence of the process operator's knowledge. *International Journal of Man-Machine Studies*, *11*(4), 411–436.

Baker, L. (1978). Processing temporal relationships in simple stories: Effects of input sequences. *Journal of Verbal Learning and Verbal Behavior, 17*, 559–572.

Balke, W. M., Hammond, K. R., & Meyer, G. D. (1973). An alternate approach to labor-management negotiations. *Administrative Science Quarterly, 18*, 311–327.

Balzer, W. K., Doherty, M. E., & O'Connor, R. O., Jr. (1989). Effects of cognitive feedback on performance, *Psychological Bulletin, 106*, 410–433.

Banaji, M. R., & Crowder, R. G. (1989). The bankruptcy of everyday memory. *American Psychologist, 44*, 1185–1193.

Barclay, S., Beach, L. R., & Braithwaite, W. P. (1971). Normative models in the study of cognition. *Organizational Behavior and Human Performance, 6*, 389–413.

Bar-Hillel, M. (1980). The base rate fallacy in probability judgments. *Acta Psychologica, 44*, 211–233.

Barker, R. G. (1968). *Ecological psychology: Concepts and methods for studying the environment of human behavior*. Stanford, CA: Stanford University Press.

Barker, R. G. (1978). *Habitats, environments, and human behavior*. San Francisco: Jossey-Bass.

Baron, J., Beattie, J., & Hershey J. C. (1988). Heuristics and biases in diagnostic reasoning II. *Congruence, Information, and Certainty, Organizational Behavior and Human Decision Processes, 42*, 88–110.

Baron, R. A., & Byrne, D. (1987). *Social psychology: Understanding human interaction* (5th ed.). Boston: Allyn and Bacon.

Bartlett, F. C. (1932). *Remembering: A study in experimental and social psychology*. Cambridge, UK: Cambridge University Press.

Beach, L. R. (1964). Recognition, assimilation, and identification of objects. *Psychological Monographs, 78*, 22–37.

Beach, L. R. (1990). *Image theory: Decision making in personal and organizational contexts*. Chichester, UK: Wiley.

Beach, L. R., Christensen-Szalanski, J., & Barnes, V. (1987). Assessing human judgment: Has it been done, can it be done, should it be done? In G. Wright & P. Ayton (Eds.), *Judgmental forecasting* (pp. 49–62). New York: Wiley & Sons.

Beach, L. R., & Mitchell, T. R. (1978). A contingency model for the selection of decision strategies. *Academy of Management Review, 3*, 439–449.

Beach, L. R., & Mitchell, T. R. (1987). Image theory: Principles, goals and plans. *Acta Psychologica, 66*, 201–220.

Beach, L. R., & Mitchell, T. R. (1990). Image theory: A behavioral theory of decisions in organizations. In B. M. Staw & L. L. Cummings (Eds.), *Research in organizational behavior* (Vol. 12). Greenwich, CT: JAI Press.

Beach, L. R., Mitchell, T. R., Paluchowski, T. F., & van Zee, E. H. (in press). Image theory: Decision framing and decision deliberation. In F. Heller (Ed.), *Leadership and decision making*. Cambridge, UK: Cambridge University Press.

Beach, L. R., Smith, B., Lundell, J., & Mitchell, T. R. (1988). Image theory:

Descriptive sufficiency of a simple rule for the compatibility test. *Journal of Behavioral Decision Making, 1,* 17–28.

Beach, L. R., & Strom, E. (1989). A toadstool among the mushrooms: Screening decisions and Image Theory's compatibility test. *Acta Psychologica, 72,* 1–12.

Beach, L. R., Vlek, C., & Wagenaar, W. A. (1988). *Models and methods for unique versus repeated decision making* (Leiden Psychological Reports: Experimental Psychology, EP04–88). Leiden, The Netherlands: Leiden University, Psychology Department.

Beatty, M. J. (1988). Increasing students' choice-making consistency: The effect of decision rule-use training. *Communication Education, 37,* 95–105.

Beer, M. (1976). The technology of organization development. In M. Dunnette (Ed.), *Handbook of industrial and organizational psychology* (pp. 937–994). New York: Wiley & Sons.

Behn, R. D., & Vaupel, J. W. (1982). *Quick analysis for busy decision makers.* New York: Basic Books.

Bell, D. E. (1981). Components of risk aversion. In J. P. Brans (Ed.), *Proceedings of the Ninth IFORS Conference* (pp. 235–242). Amsterdam: North-Holland.

Bell, D. E. (1982). Regret in decision making under uncertainty. *Operations Research, 30*(5), 961–981.

Bell, D. E. (1988). Disappointment in decision making under uncertainty. In D. E. Bell, H. Raiffa, & A. Tversky (Eds.), *Decision making: Descriptive, normative, and prescriptive interactions.* New York: Cambridge University Press.

Bell, D. E., Raiffa, H., & Tversky, A. (1988). Descriptive, normative, and prescriptive interactions in decision making. In D. E. Bell, H. Raiffa, & A. Tversky (Eds.), *Decision making: Descriptive, normative, and prescriptive interactions.* New York: Cambridge University Press.

Bellman, R. E., & Giertz, M. (1973). On the analytic formalism of the theory of fuzzy sets. *Information Sciences, 5,* 149–156.

Bennett, W. L., & Feldman, M. (1981). *Reconstructing reality in the courtroom.* New Brunswick, NJ: Rutgers University Press.

Bentham, J. (1970). *An introduction to the principles of morals and legislation.* London: Athlone. (Original work published 1789).

Ben Zur, H., & Breznitz, S. J. (1981). The effect of time pressure on risky choice behavior. *Acta Psychologica, 47,* 89–104.

Berkeley, D., & Humphreys, P. (1982). Structuring decision problems and the 'bias heuristic.' *Acta Psychologica, 50,* 201–252.

Berliner, H., Goetsch, G., Campbell, M., & Ebeling, C. (1990). Measuring the performance potential of chess programs. *Artificial Intelligence, 43,* 7–20.

Berry, D. C., & Broadbent, D. E. (1984). On the relationship between task performance and associated verbalizable knowledge. *Quarterly Journal of Experimental Psychology, 36*(A), 209–231.

Beyth-Marom, R., & Fischhoff, B. (1977). *Direct measures of availability and judgments of category frequency* (Tech. Rep. No. PTR-1042–77–3). Eugene, OR: Decision Research.

Biel, A., & Montgomery, H. (1989). Scenario analysis and energy politics: the disclosure of causal structures in decision making. In H. Montgomery & O. Svenson (Eds.), *Process and structure in human decision making* (pp. 243–260). Chichester, UK: Wiley.

Birnbaum, M. H. (1983). Base rates in Bayesian inference: Signal detection analysis of the cab problem. *American Journal of Psychology, 96*(1), 85–94.

Birnbaum, M. H., & Mellers, B. A. (1983). Bayesian inference: Combining base rates with opinions of sources who vary in credibility. *Journal of Personality and Social Psychology, 45*, 792–804.

Boyce, W. D., & Jensen, L. C. (1978). *Moral reasoning.* Lincoln, NE: University of Nebraska Press.

Bransford, J. D., & Franks, J. J. (1971). The abstraction of linguistic ideas. *Cognitive Psychology, 2*, 331–350.

Bransford, J., Sherwood, R., Vye, N., & Rieser, J. (1986). Teaching thinking and problem solving: Research foundations. *American Psychologist, 41*, 1078–1089.

Brehmer, B. (1979). Preliminaries to a psychology of inference. *Scandinavian Journal of Psychology, 20*, 193–210.

Brehmer, B. (1981). Models of diagnostic judgments. In J. Rasmussen & W. B. Rouse (Eds.), *Human detection and diagnosis of system failures* (pp. 231–241). New York: Plenum Press.

Brehmer, B. (1984). Brunswikian psychology in the 1990's. In K. M. J. Lagerspetz & P. Niemi (Eds.), *Psychology in the 1990's* (pp. 383–398). Amsterdam: Elsevier.

Brehmer, B. (1990). Strategies in real-time dynamic decision making. In R. Hogarth (Ed.), *Insights in decision making: A tribute to Hillel J. Einhorn* (pp. 262–279). Chicago: University of Chicago Press.

Brehmer, B., & Joyce, C. R. B. (Eds.). (1988). *Human judgment: The SJT view.* Amsterdam: Elsevier.

Brehmer, B., Jungermann, H., Lourens, P., & Sevon, G. (Eds.). (1986). Introduction. In *New directions in research on decision making* (pp. 1–3). New York: North-Holland.

Bronfenbrenner, U. (1979). *The Ecology of human development: Experiments by nature and design.* Cambridge, MA: Harvard University Press.

Brown, A. L., Campione, J. C., & Day, J. D. (1981). Learning to learn: On training students to learn from texts. *Educational Researcher, 10*, 14–21.

Brown, A. L., & Deloache, J. S. (1978). Skills, plans, and self-regulation. In R. S. Siegler (Ed.), *Children's thinking: What develops?* Hillsdale, NJ: Erlbaum.

Brown, J. S., Collins, A., & Duguid, P. (1989). Situated cognition and the culture of learning. *Educational Research, 18*, 32–42.

Brown, R. V. (1989a). Toward a prescriptive science and technology of decision aiding. *Annals of Operations Research, 19*, 467–483.

Brown, R. V. (1989b). Commentary, on "Implementing Decision Analysis," by H. Thomas. In I. Horowitz (Ed.), *Organization and decision theory.* Norwell, MS: Kluwer Academic Publishers.

Brown, R. V., Kahr, A. S., & Peterson, C. R. (1974). *Decision analysis for the manager.* New York: Holt, Rinehart, and Winston.

Bruggink, G. M. (1985). Uncovering the policy factor in accidents. *Air Line Pilot,* pp. 22–25.

Bruner, J. S. (1957). On perceptual readiness. *Psychological Review, 64,* 123–152.

Brunswik, E. (1934). *Wahrnehmung und gegenstandswelt: Grundlegung einer psychologie vom gegenstand her [Perception and the world of objects: The foundations of a psychology in terms of objects].* Leipzig und Vienna: Deuticke.

Brunswik, E. (1943). Organismic achievement and environmental probability. *Psychological Review, 50,* 255–272.

Brunswik, E. (1952). The conceptual framework of psychology. *International encyclopedia of unified science* (Vol. 1, No. 10, pp. 4–102). Chicago: University of Chicago Press.

Brunswik, E. (1955). Representative design and probabilistic theory in a functional psychology. *Psychological Review, 62,* 193–217.

Brunswik, E. (1956). *Perception and the representative design of psychological experiments* (2nd ed.). Berkeley, CA: University of California Press.

Brunswik, E. (1966). Reasoning as a universal behavior model and a functional differentiation between "perception" and "thinking." In K. Hammond (Ed.), *The psychology of Egon Brunswik* (pp. 487–494). New York: Holt, Rinehart, & Winston.

Bukszar, E., & Connolly, T. (1988). Hindsight bias and strategic choice. Some problems in learning from experience. *Academy of Management Journal, 31,* 628–641.

Calderwood, R., Crandall, B. W., & Baynes, T. H. (1988). *Protocols of expert/novice command decision making during simulated fire ground incidents* (KATR-858-88-02Z). Yellow Springs, OH: Klein Associates, Inc. (Prepared under contract MDA903-85-C-0327 for the U.S. Army Research Institute for the Behavioral and Social Sciences, Alexandria, VA.)

Calderwood, R., Crandall, B. W., & Klein, G. A. (1987). *Expert and novice fire ground command decisions* (KATR-858-(D)-87-02F). Yellow Springs, OH: Klein Associates, Inc.

Calderwood, R., Klein, G. A., & Crandall, B. W. (1988). Time pressure, skill, and move quality in chess. *American Journal of Psychology, 101,* 481–493.

Callan, J. R., Gwynne, J. W., Kelly, R. T., & Feher, B. (1990). Patterns of information use and performance in outer-air battle decision making. *Proceedings of 1990 Symposium on C² Research.* Monterey, CA.

Campbell, D. T., & Fiske, D. W. (1959). Convergent and discriminant validation by the multitrait-multimethod matrix. *Psychological Bulletin, 56,* 81–105.

Cannon-Bowers, J. A., Prince, C., Salas, E., Owens, J. M., Morgan, B. B., Jr., &

Gonos, G. H. (1989, November). *Determining aircrew coordination training effectiveness.* Paper presented at the 11th Annual Meeting of the Interservice/Industry Training Systems Conference, Ft. Worth, TX.

Cannon-Bowers, J. A., & Salas, E. (1990, April). *Cognitive psychology and team training: Shared mental models in complex systems.* Paper presented at the Fourth Annual Meeting of the Society for Industrial and Organizational Psychology, Miami, FL.

Cannon-Bowers, J. A., Salas, E., & Converse, S. (1990). Cognitive psychology and team training: Training shared mental models of complex systems. *Human Factors Society Bulletin, 33*(12), 1–4.

Carbonell, J. R. (1966). A queueing model of many-instrument visual sampling. *IEEE Transactions on Human Factors in Electronics, HFE-4*, 157–164.

Carbonell, J. R., Ward, J. L., & Senders, J. W. (1968). A queueing model of many-instrument visual sampling: Experimental validation. *IEEE Transactions on Man-Machine Systems, MMS-9*(3), 82–87.

Carroll, J. S. (1980). Analyzing decision behavior: The magician's audience. In T. Wallsten (Ed.), *Cognitive processes in choice and decision behavior* (pp. 68–76). Hillsdale, NJ: Erlbaum.

Cascio, W. F. (1978). *Applied psychology in personnel management.* Reston, VA: Reston Publishing Co.

Centor, R. M., Dalton, H. P., & Yates, J. F. (1984). *Are physicians' probability estimates better or worse than regression model estimates?* Paper presented at the Sixth Annual Meeting of the Society for Medical Decision Making, Bethesda, MD.

Chapanis, A., Ochsman, R. B., Parrish, R. N., & Weeks, G. D. (1972). Studies in interactive communication: I. The effects of four communication modes on the behavior of teams during cooperative problem solving. *Human Factors, 14*, 487–509.

Chapman, L. J., & Chapman, J. P. (1969). Illusory correlation as an obstacle to the use of valid diagnostic signs. *Psychological Bulletin, 74*, 271–280.

Chase, W. G., & Simon, H. A. (1973). The mind's eye in chess. In W. G. Chase (Ed.), *Visual information processing.* New York: Academic Press.

Cheng, P. W., & Holyoak, K. J. (1985). Pragmatic reasoning schemas. *Cognitive Psychology, 17*, 391–416.

Cherniak, C. (1986). *Minimal rationality.* Cambridge, MA: MIT Press.

Chi, M. T. H., Feltovich, P. J., & Glaser, R. (1981). Categorization and representation of physics problems by experts and novices. *Cognitive Science, 5*, 121–152.

Chi, M. T. H., Glaser, R., & Farr, M. J. (1988). *The nature of expertise.* Hillsdale, NJ: Erlbaum.

Chi, M. T. H., Glaser, R., & Rees, E. (1982). Expertise in problem solving. In R. Steinberg (Ed.), *Advances in the psychology of human intelligence* (Vol. 1, pp. 7–75). Hillsdale, NJ: Erlbaum.

Chidester, T. R., Kanki, B. G., Foushee, H. C., Dickinson, C. L., & Bowles, S. V. (1990). *Personality factors in flight operations: Volume I. Leadership characteristics and crew performance in a full-mission air transport sim-*

ulation (NASA Tech. Mem. No. 102259). Moffett Field, CA: NASA Ames Research Center.

Chiesi, H., Spilich, G. J., & Voss, J. F. (1979). Acquisition of domain-related information in relation to high and low domain knowledge. *Journal of Verbal Learning and Verbal Behavior, 18*, 257–273.

Choo, G. T. G. (1976). *Training and generalization in assessing probabilities for discrete events* (Tech. Rep. No. 76–5). Uxbridge, UK: Brunel Institute for Organizational and Social Studies.

Christensen-Szalanski, J. J. J. (1978). Problem-solving strategies: A selection mechanism, some implications, and some data. *Organizational Behavior and Human Performance, 22*, 307–323.

Christensen-Szalanski, J. J. J. (1980). A further examination of the selection of problem-solving strategies: The effects of deadlines and analytic aptitudes. *Organizational Behavior and Human Performance, 25*, 107–122.

Christensen-Szalanski, J. J. J. (1986). Improving the practical utility of judgment research. In B. Brehmer, H. Jungermann, P. Lourens, & G. Sevon (Eds.), *New directions for research in judgment and decision literature.* North Holland: Elsevier.

Christensen-Szalanski, J. J. J., & Beach, L. R. (1984). The citation bias: Fad and fashion in the judgment and decision literature. *American Psychologists, 39*, 75–78.

Christensen-Szalanski, J., Beck, D. E., Christensen-Szalanski, C., & Koepsell, T. (1983). Effects of expertise and experience on risk judgments. *Journal of Applied Psychology, 68*, 278–284.

Christensen-Szalanski, J., Boyce, T., Hevrill, H., & Gardner, M. (1987). Informed consent and circumcision: Is more information always better? *Medical Care, 25*, 856–867.

Christensen-Szalanski, J. J. J., & Fobian, C. S. (1988). On the significance of judgment biases. *Medical Decision Making, 8*, 265–267.

Christensen-Szalanski, J. J. J., & Fobian, C. S. (1989). Hindsight: Artifacts and treatment effects. *Medical Decision Making, 9*, 218–219.

Christensen-Szalanski, J., & Willham, C. F. (1991). The hindsight bias: A meta-analysis. *Organizational Behavior and Human Decision Processes, 48*, 147–168.

Cicourel, A. V. (1990). The integration of distributed knowledge in collaborative medical diagnoses. In J. Galegher, R. Kraut, & C. Egido (Eds.), *Intellectual teamwork: Social and technological foundations of cooperative work* (pp. 221–242). Hillsdale, NJ: Erlbaum.

Clancey, W. J. (1988). Acquiring, representing, and evaluating a competence model of diagnostic strategy. In M. T. H. Chi, R. Glaser, & M. J. Farr (Eds.), *The nature of expertise* (pp. 343–418). Hillsdale, NJ: Erlbaum.

Clancey, W. J. (1989). The frame of reference problem in cognitive modeling. *Proceedings of the 11th Annual Conference of the Cognitive Science Society.* Hillsdale, NJ: Erlbaum.

Clancey, W. J., & Letsinger, R. (1981). NEOMYCIN: Reconfiguring a rule-based expert system for application to teaching. *Proceedings of the Seventh International Joint Conference on Artificial Intelligence, 2*, 829–836.

Clancey, W. J., & Shortliffe, E. H. (Eds.). (1984). *Readings in medical artificial intelligence*. Reading, MA: Addison-Wesley.

Cohen, J. (1977). *Statistical power analysis for the behavioral sciences* (rev. ed.). New York: Academic Press.

Cohen, L. J. (1977). *The probable and the provable*. Oxford: Oxford University Press (Clarendon Press).

Cohen, L. J. (1981). Can human irrationality be experimentally demonstrated? *The Behavioral and Brain Sciences, 4*(3), 317–331.

Cohen, L. J. (1983). The controversy about irrationality. *The Behavioral and Brain Sciences, 6*(3), 510–517.

Cohen, M. D., March, J. G., & Olsen, J. P. (1972). A garbage can model of organizational choice. *Administrative Science Quarterly, 17,* 1–25.

Cohen, M. S. (1986). An expert system framework for non-monotonic reasoning about probabilistic assumptions. In L. N. Kanal & J. F. Lemmer (Eds.), *Uncertainty in artificial intelligence: Machine intelligence and pattern recognition* (Vol. 4, pp. 279–293). North Holland: Elsevier.

Cohen, M. S. (1989). Decision making "biases" and support for assumption-based higher-order reasoning. *Proceedings of the Fifth Workshop on Uncertainty in Artificial Intelligence* (pp. 71–80). Windsor, Ontario: Rockwell International.

Cohen, M. S. (1990). *Conflict resolution as a knowledge elicitation technique* (Working Paper). Reston, VA: Decision Science Consortium.

Cohen, M. S., Bromage, R. C., Chinnis, J. O., Jr., Payne, J. W., & Ulvila, J. W. (1982). *A personalized and prescriptive attack planning decision aid* (Tech. Rep. No. 82–4). Falls Church, VA: Decision Science Consortium.

Cohen, M. S., Laskey, K. B., & Tolcott, M. A. (1987). *A personalized and prescriptive decision aid for choice from a database of options* (rev.) (Tech. Rep. No. 87–18). Reston, VA: Decision Science Consortium.

Cohen, M. S., Leddo, J. M., & Tolcott, M. A. (1988). *Cognitive strategies and adaptive aiding principles in submarine command decision making* (Working Paper). Reston, VA: Decision Science Consortium.

Cohen, M. S., Schum, D. A., Freeling, A. N. S., & Chinnis, J. O., Jr. (1985). *On the art and science of hedging a conclusion: Alternative theories of uncertainty in intelligence analysis* (Tech. Rep. No. 84–6). Falls Church, VA: Decision Science Consortium.

Cole, M., & Scribner, S. (1974). *Culture and thought. A psychological introduction*. New York: Wiley.

Collingridge, D. (1982). *Critical decision-making: A new theory of social choice*. London: St. Martin's Press.

Collins, A., & Michalski, R. (1989). The logic of plausible reasoning: A core theory. *Cognitive Science, 13*(1), 1–49.

Connolly, T. (1982). On taking action seriously. In G. R. Ungson & D. N. Braunstein (Eds.), *Decision making: An interdisciplinary inquiry*. Boston: Kent.

Connolly, T. (1988). Hedge-clipping, tree-felling, and the management of ambiguity. In M. B. McCaskey, L. R. Pondy, & H. Thomas, (Eds.), *Managing the challenge of ambiguity and change*. New York: Wiley.

Connolly, T., Jessup, L. M., & Valacich, J. S. (1990). Effects of anonymity and evaluative tone on idea generation in computer-mediated groups. *Management Science, 36,* 689–703.

Connolly, T., & Wagner, W. G. (1988). Decision cycles. In R. L. Cardy, S. M. Puffer, & M. M. Newman (Eds.), *Advances in information processing in organizations* (Vol. 3, pp. 183–205). Greenwich, CT: JAI Press.

Cook, R. I., & Woods, D. D. (1990). *Characterizing the operating room domain* Columbus, OH: Cognitive Systems Engineering Laboratory, The Ohio State University. (CSEL-90-TR-03).

Cook, R. I., Woods, D. D., & Howie, M. B. (1990). The natural history of introducing new information technology into a dynamic high-risk environment. In *Proceedings of the Human Factors Society 34th Annual Meeting.* Santa Monica, CA: Human Factors Society.

Cooke, N. M., & McDonald, J. E. (1987). The application of psychological scaling techniques to knowledge elicitation. *International Journal of Man-Machine Studies, 26,* 553–550.

Cooksey, R. W., Freebody, P., & Bennett, A. (1991). The ecology of spelling: A lens model analysis of spelling errors and student judgments of spelling difficulty. *Reading Psychology, 11,* 293–322..

Coombs, C. H. (1964). *A theory of data.* New York: Wiley.

Coombs, C. H. (1975). Portfolio theory and the measurement of risk. In M. F. Kaplan & S. Schwartz (Eds.), *Human judgment and decision processes.* New York: Academic Press.

Crandall, B., & Calderwood, R. (1989). *Clinical assessment skills of experienced neonatal intensive care nurses.* Yellow Springs, OH: Klein Associates Inc. (Final Report prepared for the National Center for Nursing, NIH under Contract No. 1 R43 NR01911 01).

Crick, F. (1988). *What mad pursuit: A personal view of scientific discovery.* London: Penguin.

CSCW. (1990). *Proceedings of the Conference on Computer-supported Cooperative Work.* New York: Association for Computing Machinery.

Cyert, R. M., & March, J. G. (1963). *A behavioral theory of the firm.* Englewood Cliffs, NJ: Prentice-Hall.

Daft, R. L., & Lengel, R. H. (1986). Organizational information requirements, media richness, and structural design. *Management Science, 32,* 554–571.

Dahlstrand, U., & Montgomery, H. (1984). Information search and evaluative processes in a computer based process tracing study. *Acta Psychologica, 56,* 113–123.

Dalgleish, L. I. (1988). Decision making in child abuse cases: Applications of social judgment theory and signal detection theory. In B. Brehmer & C. R. B. Joyce (Eds.), *Human judgment: The SJT view* (pp. 317–360). Amsterdam: Elsevier.

Daniels, N. (1979). Wide reflective equilibrium and theory acceptance in ethics. *Journal of Philosophy, 76,* 256–282.

Darling, T. A., & Mumpower, J. L. (1990). Modeling cognitive influences on the dynamics of negotiation. In R. H. Sprague (Ed.), *Proceedings of the*

Twenty-Third Annual Hawaii International Conference on System Sciences (Vol. 4, pp. 22–30). Los Alamitos, CA: IEEE Computer Society Press.

Davidson, D., Suppes, P., & Siegel, S. (1957). *Decision making: An experimental approach.* Palo Alto, CA: Stanford University Press.

Davis, J. (1986). Forward. In R. Y. Hirokawa & M. S. Poole (Eds.), *Communication and group decision making* (pp. 7–12). Beverly Hills, CA: Sage.

Davis J. (1973). Group decision and social interaction: A theory of social decision schemes. *Psychological Review, 80,* 97–125.

Davis, J. H., & Stasson, M. F. (1988). Small group performance: Past and present research trends. *Advances in Group Processes, 5,* 245–277.

Dawes, R. M. (1971). A case study of graduate admissions: Application of three principles of human decision making. *American Psychologist, 34,* 571–582.

Dawes, R. M. (1979). The robust beauty of improper linear models in decision making. *American Psychologist, 34,* 571–582.

Dawes, R. M. (1982). The robust beauty of improper linear models in decision making. In D. Kahneman, P. Slovic, & A. Tversky (Eds.), *Judgment under uncertainty: Heuristics and biases* (pp. 391–407). Cambridge, UK: Cambridge University Press.

Dawes, R. M., & Corrigan, B. (1974). Linear models in decision making. *Psychological Bulletin, 81,* 95–106.

Dawkins, R. (1983). Adaptationism was always predictive and needed no defense. *The Behavioral and Brain Sciences, 6*(3), 360–361.

Dawson, N. V. (1989). Comments on a commentary. *Medical Decision Making, 9,* 68–70.

Dawson, N. V., Arkes, H. R., Siciliano, C., Blinkhorn, R., Lakshmanan, M., & Petrelli, M. (1988). Hindsight bias. An impediment to accurate probability estimation in clinicopathologic conferences. *Medical Decision Making, 8,* 259–264.

de Finetti, B. (1964). Foresight: Its logical laws, its subjective sources. English translation. In H. E. Kybert, Jr. & H. E. Smokler (Eds.), *Studies in subjective probability.* New York: Wiley. (Original work published 1937).

de Groot, A. D. (1965/1978). *Thought and choice in chess* (2nd ed.). New York: Mouton. (Original work published 1946.)

deKeyser, V. (1990). Why field studies? In M. Helander (Ed.), *Human factors in design for manufacturability and process planning.* International Ergonomics Association.

deKleer, J. (1986). An assumption-based truth maintenance system. *Artificial Intelligence, 28,* 127–162.

deKleer, J., & Brown, J. S. (1983). Assumptions and ambiguities in mechanistic mental models. In D. Gentner & A. L. Stevens (Eds.), *Mental models.* Hillsdale, NJ: Erlbaum.

Demael, J., & Levis, A. (1989). On the generation of variable structure distributed architectures for C³ systems. *Symposium on Command-and-Control Research Proceedings 1989,* 124–131.

Dennett, D. C. (1983). Intentional systems in cognitive ethology: The "Panglossian paradigm" defended. *The Behavioral and Brain Sciences, 6*(3), 343–355.

DeSanctis, G., & Gallupe, R. (1985, Winter). Group decision support systems: A new frontier. *Database,* pp. 3–10.

DeStephen, R. S. (1983, May). High and low consensus groups: A content and relational interaction analysis. *Small Group Behavior,* pp. 143–162.

Dewey, J. (1933). *How we think.* Boston: D. C. Heath.

Dewey, J., & Tufts, J. H. (1908). *Ethics.* New York: Holt.

Dierolf, D. (1990). *Dimensions of group decision making.* Unpublished Institute for Defense Analysis report for the Air Force Human Resources Laboratory, Human Factors and Logistics Division, Wright-Patterson, AFB, OH.

Doherty, M. E. (1990). Discussion of papers by Hammond and Brehmer. In R. Hogarth (Ed.), *Insights in decision making: A tribute to Hillel J. Einhorn.* Chicago: University of Chicago Press.

Doherty, M. E., & Mynatt, C. R. (1986). The magic number one. In D. R. Moates & R. Butrick (Eds.), *Proceedings of the Ohio University Interdisciplinary Inference Conference* (pp. 221–230).

Donaldson, G., & Lorsch, J. W. (1983). *Decision making at the top.* New York: Basic Books.

Dowie, J., & Elstein, A. (1988). *Professional judgment: A reader in clinical decision making.* Cambridge, UK: Cambridge University Press.

Doyle, J. (1979). A truth maintenance system. *Artificial Intelligence, 12*(3), 231–272.

Driskell, J. E. (1984. August). *Training for a hostile environment.* Paper presented at the Annual Meeting of the American Psychological Association, Toronto, Canada.

Driskell, J. E., Hogan, R., & Salas, E. (1987). *Stress and human performance* (Tech. Rep. No. TR86–002). Orlando, FL: Naval Training Systems Center.

Driskell, J. E., & Salas, E. (1991). Overcoming the effects of stress on military performance: Human factors design, training, and selection strategies. In R. Gal & A. D. Mangelsdorff (Eds.), *Handbook of military psychology.* London: Wiley.

Driskell, J. E., & Salas, E. (1992). Can you study real teams in contrived settings? The value of small group research to understanding teams. In R. Swezey & E. Salas (Eds.), *Teams: Their training and performance* (pp. 101–126). Norwood, NJ: Ablex Publishing Corp.

Duffy, L. (1990a, August). *Issues and biases in team decision making.* Paper presented at the American Psychological Association Annual Conference, Boston.

Duffy, L. (1990b, September). Team decision making and group decision support systems. *Proceedings of the 1990 Symposium on Command-and-Control Research* (pp. 335–339). McLean, VA: Science Applications International Corporation.

Duhem, P. (1962). *The aim and structure of physical theory.* New York: Atheneum. (Original work published 1914).

Duncan, K. (1981). Training for fault diagnosis in industrial process plants. In J. Rasmussen & W. B. Rouse (Eds.), *Human detection and diagnosis of system failures*. New York: Plenum Press.

Duncan, R. (1972). Characteristics of organizational environments and perceived environmental uncertainty. *Administrative Science Quarterly, 17*, 313–327.

Dvorak, D., & Kuipers, B. (1989). Model-based monitoring of dynamic systems. *Proceedings of the 11th International Joint Conference on Artificial Intelligence.*

Dyer, J. (1984a). *State-of-the-art review on team training and performance.* Fort Benning, GA: Army Research Institute Field Unit.

Dyer, J. L. (1984b). Team research and team training: A state of the art review. In F. Muckler (Ed.), *Human factors review*. Santa Monica, CA: The Human Factors Society.

Ebbesen, E. G., & Konecni, V. J. (1980). On the external validity of decision-making research: What do we know about decisions in the real world? In T. Wallsten (Ed.), *Cognitive processes in choice and decision behavior*. Hillsdale, NJ: Erlbaum.

Eddy, D. (1989). *Selected team performance measures in a C^3 environment: An annotated bibliography* (Tech. Rep. No. USAFSAM-TR-87–25). Brooks AFB, TX: USAF School of Aerospace Medicine, Human Systems Division (AFSC).

Edwards, W. (1954). The theory of decision making. *Psychological Bulletin, 51*, 380–417.

Edwards, W. (1968). Conservatism in human information processing. In B. Kleinmentz (Ed.), *Formal representation of human judgment*. New York: Wiley.

Edwards, W., & Newman, J. R. (1982). *Multiattribute evaluation*. Beverly Hills, CA: Sage.

Einhorn, H. J. (1980). Learning from experience and suboptimal rules in decision making. In T.S. Wallsten (Ed.), *Cognitive processes in choice and decision behavior*. Hillsdale, NJ: Erlbaum.

Einhorn, H. J., & Hogarth, R. M. (1981). Behavioral decision theory: Processes of judgment and choice. *Annual Review of Psychology, 32*, 53–88.

Einhorn, H. J., & Hogarth, R. M. (1986). Judging probable cause. *Psychological Bulletin, 99*, 3–19.

Einhorn, H. J., Kleinmuntz, D. N., & Kleinmuntz, B. (1979). Linear regression and process-tracing models of judgment. *Psychological Review, 86*, 465–485.

Ellsberg, D. (1961). Risk, ambiguity, and the savage axioms. *Quarterly Journal of Economics, 75*, 643–669.

Elstein, A. S. (1989). On the clinical significance of hindsight bias. *Medical Decision Making, 9*, 70.

Elstein, A. S., Shulman, L. S., & Sprafka, S. A. (1978). *Medical problem solving: An analysis of clinical reasoning*. Cambridge, MA: Harvard University Press.

Elster, J. (1977). *Ulysses and the sirens: Studies in rationality and irrationality.* Cambridge, MA: Cambridge University Press.

Ericsson, K. A., & Simon, H. A. (1980). Verbal reports as data. *Psychological Review, 87*(3), 215–251.

Ericsson, K. A., & Simon, H. A. (1984). *Protocol analysis: Verbal reports as data.* Cambridge, MA: MIT Press.

Evans, J. St. B. T. (1989). *Bias in human reasoning: Causes and consequences.* London: Erlbaum.

Feinstein, A. R. (1971). Clinical biostatistics–IX: How do we measure 'safety' and 'efficacy'? *Clinical Pharmacology and Therapeutics, 12*, 544–558.

Fidler, E. J. (1983). The reliability and validity of concurrent, retrospective, and interpretive verbal reports: An experimental study. In P. Humphreys, O. Svenson, & A. Vari (Eds.), *Analyzing and aiding decision processes.* Amsterdam: North-Holland.

Finley, Rheinlander, Thompson, & Sullivan (1972).

Fisch, H.-U., Hammond, K. R., Joyce, C. R. B., & O'Reilly, M. (1981). An experimental study of the clinical judgment of general physicians in evaluating and prescribing for depression. *British Journal of Psychiatry, 138*, 100–109.

Fischhoff, B. (1982). Debiasing. In D. Kahneman, P. Slovic, & A. Tversky (Eds.), *Judgment under uncertainty: Heuristics and biases* (pp. 422–444). New York: Cambridge University Press.

Fischhoff, B. (1983). Predicting frames. *Journal of Experimental Psychology: Learning, Memory, and Cognition, 9*, 113–116.

Fischhoff, B., & Beyth-Marom, R. (1983). Hypothesis evaluation from a Bayesian perspective. *Psychological Review, 90*, 239–260.

Fischhoff, B., & Goitein, B. (1984). Informal use of formal models. *Academy of Management Review, 9*, 505–512.

Fischhoff, B., Goitein, B., & Shapira, Z. (1982). The experienced utility of expected utility approaches. In N. Feather (Ed.), *Expectations and actions: Expectancy value models in psychology.* Hillsdale, NJ: Erlbaum.

Fischhoff, B., & Johnson, S. (1990). The possibility of distributed decision making. In National Research Council (Ed.), *Distributed decision making: Report of a workshop*, Washington, DC: National Academy Press.

Fischhoff, B., Slovic, P., & Lichtenstein, S. (1979). Subjective sensitivity analysis. *Organizational Behavior and Human Performance, 23*, 339–359.

Fitts, P. M., & Posner, M. I. (1967). *Human performance.* Belmont, CA: Brooks Cole.

Flower, L., & Hayes, J. R. (1980). The cognition of discovery: Defining a rhetorical problem. *College Composition and Communication, 31*, 21–32.

Ford, J. K., Schmitt, N., Schechtman, S. L., Hults, B. M., & Doherty, M. L. (1989). Process tracing methods: Contributions, problems, and neglected research questions. *Organizational Behavior and Human Decision Processes, 43*, 75–117.

Foushee, H. C. (1984). Dyads and triads at 35,000 feet: Factors affecting group process and aircrew performance. *American Psychologist, 39*, 885–893.

Foushee, H. C., & Helmreich, R. L. (1988). Group interaction and flight crew performance. In E. L. Wiener & D. C. Nagel (Eds.), *Human factors in aviation* (pp. 189–227). San Diego: Academic Press.

Foushee, H. C., Lauber, J. K., Baetge, M. M., & Acomb, D. B. (1986). *Crew factors in flight operations: III. The operational significance of exposure to short-haul air transport operations* (NASA Tech. Memo 88322). Mountain View, CA: NASA.

French, S. (1978). *Updating of belief in the light of someone else's opinion.* Manchester, UK: Department of Decision Theory, University of Manchester.

Friedman, L., Howell, W. C., & Jensen, C. R. (1985). Diagnostic judgment as a function of the preprocessing of evidence. *Human Factors, 27,* 665–673.

Funder, D. C. (1987). Errors and mistakes. Evaluating the accuracy of social judgment. *Psychological Bulletin, 101,* 75–90.

Gabrielcik, A., & Fazio, R. H. (1983). Priming and frequency estimation: A strict test of the availability heuristic. *Personality and Social Psychology Bulletin, 10,* 85–89.

Gagne, E., Weidemann, C., Bell, N. S., & Anders, T. D. (1984). Training thirteen-year-olds to elaborate while studying text. *Human Learning, 3,* 281–294.

Galegher, J. (1990). Intellectual teamwork and information technology: The role of information systems in collaborative intellectual work. In J. Carroll (Ed.), *Applied social psychology in organizations* (pp. 193–216). Hillsdale, NJ: Erlbaum.

Galegher, J., & Kraut, R. E. (1990). Technology for intellectual teamwork: Perspectives on research and design. In J. Galegher, R. E. Kraut, & C. Egido (Eds.), *Intellectual teamwork: Social and technological foundations of cooperative work* (pp. 1–21). Hillsdale, NJ: Erlbaum.

Gardenfors, P., & Sahlin, N. (1982). Unreliable probabilities, risk taking and decision making. *Synthese, 53.*

Garner, W. R., Hake, H. W., & Eriksen, C. W. (1956). Operationism and the concept of perception. *Psychological Review, 63,* 149–159.

Garvill, J., Gärling, T., Lindberg, E., Montgomery, H., & Svenson, O. (1990). *In search of evidence for dominance structuring in decision making* (Umeå Psychological Reports No. 188). Umeå, Sweden: University of Umeå, Department of Psychology.

Gavelek, J., & Raphael, T. E. (1985). Metacognition, instruction, and the role of questioning activities. In D. L. Forrest-Pressley, G. E. MacKinnon, & T. G. Waller (Eds.), *Metacognition, cognition, and human performance: Vol. 2—Instructional practices* (pp. 103–136). New York: Academic Press.

Gentner, D., & Stevens, A. L. (Eds.). (1983). *Mental models.* Hillsdale, NJ: Erlbaum.

Gersick, C. J. G. (1988). Time and transition in work teams: Toward a new model of group development. *Academy of Management Journal, 31,* 9–41.

Gersick, C. J. G. (1989). Marking time: Predictable transitions in task groups. *Academy of Management Journal, 32,* 274–309.

Gersick, C. J. G., & Hackman, J. R. (1990). Habitual routines in task-performing groups. *Organizational Behavior and Human Decision Processes, 47*, 65–97.

Gettys, C. F. (1983). *Research and theory on predecision processes* (Tech. Rep. No. 11–30–83). Norman, OK: University of Oklahoma, Decision Processes Laboratory.

Gettys, C. F., Fisher, S. D., & Mehle, T. (1978). *Hypothesis generation and plausibility assessment* (Tech. Rep. No. 15–10–78). Norman, OK: University of Oklahoma, Decision Process Laboratory.

Gibson, J. J. (1957). Survival in a world of probable objects [Review of *Perception and the representative design of psychological experiments*]. *Contemporary Psychology, 2*, 33–35.

Gibson, J. J. (1966). *The senses considered as perceptual systems.* Boston: Houghton-Mifflin.

Gibson, J. J. (1979). *The ecological approach to visual perception.* Boston: Houghton-Mifflin.

Gigerenzer, G. (1987). Survival of the fittest probabilist: Brunswik, Thurstone, and the two disciplines of psychology. In L. Kruger, G. Gigerenzer, & M. S. Morgan (Eds.), *The probabilistic revolution: Vol. 2. Ideas in the sciences* (pp. 49–72). Cambridge, MA: MIT Press.

Gigerenzer, G., Hell, W., & Blank, H. (1988). Presentation and content: The use of base rates as a continuous variable. *Journal of Experimental Psychology: Human Perception and Performance, 14*, 513–525.

Gigerenzer, G., & Murray, D. J. (1987). *Cognition as intuitive statistics.* Hillsdale, NJ: Erlbaum.

Gillis, J., & Schneider, C. (1966). The historical preconditions of representative design. In K. Hammond (Ed.), *The psychology of Egon Brunswik* (pp. 204–236). New York: Holt, Rinehart, & Winston.

Gingras, L., & McLean, E. R. (1982). Designers and users of information systems: A study in differing profiles. *Proceedings of the 3rd International Conference on Information Systems,* pp. 169–181.

Glaser, R. (1984). Education and knowledge: The role of thinking. *American Psychologist, 39*, 93–104.

Glaser, R. (1989). Expertise and learning: How do we think about instructional processes now that we have discovered knowledge structures? In D. Klahr & K. Kotovsky (Eds.), *Complex information processing: The impact of Herbert A. Simon* (pp. 269–282). Hillsdale, NJ: Erlbaum.

Glaser, R., Lesgold, A., Lajoie, S., Eastman, R., Greenberg, L., Logan, D., Magone, M., Weiner, A., Wolf, R., & Yengo, L. (1985). *Cognitive task analysis to enhance technical skills training and assessment.* Pittsburgh: University of Pittsburgh, Learning Research and Development Center.

Glickman, A. S., Zimmer, S., Montero, R. C., Guerette, P. J., Campbell, W. J., Morgan, B. B., Jr., & Salas, E. (1987). *The evolution of team skills: An empirical assessment with implications for training* (Tech. Rep. No. NTSC87–016). Orlando, FL: Naval Training Systems Center.

Glymour, C. (1980). *Theory and evidence.* Princeton, NJ: Princeton University Press.

Glymour, C., Scheines, R., Spirtes, P., & Kelly, K. (1987). *Discovering causal structure: Artificial intelligence, philosophy of science, and statistical modeling.* New York: Academic Press.

Goguen, J., Linde, C., & Murphy, M. (1986). *Crew communication as a factor in aviation accidents* (NASA Tech. Memo 88254). Mountain View, CA: NASA.

Goldberg, L. R. (1968). Simple models or simple processes? Some research on clinical judgments. *American Psychologist, 23,* 483–496.

Goodman, N. (1965). *Fact, fiction and forecast* (2nd ed.). Indianapolis, IN: Bobbs-Merrill.

Gopher, D., Weil, M., Bareket, T., & Caspi, S. (1988a). *Fidelity of task structure as a guiding principle in the development of skill trainers based upon complex computer games.* Paper presented at the Annual Meeting of the Human Factors Society, Anaheim, CA.

Gopher, D., Weil, M., Bareket, T., & Caspi, S. (1988b, August). *Using complex computer games as task simulators in the training of flight skills.* Paper presented at the IEEE International Conference on Systems, Man, & Cybernetics, China.

Gore, W. J. (1964). *Administrative decision making: A heuristic model.* New York: Wiley.

Gould, S. J., & Lewontin, R. (1979). The spandrels of San Marco and the Panglossian paradigm: A critique of the adaptationist programme. *Proceedings of the Royal Society (London), B205,* 581–598.

Gowin, R., & Novak, J. D. (1984). *Learning how to learn.* New York: Cambridge University Press.

Greenwald, A. G., Pratkanis, A. R., Leippe, M. R., & Baumgardner, M. H. (1986). Under what conditions does theory obstruct research progress? *Psychological Review, 93,* 216–229.

Grice, H. P. (1975). Logic and conversation. In D. Davidson & G. Harman (Eds.), *The logic of grammar.* Encino, CA: Dickenson.

Groen, G. J., & Patel, V. L. (1988). The relationship between comprehension and reasoning in medical expertise. In M. T. H. Chi, R. Glaser, & M. J. Farr (Eds.), *The nature of expertise* (pp. 287–310). Hillsdale, NJ: Erlbaum.

Hackman, J. R. (1985). The design of work teams. In J. W. Lorsch (Ed.), *Handbook of organizational behavior.* Englewood Cliffs, NJ: Prentice-Hall.

Hackman, J. R. (1986). Group-level issues in the design and training of cockpit crews. *Cockpit resource management training* (NASA Conference Publication 2455). Moffett Field, CA: NASA-Ames Research Center.

Hackman, J. R. (1988, February). *Resource management training and cockpit crew coordination.* Invited address to the General Flight Crew Training Meeting, International Air Transport Association, Washington, DC.

Hackman, J. R. (1990). *Groups that work (and those that don't).* San Francisco: Jossey-Bass.

Hadamard, J. L. (1945). *The psychology of invention in the mathematical field.* Princeton, NJ: Princeton University Press.

Hall, E. R., & Rizzo, W. A. (1975). *An assessment of U. S. Navy tactical team training* (TAEG Report No. 18). Orlando, FL: Training Analysis and Evaluation Group.

Hamm, R. M. (1988). Moment-by-moment variation in experts' analytic and intuitive cognitive activity. *IEEE Transactions on Systems, Man, and Cybernetics, SMC-18*(5), 757–776.

Hammond, K. R. (1955). Probabilistic functionalism and the clinical method. *Psychological Review, 62*, 255–262.

Hammond, K. R. (1966a). Probabilistic functionalism: Egon Brunswik's integration of the history, theory, and methodology of psychology. In K. R. Hammond (Ed.), *The psychology of Egon Brunswik.* New York: Holt, Rinehart, & Winston.

Hammond, K. R. (1966b). *The psychology of Egon Brunswik.* New York: Holt, Rinehart, and Winston.

Hammond, K. R. (1980a). *The integration of research in judgment and decision theory* (Tech. Rep. No. 226). Boulder, CO: University of Colorado, Center for Research on Judgment and Policy.

Hammond, K. R. (1980b). Introduction to Brunswikian theory and methods. In K. R. Hammond & N. E. Wascoe (Eds.), *Realizations of Brunswik's experimental design.* San Francisco: Jossey-Bass.

Hammond, K. R. (1986a). Generalization in operational contexts: What does it mean? Can it be done? *IEEE Systems, Man, and Cybernetics, SMC-16*, 428–433.

Hammond, K. R. (1986b). *A theoretically based review of theory and research in judgment and decision making* (Tech. Rep. No. 260). Boulder, CO: University of Colorado, Center for Research on Judgment and Policy.

Hammond, K. R. (1988). Judgment and decision making in dynamic tasks. *Information and Decision Technologies, 14*, 3–14.

Hammond, K. R. (1990). Functionalism and illusionism: Can integration be usefully achieved? In R. M. Hogarth (Ed.), *Insights in decision making: A tribute to Hillel J. Einhorn* (pp. 227–261). Chicago: University of Chicago Press.

Hammond, K. R., & Adelman, L. (1976). Science, values, and human judgment. *Science, 194*, 389–396.

Hammond, K. R., & Brehmer, B. (1973). Quasi-rationality and distrust: Implications for international conflict. In L. Rappoport & D. A. Summers (Eds.), *Human judgment and social interaction* (pp. 338–391). New York: Holt, Rinehart, & Winston.

Hammond, K. R., Frederick, E., Robillard, N., & Victor, D. (1989). Application of cognitive theory to the student-teacher dialogue. In D. A. Evans & V. L. Patel (Eds.), *Cognitive science in medicine* (pp. 173–210). Cambridge, MA: MIT Press.

Hammond, K. R., & Grassia, J. (1985). The cognitive side of conflict: From theory to resolution of policy disputes. In S. Oskamp (Ed.), *Applied social psychology annual: Vol. 6. International conflict and national public policy issues* (pp. 233–254). Beverly Hills, CA: Sage.

Hammond, K. R., Hamm, R. M., Grassia, J., & Pearson, T. (1987). Direct comparison of the efficacy of intuitive and analytical cognition in expert judgment. *IEEE Transactions on Systems, Man, and Cybernetics, SMC-17*(5), 753–770.

Hammond, K. R., Hursch, C. J., & Todd, F. J. (1964). Analyzing the components of clinical inference. *Psychological Review, 71,* 438–456.

Hammond, K. R., McClelland, G. H., & Mumpower, J. (1980). *Human judgment and decision making: Theories, methods and procedures.* New York: Praeger.

Hammond, K. R., Stewart, T. R., Brehmer, B., & Steinmann, D. O. (1975). Social judgment theory. In M. F. Kaplan & S. Schwartz (Eds.), *Human judgment and decision processes* (pp. 271–312). New York: Academic Press.

Hammond, K. R., & Summers, D. A. (1972). Cognitive control. *Psychological Review, 79,* 58–67.

Hammond, K. R., & Wascoe, N. E. (Eds.). (1980). *New directions for methodology of social and behavioral science: Realizations of Brunswik's representative design.* San Francisco: Jossey-Bass.

Harmon, J., & Rohrbaugh, J. (1990). Social judgment analysis and small group decision making: Cognitive feedback effects on individual and collective performance. *Organizational Behavior and Human Decision Processes, 46,* 34–54.

Harris, J. E., & Morris, P. E. (1984). *Everyday memory: Actions and absentmindedness.* London: Academic Press.

Harvey, J. B. (1974, Summer). The Abilene Paradox. *Organizational Dynamics,* pp. 64–83.

Harvey, J. B. (1988). *The Abilene Paradox.* Lexington, MA: Lexington Books.

Hastie, R. (1981). Schematic principles in human memory. In E. T. Higgens, C. P. Herman, & M. P. Zanna (Eds.), *Social cognition: The Ontario symposium on personality and social psychology.* Hillsdale, NJ: Erlbaum.

Hastie, R., & Park, B. (1986). The relationship between memory and judgment depends on whether the judgment task is memory-based or on-line. *Psychological Review, 93,* 258–268.

Hayes, J. R. (1980). Teaching problem-solving mechanisms. In D. T. Tuma & F. Reif (Eds.), *Problem solving and education: Issues in teaching and research* (pp. 141–147). Hillsdale, NJ: Erlbaum.

Heath, S. B. (1991). "It's about winning!" The language of knowledge in baseball. In L. Resnick, J. Levine, & S. Behrend (Eds.), *Shared cognition. Thinking as social practice.* Washington, DC: American Psychological Association.

Helmreich, R. L., (1990, April). *Studying flightcrew interaction: The intersection of basic and applied research.* Talk presented at the dedication of the NASA-Ames Research center Human Performance Research Laboratory.

Helmreich, R. L. (1990, April). *Studying flightcrew interaction: The intersection of basic and applied research.* Talk presented at the dedication of the NASA-Ames Research Center Human Performance Research Laboratory.

Helmreich, R. L., Chidester, T. R., Foushee, H. C., Gregorich, S., & Wilhelm, J. A. (1989). *How effective is cockpit resource management training: Issues in evaluating the impact of programs to enhance crew coordination* (NASA/UT Tech. Rep. No. 89, Draft 6.0). Moffett Field, CA: NASA Ames Research Center.

Hempel, C. G. (1965). Studies in the logic of confirmation. In *Aspects of scientific explanation*. New York: Free Press. (Original work published 1945).

Hendrickx, L., Vlek, C., & Oppewal, H. (1989). Relative importance of scenario information and frequency information in the judgment of risk. *Acta Psychologica, 72*, 41–63.

Herrnstein, R. J., Nickerson, R. S., Sanchez, M., & Swets, J. A. (1986). Teaching thinking skills. *American Psychologist, 41*, 1279–1289.

Hickson, D. J., Butler, R. J., Cray, D., Mallory, G. R., & Wilson, D. C. (1986). *Top decisions: Strategic decision-making in organizations*. San Francisco: Jossey-Bass.

Hildebrand, J. H. (1957). *Science in the making*. New York: Columbia University Press.

Hinsz, V. B. (1990a). *A conceptual framework for a research program on groups as information processors* (Tech. Rep.). Submitted to the Logistics and Human Factors Division, AF Human Resources Laboratory, Wright-Patterson AFB, OH.

Hinsz, V. B. (1990b). *Considerations in the assessment and evaluation of mental models* (Tech. Rep.). Submitted to the Logistics and Human Factors Division, AF Human Resources Laboratory, Wright-Patterson AFB, OH.

Hinsz, V. B. (1990c). Cognitive and consensus processes in group recognition memory performance. *Journal of personality and Social Psychology, 59*, 705–718.

Hinsz, V. B., Tindale, R. S., Nagao, D. H., Davis, J. H., & Robertson, B. A. (1988). The influence of the accuracy of individuating information on the use of base rate information in probability judgement. *Journal of Experimental Social Psychology, 24*, 127–145.

Hintzman, D. L. (1986). Schema abstraction in a multiple-trace memory model. *Psychological Review, 93*, 411–428.

Hirokawa, R. Y. (1983). Group communication and problem solving effectiveness: An investigation of group phases. *Human Communication Research, 9*, 291–305.

Hoc, J. M., & Leplat, J. (1983). Evaluation of different modalities of verbalization in a sorting task. *International Journal of Man-Machine Studies, 18*, 283–306.

Hoch, S. J. (1985). Counterfactual reasoning and accuracy in predicting personal events. *Journal of Experimental Psychology: Learning, Memory, and Cognition, 11*(4), 719–731.

Hoch, S. J., & Tschirgi, J. E. (1983). Cue redundancy and extra logical inferences in a deductive reasoning task. *Memory and Cognition, 11*, 200–209.

Hoffman, P. J. (1960). The paramorphic representation of clinical judgment. *Psychological Bulletin, 57*, 116–131.

Hogarth, R. M. (1981). Beyond discrete biases: Functional and dysfunctional aspects of judgmental heuristics. *Psychological Bulletin, 90*, 197–217.

Hogarth, R. M. (1986). Generalization in decision research: The role of formal models. *IEEE Systems, Man, and Cybernetics, SMC-16*, 439–449.

Hogarth, R. M. (1987). *Judgment and choice: The psychology of decisions*. New York: Wiley.

Hogarth, R. M., & Makridakis, S. (1981). Forecasting and planning: An evaluation. *Management Science, 27*(2), 115–138.

Hogarth, R., & Reder, M. (1986). The behavioral foundations of economic theory. *The Journal of Business, 59*, S181-S505.

Hogarth, R. M., Michaud, C., & Mery, J. L. (1980). Decision behavior in urban development: A methodological approach and substantive considerations. *Acta Psychologica, 45*, 95–117.

Hollnagel, E., Pederson, O. M., & Rasmussen, J. (1981). *Notes on human performance analysis* (Tech. Rep. Riso-M-2285). Riso National Laboratory.

Horwich, P. (1982). *Probability and evidence.* Cambridge, UK: Cambridge University Press.

Huber, G. P. (1980). *Managerial decision making.* Glenview, IL: Scott Foresman.

Huber, G. P. (1990). A theory of the effects of advanced information technologies on organization design, intelligence, and decision making. *Academy of Management Review, 15*(1), 47–71.

Huber, O. (1986). Decision making as a problem solving process. In B. Brehmer, H. Jungermann, P. Lourens, & G. Sevon (Eds.), *New directions in research on decision making* (pp. 109–138). New York: North-Holland.

Huffman, M. D. (1978). *The effect of decision task characteristics on decision behavior* (Tech. Rep. No. 78-16). Seattle: University of Washington, Department of Psychology.

Hughes, W. P. (1986). Garbage cans at sea. In J. G. March, & R. Weissinger-Baylon (Eds.), *Ambiguity and command: Organizational perspectives on military decision making* (pp. 249–257). Marshfield, MA: Pitman Publishing.

Humphreys, P., & Berkley, D. (1985). Handling uncertainty: Levels of analysis of decision problems. In G. Wright (Ed.), *Behavioral decision-making.* New York: Plenum Press.

Hunter, J. E., & Schmidt, F. L. (1989). *Methods of meta-analysis: Correcting error and bias in research findings.* Beverly Hills, CA: Sage.

Hunter, J. E., Schmidt, F. L., & Jackson, G.B. (1982). *Meta-analysis: Cumulating research findings across studies.* Beverly Hills, CA: Sage.

Hutchins, E. (1980). *Culture and inference.* Cambridge, MA: Harvard University Press.

Hutchins, E. (1983). Understanding micronesian navigation. In D. Gentner & A. L. Stevens (Eds.), *Mental models.* Hillsdale, NJ: Erlbaum.

Hutchins, E. (1989). The technology of team navigation. In J. Galegher, R. E. Kraut, & C. Egido (Eds.), *Intellectual teamwork: Social and technical bases of cooperative work* (pp. 191–220). Hillsdale, NJ: Erlbaum.

Hutchins, E., & Klausen, T. (1991). *Distributed cognition in an airline cockpit.* Unpublished manuscript, University of California, Dan Diego, CA.

Isenberg, D. J. (1984, November/December). How senior managers think. *Harvard Business Review,* pp. 81–90.

Isenberg, D. J. (1985). Some hows and whats of managerial thinking: Implications for future army leaders. In J. G. Hunt & J. Blair (Eds.), *Military leadership in the future battlefield.* New York: Pergammon Press.

James, W. (1890). *Principles of psychology*. New York: Holt.

Janis, I. L. (1972). *Victims of groupthink*. Boston: Houghton-Mifflin.

Janis, I. L. (1989). *Crucial decision making*. New York: Free Press.

Janis, I. L., & Mann, L. (1977). *Decision making: A psychological analysis of conflict, choice, and commitment*. New York: The Free Press.

Johnson, E. J. (1988). Expertise and decision under certainty: Performance and process. In M. Chi, R. Glaser, & M. Farr (Eds.), *The nature of expertise*. Hillsdale, NJ: Erlbaum.

Johnson, E. J., Payne, J. W., & Bettman, J. R. (1988). Information displays and preference reversals. *Organizational Behavior and Human Decision Processes, 42*, 1–21.

Johnson, P. E., Duran, F., Hassenbrock, A., Moller, J., Prietula, M., Feltovich, P., & Swanson, D. (1981). Expertise and error in diagnostic reasoning. *Cognitive Science, 5*, 235–283.

Johnson, P.E., Zualkernan, I., & Garber, S. (1987). Specification of expertise. *International Journal of Man-Machine Studies, 26*, 161–182.

Johnson-Laird, P. N. (1983). *Mental model: Towards a cognitive science of language, inference, and consciousness*. Cambridge, MA: Harvard University Press.

Johnson-Laird, P. N., Legrenzi, P., & Legrenzi, M. S. (1972). Reasoning and a sense of reality. *British Journal of Psychology, 63*, 305–400.

Jungermann, H. (1983). The two camps on rationality. In R. W. Scholz (Ed.), *Decision making under uncertainty*. North Holland: Elsevier.

Jungermann, H., & Thuring, M. (1987). The use of mental models for generating scenarios. In G. Wright & P. Ayton (Eds.), *Judgmental forecasting* (pp. 245–265). New York: Wiley.

Kadane, J. B., & Lichtenstein, S. (1982). *A subjectivist view of calibration* (Rep. 82-6). Eugene, OR: Decision Research.

Kahneman, D., & Miller, D. T. (1986). Norm theory: Comparing reality to its alternatives. *Psychological Review, 93*, 136–153.

Kahneman, D., Slovic, P., & Tversky, A. (Eds.). (1982). *Judgment under uncertainty: Heuristics and biases*. Cambridge, UK: Cambridge University Press.

Kahneman, D., & Tversky, A. (1972). Subjective probability: A judgment of representativeness. *Cognitive Psychology, 3*, 430–454.

Kahneman, D., & Tversky, A. (1973). On the psychology of prediction. *Psychological Review, 80*, 237–251.

Kahneman, D., & Tversky, A. (1979). Prospect theory: An analysis of decision under risk. *Econometrica, 47*(2), 263–291.

Kahneman, D., & Tversky, A. (1982a). On the study of statistical intuitions. *Cognition, 11*, 123–141.

Kahneman, D., & Tversky, A. (1982b). The simulation heuristic. In D. Kahneman, P. Slovic, & A. Tversky (Eds.), *Judgment under uncertainty: Heuristics and biases*. Cambridge, UK: Cambridge University Press.

Kanal, L. N., & Lemmer, J. F. (Eds.). (1986). *Uncertainty in artificial intelligence: Machine intelligence and pattern recognition* (Vol. 4). North Holland: Elsevier.

Kanki, B. G., Lozito, S., & Foushee, H. C. (1989). Communication indices of crew coordination. *Aviation, Space and Environmental Medicine, 60,* 56–60.

Kaplan, J. (1978). *Criminal justice: Introductory cases and materials* (2nd ed.). Mineola, Foundation Press.

Kaplan, M. F., & Schwartz, S. (1975). *Human judgment and decision processes.* New York: Academic Press.

Kassirer, J. P. (1989). Diagnostic reasoning. *Annals of Internal Medicine, 110,* 893–900.

Kassirer, J. P., & Kopelman, R. I. (1987, June). Derailed by the availability heuristic. *Hospital Practice,* pp. 56–69.

Kassirer, J. P., & Kopelman, R. I. (1989). Cognitive errors in diagnosis: Instantiation, classification, and consequences. *The American Journal of Medicine, 86,* 433–441.

Kassirer, J. P., Kuipers, B. J., & Gorry, G. A. (1982). Toward a theory of clinical expertise. *American Journal of Medicine, 73,* 251–259.

Kato, T. (1986). What "question-asking protocols" can say about the user interface. *International Journal of Man-Machine Studies, 25,* 659–673.

Katsoff, L. O. (1965). *Making moral decisions.* The Hague: Nijhoff.

Keeney, R. L. (1973). A decision analysis with multiple objectives: The Mexico City airport. *Bell Journal of Economics and Management Science, 4,* 101–117.

Keeney, R. L. (1982). Decision analysis: An overview. *Operations Research, 30,* 803–838.

Keeney, R. L., & Raiffa, H. (1976). *Decisions with multiple objectives: Preferences and value tradeoffs.* New York: Wiley & Sons.

Keinan, G. (1987). Decision making under stress: Scanning of alternatives under controllable and uncontrollable threats. *Journal of Personality and Social Psychology, 52,* 639–644.

Kelley, H. H. (1973). The processes of causal attribution. *American Psychologist, 28,* 107–128.

Keren, G. B., & Wagenaar, W. A. (1985). On the psychology of playing blackjack: Normative and descriptive considerations with implications for decision theory. *Journal of Experimental Psychology: General, 114,* 133–158.

Keren, G. B., & Wagenaar, W. A. (1987). Violation of utility theory in unique and repeated gambles. *Journal of Experimental Psychology: Learning, Memory and Cognition, 13,* 387–396.

Kirlik, A., Miller, R. A., & Jagacinski, R. (1989). A process model of skilled human performance in a dynamic uncertain environment. *Proceedings of IEEE Conference on Systems, Man, and Cybernetics, IEEE.* New York: Institute of Electrical and Electronic Engineers, Inc.

Kirwan, J., Chaput de Saintonge, D. M., Joyce, C. R. B., & Currey, H. L. F. (1984). Clinical judgment in rheumatoid arthritis. III: British rheumatologists' judgments of "change in response to therapy." *Annals of the Rheumatic Diseases, 43,* 686–694.

Klawans, H. L. (1988). *Toscanini's fumble.* New York: Comtemporary Books.

Klayman, J., & Ha, Y. W. (1987). Confirmation, disconfirmation and information in hypothesis testing. *Psychological Review, 94,* 211–228.

Klein, G. A. (1980). Automated aids for the proficient decision maker. *IEEE Transactions on Systems, Man, and Cybernetics*, pp. 301-304.

Klein, G. A. (1987). Applications of analogical reasoning. *Metaphor and Symbolic Activity*, 2, 201–218.

Klein, G. A. (1989a). Recognition-primed decisions. In W.B. Rouse (Ed.), *Advances in man-machine system research* (Vol. 5, pp. 47–92). Greenwich, CT: JAI Press.

Klein, G. A. (1989b). Do decision biases explain too much? *Human Factors Society Bulletin, 32*(5), 1–3.

Klein, G. A., & Calderwood, R. (1987). Decision models: Some lessons from the field. *Proceedings of the 1987 International Conference on Systems, Man, and Cybernetics, 1*, 247–251. (Received the *Franklin V. Taylor Award* for best paper presentation at the 1987 SMC Conference, October 20–23.)

Klein, G. A., & Calderwood, R. (in press). Decision models: Some lessons from the field. *IEEE Transactions on Systems, Man, and Cybernetics.*

Klein, G. A., Calderwood, R., & Clinton-Cirocco, A. (1986). Rapid decision making on the fire ground. *Proceedings of the Human Factors Society 30th Annual Meeting, 1*, 576–580.

Klein, G. A., Calderwood, R., & MacGregor, D. (1989). Critical decision method for eliciting knowledge. *IEEE Systems, Man, and Cybernetics, 19*(3), 462–472.

Klein, G. A., & Thordsen, M. L. (1989a). *Cognitive processes of the team mind* (Final Report submitted to NASA-Ames Research Center under PO#A72145C). Yellow Springs, OH: Klein Associates.

Klein, G. A., & Thordsen, M. L. (1989b). Recognitional decision making in C² organizations. *Proceedings of the 1989 Symposium on Command-and-Control Research* (pp. 239–244). McLean, VA: Science Applications International Corporation.

Kleinman, D. L., Luh, P. B., Pattipati, K. R., & Serfaty, D. (1992). Mathematical models of team performance: A distributed decision making approach. In R. W. Swezey & E. Salas (Eds.), *Teams: Their training and performance* (pp. 177–218). Norwood, NJ: Ablex Publishing Corp.

Kleinman, D. L. & Serfaty, D. (1989). Team performance assessment in distributed decision making. In R. Gilson, J. P. Kincaid, & B. Goldiez (Eds.), *Proceedings of the Interactive Networked Simulation for Training Conference.* Orlando, FL: Naval Training Systems Center.

Kleinmuntz, D. N., & Thomas, J. B. (1987). The value of action and inference in dynamic decision making. *Organizational Behavior and Human Decision Processes, 39*, 341–364.

Koriat, A., Lichtenstein, S., & Fischhoff, B. (1980). Reasons for confidence. *Journal of Experimental Psychology: Human Learning and Memory, 6*(2), 107–118.

Kowalski, B., & VanLehn, K. (1988). Cirrus: Inducing subject models from protocol data. *Proceedings of the Tenth Annual Conference of the Cognitive Science Society.* Hillsdale, NJ: Erlbaum.

Kraemer, K., & King, J. (1988). Computer-based systems for cooperative work and group decision making. *ACM Computing Surveys, 20*(2), 115–146.

Krahenbuhl, G. S., Marett, J. R., & Reid, G. B. (1978). Task-specific simulator pretraining and in-flight stress on student pilots. *Aviation, Space, and Environmental Medicine, 49*, 1107–1110.

Kuhn, D., Ansel, E., & O'Laughlin, M. (1988). *The development of scientific thinking skills.* San Diego: Academic Press.

Kuhn, T. (1962). *The structure of scientific revolutions.* Chicago: University Press of Chicago.

Kuipers, B., & Kassirer, J. P. (1984). Causal reasoning in medicine: Analysis of a protocol. *Cognitive Science, 8*, 363–385.

Kyburg, H. E. (1988). Bets and beliefs. In P. Gardenfors & N.-E. Sahlin (Eds.), *Decision, probability, and utility: Selected readings.* Cambridge, UK: Cambridge University Press.

Laird, J., Rosenbloom, P., & Newell, A. (1987). SOAR: An architecture for general intelligence. *Artificial Intelligence, 33*, 1–64.

Lanir, Z. (1991). The reasonable choice of disaster. In J. Rasmussen, B. Brehmer, & J. Leplat (Eds.), *Distributed decision making: Cognitive models for cooperative work* (pp. 215–230). London: Wiley.

Lanzetta, J. T., & Roby, T. B. (1960). The relationship between certain group process variables and group problem solving efficiency. *Journal of Social Psychology, 52*, 135–148.

Larkin, J. H. (1977). *Problem solving in physics* (Tech. Rep.). Berkeley, CA: University of California, Group in Science and Mathematics Education.

Larkin, J. H. (1981). Enriching formal knowledge: A model for learning to solve textbook physics problems. In J. R. Anderson (Ed.), *Cognitive skills and their acquisition.* Hillsdale, NJ: Erlbaum.

Larkin J. H. (1983). The role of problem representation in physics. In D. Gentner & A. L. Stevens (Eds.), *Mental models.* Hillsdale, NJ: Erlbaum.

Larkin, J., McDermott, J., Simon, D. P., & Simon, H. A. (1980). Expert and novice performance in solving physics problems. *Science, 20*(208), 1335–1342.

Laskey, K. B., Leddo, J. M., & Bresnick, T. A. (1989). *Executive thinking and decision skills: A characterization and implications for training* (Tech. Rep. No. TR89–12). Reston, VA: Decision Science Consortium.

Lassiter, D. L., Vaughn, J. S., Smaltz, V. E., Morgan, B. B., Jr., & Salas, E. (1990). *A comparison of two types of training interventions on team communication performance.* Paper presented at the 1990 Meeting of the Human Factors Society, Orlando, FL.

Laughlin, P. (1980). Social combination processes in cooperative problem-solving groups on verbal intellective tasks. In M. Fishbein (Ed.), *Progress in social psychology* (pp. 127–155).

Laughlin, P., & McGlynn, R. (1986). Collective induction: Mutual group and individual influence by exchange of hypotheses and evidence. *Journal of Experimental Social Psychology, 22*, 567–589.

Lave, J. (1988). *Cognition in practice.* New York: Cambridge University Press.

Lave, J., Murtaugh, M., & de la Roche, O. (1984). The dialectic of arithmetic in grocery shopping. In B. Rogoff & J. Lave (Eds.), *Everyday cognition: Its development in social context.* Cambridge, MA: Harvard University Press.

Leathers, D. (1969). Process disruption and measurement in small group communication. *Quarterly Journal of Speech, 55,* 287–300.

Leathers, D. (1972). Quality of group communication as a determinant of group product. *Speech Monographs, 39,* 166–173.

LeCompte, M. D., & Goetz, J. P. (1982). Problems of reliability and validity in ethnographic research. *Review of Educational Research, 52*(1), 31–60.

Leddo, J., Abelson, R. P., & Gross, P. H. (1984). Conjunctive explanations: When two reasons are better than one. *Journal of Personality and Social Psychology, 47*(5), 933–943.

Leddo, J., Chinnis, J. O., Jr., Cohen, M. S., & Marvin, F. F. (1987). *The influence of uncertainty and time stress on decision making* (Tech. Rep. No. 87–1). Falls Church, VA: Decision Science Consortium.

Lee, W. (1971). *Decision theory and human behavior.* New York: Wiley & Sons.

Leon, M., & Anderson, N. H. (1974). A ratio-rule from integration theory applied to inference judgments. *Journal of Experimental Psychology, 102,* 27–36.

Leplat, J., & Hoc, J. M. (1981). Subsequent verbalization in the study of cognitive processes. *Ergonomics, 24,* 743–755.

Lesgold, A. (1989). Context-specific requirements for models of expertise. In D. A. Evans & V. L. Patel (Eds.), *Cognitive science in medicine.* Cambridge, MA: MIT Press.

Lesgold, A., Feltovich, P. J., Glaser, R., & Wang, M. (1981). *The acquisition of perceptual diagnostic skill in radiology* (Tech Rep. No. PDS-1). Pittsburgh: University of Pittsburgh, Learning Research and Development Center.

Lesgold, A., Glaser, R., Rubinson, H., Klopfer, D., Feltovich, P., & Wang, Y. (1988). Expertise in a complex skill: Diagnosing x-ray pictures. In M. T. H. Chi, R. Glaser, & M. J. Farr (Eds.), *The nature of expertise* (pp. 311–342). Hillsdale, NJ: Erlbaum.

Lesgold, A., Lajoie, S., Bunzo, M., & Eggan, G. (1988). *SHERLOCK: A coached practice environment for an electronics troubleshooting job.* Pittsburgh: University of Pittsburgh, Learning Research and Development Center.

Levi, I. (1986). *Hard choices: Decision making under unresolved conflict.* New York: Cambridge University Press.

Levine, J. M., & Moreland, R. L. (1985). Innovation and socialization in small groups. In S. Moscovici, G., Mugny, & E. van Avermaet (Eds.), *Perspectives on minority influence.* Cambridge: Cambridge University Press.

Levine, J. M., & Moreland, R. L. (1990). Progress in small group research. *Annual Review of Psychology, 41,* 585–634.

Lewicka, M. (1990, August). *Mood related differences in predecisional information search strategies.* Paper presented at the 98th Annual Convention of the American Psychological Association, Boston.

Lewis, C. H. (1988). Why and how to learn why: Analysis-based generalization of procedures. *Cognitive Science, 12,* 211–256.

Lichtenstein, S., & Fischhoff, B. (1980). Training for calibration. *Organizational Behavior and Human Performance, 26,* 149–171.

Lichtenstein, S., Fischhoff, B., & Phillips, L. D. (1982). Calibration of probabilities: The state of the art to 1980. In D. Kahneman, P. Slovic, & A. Tversky (Eds.), *Judgment under uncertainty: Heuristics and biases.* New York: Cambridge University Press.

Lindberg, E., Gärling, T., & Montgomery, H. (1988). People's beliefs and values as determinants of housing preferences and simulated choices. *Scandinavian Housing and Planning Research, 5,* 181–197.

Lindberg, E., Gärling, T., & Montgomery, H. (1989). Differential predictability of preferences and choice. *Journal of Behavioral Decision Making, 2,* 205–219.

Lindberg, E., Gärling, T., & Montgomery, H. (1990a). *Preferences for and choices among incompletely described housing alternatives* (Umeå Psychological Reports, No. 196). Umeå, Sweden: University of Umeå, Department of Psychology.

Lindberg, E., Gärling, T., & Montgomery, H. (1990b). *Intra-urban mobility: Subjective belief-value structures as determinants of residential preferences and choices* (Umeå Psychological Reports, 197). Umeå, Sweden: University of Umeå, Department of Psychology.

Lindblom, C. E. (1959). The science of "muddling through." *Public Administration Review, 19*(2), 79–88.

Lindley, D. V. (1982). Scoring rules and the inevitability of probability. *International Statistical Review, 50,* 1–26.

Lipshitz, R. (1989). *Decision making as argument driven action.* Boston: Boston University Center for Applied Social Science.

Lipshitz, R. (1989). *Making sense of decision making: Towards an integrative approach understanding and improving decisions.* Haifa: University of Haifa.

Lodico, M. G., Ghatala, E. S., Levin, J. R., Pressley, M., & Bell, J. A. (1983). The effects of strategy-monitoring training on children's selection of effective memory strategies. *Journal of Experimental Child Psychology, 35,* 263–277.

Loomis, G., & Sugden, R. (1982). Regret theory: An alternative theory of rational choice under uncertainty. *Economic Journal, 92,* 805–824.

Lopes, L. L. (1981). Decision making in the shortrun. *Journal of Experimental Psychology: Human Learning and Memory, 1,* 377–385.

Lopes, L. L. (1982a). Doing the impossible: A note on induction and the experience of randomness. *Journal of Experimental Psychology: Learning, Memory, and Cognition, 8*(6), 626–636.

Lopes, L. L. (1982b). *Toward a procedural theory of judgment* (Tech. Rep. No. 17). Madison, WI: Wisconsin Human Information Processing Program.

Lopes, L. L. (1983). Observations: Some thoughts on the psychological concept of risk. *Journal of Experimental Psychology: Human Perception and Performance, 9*(1), 137–144.

Lopes, L. L. (1988). *The rhetoric of irrationality.* Madison, WI: University of Wisconsin.

Lopes, L. L., & Oden, G. C. (in press). The rationality of intelligence. In E. Eells & T. Maruszewski (Eds.), *Rationality and reasoning.* Amsterdam: Rodopi.

Lord, R. G. (1985). An information processing approach to social perceptions, leadership, and behavioral measurement in organizations. In L. L. Cummings & B. M. Staw (Eds.), *Research in organizational behavior* (Vol. 7, pp. 87–128). Greenwich, CT: JAI Press.

Lord, R. G., & Maher, K. J. (1989). Cognitive processes in industrial and organizational psychology. *International Review of Industrial and Organizational Psychology*, pp. 49–91.

Lorenz, K. (1966). *On aggression*. New York: Harcourt, Brace, & World.

Luce, R. D. (1959). *Individual choice behavior. A theoretical analysis*. New York: Wiley.

Luce, R. D. (1977). The choice axiom after twenty years. *Journal of Mathematical Psychology, 15*, 215–233.

Lusk, C. M., & Hammond, K. R. (1991). Judgment in a dynamic task: Microburst forecasting. *Journal of Behavioral Decision Making, 4*, 55–73.

Lusk, C. M., Mross, E. F., & Hammond, K. R. (1989). *Judgment and decision making under stress: A preliminary study of convection forecasts*. U.S. Army Research Institute progress report.

Lusk, C. M., Stewart, T. R., & Hammond, K. R. (1988). *Toward the study of judgment and decision making in dynamic tasks: The case of forecasting the microburst*. Boulder, CO: University of Colorado, Center for Research on Judgment and Policy.

Lusk, C. M., Stewart, T. R., Hammond, K. R., & Potts, R. J. (1990). Judgment and decision making in dynamic tasks: The case of forecasting the microburst. *Weather and Forecasting, 5*, 627–639.

MacCrimmon, K. R., & Taylor, R. N. (1976). Decision making and problem solving. In M. D. Dunnette (Ed.), *Handbook of industrial and organizational psychology* (pp. 1397–1454). New York: Wiley & Sons.

Macdonald, R. R. (1986). Credible conceptions and implausible probabilities. *British Journal of Mathematical and Statistical Psychology, 39*, 15–27.

MacDougall, R. (1922). *The general problems of psychology*. New York: New York University Press. (Cited in Gillis, J., & Schneider, C. (1966). The historical preconditions of representative design. In K. Hammond (Ed.), *The psychology of Egon Brunswik* (pp. 204–236). New York: Holt, Rinehart, & Winston.)

Machina, M. J. (1982). "Expected utility" analysis without the independence axiom. *Econometrica, 50*, 277–332.

Mackie, D. M., & Goethals, G. R. (1987). Individual and group goals. *Review of Personality and Social Psychology, 8*, 144–167.

Makridakis, S., & Hibon, M. (1979). Accuracy of forecasting: An empirical investigation. *Journal of the Royal Statistical Society, A142*(2), 97–125.

Mandler, J. M. (1980). Categorical and schematic organization in memory. In C. R. Puff (Ed.), *Memory organization and structure*. New York: Academic Press.

Mann, L., Janis, I. L., & Chaplin, R. (1969). The effects of anticipation of forthcoming information on predecisional processes. *Journal of Personality and Social Psychology, 11*, 10–16.

Manu, P., Runge, L. A., & Lee, J. Y. (1984). Judged frequency of complications after invasive diagnostic procedures. *Medical Care, 22*, 366–368.

March, J., & Weissinger-Baylor, R. (1986). *Ambiguity and command: Organizational perspectives on military decision making.* Marshfield, MA: Pitman Publishing.

March, J. G. (1978). Bounded rationality, ambiguity, and the engineering choice. *Bell Journal of Economics, 9,* 587–608.

March, J. G. (1988). Bounded rationality, ambiguity, and the engineering of choice. In D. E. Bell, H. Raiffa, & A. Tversky (Eds.), *Decision making: Descriptive, normative, and prescriptive interactions.* Cambridge, UK: Cambridge University Press.

March, J. G., & Olsen, J. P. (1976). *Ambiguity and choice in organizations.* Bergen: Universitetsforlaget.

March, J. G., & Olsen, J. P. (1986). Garbage can models of decision making in organizations. In J. G. March & R. Weissinger-Baylon (Eds.), *Ambiguity and command: Organizational perspectives on military decision making.* Cambridge, MA: Ballinger.

March, J. G., & Simon, H. A. (1958). *Organizations.* New York: Wiley.

Marks, M., Hammond, K., & Converse, T. (1989). Planning in an open world: A pluralistic approach. *Proceedings of the 11th Annual Conference of the Cognitive Science Society.* Hillsdale, NJ: Erlbaum.

Marks, R. W. (1951). The effect of probability, desirability, and 'privilege' on the stated expectations of children. *Journal of Personality, 19,* 332–351.

Mason, R. O., & Mitroff, I. I. (1981). *Challenging strategic planning assumptions.* New York: Wiley.

Maule, A. J. (1989). Positive and negative decision frames: A verbal protocol analysis of the Asian disease problem of Tversky and Kahneman. In H. Montgomery & O. Svenson (Eds.), *Process and structure in human decision making.* New York: Wiley.

May, R. S. (1986). Inferences, subjective probability and frequency of correct answers: A cognitive approach to the overconfidence phenomenon. In B. Brehmer, H. Jungermann, P. Lourens, & G. Sevon (Eds.), *New directions in research on decision making.* New York: North-Holland.

McAllister, D., Mitchell, T. R., & Beach, L. R. (1979). The contingency model for selection of decision strategies: An empirical test of the effects of significance, accountability, and reversibility. *Organizational Behavior and Human Performance, 24,* 228–244.

McCartt, A. T., & Rohrbaugh, J. (1989). Evaluating group decision support system effectiveness: A performance study of decision conferencing. *Decision Support Systems, 5,* 243–253.

McCoch, A. M. (1990). Supporting group decisions in bond trading. In K. Borcherding, O. I. Larichev, & D. M. Messick (Eds.), *Contemporary issues in decision making* (pp. 333–351). Amsterdam: North-Holland.

McDermott, J. (1982). R1: A rule-based configurer of computer systems. *Artificial Intelligence, 19,* 39–88.

McDonald, P. (1990). *Group support technologies.* Report written for the Organizational Planning and Development Division, Office of Human Resource Management, Federal Aviation Administration, U. S. Dept. of Transportation, Transportation Systems Center, Strategic Management Division, Cambridge, MA.

McFarren, M. R. (1987). *Using concept maps to define problems and identify key kernels during the development of a decision support system.* Unpublished Master's thesis, Air Force Institute of Technology, Dayton, OH.

Mcgrath, J. E. (1964). *Social psychology: A brief introduction.* New York: Holt.

McGrath, J. (1984). *Groups: Interaction and performance.* Englewood Cliffs, NJ: Prentice-Hall.

McGrath, J. E. (1991). Time, interaction, and performance (TIP): A theory of groups. *Small Group Research, 22,* 147–174.

McIntyre, R. M., Morgan, B. B., Jr., Salas, E., & Glickman, A. S. (1988). *Team research in the eighties: Lessons learned.* Unpublished manuscript. Orlando, FL: Naval Training Systems Center.

Means, B. (1983, April). *How to choose the very best: What people know about decision-making strategies.* Paper presented at the Annual Meeting of the American Educational Research Association, Montreal, Canada.

Means, B., & Gott, S. P. (1988). Cognitive task analysis as a basis for tutor development: Articulating abstract knowledge representations. In J. Psotka, L. D. Massey, & S. A. Mutter (Eds.), *Intelligent tutoring systems: Lessons learned* (pp. 35–57). Hillsdale, NJ: Erlbaum.

Meehl, P. E. (1978). Theoretical risks and tabular asterisks: Sir Karl, Sir Ronald, and the slow progress of soft psychology. *Journal of Consulting and Clinical Psychology, 46,* 806–834.

Meehl, P. (1990). *Corroboration and verisimilitude: Against Lakatos's "sheer leap of faith."* Minneapolis, MN: University of Minnesota, Minnesota Center for Philosophy of Science.

Michaelsen, L. K., Watson, W. E., & Black, R. H. (1989). A realistic test of individual versus group consensus decision making. *Journal of Applied Psychology, 74*(5), 834–839.

Miller, G. A., Galanter, E., & Pribram, K. H. (1960). *Plans and the structure of behavior.* New York: Holt, Rinehart, & Winston.

Milliken, F. C. (1987). Three types of perceived uncertainty about the environment: State, effect, and response uncertainty. *Academy of Management Review, 12* (1), 133–143.

Milter, R. G., & Rohrbaugh, J. (1988). Judgment analysis and decision conferencing for administrative review: A case study of innovative policy making in government. *Advances in Information Processing in Organizations, 3,* 245–262.

Minsky, M. (1968). *Semantic information processing.* Cambridge, MA: MIT Press

Minsky, M. (1975). A framework for representing knowledge. In P. Winston (Ed.), *The psychology of computer vision.* New York: McGraw-Hill.

Mintzberg, H. (1975, July/August). The manager's job: Folklore and fact. *Harvard Business Review,* pp. 49–61.

Mitchell, C. M., & Miller, R. A. (1986). A discrete control model of operator function: A methodology for information display design. *IEEE Systems, Man, and Cybernetics, SMC-16,* 343–357.

Mitchell, T. R., & Beach, L. R. (1990). ". . . Do I love thee? Let me count. . . " Toward an understanding of intuitive and automatic decision making. *Organizational Behavior and Human Decision Processes, 47,* 1–20.

Miyake, N. (1986). Constructive interaction and the iterative process of understanding. *Cognitive Science, 10,* 151–177.

Modrick, J. A. (1986). Team performance and training. In J. Zeidner (Ed.), *Training and human factors in systems design: Human productivity enhancement* (Vol. 1, pp. 130–166). New York: Praeger.

Montgomery, H. (1983). Decision rules and the search for a dominance structure: Towards a process model of decision making. In P. Humphreys, O. Svenson, & A. Vari (Eds.), *Advances in psychology.* Amsterdam: North-Holland.

Montgomery, H. (1989a). From cognition to action: The search for dominance in decision making. In H. Montgomery & O. Svenson (Eds.), *Process and structure in human decision making.* Chichester, UK: Wiley.

Montgomery, H. (1989b). The search for a dominance structure: Simplification and elaboration in decision making. In D. Vickers & P. L. Smith (Eds.), *Human information processing: Measures, mechanisms, and models* (pp. 471–483). Amsterdam: North-Holland.

Montgomery, H., Selart, M., Gärling, T., & Lindberg, E. (1991, August). *The judgment-choice discrepancy: Response incompatibility and/or dominace structuring?* Paper presented at the 13th European Research Conference of Subjective Probability, Utility, and Decision Making, Fribourt, Switzerland.

Montgomery, H., & Svenson, O. (1976). On decision rules and information processing strategies for choices among multiattribute alternatives. *Scandinavian Journal of Psychology, 17,* 283–291.

Montgomery, H., & Svenson, O. (1983). Think aloud study of dominance structuring in decision processes. In R. Tietz (Ed.), *Aspiration level in bargaining and economic decision making.* Berlin: Springer Verlag.

Montgomery, H., & Svenson, O. (Eds.). (1989a). *Process and structure in human decision making,* Chichester, UK: Wiley.

Montgomery, H., & Svenson, O. (1989b). A think aloud study of dominance structuring. In H. Montgomery & O. Svenson (Eds.), *Process and structure in human decision making* (pp. 135–150). Chichester, UK: Wiley.

Moreland, R. L., & Levine, J. M. (1988). Group dynamics over time: Development and socialization in small groups. In J. E. McGrath (ed.), *The social psychology of time: New perspectives* (pp. 151–181). Newbury Park, CA: Sage Publications.

Morgan, B. B., Glickman, A. S., Woodard, E. A., Blaiwes, A. S., & Salas, E. (1986). *Measurement of team behaviors in a Navy environment* (Tech. Rep. No. NTSC TR-86–014). Orlando, FL: Naval Training Systems Center.

Morrison, J., Morrison, M., Sheng, O. R., Vogel, D. R., & Nunamaker, J. F. (1990). *Development of a prototype software system to support distributed team collaboration.* Working Paper for the Department of Management Information Systems, College of Business and Public Administration, University of Arizona, Tucson, AZ.

Mosteller, F., & Nogee, P. (1951). An experimental measurement of utility. *Journal of Political Economics, 59,* 371–404.

Mumpower, J. L., Schuman, S. P., & Zumbolo, A. (1988). Analytical mediation: An application in collective bargaining. In R. M. Lee, A. M. McCosh, & P. Migliarese (Eds.), *Organisational decision support systems* (pp. 61–73). Amsterdam: Elsevier.

Murphy, G. L., & Medin, D. L. (1985). The role of theories in conceptual coherence. *Psychological Review, 92*, 289–316.

Murphy, M. R., & Awe, C. A. (1985). Aircrew coordination and decision making: Performance ratings of video tapes made during a full mission simulation. *Proceedings of the 21st Annual Conference on Manual Control.* Columbus, OH: Ohio State University.

Myers, D. G., & Lamm, H. (1976). The group polarization phenomenon. *Psychological Bulletin, 83*, 602–627.

Nance, J. J. (1984). *Splash of colors: The self-destruction of Braniff International.* New York: Morrow Publishers.

Nannestad, D. (1989). *Reactive voting in Danish general elections 1971–1979: A revisionist interpretation.* Aarhus, DK: Aarhus University Press.

National Research Council. (1990). *Distributed decision making: Report of a workshop.* Washington, DC: National Academy Press.

Nau, R. F. (1986). *A new theory of indeterminate probabilities and utilities* (Fucqua School of Business Working Paper #8609). Durham, NC: Fucqua School of Business, Duke University.

Neisser, U. (1976). *Cognition and reality.* San Francisco: Freeman.

Neisser, U. (1978). Memory: What are the important questions: In M. M. Gruneberg, P. E. Morris, & R. N. Sykes (Eds.), *Practical aspects of memory* (pp. 3–24). London: Academic Press.

Newell, A. (1982). The knowledge level. *Artificial Intelligence, 18*, 87–127.

Newell, A., & Simon, H. A. (1972). *Human problem solving.* Englewood Cliffs, NJ: Prentice-Hall.

Nichols-Hoppe, K. T., & Beach, L. R. (1990). The effects of test anxiety and task variables on predecisional information search. *Journal of Research in Personality, 24*, 163–172.

Niiniluoto, I. (1981). L. J. Cohen versus Bayesianism. *The Behavioral and Brain Sciences, 4*(3), 349.

Nisbett, R. E., & Ross, L. (1980). *Human inference: Strategies and shortcomings of social judgment.* Englewood Cliffs, NJ: Prentice-Hall.

Nisbett, R. E., Borgida, E., Crandall, R., & Reed, H. (1976). Popular induction: Information is not necessarily informative. In J. S. Carroll & J. W. Payne (Eds.), *Cognition and social behavior.* Hillsdale, NJ: Erlbaum.

Nisbett, R. E., Krantz, D. H., Jepson, C., & Fong, T. (1982). Improving inductive inference. In D. Kahneman, P. Slovic, & A. Tversky (Eds.), *Judgment under uncertainty: Heuristics and biases.* Cambridge, MA: Cambridge University Press.

Nisbett, R. E., Krantz, D. H., Jepson, C., & Kunda, Z. (1983). The use of statistical heuristics in every day inductive reasoning. *Psychological Review, 90*(4), 339–363.

Nisbett, R. E., & Wilson, T. D. (1977). Telling more than we can know: Verbal reports on mental processes. *Psychological Review, 84*, 231–159.

Noble, D. (1989). *Application of a theory of cognition to situation assessment.* Vienna, VA: Engineering Research Associates.

Noble, D., Boehm-Davis, D., & Grosz, C. G. (1986). *A schema-based model of information processing for situation assessment* (NTIS No. ADA163150). Vienna, VA: Engineering Research Associates.

Noble, D., Grosz, C., & Boehm-Davis, D. (1987). *Rules, schema and decision making.* Vienna, VA: Engineering Research Associates.

Noble, D., & Mullen, R. (1987). *The adaptation of schema-based information processing theory to plan recognition.* Vienna, VA: Engineering Research Associates.

Noble, D., Truelove, J., Grosz, C. G., & Boehm-Davis, D. (1989). *A theory of information presentation for distributed decision making* (NTIS No. ADA216219). Vienna, VA: Engineering Research Associates.

Norman, D. A. (1990). The 'problem' of automation: Inappropriate feedback and interaction, not 'over-automation.' *Philosophical Transactions of the Royal Society of London, B327.*

Norman, G. R., & Brooks, L. R. (1989). Comment on the hindsight bias. *Medical Decision Making, 9,* 217–218.

Nunamaker, J., Applegate, L., & Kosynski, B. (1988, November-December). Computer aided deliberation: Model management and group decision support. *Journal of Operations Research,* pp. 826–848.

Olshavsky, R. W. (1979). Task complexity and contingent processing in decision making: A replication and extension. *Organizational Behavior and Human Performance, 24,* 300–316.

Orasanu, J. (1990). *Shared mental models and crew decision making* (Tech. Rep. No. 46). Princeton, NJ: Princeton University, Cognitive Sciences Laboratory.

Orr, J. (1985). *Social aspects of expertise.* Palo Alto, CA: Xerox PARC.

Palincsar, A. S., & Brown, A. L. (1984). Reciprocal teaching of comprehension-fostering and monitoring activities. *Cognition and Instruction, 1,* 117–175.

Paquette, L., & Kida, T. (1988). The effect of decision strategy and task complexity on decision performance. *Organizational Behavior & Human Decision Processes, 41,* 128–142.

Parsons, H. M. (1972). *Man-machine systems experiments.* Baltimore, MD: John Hopkins Press.

Patil, R. S., Szolovits, P., & Schwartz, W. B. (1981). Causal understanding of patient illness in medical diagnosis. *Proceedings of the Seventh International Joint Conference on Artificial Intelligence* (pp. 893–899). Vancouver, BC, Canada.

Payne, J. W. (1976). Task complexity and contingent processing in decision making: An information search and protocol analysis. *Organizational Behavior and Human Performance, 16,* 366–387.

Payne, J. W. (1982). Contingent decision behavior. *Psychological Bulletin, 92,* 382–402.

Payne, J. W., Bettman, J. R., & Johnson, E. J. (1988). Adaptive strategy selection in decision making. *Journal of Experimental Psychology: Learning, Memory and Cognition, 14,* 534–552.

Payne, J. W., Bettman, J. R., & Johnson, E. J. (1989). *The adaptive decision-maker: Effort and accuracy in choice* (ONR Tech. Rep. No. 89–1). Durham, NC: The Fucqua School of Business, Duke University.

Payne, J. W., Johnson, E. J., Bettman, J. R., & Coupey, E. (1990). Understanding contingent choice: A computer simulation approach. *IEEE Systems, Man, and Cybernetics, SMC-20,* 296–309.

Pearl, J. (1988). *Probabilistic reasoning in intelligent systems: Networks of plausible inference.* San Mateo, CA: Morgan Kaufmann.

Pence, A. R. (1988). *Ecological research with children and families.* New York: Teachers College Press.

Pennington, N. (1981). *Causal reasoning and decision making: The case of juror decisions.* Unpublished doctoral dissertation, Harvard University, Cambridge, MA.

Pennington, N., & Hastie, R. (1980, June). *Representation and inference in juror reasoning: Two illustrative analysis.* Paper presented at the Second Annual Meeting of the Cognitive Science Society, New Haven, CT.

Pennington, N., & Hastie, R. (1981). Juror decision making models: The generalization gap. *Psychological Bulletin, 89,* 246–287.

Pennington, N., & Hastie, R. (1986). Evidence evaluation in complex decision making. *Journal of Personality and Social Psychology, 51,* 242–258.

Pennington, N., & Hastie, R. (1988). Explanation-based decision making: Effects of memory structure on judgment. *Journal of Experimental Psychology: Learning, Memory, & Cognition, 14*(3), 521–533.

Pennington, N., & Hastie, R. (in press). Explaining the evidence: Tests of the story model for juror decision making. *Joural of Personality and Social Psychology.*

Pepitone, D., King, T., & Murphy, M. (1988). *The role of flight planning in aircrew decision performance* (Society for Automotive Engineers Technical Paper Series #881517).

Pepper, S. C. (1942). *World hypotheses*: A study in evidence. Berkeley, CA: University of California Press.

Perkins, D. N., & Salomon, G. (1989). Are cognitive skills context-bound? *Educational Researcher, 18,* 16–25.

Perrow, C. (1970). *Organizational analysis: A sociological view.* Monterey, CA: Brooks/Cole.

Peters, T. J. (1979, November/December). Leadership: Sad facts and silver linings. *Harvard Business Review,* pp. 164–172.

Peterson, C. R., & Beach, L. R. (1967). Man as an intuitive statistician. *Psychological Bulletin, 68,* 29–46.

Petrinovich, L. (1980). Brunswikian behavioral biology. In K. R. Hammond & N. E. Wascoe (Eds.), *New directions for methodology of social and behavioral science* (Vol. 3, pp. 85–94). San Francisco: Jossey-Bass.

Petrinovich, L. (1989). Representative design and the quality of generalization. In L. W. Poon, D. C. Rubin, & B. A. Wilson (Eds.), *Everyday cognition in adulthood and late life* (pp. 11–24). Cambridge, UK: Cambridge University Press.

Pew, R. W., Miller, D. C., & Feehrer, C. E. (1982). *Evaluation of proposed control room improvements through analysis of critical operator decisions.* Palo Alto, CA: Electric Power Research Institute, NP-1982.

Phillips, L. (1982). Applications of inference theory and analysis of artificial intelligence to problems in intelligence analysis. In *Intelligence Production Laboratory Conference Proceedings.* Rosslyn, VA: Analytic Methodology Research Division, Office of Research and Development, Central Intelligence Agency.

Phillips, L. D. (1985, April). Systems for solutions. *Datamation Business*, pp. 26–29.

Phillips, L. D. (1986, October). Computing to consensus. *Datamation*, pp. 2–6.

Phillips, L. D. (1989). Requisite decision modelling for technical projects. In C. Vlek & G. Cvetkovich (Eds.), *Social decision methodology for technical projects.* Dordrecht: Kluwer.

Pinsonneault, A., & Kraemer, K. L. (1990). The effects of electronic meetings on group process and outcomes: An assessment of the empirical research. *European Journal of Operations Research*, 46, 143–161.

Pitz, G. F. (1974). Subjective probability distributions for imperfectly known quantities. In L. W. Gregg (Ed.), *Knowledge and cognition.* New York: Wiley.

Pitz, G. F., & Sachs, N. J. (1984). Judgment and decision: Theory and application. *The Annual Review of Psychology*, 35, 139–163.

Polya, G. (1945). *How to solve it.* Princeton, NJ: Princeton University Press.

Poole, M. S. & DeSanctis, G. (1990). Understanding the use of group decision support systems: The theory of adaptive structuration. In J. Fulk & C. Steinfield (Eds.), *Organizations and communication technology* (pp. 173–193). Beverly Hills, CA: Sage Publications.

Poole, M. S., & Doelger, J. A. (1986). Developmental processes in group decision making. In R. Y. Hirokawa & M. S. Poole (Eds.), *Communication and group decision making* (pp. 35–61). Beverly Hills, CA: Sage.

Poon, L. W., Rubin, D. C., & Wilson, B. A. (Eds.). (1989). *Everyday cognition in adulthood and late life.* Cambridge, UK: Cambridge University Press.

Pople, H. E., Jr. (1982). Heuristic methods for imposing structure on ill-structured problems: The structuring of medical diagnostics. In P. Szolovits (Ed.), *Artificial intelligence in medicine.* Boulder, CO: Westview Press.

Popper, K. (1959). *The logic of scientific discovery.* New York: Basic Books.

Popper, K. (1969). *Conjectures and refutations.* New York: Harper & Row.

Popper, K. R. (1962). *Conjectures and refutations: The growth of scientific knowledge.* New York: Basic Books.

Posner, M. I. (1982). Cumulative development of attention theory. *American Psychologist*, 37, 168–179.

Praetorius, N., & Duncan, K. D. (1988). Verbal reports: A problem in research design. In L. P. Goodstein, H. B. Andersen, & S. E. Olsen (Eds.), *Tasks, errors and mental models.* London: Taylor & Francis.

Pratt, J. W. (1986). Comment. *Statistical Science, 1,* 498–499.

Prince, C., Chidester, T. R., Cannon-Bowers, J. A., & Bowers, C. (1992). Aircrew coordination: Achieving teamwork in the cockpit. In R. Swezey & E. Salas (Eds.), *Teams: Their training and performance* (pp. 329–354). Norwood, NJ: Ablex Publishing Corp.

Quine, W. (1960). *Word and object.* Cambridge, MA: MIT Press.

Quine, W. V. O. (1961). *Two dogmas of empiricism. From a logical point of view* (2nd rev. ed., pp. 20–46). New York: Harper and Row.

Quinn, J. B. (1980). *Strategies for change: Logical incrementalism.* Homewood, IL: Irwin.

Raiffa, H. (1968). *Decision analysis: Introductory lectures on choices under uncertainty.* Reading, MA: Addison-Wesley.

Rasmussen, J. (1983). Skill, rules and knowledge: Signals, signs, and symbols, and other distinctions in human performance models. *IEEE Transactions on Systems, Man and Cybernetics, SMC-13*(3), 257–266.

Rasmussen, J. (1985). The role of hierarchical knowledge representation in decision making and system management. *IEEE Transactions on Systems, Man and Cybernetics, 15,* 234–243.

Rasmussen, J. (1986). *Information processing and human-machine interaction: An approach to cognitive engineering.* Amsterdam: North-Holland.

Rasmussen, J. (1989). Mental models and the control of actions in complex environments. In J. M. Tauber & D. Ackermann (Eds.), *Mental models and human computer-interaction.* Amsterdam: North-Holland. Also in Tech. Rep. Risd-M-2656, 1987).

Rasmussen, J., & Jensen, A. (1974). Mental procedures in real-life tasks: A case of electronic trouble shooting. *Ergonomics, 17,* 293–307.

Rawls, J. (1971). *A theory of justice.* Cambridge, MA: Bellknap.

Reagan, P., & Rohrbaugh, J. (in press). Decision conferencing: A unique approach to the behavioral aggregation of expert judgment. In G. Wright & F. Bolger (Eds.), *Expertise and decision support.* New York: Plenum.

Reason, J. (1990). *Human error.* Cambridge, UK: Cambridge University Press.

Reason, J., & Mycielska, K. (1982). *Absent minded? The psychology of mental lapses and everyday errors.* Englewood Cliffs, NJ: Prentice-Hall.

Reilly, B. A., & Doherty, M. E. (1989). A note on the assessment of self-insight in judgment research. *Organizational Behavior and Human Decision Processes, 44,* 123–131.

Reilly, B. A., & Doherty, M. E. (in press). Self-insight in judgment. *Organizational Behavior and Human Decision Processes.*

Rentsch, J. R. (1990). Climate and culture: Interaction and qualitative differences in organizational meanings. *Journal of Applied Psychology, 75*(6), 668–681.

Rentsch, J. R., & Duffy, L. (1990, September). *An organizational climate and culture perspective on shared mental models of team members.* Paper presented at the 1990 International Conference on Self-managed Work Teams, Denton, TX.

Resnick, L. (1987). Learning in school and out. *Educational Researcher, 16,* 13–20.

Reuben, D. B. (1984). Learning diagnostic restraint. *New England Journal of Medicine, 310,* 591–593.

Ribot, T. (1886). *German psychology of today.* New York: Scribner.

Riesbeck, C. K. (1984). Knowledge reorganization and reasoning style. *International Journal of Man-Machine Studies, 20,* 45–61.

Rigney, J. W., Towne, D. M., & Mason, A. K. (1968). *An analysis of the structure and errors in corrective maintenance work* (Tech. Rep. No. 55, 1–79). Los Angeles: University of Southern California, Electronics Personnel Group.

Rips, L. J. (1986). Mental muddles. In M. Brand & R. M. Harnish (Eds.), *The representation of knowledge and belief* (pp. 258–286). Tucson, AZ: University of Arizona Press.

Rips, L. J. (1989). Similarity, typicality, and categorization. In S. Vosniadu & A. Ortony (Eds.), *Similarity and analogy.* Cambridge, UK: Cambridge University Press.

Roberts, K. H., & Rousseau, D. M. (1989). Research in nearly failure-free, high reliability systems: "Having the bubble." *IEEE Transactions on Engineering Management, 36,* 132–139.

Rochlin, G. I. (1986, September). High-reliability organizations and technical change: Some ethical problems and dilemmas. *IEEE Technology and Society Magazine.*

Rochlin, G. I. (1988, October). *Technology, hierarchy, and organizational self-design: U. S. Naval Flight Operations as a case study.* Discussion paper presented to World Bank Workshop on Safety Control and Risk Management, Washington, DC.

Rochlin, G. I., La Porte, T. R., & Roberts, K. H. (1987, Autumn). The self designing high-reliability organization: Aircraft carrier flight operations at sea. *Naval War College Review,* pp. 76–90.

Rogoff, B., & Lave, J. (1984). *Everyday cognition: Its development in social context.* Cambridge, MA: Harvard University Press.

Rohrbaugh, J. (1984). Making decisions about staffing standards. In L. G. Nigro (Ed.), *Decision making in the public sector* (pp. 93–115). New York: Marcel Dekker, Inc.

Rohrbaugh, J. (1988). Cognitive conflict tasks and small group processes. In B. Brehmer & C. R. B. Joyce (Eds.), *Human judgment: The SJT view* (pp. 199–226). Amsterdam: Elsevier.

Roose, J., & Doherty, M. E. (1976). Judgment theory applied to the selection of life insurance salesmen. *Organizational Behavior and Human Performance, 16,* 231–249.

Rosch, E., & Mervis, C. B. (1975). Family resemblances: Studies in the internal structure of categories. *Journal of Cognitive Psychology, 7,* 573–605.

Rosch, E., Mervis, C. B., Gray, W. D., Johnson, D. M., & Boyes-Braem, P. (1976). Basic objects in natural categories. *Cognitive Psychology, 8,* 382–439.

Rosenthal, R. (1984). *Meta-analytic procedures for social research.* Beverly Hills, CA: Sage.

Rosenthal, R., & Rubin, D. (1982). A simple, general purpose display of magnitude of experimental effect. *Journal of Educational Psychology, 74,* 166–169.

Roth, E. M., Bennett, K. B., & Woods, D. D. (1987). Human interaction with an 'intelligent' machine. *International Journal of Man-Machine Studies, 27,* 479–525.

Roth, E. M., & Woods, D. D. (1989). Cognitive task analysis: An approach to knowledge acquisition for intelligent system design. In G. Guida & C. Tasso (Eds.), *Topics in expert system design.* New York: North-Holland.

Rothstein, H. G. (1986). The effects of time pressure on judgment in multiple cue probability learning. *Organizational Behavior and Human Decision Making, 37,* 83–92.

Rouse, S. H., Rouse, W. B., & Hammer, J. M. (1982). Design and evaluation of an onboard computer-based information system for aircraft. *IEEE Transactions on Systems, Man, and Cybernetics, 12,* 451–463.

Rouse, W. B. (1974). Optimal selection of acquisition sources. *Journal of the American Society for Information Science, 25,* 227–231.

Rouse, W. B. (1975). Optimal resource allocation in library systems. *Journal of the American Society for Information Science, 26,* 157–165.

Rouse, W. B. (1990). *Design for success: A human-centered approach to designing successful products and systems.* New York: Wiley.

Rouse, W. B., Geddes, N. D., & Curry, R. E. (1988). An architecture for intelligent interfaces: Outline of an approach to supporting operators of complex systems. *Human-Computer Interaction, 3,* 87–122.

Rouse, W. B., Geddes, N. D., & Hammer, J. M. (1990). Computer-aided fighter pilots. *IEEE Spectrum, 27,* 38–41.

Rouse, W. B., & Morris, N. M. (1986). On looking into the black box: Prospects and limits on the search for mental models. *Psychological Bulletin, 100,* 349–363.

Rubin, K. S., Jones, P. M., & Mitchell, C. M. (1988). OFMspert: Application of a blackboard architecture to infer operator intentions in real time decision making. *IEEE Systems, Man, and Cybernetics, SMC-18,* 618–637.

Rumelhart, D. E. (1977). Understanding and summarizing brief stories. In D. LaBerge & S. J. Samuels (Eds.), *Basic processes in reading: Perception and comprehension.* Hillsdale, NJ: Erlbaum.

Rumelhart, D. E. (1980). Schema: The building blocks of cognition. In R. J. Spior, B. C. Bruce, & W. F. Brewer (Eds.), *Theoretical issues in reading comprehension.* Hillsdale, NJ: Erlbaum.

Rumelhart, D. E. (1984). Understanding understanding. In J. Flood (Ed.), *Understanding reading comprehension* (pp. 1–20). Newark, DE: International Reading Association.

Russo, J. E., Johnson, E. J., & Stephens, D. (1989). The validity of verbal protocols. *Memory & Cognition, 17,* 759–769.

Sage, A. P. (1981). Behavioral and organizational considerations in the design of information systems and processes for planning and decision support. *IEEE Transactions on Systems, Man, and Cybernetics, SMC-11(9),* 640–678.

Salas, E., Dickinson, T. L., Tannenbaum, S., & Converse, S. A. (1991). *A meta-analytic review of the team training and performance literature.* Unpublished manuscript. Naval Training Systems Center, Orlando, FL.

Salas, E., & Morgan, Jr. B. B., (1989, August). *Role of teamwork in the develop-*

ment of effective work groups. Paper presented at the Annual Meeting of the American Psychological Association, New Orleans.

Salter, W. (1983). *The structure and content of tacit theories of economics.* Unpublished doctoral dissertation, Yale University, New Haven, CT.

Sanders, G. S., & Mullen, B. (1983). Accuracy in perceptions of concensus: Differential tendencies of people with majority and minority positions. *European Journal of Social Psychology, 13,* 57–70.

Savage, L. J. (1972). *The foundations of statistics.* New York: Dover. (Original work published 1954).

Scardamalia, M., & Bereiter, C. (1985). Fostering the development of self-regulation in children's knowledge processing. In S. F. Chipman, J. W. Segal, & R. Glaser (Eds.), *Thinking and learning skills* (Vol. 2, pp. 563–577). Hillsdale, NJ: Erlbaum.

Schank, R. C., & Abelson, R. P. (1977). *Scripts, plans, goals and understanding: An inquiry into human knowledge structures.* Hillsdale, NJ: Erlbaum.

Schank, R. C., Collins, G. C., & Hunter, L. E. (1986). Transcending inductive category formation in learning. *The Behavioral and Brain Sciences, 9,* 639–686.

Schlatter, T. W. (1985). A day in the life of a modern mesoscale forecaster. *ESA Journal, 9,* 235–256.

Schneider, S. L., & Lopes, L. L. (1985). *Reflection in preferences for multioutcome lotteries* (WHIPP22). Madison, WI: University of Wisconsin.

Schneider, W. (1982). *Automatic/control processing concepts and their implications for the training of skills* (Tech. Rep. No. HARL-ONR-8101). Champaign, IL: University of Illinois, Human Attention Research Laboratory.

Schneider, W. (1985). Training high-performance skills: Fallacies and guidelines. *Human Factors, 27,* 285–300.

Schneider, W., & Detweiler, M. (1988). The role of practice in dual-task performance: Toward workload modeling in a connectionist/control architecture. *Human Factors, 30,* 539–566.

Schneider, W., & Shiffrin, R. M. (1977). Controlled and automatic human information processing: I. Detection, search, and attention. *Psychological Review, 84,* 1–66.

Schoemaker, P. J. H. (1982). The expected utility model: Its variants, purposes, evidence, and limitations. *Journal of Economic Literature, 20,* 529–563.

Schoenfeld, A. H. (1985). *Mathematical problem solving.* Orlando, FL: Academic Press.

Schoenfeld, A. H., & Herrman, D. J. (1982). Problem perception and knowledge structure in expert and novice mathematical problem solvers. *Journal of Experimental Psychology: Learning, Memory and Cognition, 8,* 484–494.

Scholz, R. W. (1983). Biases, fallacies, and the development of decision making. In R. W. Scholtz (Ed.), *Decision making under uncertainty* (pp. 3–18). Amsterdam: Elsevier.

Schon, D. A. (1983). *The reflective practitioner.* New York: Basic Books.

Schwartz, D. R., & Howell, W. C. (1985). Optional stopping performance under graphic and numeric CRT formatting. *Human Factors, 27,* 433–444.

Seeger, J. A. (1983). No innate phases in group problem solving. *Academy of Management Review, 8*(4), 683–689.

Segal, L. (1989). *Effects of aircraft cockpit design on crew communication.* Urbana-Champaign: Prepared for Aviation Research Laboratory, University of Illinois.

Selznick, P. (1957). *Leadership in administration: A sociological interpretation.* Evanston, IL: Row, Peterson.

Senders, J. W. (1964). The human operator as a monitor and controller of multi-degree of freedom systems. *IEEE Transactions on Human Factors in Electronics, HFE-5,* 2–5.

Senders, J. W. (1966). A reanalysis of pilots eye movement data. *IEEE Transactions on Human Factors in Electronics, HFE-7,* 103–106.

Senders, J. W., & Posner, M. J. M. (1976). A queueing model of monitoring and supervisory behavior. In T. Sheridan & G. Johannsen (Eds.), *Monitoring behavior and supervisory control.* New York: Plenum Press.

Shafer, G. (1976). *A mathematical theory of evidence.* Princeton, NJ: Princeton University Press.

Shafer, G. (1981). Jeffrey's rule of conditioning. *Philosophy of Science, 48,* 337–362.

Shafer, G. (1986). Savage revisited. *Statistical Science, 1,* 463–501.

Shafer, G. (1988). Savage revisited. In D. E. Bell, H. Raiffa, & A. Tversky (Eds.), *Decision making: Descriptive, normative, and prescriptive interactions.* Cambridge, UK: Cambridge University Press.

Shafer, G., & Tversky, A. (1988). Languages and designs for probability judgment. In D. E. Bell, H. Raiffa, & A. Tversky (Eds.), *Decision making: Descriptive, normative, and prescriptive interactions* (pp. 237–265). Cambridge, UK: Cambridge University Press.

Shanteau, J. (1987). Psychological characteristics of expert decision makers. In J. Mumpower et al. (Eds.), *Expert judgment and expert systems.* Berlin: Springer-Verlag.

Shanteau, J. (1989). Cognitive heuristics and biases in behavioral auditing: Review, comments and observations. *Accounting Organizations and Society, 14*(1/2), 165–177.

Shanteau, J., & Phelps, R. H. (1977). Judgment and swine: Approaches and issues in applied judgment analysis. In M. F. Kaplan & S. Schwartz (Eds.), *Human judgment and decision processes in applied settings.* New York: Academic Press.

Sherif, M. (1935). A study of some social factors in perception. *Archives of Psychology, 27,* 5–60.

Short, J., Williams, E., & Christie, B. (1976). *The social psychology of telecommunications.* Chichester, UK: Wiley.

Shortliffe, E. H. (1976). *Computer-based medical consultations: MYCIN.* New York: Elsevier.

Simon, H. A. (1955). A behavioral model of rational choice. *Quarterly Journal of Economics, 69,* 99–118.

Simon, H. A. (1969). *The sciences of the artificial.* Cambridge, MA: MIT Press.

Simon, H. A. (1972). Theories of bounded rationality. In C. B. Radner & R.

Radner (Eds.), *Decision and organization* (pp. 161–176). Amsterdam: North Holland.

Simon, H. A. (1976). *Administrative behavior*. New York: Macmillan.

Simon, H. A. (1978). Information-processing theory of human problem solving. In W. K. Estes (Ed.), *Handbook of learning and cognitive processes*, Vol. 5, *Human information processing*. Hillsdale, NJ: Erlbaum.

Simon, H. A. (1983). *Reason in human affairs*. Palo Alto, CA: Stanford University Press.

Simon, H. A., & Hayes, J. R. (1976). The understanding process: Problem isomorphs. *Cognitive Psychology, 8*, 165–190.

Sloboda, J. A. (1976). Visual perception of musical notations: Registering pitch symbols in memory. *Quarterly Journal of Experimental Psychology, 28*, 1–16.

Slovic, P. (1966). Value as a determiner of subjective probability. *IEEE Transactions of Human Factors in Electronics, HFE-7*, 22–28.

Slovic, P., Fischhoff, B., & Lichtenstein, S. (1977). Behavioral decision making. *Annual Review of Psychology, 28*, 1–39.

Slovic, P., & Lichtenstein, S. (1971). Comparison of Bayesian and regression approaches to the study of human information processing in judgment. *Organizational Behavior and Human Performance, 6*, 649–744.

Slovic, P., & Tversky, A. (1974). Who accepts Savage's axiom? *Behavioral Science, 19*, 368–373.

Smith, E. E., & Medin, D. L. (1981). *Categories and concepts*. Cambridge, MA: Harvard University Press.

Smith, J. F., Mitchell, T. R., & Beach, L. R. (1982). A cost-benefit mechanism for selecting problem solving strategies: Some extensions and empirical tests. *Organizational Behavior and Human Performance, 29*, 370–396.

Smith, L. D. (1986). *Behaviorism and logical positivism*. Stanford, CA: Stanford University Press.

Smithson, M. (1989). *Ignorance and uncertainty: Emerging paradigms*. New York: Springer-Verlag.

Soelberg, P. (1967). Unprogrammed decision making. *Management Review, 3*, 19–29.

Sorkin, R. D., & Woods, D. D. (1985). Systems with human monitors: A signal detection analysis. *Human-Computer Interaction, 1*, 49–75.

Spiro, R., Coulson, R., Feltovich, P., & Anderson, D. (1988). Cognitive flexibility theory: Adavanced knowledge acquisition in ill-structured domains. *Proceedings of the 10th Annual Conference of the Cognitive Science Society*. Hillsdale, NJ: Erlbaum.

Stammers, R. B., & Hallum, J. (1985). Task allocation and balancing of task demands in the multi-man-machine system: Some case studies. *Applied Ergonomics, 16*(4), 251–257.

Stasser, G., & Titus, W. (1985). Pooling of unshared information in group decision making: Biased information sampling during discussion. *Journal of Personality and Social Psychology, 48*(6), 1467–1478.

Stasser, G., & Titus, W. (1987). Effects of information load and percentage of shared information on the dissemination of unshared information during group discussion. *Journal of Personality and Social Psychology, 53,* 81–93.

Stasser, G., Taylor, L. A., & Hanna, C. (1989). Information sampling in structured and unstructured discussions of three- and six-person groups. *Journal of Personality and Social Psychology, 57,* 67–78.

Staw, B. M. (1981). The escalation of commitment to a course of action. *Academy of Management Review, 6,* 577–587.

Stein, N. L., & Glenn, C. G. (1979). An analysis of story comprehension in elementary school children. In R. O. Freedle (Ed.), *New directions in discourse processing* (Vol. 2). Norwood, NJ: Ablex Publishing Corp.

Steinbruner, J. D. (1974). *The cybernetic theory of decision.* Princeton, NJ: Princeton University Press.

Steiner, I. D. (1972). *Group process and productivity.* New York: Academic Press.

Steiner, I. D. (1976). Paradigms and groups. *Advances in Experimental Social Psychology, 19,* 251–289.

Sternberg, R. J. (1985, November). Teaching critical thinking, Part I: Are we making critical mistakes? *Phi Delta Kappa,* pp. 194–98.

Sternberg, R. J. (1986). *Intelligence applied: Understanding and increasing your intellectual skills.* San Diego: Harcourt, Brace, & Jovonovich.

Stewart, T. R., Middleton, P., & Ely, D. (1983). Urban visual air quality judgements: Reliability and validity. *Journal of Environmental Psychology, 3,* 129–145.

Stich, S. P., & Nisbett, R. E. (1980). Justification and the psychology of human reasoning. *Philosophy of Science, 47,* 188–202.

Suchman, L. A. (1987). *Plans and situated actions: The problem of human-machine communication.* Cambridge, UK: Cambridge University Press.

Sundstrom, E., DeMeuse, K. P., & Futrell, D. (1990). Work teams: Applications and effectiveness. *American Psychologist, 45*(2), 120–133.

Svenson, O. (1979). Process descriptions of decision making. *Organizational Behavior and Human Performance, 23,* 86–112.

Svenson, O. (1990). Some propositions for the classification of decision situations. In K. Borcherding, O. I. Larichev, & D. M. Messick (Eds.), *Contemporary issues in decision making* (pp. 17–31). Amsterdam: North-Holland.

Swets, J. A. (1961). Is there a sensory threshold? *Science, 134,* 168–177.

Swezey, R. W., & Salas, E. (1989). Development of design guidelines for team training systems. *Proceedings of the 11th Interservice/Industry Training Systems Conference* (pp. 422–426). Ft. Worth, TX: American Defense Preparedness Association.

Swezey, R. W., & Salas, E (Ed.). (1992). *Teams: Their training and performance.* Norwood, NJ: Ablex Publishing Corp.

Taylor, S. E., & Crocker, J. (1981). Schematic bases of social information processing. In E. T. Higgens, C. P. Herman, & M. P. Zanna (Eds.), *Social cognition: The Ontario Symposium.* Hillsdale, NJ: Erlbaum.

Taynor, J., Crandall, B., & Wiggins, S. (1987). *The reliability of the critical decision method* (KATR-863(B)-87–07F). (Prepared under contract

MDA903–86-C-0170 for the U.S. Army Research Institute Field Unit.) Yellow Springs, OH: Klein Associates Inc.

Teger, A. (1980). *Too much invested to quit*. New York: Pergammon Press.

Tetlock, P. E. (1985). Accountability: The neglected social context of judgement and choice. *Research in Organizational Behavior, 7*, 297–332.

Thagard, P. (1988). *Computational philosophy of science*. Cambridge, MA: MIT Press.

Thompson, W. B., Johnson, P. E., & Moen, J. B. (1983). Recognition-based diagnostic reasoning. *Proceedings of the Eighth International Joint Conference on Artificial Intelligence*. Karlsruhe, FRG.

Thordsen, M. L., & Klein, G. A. (1990, April). Cognitive analysis of C^2 decision making. *Proceedings of The Seventh Annual Workshop on Command-and-Control Decision Aiding*. Dayton, OH.

Thordsen, M. L., Galushka, J., Klein, G. A., Young, S., & Brezovic, C. P. (1990). *A knowledge elicitation study of military planning* (Tech. Rep. No. 876). Alexandria, VA: U.S. Army Research Institute for the Behavioral and Social Sciences.

Thorndyke, P. (1984). Applications of schema theory in cognitive research. In J. Anderson & S. Kosslyn (Eds.), *Tutorials in learning and memory*. New York: W. H. Freeman and Co.

Thorngate, W. (1980). Efficient decision heuristics. *Behavioral Science, 25*, 219–225.

Thuring, M., & Jungermann, H. (1986). Constructing and running mental models for inferences about the future. In B. Brehmer, H. Jungermann, P. Lourens, & G. Sevon (Eds.), *New directions in research on decision making*. New York: North-Holland.

Tolcott, M. A., & Marvin, F. F. (1988). *Reducing the confirmation bias in an evolving situation* (Tech. Rep. No. 88–11). Reston, VA: Decision Science Consortium.

Tolcott, M. A., Marvin, F. F., & Bresnick, T. A. (1989a). The confirmation bias in evolving decisions. *Proceedings of the 1989 Symposium on Command-and-Control Research* (pp. 232–238). McLean, VA: Science Applications International Corporation.

Tolcott, M. A., Marvin, F. F., & Bresnick, T. A. (1989b). *The confirmation bias in military situation assessment*. Reston, VA: Decision Science Consortium.

Tolcott, M. A., Marvin, F. F., & Lehner, P. E. (1987). *Effects of early decisions on later judgments in an evolving situation* (Tech. Rep. No. 87–10). Falls Church, VA: Decision Science Consortium.

Tolman, E. C., & Brunswik, E. (1935). The organism and the causal texture of the environment. *Psychological Review, 42*, 43–77.

Torrance, E. P. (1953). The behavior of small groups under the stress conditions of "survival." *American Sociological Review, 19*, 751–755.

Torrance, E. P. (1954). Some consequences of power differences on decision making in permanent and temporary 3-man groups. *Research Studies, State College of Washington, 22*, 130–140.

Toulmin, S. (1958). *The uses of argument*. Cambridge, UK: Cambridge University Press.

Trabasso, T., & van den Broek, P. (1985). Causal thinking and the representation of narrative events. *Journal of Memory and Language, 24*, 612–630.

Tribe, L. H. (1971). Trial by mathematics: Precision and ritual in the legal process. *Harvard Law Review, 84*(6), 1329–1393.

Tucker, L. R. (1964). A suggested alternative formulation in the developments by Hursch, Hammond, & Hursch, and Hammond, Hursch, & Todd. *Psychological Review, 71*, 528–530.

Tversky, A. (1967). Additivity, utility, and subjective probability. *Journal of Mathematical Psychology, 4*, 175–201.

Tversky, A. (1972). Elimination by aspects: A theory of choice. *Psychological Review, 79*(4), 281–299.

Tversky, A., & Kahneman, D. (1972). Availability: A heuristic for judging frequency and probability. *Cognitive Psychology, 4*, 207–232.

Tversky, A., & Kahneman, D. (1974). Judgment under uncertainty: Heuristics and biases. *Science, 185*, 1124–1131.

Tversky, A., & Kahneman, D. (1980). Causal schemas in judgments under uncertainty. In M. Fishbein (Ed.), *Progress in social psychology* (Vol. I). Hillsdale, NJ: Erlbaum.

Tversky, A., & Kahneman, D. (1981). The framing of decisions and the psychology of choice. *Science, 211*, 453–458.

Tversky, A., & Kahneman, D. (1982). Evidential impact of base rates. In D. Kahneman, P. Slovic, & A. Tversky (Eds.), *Judgment under uncertainty: Heuristics and biases*. New York: Cambridge University Press.

Tversky, A., & Kahneman, D. (1983). Extensional versus intuitive reasoning: The conjunction fallacy in probability judgment. *Psychological Review, 90*, 293–315.

Tweney, R. D. (1985). Faraday's discovery of induction: A cognitive approach. In D. Gooding & F. James (Eds.), *Faraday rediscovered: Essays on the life and work of Michael Faraday*. London: Macmillan.

Tweney, R. D., Doherty, M. E., & Mynatt, C. R. (1981). *On scientific thinking*. New York: Columbia University Press.

Tyszka, T. (1980). Contextual multiattribute decision rules. In L. Sjöberg, T. Tyszka, & J. Wise (Eds.), *Decision processes and decision analysis*. Lund: Doxa.

Tyszka, T. (1981). Simple decision strategies vs. multi-attribute utility theory approach to complex decision problems. *Praxiology Yearbook, 2*, 159–172.

Tyszka, T., & Wielochoski, M. (1990). *Must boxing verdicts be partial?* Manuscript submitted for publication. Warszawa: Academy of Sciences, Department of Psychology.

Ullman, D. G., & Doherty, M. E. (1984). Two determinants of the diagnosis of hyperactivity: The child and the clinician. In M. Wolraich & D. K. Routh (Eds.), *Advances in behavioral pediatrics*. Greenwich, CT: JAI Press.

Ulvila, J. W., & Brown, R. V. (1982, September-October). Decision analysis comes of age. *Harvard Business Review*, pp. 130-140. (Reprinted in *A sampling of quantitative methods for managers, Harvard Business Review Book*, No. 13016, pp. 3–14.)

Valusek, J. R. (1988). Adaptive design of DSSs: A user perspective. In E. S. Weber (Ed.), *DSS-88 transactions: Eighth international conference on decision support systems* (pp. 105–112). TIMS College on Information Systems.

van Zee, E. H., Paluchowski, T. F., & Beach, L. R. (in press). The 'screening effect' and the 'task partitioning effect' in pre-choice information use. *Journal of Behavioral Decision Making.*

Vicente, K. J., & Rasmussen, J. (in press). Ecological interface design: Theoretical foundations. *IEEE Transactions on Systems, Man, and Cybernetics.*

Vidulich, M., Yeh, Y., & Schneider, W. (1983). Time-compressed components for air-intercept control skills. *Proceedings of the Human Factors Society 27th Annual Meeting*, pp. 161–164.

von Neumann, J., & Morgenstern, O. (1947). *Theory of games and economic behavior.* Princeton, NJ: Princeton University Press.

von Winterfeldt, D., & Edwards, W. (1973). *Flat maxima in linear optimization models* (Tech. Rep. No. 011313–4-T). Ann Arbor, MI: University of Michigan Engineering Psychology Laboratory, Institute of Science and Technology.

von Winterfeldt, D., & Edwards, W. (1975). *Error in decision analysis: How to create the possibility of large losses by using dominated strategies* (Res. Rep. 75–4). Los Angeles: University of Southern California Social Science Research Institute.

von Winterfeldt, D., & Edwards, W. (1986). *Decision analysis and behavioral research.* New York: Cambridge University Press.

Voss, J. F., Perkins, D., & Segal, J. (1990). *Informal reasoning and education.* Hillsdale, NJ: Erlbaum.

Voss, J. F., Tyler, S. W., & Yengo, L. A. (1983). Individual differences in the solving of social science problems. In R. F. Dillon & R. R. Schmeck (Eds.), *Individual differences in cognition* (Vol. 1). New York: Academic Press.

Vroom, V. E. (1976). Leadership. In M. D. Dunnette (Ed.), *Handbook of industrial and organizational psychology* (pp. 1527–1552). New York: Wiley & Sons.

Vroom, V. E., & Yetton, P. W. (1973). *Leadership and decision making.* Pittsburgh, PA: University of Pittsburgh Press.

Vygotsky, L. S. (1978). *Mind in society: The development of higher psychological processes.* Cambridge, MA: Harvard University Press.

Wagenaar, W. A. (1972). Generation of random sequences by human subjects: A critical survey of literature. *Psychological Bulletin, 77*, 65–72.

Wagenaar, W. A. (1988). *Paradoxes of gambling behavior.* Hillsdale, NJ: Erlbaum.

Wagenaar, W. A., & Keren, G. B. (1988). Chance and luck are not the same. *Journal of Behavioral Decision Making, 1*, 65–75.

Wagenaar, W. A., Keren, G. B., & Lichtenstein, S. (1988). Islanders and hostages: Deep and surface structures of decision problems. *Acta Psychologica, 68*, 175–189.

Wagenaar, W. A., Keren, G. B., & Pleit-Kuiper, A. (1984). The multiple objectives of gamblers. *Acta Psychologica, 56*, 167–178.

Waller, W. S., & Mitchell, T. R. (1984). The effects of context on the selection of decision strategies for the cost variance investigation. *Organizational Behavior and Human Performance, 33,* 397–413.

Wallsten, T. S. (1983). The theoretical status of judgmental heuristics. In R. W. Scholz (Ed.), *Decision making under uncertainty.* Amsterdam: North-Holland.

Wallsten, T. S., & Barton, C. (1982). Processing probabilistic multidimensional information for decisions. *Journal of Experimental Psychology: Learning, Memory, and Cognition, 8,* 361–384.

Warneryd, K. E. (1986). Economic and psychological approaches to the study of economic behavior. Similarities and differences. In B. Brehmer, H. Jungermann, P. Lourens, & G. Sevon (Eds.), *New directions in research on decision making* (pp. 29–58). New York: North-Holland.

Wason, P. C. (1960). On the failure to eliminate hypotheses in a conceptual task. *Quarterly Journal of Experimental Psychology, 12,* 129–140.

Wason, P. C. (1968). Reasoning about a rule. *Quarterly Journal of Experimental Psychology, 20,* 273–281.

Wason, P. C., & Johnson-Laird, P. N. (1972). *Psychology or reasoning: Structure and content.* Cambridge, MA: Harvard University Press.

Watzlawick, P., Weakland, J., & Fisch, R. (1974). *Change: Principles of problem formation and problem resolution.* New York: Norton.

Webster, E. C. (1964). *Decision making in the employment interview.* Montreal: Eagle Publishers, Ltd.

Wechsler, J. (Ed.). (1978). *On aesthetics in science.* Cambridge, MA: MIT Press.

Wegner, D. (1987). Transactive memory: A contemporary analysis of group mind. In B. Mullen & G. R. Goethals (Eds.), *Theories of group behavior* (pp. 185–208). New York: Springer-Verlag.

Weick, K. E. (1979). *The social psychology of organizing.* Reading, MA: Addison-Wesley.

Weick, K. E. (1983). Managerial thought in the context of action. In S. Srivastva (Ed.), *The executive mind.* San Francisco: Jossey-Bass.

Weiss, S. M., Kulikowski, C. A., Amarel, S., & Safir, A. (1978). A model-based approach for computer-aided medical decision-making. *Artificial Intelligence, 11,* 145–172.

Wellens, A. R. (1989, September). Effects of telecommunication media upon information sharing and team performance: Some theoretical and empirical observations. *IEEE AES Magazine,* pp. 13–19.

Wellens, A. R. (1990a). *Assessing multi-person and person-machine distributed decision making using an extended psychological distancing model.* Final University Resident Research Program Report for the Air Force Office of Scientific Research.

Wellens, A. R. (1990b, August). *Group situation awareness and distributed decision making.* Paper presented at the American Psychological Association Annual Conference, Boston.

Wellens, A. R., & Ergener, D. (1988). The C.I.T.I.E.S. game: A computer-based situation assessment for studying distributed decision making. *Simulation and Games, 19*(3), 304–327.

Wertsch, J. V. (1985). *Vygotsky and the social formation of mind.* Cambridge, MA: Harvard University Press.

Wheeler, D. D., & Janis, I. L. (1980). *A practical guide for making decisions.* New York: The Free Press.

Whittlesea, B. W. A. (1987). Preservation of specific experiences in the representation of general knowledge. *Journal of Experimental Psychology: Learning, Memory, and Cognition, 13,* 3–17.

Wigton, R. W. (1988). Applications of judgment analysis and cognitive feedback to medicine. In B. Brehmer & C. R. B. Joyce (Eds.), *Human judgment: The SJT view* (pp. 227–245). Amsterdam: Elsevier.

Wigton, R., Poses, R., Collins, M., & Cebul, R. (1990). Teaching old dogs new tricks: Using cognitive feedback to improve physicians' judgments on simulated cases. *Academic Medicine, 65,* S5–6.

Wilensky, R. (1983). *Planning and understanding: A computational approach to human reasoning.* Reading, MA: Addison-Wesley.

Wilkins, A. J., & Baddeley, A. D. (1978). Remembering to recall in everyday life: An approach to absent-mindedness. In M. M. Gruneberg, P.E. Morris, & R. N. Sykes (Eds.), *Practical aspects of memory* (pp. 27–34). London: Academic Press.

Willems, E. P., & Raush, H. L. (Eds.). (1969). *Naturalistic viewpoints in psychological research.* New York: Holt, Rinehart, & Winston.

Williges, R. C., Johnston, W. A., & Briggs, G. E. (1966). Role of verbal communication in teamwork. *Journal of Applied Psychology, 50,* 473–478.

Winograd, T. (1987). *Three responses to situation theory* (Tech. Rep. No. CSLI-87–106). Stanford, CA: Stanford University, Center for the Study of Language and Information.

Wohl, J. G. (1981). Force management requirements for Air Force tactical command and control. *IEEE Transactions and Systems, Man, and Cybernetics, SMC11*(9), 618–639.

Woodcock, A. E. R., Cobb, L., Familant, M. E., & Markey, J. (1988). *I&W applications of catastrophe theory* (Tech. Rep. No. RADC-TR-88–212). Rome, NY: Synectics Corporation.

Woods, D. D. (1988). Coping with complexity: The psychology of human behavior in complex systems. In L. P. Goodstein, H. B. Andersen, & S. E. Olsen (Eds.), *Tasks, errors, and mental models.* London: Taylor & Francis.

Woods, D. D., O'Brien, J., & Hanes, L. F. (1987). Human factors challenges in process control: The case of nuclear power plants. In G. Salvendy (Ed.), *Handbook of human factors/ergonomics.* New York: Wiley.

Woods, D. D., & Roth, E. M. (1988). Cognitive systems engineering. In M. Helander (Ed.), *Handbook of human-computer interaction.* New York: North-Holland.

Woods, D. D., Roth, E. M., & Pople, H. E. (1987). *Cognitive environment simulation: An artificial intelligence system for human performance assessment* (NUREG-CR-4862). Washington, DC: U. S. Nuclear Regulatory Commission.

Wright, J. C., & Murphy, G. L. (1984). The utility of theories in intuitive statistics: The robustness of theory-based judgments. *Journal of Experimental Psychology: General, 113*, 301–322.

Wright, P. (1974). The harassed decision maker: Time pressures, distractions and the use of evidence. *Journal of Applied Psychology, 59*(5), 555–561.

Xu, Y. (1987, January). *From the technical level to the conceptual level: Development of expertise in statistics.* Paper presented at the Third International Conference on Thinking, Honolulu.

Yates, J. F. (1982). External correspondence. Decomposition of the mean probability score. *Organizational Behavior and Human Performance, 30*, 132–156.

York, K. M., Doherty, M. E., & Kamouri, J. (1987). The influence of cue unreliability on judgment in a multiple cue probability learning task. *Organizational Behavior and Human Decision Processes, 39*, 303–317.

Zadeh, L. A. (1965). Fuzzy sets. *Information and Control, 8*, 338–353.

Zadeh, L. A. (1984). Review of Shafer's, A mathematical theory of evidence. *AI Magazine, 5*(3), 81-83.

Zakay, D., & Wooler, S. (1984). Time pressure, training, and decision effectiveness. *Ergonomics, 27*, 273–284.

Zimmer, A. (1983). Verbal versus numerical processing of subjective probabilities. In R. W. Scholz (Ed.), *Decision making under uncertainty*. North Holland: Elsevier.

Zimmerman, S. K., Ono, K., Stasson, M., & Davis, J. H. (1985, August). *Schema synchronization: Cognitive reorganization of social information through group interaction.* Paper presented at the American Psychological Association Conference, Los Angeles, CA.

Author Index

Subject Index